Balkan Justice

Balkan Justice

The Story Behind the First International War Crimes Trial Since Nuremberg

Michael P. Scharf

CAROLINA ACADEMIC PRESS
Durham, North Carolina

Library of Congress Cataloging-in-Publication Data
Scharf, Michael P., 1963–
Balkan justice: the story behind the first international war crimes trial since Nuremberg / Michael P. Scharf.
p. cm.
Includes bibliographical references and index.
ISBN 0-89089-919-3 hard cover
ISBN 0-89089-918-5 paperback
1. Tadic, Dusko—Trials, litigation, etc. 2. War crime trials—Netherlands—Hague. 3. War crimes—Bosnia and Hercegovina. 4. Yugoslav War, 1991– —Atrocities. I. Title.
JX5445.S33 1997
341.6'9'0268—dc21 96-45266
CIP

Carolina Academic Press
700 Kent Street
Durham, North Carolina 27701
Telephone (919) 489-7486
Fax (919) 493-5668
Email www.cap-press.com

Printed in the United States of America

To my wife Trina,
for her love and support

To my son Garrett,
for his inspiration

And to the memory of
Joseph Kruzel, 1945–1995,
who gave his life in Bosnia
in the cause of bringing peace and justice
to that troubled country

Contents

Maps on pages 18, 19 and 91.

Acknowledgments

SEVERAL PEOPLE AND ENTITIES deserve special recognition for the assistance they have furnished me in writing this book. Foremost among those is Virginia Morris of the United Nations Office of Legal Affairs, with whom I previously co-authored a two-volume textbook entitled *An Insider's Guide to the International Tribunal for the Former Yugoslavia.* That book provides a detailed legal analysis of the Statute and Rules of the Tribunal, while the focus of this work is on the politics, personalities, and strategies involved in creating the Tribunal and trying the first case before it. Nevertheless, many of the insights I gained from our countless hours of discussions have found their way into this text as well. In addition, I would like to express my gratitude to the staff of Court TV for supplying me their daily reports of the Tadic trial, which were instrumental in the preparation of Chapters 7 through 9 of this book. I would also like to thank Professor Cherif Bassiouni, Chairman of the U.N. War Crimes Commission, who shared his insights with me from Chicago; Justice Richard Goldstone, the Prosecutor of the Yugoslavia Tribunal, who met with me in Brussels; Graham Blewitt, the Tribunal's Deputy Prosecutor, Grant Niemann, the lead prosecuting attorney in the Tadic case, and Mike Keegan of the Office of the Prosecutor, who met with me at their office at the Tribunal Building in The Hague; and Tadic's defense lawyers—Michail Wladimiroff, Steven Kay, and Sylvia de Bertodano—who provided me an insightful interview over an unforgettable dinner at The Hague. Finally, I would like to thank my research assistant, Craig Silverman, whose enthusiasm was contagious; the New England School of Law, for its support of this project; and Keith Sipe, Linda Lacy and their colleagues at Carolina Academic Press, for their extra efforts to ensure the timely publication of this work.

Bal·kan*adjective*: of or relating to the Balkan peninsula in southeastern Europe; *also* **bal·kan·ize**, *verb*: to break a territory up into small conflicting units.

Jus·tice*noun*, 1: the administration of law by impartial adjudication; 2: the infliction of deserved punishment.

Prologue

June 18, 1992
Omarska Detention Center
Prijedor, Northern Bosnia

THIS IS NOT A TALE for the faint of heart. In the summer of 1992, ethnic violence engulfed Bosnia-Herzegovina (Bosnia). Thousands of Muslim men and women were forced from their homes and incarcerated in Serb-run concentration camps. The worst of these was located at the Omarska iron ore mine in northeast Bosnia. Omarska was known as a "death camp" and, in fact, more than half of those interned there never left alive. Sanitary conditions were appalling. Food was scarce. Medical care was nonexistent. The jailers were brutal. One in particular—Dusko Tadic (pronounced DOO-shko TAH-ditch)—became widely known as "The Butcher."

Survivors of Omarska report that Tadic personally raped one woman detainee, murdered thirteen men, and tortured scores of others. It is said that he used a large hammer to smash inmates' heads; that he beat other prisoners with iron bars, wooden clubs, and the butt of his rifle; that he forced prisoners to drink motor oil and mud from puddles; and, on one occasion, that he discharged the contents of a fire extinguisher into the mouth of one of the inmates. Then, on the afternoon of June 18, Tadic is alleged to have participated in an act so vile that news of it quickly spread throughout the world.

That day, five prisoners were summoned to Omarska's garage building, known as "the hangar." Among these prisoners was a Muslim policeman named Fikret Harambasic (Hari). When Hari arrived at the hangar, Tadic and a group of Serbs allegedly beat him and the other prisoners with truncheons and forced them to wallow naked and bloody in the sump oil collected in the garage service pits. Two of the prisoners died in the course of the beatings; Hari lapsed in and out of consciousness. But the Serbs soon grew bored and decided to try something new—something dreadfully new.

According to witnesses, one of the prisoners was ordered at knife point to bite off Hari's testicles. The Serbs were yelling, "Bite, harder,

harder," as Hari was sexually mutilated; all the while a tape recorder insidiously played the popular Muslim song, "Let Me Live, Don't Take Away My Happiness." Dozens of witnesses throughout the camp heard Hari's inhuman screams of pain over the music and the cheering of his Serb tormentors. Hari did not survive the night. The next morning his body was tossed with dozens of others onto a garbage truck destined for a mass grave somewhere in the nearby countryside.

This vicious incident has become a symbol for the entire Bosnian Muslim experience at the hands of their Serb neighbors during the bloody summer of 1992. It was the one documented atrocity that, more than any other, defined the horrors of Omarska. And it was the revelation of those horrors that finally prodded the international community to action in Bosnia.

Four years later, Dusko Tadic, a forty-year-old Bosnian Serb pub owner and karate instructor, would find himself in a similar situation to that of Hermann Goering following the Second World War. He would become the first person in fifty years to stand trial before an international tribunal for crimes against humanity. Millions around the world tuned in to the televised proceedings—billed by the media as "the trial of the century"—to find out whether Tadic was the sadistic instrument of the Serb policy of "ethnic cleansing" that the prosecution made him out to be, or just a scapegoat for people who had suffered terribly and were looking for revenge as the defense contended. At stake was no less than the future of international humanitarian law. This is the true story behind this landmark trial.

Introduction

> The wrongs which we seek to condemn and punish have been so calculated, so malignant and so devastating, that civilization cannot tolerate their being ignored, because it cannot survive their being repeated.
>
> —Robert H. Jackson
> *Opening Speech for the Prosecution at Nuremberg, 21 November 1945*

During the twentieth century, four times as many civilians have been victims of war crimes and crimes against humanity than the number of soldiers killed in all the international wars combined.* After the Nazis exterminated six million Jews during the Holocaust, the world community said "never again." The victorious Allied powers set up an international tribunal at Nuremberg to prosecute the Nazi leaders for their monstrous deeds. There was hope that the legacy of Nuremberg would be the institutionalization of a judicial response to atrocities committed by anyone, anywhere around the globe.

Yet, the pledge of "never again" quickly became the reality of "again and again" as the world community failed to take action to bring those responsible to justice when 4 million people were murdered in Stalin's purges (1937–1953), 5 million were annihilated in China's Cultural Revolution (1966–1976), 2 million were butchered in Cambodia's killing fields (1975–1979), 30,000 disappeared in Argentina's Dirty War (1976–1983), 200,000 were massacred in East Timor (1975–1985), 750,000 were exterminated in Uganda (1971–1987), 100,000 Kurds were gassed in Iraq (1987–1988), and 75,000 peasants

* Professor Rudi Rummel documents that as many as 170 million persons have been murdered by their own governments. R.J. Rummel, *Death by Government* (1994), p. 9.

were slaughtered by death squads in El Salvador (1980–1992).[1] The U.N. High Commissioner for Human Rights summed up the state of affairs when he recently said, "A person stands a better chance of being tried and judged for killing one human being than for killing 100,000."[2]

Then, in the summer of 1992, the world learned of the existence of Serb-run concentration camps in Bosnia-Herzegovina, with conditions reminiscent of the Nazi-run camps of World War II. Daily reports of acts of unspeakable barbarity committed in the Balkans began to fill the pages of our newspapers. The city of Sarajevo, which had recently impressed the world as host of the 1984 Winter Olympics, was transformed from a symbol of ethnic harmony into a bloody killing ground. For the first time since World War II, genocide had returned to Europe. The international outcry was deafening.

I was, at the time, the Attorney-Adviser for United Nations Affairs at the U.S. Department of State. I had previously served as counsel to the Counter-Terrorism Bureau and when I was promoted to my new position in 1991, I requested to work on the hot issue of the day—the Persian Gulf War. But my superior felt that I should first gain some experience in a "less critical area," and accordingly assigned me responsibility for the situation in Yugoslavia. In this capacity, over the next two years, I participated in and observed first-hand the policy formulation, negotiation, and compromises that shaped the United States' and United Nations' responses to the unfolding crisis in the former Yugoslavia. During this time, it fell on me to draft the Security Council resolution that established a War Crimes Commission to investigate and document the Yugoslav atrocities, the U.S. proposal for the statute of an International War Crimes Tribunal, and ultimately the Security Council resolution establishing the Tribunal and the crucial interpretive statement delivered by Ambassador Madeleine Albright at the time that resolution was adopted.

For me, the Yugoslavia crisis began as an exciting legal and policy challenge. The growing casualty figures—250,000 civilians murdered, 20,000 women raped, 2 million people driven from their homes—were little more than numbers. I did not begin to really comprehend the horror of the situation or perceive the pain of the victims until I was asked in the fall of 1992 to help write the U.S. reports to the newly established U.N. War Crimes Commission describing the specific information in the possession of the United States government concerning atrocities in the former Yugoslavia. Through this undertaking, I was exposed to the first-hand accounts of individual victims, like that of a twenty-eight-year-old Bosnian Muslim woman who had been raped by a succession of a dozen Serb fighters in an outdoor sports stadium in full view of her family and other detainees until she mercifully lost consciousness. And this is where I first learned of the story of Dusko Tadic and the Omarska camp atrocities which are described in the Prologue.

Most observers believe that the Security Council, led by the United States, could have put an early halt to the bloodshed in the Balkans, but that the members of the council lacked the political will to take the necessary measures, such as air strikes and committing troops to a combat situation which had the potential of turning into a quagmire like Vietnam. Consequently, the idea of a war crimes tribunal appealed to the members of the council as a means of countering accusations that they tolerated massive violations of international humanitarian law in the former Yugoslavia and stood by idly while a defenseless Bosnia succumbed to Serb and Croat aggression. Yet, all the members of the council did not share the same enthusiasm for such an undertaking. While U.S. President Bill Clinton took the position that the effective operation of the Tribunal should be "a top United Nations priority," Britain and France attributed greater importance to a peace settlement than to war crimes trials which could impede the peace process. The Chinese were concerned about a precedent that might one day be used against them, and the Russians were uncomfortable with putting their historic allies—the Serbs—on trial.

Against great odds, the Yugoslavia War Crimes Tribunal was established on May 25, 1993. Within a year and a half, the judges had been elected, a prosecutor and his staff appointed, a courtroom and detention center erected, the Rules of Procedure promulgated, and the first indictments issued. Among the first to be charged by the Tribunal was Dusko Tadic, who had recently moved to Germany where he was taken into custody after being identified as the "Butcher of Omarska" by Bosnian refugees who had been interned there. He was charged with thirty-four counts of crimes against humanity and grave breaches of the Geneva Conventions, including the murder, rape and torture of Muslim men and women within and outside the Omarska camp.

Tadic's trial, the first before the new international war crimes tribunal, began on May 7, 1996. Over one hundred witnesses testified during the seven-month trial.

This book provides the inside story of the creation of the Yugoslavia War Crimes Tribunal and chronicles the case of Dusko Tadic, from indictment to judgment. To the extent possible, consistent with State Department rules of confidentiality, I have filled these pages with behind-the-scenes information gleaned from my days at the State Department and from subsequent interviews with the major players involved in this international judicial drama. I must stress, of course, that the views expressed herein are solely my own and do not reflect those of the United States government.

The descriptions of the highlights of the Tadic trial contained in Chapters 7 through 9 of this book are derived both from my first-hand observations of parts of the trial at The Hague and from viewing the gavel-to-gavel television coverage of the trial broadcast on Court TV, as well as from the daily trial reports prepared by the staff of Court TV. The depiction is meant only to provide a flavor of the trial, not to be a comprehensive and precise account, which awaits historical writing when the official trial transcript has been made publicly available.

The reader may note that although Appendix C, the reproduction of the indictment of Dusko Tadic, contains diacritical marks on Serbo-Croatian names, these accents have been omitted in the text for ease of reading. One should also note that name and place spellings occasionally vary (Herzegovina or Hercegovina, for instance) depending on how the Serbo-Croatian was transliterated.

It is my hope that this book will help readers understand how the masses of ordinary people in Bosnia could be incited to turn on their neighbors in such a bloodthirsty way, as well as the politics behind the United Nations Security Council's response to the Balkan crisis. The book is intended also to educate readers about international humanitarian law and international criminal procedure, and help them appreciate the complexities and challenges involved in creating a novel international institution and trying the first case before it. Finally, it provides the first published gavel-to-gavel account of one of the most significant trials of the twentieth century.

In researching and writing this book, I often reflected on something Dr. Joseph Kruzel, my international relations professor at Duke

University, said back in 1982: "There can be no real peace without justice." Thirteen years later, on August 19, 1995, the same Joe Kruzel, now Deputy Assistant Secretary of Defense, became the first U.S. official to be killed in Bosnia as his car skidded off a narrow mountain road near Sarajevo while on the way to peace talks, which had reached a pivotal stage. Shocked by the news of Kruzel's death, President Clinton vowed to intensify efforts to induce a settlement, and on November 22, 1995, in Dayton, Ohio, the parties to the Yugoslav conflict signed a comprehensive peace accord. The accord included a key provision requiring their cooperation with the Yugoslav War Crimes Tribunal in the investigation and prosecution of war crimes. "Joe Kruzel achieved something given only a few men," said Secretary of Defense William Perry at a memorial service. "He left the world better than he found it." This book is dedicated to the memory of this outstanding educator and public servant, and the important principle for which he gave his life.

Balkan Justice

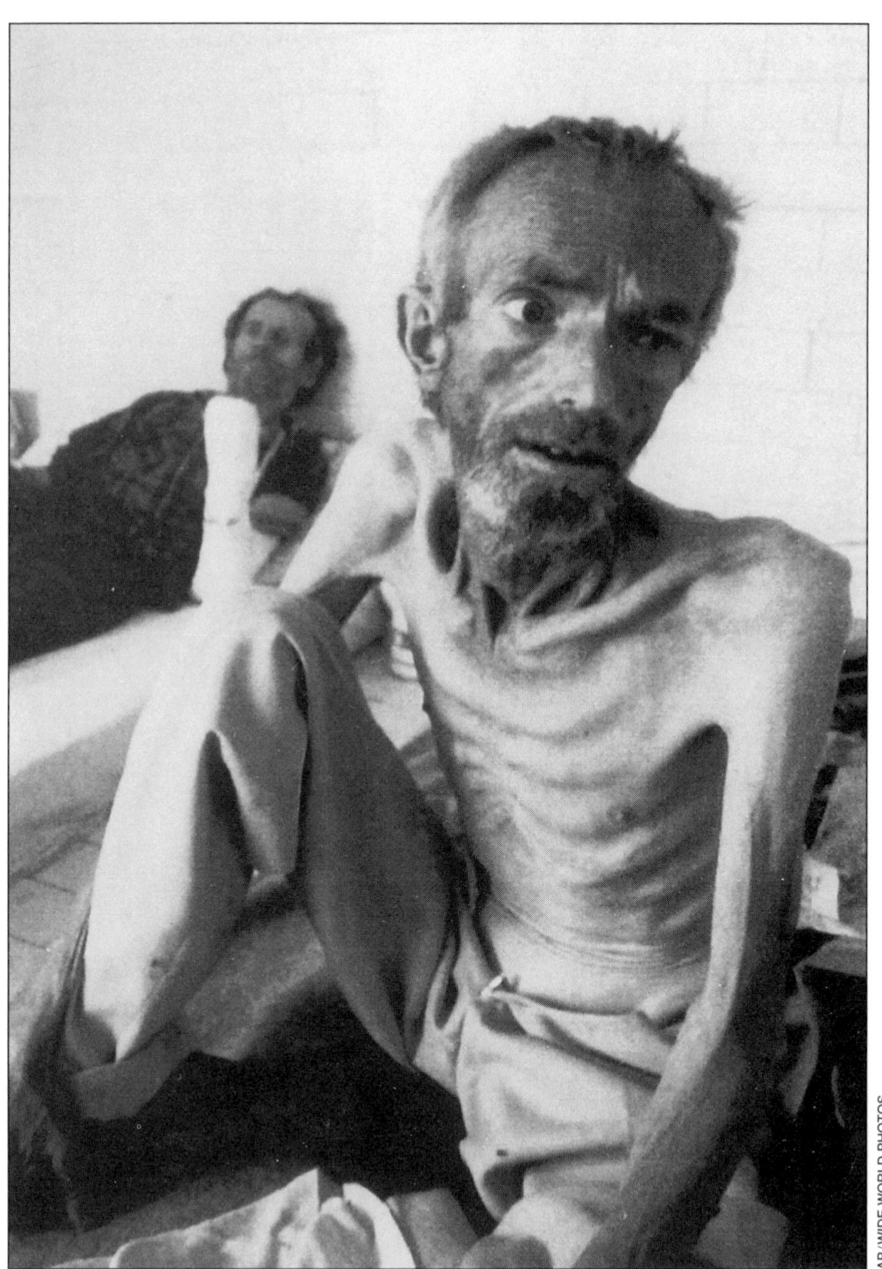

AP/WIDE WORLD PHOTOS

In the summer of 1992, thousands of Muslim men and women were forced from their homes and incarcerated in Serb-run concentration camps where conditions were appalling and the jailers were brutal.

Chapter 1

From Nuremberg to Bosnia

Many mistakes have been made and many inadequacies must be confessed. But I am consoled by the fact that in proceedings of this novelty, errors and missteps may also be instructive to the future.

—Robert H. Jackson
Report to the President,
October 7, 1946

1

History's first international criminal court was the Nuremberg Tribunal, created by the victorious Allies after World War II to prosecute the major German war criminals. Fifty years would pass since the Nuremberg war crimes trials before another international criminal court would be established. To understand the recently established Yugoslavia War Crimes Tribunal, one must first know something about its predecessor, the Nuremberg Tribunal. Moreover, to highlight the relevance of the Nuremberg legacy to the Yugoslavia War Crimes trials, many of the chapters of this book are preceded by prophetic quotes from Robert Jackson, the chief prosecutor at Nuremberg.

The events that prompted the formation of the Nuremberg Tribunal in 1945 are probably more familiar to most people than those which led to the creation of the Yugoslavia War Crimes Tribunal a half century later. Between 1933 and 1940, the Nazi regime established concentration camps where Jews, Communists, and opponents of the regime were incarcerated without trial; it progressively outlawed the Jews, stripped them of citizenship, and made marriage or sexual intimacy between Jews and German citizens a criminal offense; it forcibly annexed Austria and Czechoslovakia; it invaded and occupied Poland, Denmark, Norway, Luxembourg, Holland, Belgium, and France; and it then set in motion "the final solution to the Jewish problem" by establishing death camps such as Auschwitz and Treblinka, where six million Jews were killed.

As Allied forces pressed into Germany and an end to the fighting in Europe came into sight, the Allied powers faced the task of establishing an acceptable procedure for dealing with the surviving Nazi leadership. The initial step in that direction was the establishment in 1942 of the "United Nations War Crimes Commission." The phrase "United Nations" had been adopted by the alliance of Britain, the United States, the Soviet Union, China, and twenty-two other nations united against the Axis Powers—Germany, Italy, and Japan. The War Crimes Commission was supposed to investigate and collect evidence of war crimes, but it had no investigatory staff and no resources. Foreshadowing the difficulties faced by its namesake for the former Yugoslavia fifty years later, the U.N. War Crimes Commission ended up doing little more than recording a few cases referred to it by the Allied governments. Britain, in particular, failed to provide much in the way of cooperation. On March 30, 1944, Sir Cecil Hurst, the chairman of the commission, reported that no evidence of the massacre of Jews in Poland had been received by the commission, despite the fact that the British Foreign Minister had publicly disclosed fifteen months earlier that proof of such massacres was in the British government's hands.[1] The commission thus turned its attention to the academic exercise of determining whether launching an aggressive war should be considered a crime under international law; whether atrocities committed by a government against its own citizens should be regarded as an international crime; and whether an international tribunal should be created for the trial of war crimes. Unfortunately, the members of the commission were so evenly divided on these issues that no consensus was ever reached.

The British government initially opposed the establishment of any tribunal for the trial of the civilian and military leaders of Nazi Germany on the ground that their "guilt was so black" that it was "beyond the scope of judicial process."[2] British Prime Minister Winston Churchill therefore proposed the summary execution of the major Nazis on the basis of a political decision of the Allies. This came to be referred to in government circles as the "Napoleonic precedent," since the one-time emperor of the French had, after his defeat at Waterloo in 1815, been exiled to St. Helena for life without trial. This political decision had been made by the victorious governments of Britain, Austria, and Russia.[3] The Soviet Premier, Joseph Stalin, also favored applying the Napoleonic precedent, and reportedly had his subordinates draw up a list of fifty thousand Nazi War criminals for execution. At a banquet attended by Roosevelt and Churchill, Stalin proposed a toast, stating, "I drink to the quickest possible justice for all German war criminals. I drink to the justice of a firing squad... Fifty thousand must be shot."[4]

Surprisingly, President Roosevelt appeared willing to go along with this approach.* But its prospects perished with Roosevelt's death in April 1945. Upon taking office, President Harry Truman made it clear that he opposed summary execution. Instead, at the urging of U.S. Secretary of War, Henry Stimson, Truman pushed for the establishment of an international tribunal to try the Nazi leaders. The Soviets declared that they could accept such a judicial approach so long as the Tribunal's task was "only to determine the measure of guilt of each particular person and mete out the necessary punishment."[5] But the United States made clear to the Soviets that "if we are going to have a trial, then it must be an actual trial."[6]

The United States ultimately convinced the British, French, and Soviets that the establishment of an international tribunal would serve several shared objectives. First, judicial proceedings would avert future hostilities which would likely result from the execution, without trial, of German leaders. Legal proceedings, moreover, would bring German atrocities to the attention of all the world, thereby legitimizing Allied conduct during and after the war. Finally, such a trial would

---

* On September 15, 1944, President Roosevelt approved a memorandum supporting Churchill's plan for the German leaders and agreeing to "concert with him a list of names" for execution. Telford Taylor, *The Anatomy of the Nuremberg Trials* (1992), p. 31.

permit the Allied powers, and the world, to exact a penalty from the Nazi leadership rather than from Germany's civilian population.[7]

Thus, in the summer of 1945, representatives from the four countries gathered in London to draw up a charter for the "International Military Tribunal" to try the German civilian and military leadership for war crimes, the crime of waging a war of aggression, and crimes against humanity.[8] Nuremberg was chosen as the site of the Tribunal for symbolic reasons—it was there that the Nazi Party had staged its annual mass demonstrations and that the anti-Semitic "Nuremberg Laws" had been decreed in 1935.[9]

2

THE FIFTEEN NEGOTIATING SESSIONS from June 26 to August 8, 1945 leading up to the adoption of the Charter of the Nuremberg Tribunal ranged from turbulent to tumultuous. The problem was that the negotiators brought to the table their own legal conceptions and the experiences of their respective legal systems: the common law adversarial system as it had evolved differently in England and in the United States and variations of the civil law inquisitorial system employed in France and Russia. The task of creating an entirely new judicial entity which blended elements from the two systems and was acceptable to the four parties proved an incredible challenge for the negotiators. "With dissimilar backgrounds in both penal law and international law it is less surprising that clashes developed at the Conference than that they could be reconciled," wrote the chief U.S. negotiator, Robert Jackson, in the preface to his *Report* containing a summary of the Charter's negotiating history.[10]

Under the Continental system, most of the documentary and testimonial evidence is presented to an examining magistrate who assembles it in a dossier, copies of which are provided to the defendant and to the court prior to trial. The court, either on its own motion or at the request of one of the parties, will question witnesses directly, and cross examination by opposing counsel is a rarity. There is no rule against hearsay evidence, and trials in absentia are permitted. In the Anglo-American system, in contrast, the indictment contains only a summary of the facts alleged and evidence is presented in open court by lawyers who examine and cross-examine the witnesses. Most importantly, under the adversarial system, the defendant has a right to confront his accusers—a right that limits the use of hearsay evidence and ex parte affidavits (depositions taken out of the presence of the accused or his lawyer) and requires the presence of the accused at trial.

The charter that the negotiators eventually came up with represented a blend of the two systems. Mixing elements from both systems, the Nuremberg Charter required (contrary to the Anglo-American practice) that the indictment "shall include full particulars specifying in detail the charges against the defendants," and that there be "documents" submitted with the indictment. But, contrary to the Continental practice, it did not require that the prosecution present all of its evidence with the indictment. Also contrary to Continental practice, defendants could testify as witnesses in their own behalf, but in contrast to Anglo-American practice, defendants could be compelled to testify by the Tribunal and they were permitted to make an unsworn statement at the end of the trial.[11]

The negotiators agreed, moreover, that the technical rules of evidence developed under the common law system of jury trials to prevent the jury from being influenced by improper evidence would be unnecessary for a trial where no jury would be used.[12] Accordingly, the Nuremberg Charter adopted the principle that the Nuremberg Tribunal should admit any evidence which it deemed to have a probative value and should not be bound by technical rules of evidence, such as the notion of "hearsay." Commenting on the evidentiary and procedural compromises, Robert Jackson wrote: "The only problem was that a procedure that is acceptable as a fair trial in countries accustomed to the Continental system of law may not be regarded as a fair trial in common-law counties. What is even harder for Americans to recognize is that trials which we regard as a fair and just may be regarded in Continental countries as not only inadequate to protect society but also as inadequate to protect the accused individual."[13]

As for the Nuremberg Tribunal's substantive law, two particularly controversial compromises were made which resulted in depriving the Tribunal of jurisdiction over the Nazis' pre-war atrocities against the Jews. The first concerned the concept of conspiracy. The United States had proposed inclusion of a charge of conspiracy to commit any of the crimes within the jurisdiction of the Tribunal* in order to reach prewar Nazi outrages against German Jews. While these early acts could not be treated as war crimes, they could be punishable as initial steps in a conspiracy to commit war crimes after the war had begun. The other parties were reluctant to accept this proposal, particularly since the Anglo-American concept of conspiracy was not recognized in any of the Continental European legal systems at that time. At the Soviets' insistence, the proposed language was amended to make the conspiracy charge applicable only to the crime of initiating aggressive war. The United States accepted this revision but then sought to ignore it by persuading the Nuremberg prosecutors to include in the indictment a charge of conspiracy to commit all three of the offenses contained in the Nuremberg Charter. The attempt by the United States to circumvent the limited notion of conspiracy contained in the Charter proved unsuccessful, however. In its judgment, the Nuremberg Tribunal narrowly interpreted the wording of the charter and ruled that the notion of conspiracy only applied to the crime of aggression, thus precluding a general finding that prewar atrocities were punishable.[14]

The second substantive compromise concerned a dispute about whether a comma or a semicolon should be used in the wording of Article 6(C) of the Nuremberg Charter's definition of crimes against humanity:

> Crimes Against Humanity: namely, murder, extermination, enslavement, deportation, and other inhumane acts committed against any civilian population, before or during the war[;][,] or persecutions on political, racial or religious grounds, in execution of or in connection with any crime within the jurisdiction of the Tribunal, whether or not in violation of the domestic law of the country where perpetrated.

In the English and French official texts of the charter, a semicolon appeared between the phrase "the war" and the phrase "or persecutions," while the Russian text had a comma in the corresponding place. At the Soviet Union's insistence, the four governments signed a protocol to the Nuremberg Charter, which replaced the semicolon with a

---

* The Nuremburg Tribunal had jurisdiction over (1) war crimes, (2) the crime of initiating an aggressive war, and (3) crimes against humanity.

comma in all the texts. As a consequence of this seemingly minor grammatical change, the phrase "in execution of or in connection with any crime within the jurisdiction of the Tribunal" became a limitation on all crimes against humanity, not just "persecutions" as originally written. This substantially limited the jurisdiction of the Nuremberg Tribunal with respect to crimes against humanity committed before the German invasion of Poland in 1939 (which the Tribunal determined to be the start of the war).[15] While the public perception is that the Nuremberg trial provided a comprehensive account of the Holocaust, in fact that was the one thing the Nuremberg Tribunal was legally precluded from doing.

There is no record of the discussion of this matter between the four countries, and historians disagree as to whether the United States' acceptance of the change to a comma reflected a change of position or merely recognition of an earlier mechanical error in drafting.[16] To add to the mystery, the Allies did not include the linkage to war in the definition of crimes against humanity contained in Control Council Law No. 10, which was adopted after the Nuremberg Charter to provide a uniform basis for the trial of German war criminals other than the major war criminals tried by the Nuremberg Tribunal.[17] This resulted in confused judicial pronouncements by the post-Nuremberg war crimes tribunals: in the *Einsatzgruppen* case and the *Justice* case, the tribunals recognized that crimes against humanity could be committed during peacetime. However, in the *Flick* case and the *Ministries* case, the tribunals followed the precedent of the Nuremberg Tribunal and required the connection to war, notwithstanding the differences in the Nuremberg Charter and Control Council Law No. 10.[18] This has led to an enduring controversy over whether crimes against humanity under international law can be committed during peacetime, or only during war—a controversy that would have a profound effect on the jurisprudence of the Yugoslavia war crimes trials fifty years later.

3

ALTHOUGH HITLER, HIMMLER, AND GOEBBELS escaped prosecution by committing suicide, many of the most notorious German leaders were tried before the Nuremberg Tribunal. The list of the Nuremberg defendants reads like a "Who's Who" of the Third Reich: Hitler's second-in-command, Hermann Goering; armaments minister Albert Speer; Foreign Minister Joachim von Ribbentrop; Ribbentrop's predecessor as Foreign Minister, Constantin von Neurath; Interior Minister Wilhelm Frick; Minister of Economics Hjalmar Schacht; Schacht's successor as Minister of Economics, Walter Funk; Vice Chancellor Franz von Papen; chief military advisers Wilhelm Keitel and Alfred Jodl; Grand Admiral Erich Raeder, Commander in Chief of the German Navy until 1943; Raeder's successor as Commander in Chief of the Navy, Admiral Karl Doenitz; Fritz Sauckel, the primary figure in the foreign forced-labor program; Hans Fritzsche, Goebbels' Deputy for Propaganda; Julius Streicher, a Nazi Party leader and editor of the virulently anti-Semitic newspaper *Der Stuermer*; Alfred Rosenberg, the official Nazi ideologist and Minister of German-occupied eastern territories; Baldur von Schirach, the Nazi Youth leader; Hans Frank, the Governor-General of occupied Poland; Arthur Seyss-Inquart, Commissioner for the occupied Netherlands; Ernst Kaltenbrunner, the senior surviving official of the SS and Gestapo; and Rudolf Hess, the Deputy Führer who had flown to Scotland on a purported peace mission in 1941. In addition, the Nuremberg Tribunal tried Martin Bormann, Hitler's Deputy for Nazi Party Affairs, in absentia, though he was probably dead at the time.

After a trial that lasted 284 days, nineteen of the twenty-two German officials tried at Nuremberg were found guilty, and twelve were sentenced to death by hanging.[19] Of even more importance, in the words of the United States' chief prosecutor Robert Jackson, the Nuremberg Tribunal documented the Nazi atrocities "with such authenticity and in such detail that there can be no responsible denial of these crimes in the future and no tradition of martyrdom of the Nazi leaders can arise among informed people."[20] The jurisprudence of the Nuremberg Tribunal also laid the foundation for trial by military tribunals in occupied zones in Germany and in the liberated or allied nations of over a thousand other German political and military officers, businessmen, doctors, and jurists under Control Council Law No. 10.[21] Major Japanese war criminals were tried before the International Military Tribunal for the Far East whose charter was based largely on the charter of the Nuremberg Tribunal.[22]

Like any novel endeavor, however, the Nuremberg Tribunal was not above reproach.[23] In the years following its judgment there have been three main criticisms levied on the Nuremberg Tribunal: first, that it was a victor's tribunal before which only the vanquished were called to account for violations of international humanitarian law committed during the war; second, that the defendants were prosecuted and punished for crimes expressly defined for the first time in an instrument adopted by the victors at the conclusion of the war; and third, that the Nuremberg Tribunal functioned on the basis of limited procedural rules that inadequately protected the rights of the accused.

These criticisms are not without foundation. It was true, for example, that only victorious states were represented on the Nuremberg Tribunal. Many commentators have criticized the Allies' failure to appoint a judge from a neutral country or from Germany to the Nuremberg Tribunal.[24] It has been suggested that the post-Nuremberg trials administered by the German courts (including the conviction of the three defendants who were acquitted by the Nuremberg Tribunal) attest to the fact that a German judge could have dealt justly with the accused.[25]

Moreover, the Nuremberg judges oversaw the collection of evidence and judged the defendants in a necessarily political arena, thereby raising questions about their ability to objectively preside over the trials. Most astonishing of all, however, was the fact that two of the judges of the Nuremberg Tribunal, General Nikitchenko (Soviet Union) and Robert Falko (alternate, France), had served earlier as members of the committee that drafted the Nuremberg Charter and the indictments.[26] Having written the law to be applied and selected the defendants to be tried, it is hard to believe they could be sufficiently impartial and unbiased. And yet, they were insulated from challenge since the Nuremberg Charter stipulated that neither the court, nor its members, could be challenged by the prosecution or the defendants.

In addition, the states that tried the Nuremberg defendants were guilty of many of the same crimes for which they convicted and hung their former adversaries. American judges convicted defendants for crimes against humanity despite the dropping of the atomic bombs and the firebombing of civilian centers; and German Admiral Karl Doenitz was tried for violating the laws of war by conducting unrestricted submarine warfare, despite the fact that the American Forces engaged in similar conduct throughout the war. Soviet judges, moreover, convicted defendants for waging aggressive war and for mistreating prisoners, despite the forcible Soviet annexation of the Baltic States and the appalling record of the Soviets regarding the treatment of their POWs. Most reprehensible of all, however, was the Soviet Union's insistence that the defendants be charged with responsibility for the Katyn Forest Massacre in which 14,700 Polish prisoners of war were murdered in 1941—when the true perpetrators of this atrocity, we now know, were the Soviets not the Germans.[27]

Perhaps the most often heard criticism of Nuremberg was its perceived application of ex post facto laws by holding individuals responsible for the first time in history for waging a war of aggression and by applying the concept of conspiracy which had never before been recognized in continental Europe. One of the first to voice this criticism was Senator Robert Taft of Ohio in 1946, but it was not until John F. Kennedy reproduced Taft's speech in his Pulitzer Prize-winning 1956 book, *Profiles of Courage*, that this criticism became part of the public legacy of Nuremberg. To this day, articles appear in the popular press deriding Nuremberg as "a retroactive jurisprudence that would surely be unconstitutional in an American court."[28]

The other major criticism was that the Nuremberg Charter failed to provide sufficient due process guarantees and that those it did provide were circumscribed by several pro-prosecution judicial rulings. The most notable of such rulings was the Tribunal's decision to allow the prosecutors to introduce ex parte affidavits of persons who were in fact available to testify at trial. During the proceedings, the Nuremberg Tribunal took statements from 240 witnesses, and received 300,000 ex parte affidavits into evidence.[29] As Telford Taylor, one of the prosecutors at Nuremberg, wrote: "Total reliance on... untested depositions by unseen witnesses is certainly not the most reliable road to factual accuracy.... Considering the number of deponents and the play of emotional factors, not only faulty observation but deliberate exaggeration must have warped many of the reports."[30] Such ex parte affidavits seriously undermined the right of the defendants to confront the witnesses against them. The U.S. Supreme Court has expressed the importance of this right as follows: "Face-to-face confrontation generally serves to enhance the accuracy of fact finding by reducing the risk that a witness will wrongfully implicate an innocent person."[31] Telford Taylor also criticized the Nuremberg Tribunal's rulings preventing the defendants from having access to the Tribunal's evidentiary archives assembled by the Allies and allowing only the prosecution the right to object to witnesses before questioning.[32]

Such rulings were particularly troubling since the Tribunal did not provide for a right of appeal. Interestingly, those who were acquitted by the Nuremberg Tribunal (Hjalmar Schacht, Franz von Papen, and Hans Fritzsche) fared little better than those convicted since, in the absence of a double jeopardy provision in the Nuremberg Charter, they were subsequently tried and found guilty by German national courts for the same crimes for which they were tried and found not guilty at Nuremberg.[33]

Yet Nuremberg must be judged, not by contemporary standards, but through the prism of history. Viewed within the historic context described above, it was extraordinary that the major German war criminals were even given a trial (albeit an imperfect one), rather than summarily executed as had been proposed by Churchill and Stalin. With this in mind, Justice Robert Jackson, the chief prosecutor of Nuremberg, began his opening speech for the prosecution by stating: "That four great nations, flushed with victory and stung with injury, stay the hand of vengeance and voluntarily submit their captive enemies to the judgment of the law is one of the most significant tributes that Power has ever paid to Reason."[34] This is not meant to exonerate Nuremberg or excuse its shortcomings. Even Justice Jackson acknowledged at the conclusion of the Nuremberg Trials that "many mistakes have been made and many inadequacies must be confessed."[35] But he went on to say that he was "consoled by the fact that in proceedings of this novelty, errors and missteps may also be instructive to the future."

4

DESPITE SUCH ERRORS AND MISSTEPS, the Nuremberg precedent demonstrated that the creation of an international criminal tribunal was feasible, and the substantive principles of the Nuremberg Charter and judgment were unanimously affirmed by the United Nations

General Assembly in 1946.[36] The definition of war crimes contained in the Nuremberg Charter was later codified and elaborated in the four Geneva Conventions of 1949 for the protection of war victims,[37] and the Nuremberg Charter's definition of crimes against humanity led to the adoption in 1948 of the Convention on the Prevention and Punishment of the Crime of Genocide.[38]

In the aftermath of the Nuremberg trial, the world community began to direct its energies toward the establishment of a permanent international criminal court. To this end, in 1948 the United Nations General Assembly invited the International Law Commission "to study the desirability and possibility of establishing an international judicial organ for the trial of persons charged with genocide or other crimes over which jurisdiction will be conferred upon that organ by international conventions."* After considering the matter, the commission concluded that the establishment of such an organ was both desirable and possible. As a result, in 1950 the General Assembly set up the Committee on International Criminal Jurisdiction consisting of representatives of seventeen member states.[39] The committee was charged with preparing concrete proposals for the establishment of an international criminal court that could administer the Code of Crimes Against the Peace and Security of Mankind, which the International Law Commission was simultaneously drafting. The committee submitted a draft statute in 1951 which was amended by a second committee in 1953.[40]

The 1953 draft statute was permanently shelved due to the absence of an internationally accepted definition of the crime of "aggression" and the resulting failure to complete the Draft Code of Crimes Against the Peace and Security of Mankind, which was to have defined the subject matter jurisdiction of the International Criminal Court.[41] The General Assembly finally adopted a definition of "ag-

* The International Law Commission was established by the General Assembly in 1947 pursuant to its obligation to encourage the codification and progressive development of international law under Article 13, paragraph 1 of the United Nations Charter. The ILC consists of thirty-four members who are persons of recognized competence in international law. The members are elected by the General Assembly bearing in mind the need to ensure representation of the principal legal systems of the world. See United Nations, *The Work of the International Law Commission* (4th ed., 1988), pp. 4 and 28.

gression" in 1974, but it would be almost twenty years before the United Nations would return to the project of creating an international criminal court.[42]

There are several reasons why the initial efforts of the United Nations to create an international criminal court never got off the ground. First, since World War II, there has not been a repeat of the unique circumstances that made the Nuremberg and Tokyo Tribunals possible. That is, there have been no wars in which a coalition broadly supported by other members of the international community has defeated an obvious aggressor and violator of the laws of war and humanity so decisively as to bring about its complete defeat and subjugation. Second, an international criminal court whose goals included the punishment of aggressive warfare was seen in the context of the cold war as a threat to national sovereignty. For the major powers in particular, the power to review the legitimacy of the use force or to supersede the criminal jurisdiction of national courts was simply more than they were willing to cede to any international judicial body. Finally, the formulation of the United Nations Draft Statute for an International Criminal Court in 1953 had the paradoxical effect of setting back the effort to create such a court. Once the document was drafted, the debate shifted from whether to establish an international criminal court to whether to adopt the 1953 draft statute, which was extremely ambitious in the powers it conferred on the court with respect to states. In addition, the draft statute was tied inextricably to the Draft Code of Crimes Against the Peace and Security of Mankind, which was strongly opposed by many countries.

5

WITH THE END OF THE COLD WAR in the late 1980s, the United Nations returned to its project to create a permanent international criminal court. In 1989 the issue was reintroduced into the agenda of the General Assembly at the urging of a coalition of sixteen Caribbean and Latin American nations, led by Trinidad and Tobago, that saw such a court as a way to solve the difficulties which they encountered in prosecuting or extraditing narco-terrorists.[43]

The United States, however, decided to try to block the initiative for a variety of reasons. First, there existed residual mistrust of international tribunals among the members of the bureaucracy stemming in part from the recent International Court of Justice's adverse ruling in the *Nicaragua* case.[44] This ruling had resulted in the United States' withdrawal from the compulsory jurisdiction of the World Court. As then State Department Legal Adviser Abraham Sofaer testified to the Senate Foreign Relations Committee, "The ICJ betrayed a predisposition to find that it had jurisdiction and that Nicaragua's claims were justiciable, regardless of the overwhelming legal case to the contrary."[45] One of my colleagues in the Office of the Legal Adviser at the State Department put the point bluntly to me one day, when she said half-jokingly: "No matter how careful the selection process, you just can't trust international judges; it's as if there's something in the water at The Hague."

The second reason for the United States executive branch's decision was that it was strongly opposed to the creation of any international court that could potentially assert jurisdiction over U.S. officials for internationally controversial acts committed by U.S. forces such as the 1983 invasion of Grenada, the 1986 bombing of Tripoli, or the 1989 invasion of Panama.[46] In addition, there was concern that the establishment of an international criminal court would undermine the government's existing international law enforcement efforts and authorities. At that time, the *Alvarez Machain* case was pending before the U.S. Supreme Court. In that case, the U.S. government took the position that it was appropriate for it to kidnap foreign citizens from other countries to subject them to trial in the United States.[47]

Yet, because the Trinadadian proposal had widespread international support, a frontal assault was out of the question. Consequently, the U.S. government adopted the strategy of trying to prolong, without progress, the debate on a permanent international criminal court. Given the penchant of the U.N. International Law Commission to conduct decade-long studies on issues referred to it, the United States eagerly proposed that the question be sent to the commission. The alternative would have been to convene a preparatory conference to prepare a text of a treaty establishing an international criminal court, which would then be considered by a conference of plenipotentiaries and ratified by governments, perhaps within a span of three to five years. The United States succeeded in convincing the General Assembly to put the breaks on the project, and the issue was sent to the International Law Commission for study.

To the United States' surprise, after just one year of examining the question, the International Law Commission submitted an interim report to the General Assembly containing preliminary conclusions.[48] In keeping with its strategy, the United States identified a number of issues the commission's report failed adequately to address and proposed that the commission be requested to conduct further study of these issues.[49] The United States' proposal was adopted by consensus,[50] and the commission went back to the drawing board. The U.S. strategy appeared to be working, and the commission might well still be debating the matter to this day if it were not for the developments in the Balkans in the summer of 1992.

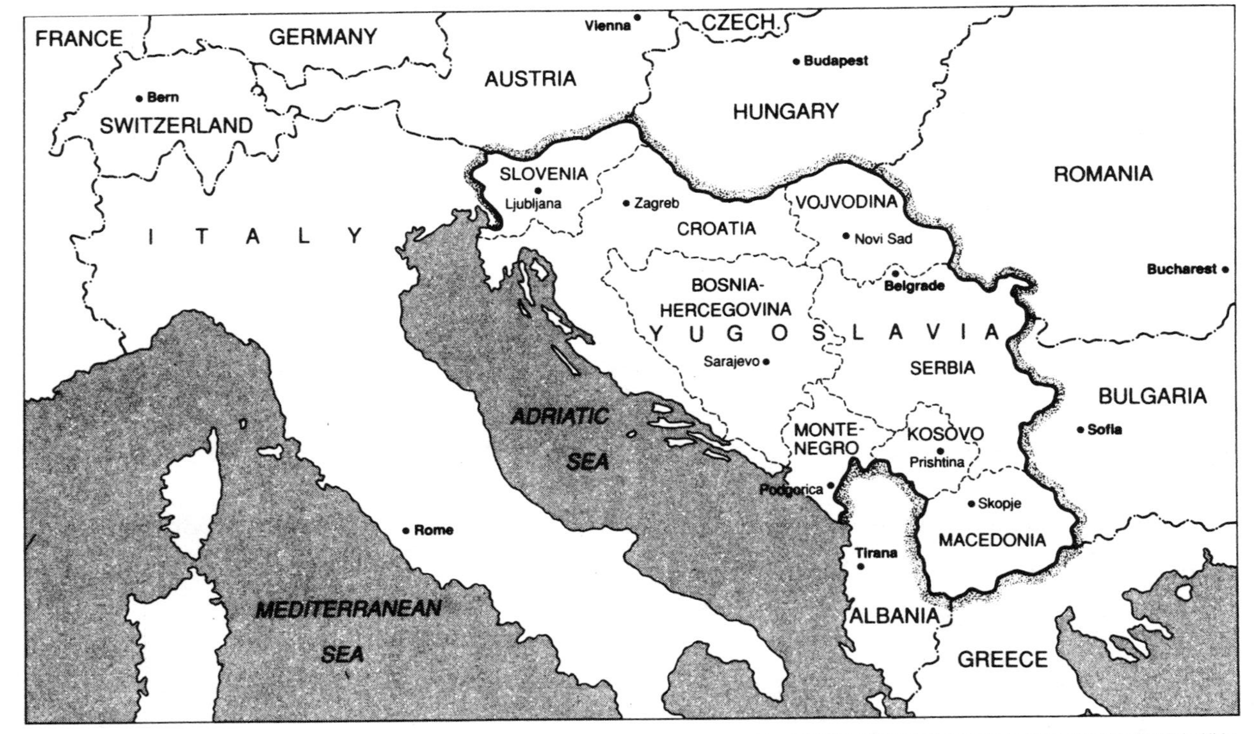

The republics of the former Yugoslavia

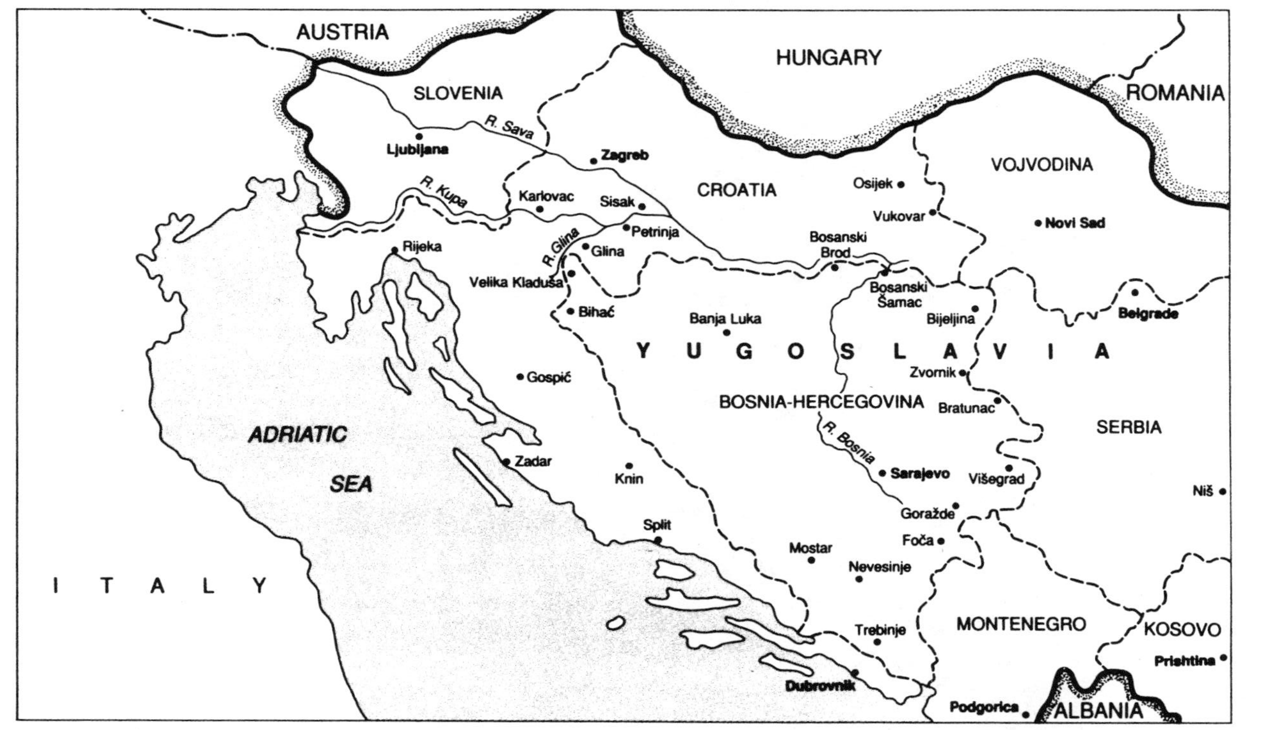

The republics of Croatia and Bosnia-Hercegovina

AP/WIDE WORLD PHOTOS

The U.N.'s efforts to mediate peace in the Balkans limped on from 1992–1995 without a major breakthrough under the co-chairmanship of former U.S. Secretary of State Cyrus Vance and Lord David Owen of Britain. Vance (center) and Owen (left) are shown above with Bosnian Serb leader Radovan Karadzic (right), the principal architect of ethnic cleansing in Bosnia.

Chapter 2

History of the Yugoslav Crisis

These characters are locked in history.

—Lord David Owen
PBS Interview
June 14, 1994

1

Prior to its dissolution in 1991, Yugoslavia was not so much an ethnic melting pot as a boiling cauldron of ethnic tension with deep historic roots.[1] Although the people of the different regions of the former Yugoslavia shared a common language (Serbo-Croatian) and physical characteristics (Slavic), differences among their religions and historical experiences led to the growth of strong separate ethnic identities. The region's strategic position at the southern crossroads of Europe and Asia has been the source of its historic turmoil. Since recorded time, the region has been invaded, contested, and ruled successively or concurrently by the Macedonian, Roman, Byzantine, Slav, Bulgar, Venetian, Austro-Hungarian, Ottoman, and the Nazi German empires.

By the ninth century, Christianity had become the predominant faith throughout the region, with the western portion (what is now Croatia and Slovenia) largely Roman Catholic, and the eastern section (Bosnia-Herzegovina, Serbia, Montenegro, and Macedonia) mostly Eastern Orthodox. The defining moment in the early history of the region occurred on St. Vitus Day (June 28) in 1389, when the Ottoman Turks defeated Serbian forces at the battle of Kosovo Polje (Field of the Blackbirds). Thereafter, the eastern portion of the Balkans were plunged into a period of Ottoman occupation from which they did not emerge until the early twentieth century. During the Ottoman subjugation, many of the Balkan people were able to preserve their culture by accepting second-class status within the Ottoman Empire. Others (predominantly in the cities of what is now Bosnia) converted to Islam to avoid persecution and the oppressive taxes required of non-Muslims. Current-day Serbian hostility toward Bosnian Muslims stems in large part from what they believe was betrayal of the true faith by their ancestors over six hundred years ago.[2] While Serbia and Bosnia existed under five centuries of Ottoman domination, the Catholic Slovenes and Croats were absorbed by the Hapsburg Empire and were influenced by centuries of close contact with Austria, Hungary, and Italy.

Two Balkan wars were fought in 1912 and 1913, which resulted in the liberation of the Balkan peninsula from Ottoman control. During these conflicts, Serbian nationalists resorted to ethnic violence on a massive scale. As the International Commission to Inquire into the Causes and Conduct of the Balkan Wars reported in 1914, "houses and whole villages [were] reduced to ashes, unarmed and innocent populations [were] massacred en masse, incredible acts of violence, pillage and brutality of every kind—such were the means which were employed by the Serbo-Montenegrin soldiery, with a view to the entire transformation of the ethnic character of these regions."[3]

Having expelled the Turks, Serb nationalists turned their attention to the Hapsburg empire, which had annexed Bosnia-Herzegovina in 1908. World War I began when Gavrilo Princip, a Bosnian Serbian nationalist, assassinated Austrian Archduke Ferdinand in Sarajevo on June 28, 1914. It was no coincidence that the archduke, who was heir to the Hapsburg throne, was killed on the anniversary of the Battle of Kosovo. Independence from foreign domination was finally realized after the First World War when King Alexander of Serbia proclaimed the Kingdom of Serbs, Croats, and Slovenes, which became known as Yugoslavia, meaning "Land of the South Slavs."

2

THE UNITY ACHIEVED UNDER KING ALEXANDER was fragile, with the Croats pushing for ever greater self-government within a looser confederation. In 1929, with the support of Italian dictator Benito Mussolini, the Ustasha (meaning "uprising") movement was born with the goal of Croatian independence—if necessary through violence. In 1934, a member of the Ustasha assassinated King Alexander, and a weak regency was appointed to rule in place of Alexander's ten-year-old son. This set the stage for the invasion of Yugoslavia by the Axis powers in 1941.

During World War II, the Axis powers occupied Yugoslavia and partitioned the country into German and Italian spheres of influence. Croatia became a puppet state (comprised of today's Croatia and Bosnia-Herzegovina) of Hitler's Nazi Germany, with the Ustasha leader, Ante Pavelic, placed in charge. The Ustasha regarded Croatia's two million Serbs as a threat and set about to eliminate them through mass extermination.[4] To that end, Pavelic stated "the Slavoserbs are the rubbish of a nation, the type of people who will sell themselves to anyone and at any price, and to every buyer."[5] Mile Budak, one of Pavelic's chief deputies, declared the Ustasha plan for the Croatian and Bosnian Serbs on July 22, 1941: "We shall slay one-third of the Serbian population, drive away another third, and the rest we shall convert to the Roman Catholic faith and thus assimilate into Croats. Thus we will destroy every trace of theirs and all that which will be left will be an evil memory of them."[6] Echoing this policy, the governor of western Bosnia, Victor Gutisch, urged that the territory under his control be "thoroughly cleansed of Serbian dirt."[7] Hence, the term "ethnic cleansing" was first coined, not by the Serbs, but by the Croats and Bosnians during World War II.

To accomplish its goal, the Ustasha established an extermination camp at Jasenovac which rivaled the infamous Nazi death camp at Auschwitz in its brutal efficiency.[8] In all, a million and a half Serbs were "ethnicly cleansed" by the Ustasha during the Second World War—over five hundred thousand were killed and a million were driven from the territory to seek refuge in other countries. At one point, the German authorities were reportedly forced to close the Danube to swimming because of the large number of Serb corpses being thrown into the river by the Croatian Ustasha.[9]

Resistance to the Axis occupation of Yugoslavia came from the communist Partisan forces, led by the Croatian-born Josip Broz Tito. With the support of the Allies, Tito's partisans eventually secured control over the entire Yugoslav territory. In revenge for the Croat atrocities, the partisans murdered over one hundred thousand Croatian prisoners when the Ustasha surrendered in May 1946.[10]

After the war, Tito established a federal system in Yugoslavia consisting of six republics—Serbia, Croatia, Slovenia, Bosnia-Herzegovina, Macedonia, and Montenegro—and two autonomous provinces (Kosovo and Vojvodina) within the Republic of Serbia. The reordered internal boundaries were aimed at containing Serbian nationalism by stranding Serb minorities in each of the republics outside Serbia itself. In addition, Tito successfully dealt with ethnic tensions within and among the republics through stern repression at the hands of the secret police known as the GZNA.

In 1948, the Soviet Premier, Joseph Stalin, expelled Yugoslavia from the Cominform, an organization of eastern Communist nations, for "pursuing an unfriendly policy towards the Soviet Union."[11] This action led to fears of a Soviet attack, fears which intensified after the Soviet invasion of Czechoslovakia in 1968. As much as anything else, the Soviet threat provided the glue which held Tito's Yugoslavia together. To counter this threat, Tito initiated a doctrine known as "Total National Defense" which required universal military service and coordinated training in guerrilla warfare. Training facilities, weapons caches, and supply stores were placed throughout the country, and the military organized reserve units around work places to provide the wide distribution of forces and weapons.[12] The Yugoslav National Army became the third-largest in all of Europe.

Tito's death on May 4, 1980, and the collapse of the Soviet threat in the late 1980s, unleashed the long-festering centrifugal forces which would soon lead to Yugoslavia's disintegration. After the break up of Yugoslavia, the Total National Defense system would be used not against a foreign invader, but against Yugoslavia's own republics. An emphasis on guerrilla warfare, a decentralized command system, and the enlistment of civilian volunteers would reappear in the tactics of each of the warring factions.

3

THE HISTORY OF THE REGION might suggest that the war that began in 1991 was little more than a continuation of the endemic ethnic strife in the area. Yet to attribute the tragedy of Yugoslavia solely to unstoppable historic forces is to turn a blind eye to the critical role played by the rise of Serb nationalism among Belgrade intellectuals in the mid-1980s and the subsequent harnessing of nationalist rhetoric by Slobodan Milosevic. As Warren Zimmermann, then U.S. ambassador to Belgrade put it, "The breakup of Yugoslavia was a classic example of nationalism from the top down."[13]

In 1986, members of the Serbian Academy of Arts and Sciences prepared a Manifesto attacking the Yugoslavia Constitution. The document, known as the SAAS Memorandum, argued that Tito had consistently discriminated against the Serbs and that Serbia had been subject to economic domination by Croatia and Slovenia. It spoke of the "physical, political, legal and cultural genocide against the Serb population in Kosovo" as well as discrimination against Serbs who resided in other Republics.[14]

Later that year, Slobodan Milosevic, riding a wave of Serbian nationalism, became Serbian Communist Party chief. Milosevic solidified his position by provoking and then using federal troops to ruthlessly crush successive crises in the region of Serbia known as Kosovo, where Albanians outnumbered Serbs ten to one. Kosovo became Milosevic's launching pad in his quest to extend his power to the rest of Yugoslavia. If, as one commentator put it, "the hatred that astounded the world in Yugoslavia was engineered, not innate,"[15] it was Milosevic who was the chief engineer. According to Ambassador Zimmermann, "Those who argue that ancient Balkan hostilities account for the violence that overtook and destroyed Yugoslavia ignore the power of television in the service of officially provoked racism."[16] Through a barrage of propaganda via the state-owned media, Milosevic played on Serb fears and feelings of victimization, going back to their defeat by the Ottomans at Kosovo in 1389 and emphasizing their treatment at the hands of the Ustasha during World War II. "The virus of television," Ambassador Zimmermann recounts, "spread ethnic hatred like an epidemic."[17]

The ascent of a hardline Serbian nationalist government in Serbia fanned anti-Serb nationalism in the republics of Croatia and Slovenia. At the same time, Milosevic's efforts to create a more centralized Yugoslavia under Serbian dominance engendered strident resistance from the leaders of Croatia and Slovenia, Franjo Tudjman and Milan Kucan, who desired to convert Yugoslavia into a loose confederation that would dilute Serbian influence. Flexing his political muscle in the spring of 1991, Milosevic blocked Stipe Mesic, a Croat, from assuming the federal presidency, despite the fact that the constitution provided that the presidency rotate annually among the republics and it was Croatia's turn.

After a series of negotiations with Milosevic over a new Yugoslav constitution proved futile, Croatia and Slovenia declared their independence on June 25, 1991, without offering concrete guarantees for the security of the five hundred thousand Serbs living within their borders. While visiting Belgrade a week earlier, U.S. Secretary of State James Baker had warned of the "dangers of disintegration." He urged that Yugoslavia maintain "territorial integrity" and said that the United States "would not recognize unilateral declarations of independence."[18] Milosevic took this as a green light to use force to halt secession and to protect the Serbs living in Croatia and Slovenia. "What they read between the lines of the Baker visit," writes Ambassador Zimmermann, "was that the United States had no intention of stopping them by force."[19] Milosevic began by sending the Serb-dominated Yugoslav National Army (JNA) into Slovenia to crush that republic's nascent militia. After the Slovenes withstood repeated attacks and actually defeated the JNA in several engagements, Milosevic agreed to a European Community-brokered cease-fire, while he turned his attention to Croatia.

The JNA, aided by local Serbian insurgents, inflicted heavy casualties on the inexperienced and outgunned Croatian forces and quickly took control of one-third of Croatia's territory. On November 20, 1991, one of the Yugoslav conflict's most egregious acts was committed when Serb forces captured the Croatian town of Vukovar. Upon entering the city, Serb forces massacred some two hundred Croatian patients (mostly wounded soldiers) in the Vukovar hospital and disposed of their bodies in a mass grave that was later discovered by U.N. forensic investigators.[20]

For six months, repeated efforts by the European Community and the Conference on Security and Cooperation in Europe to broker a durable cease fire in Croatia failed to yield tangible success. Finally, in January of 1992, after thousands had been killed in the fighting, Croatia and Serbia agreed to the deployment of a United Nations peacekeeping force (known as UNPROFOR) to oversee the withdrawal of the JNA and the disarming of local forces in the areas of conflict inside Croatia.[21] Later that month, the European Community formally recognized the new independent state of Croatia. During the next four years, Croatia, under cover of the United Nations and backed by Germany, would arm and make preparations for a successful campaign to retake its lost territory.

In the meantime, the Bosnians were forced to choose between remaining in what had become a Serbian ethnic dictatorship or seeking a hazardous independence. The leader of the Bosnian Serb political party, a psychiatrist named Radovan Karadzic, warned that pursuing independence would "make the Muslim people disappear, because the Muslims cannot defend themselves if there is war."[22] But his warning (or threat) was not heeded. On February 29 and March 1, 1992, the Muslim and Croatian people of Bosnia-Herzegovina voted overwhelmingly for independence. At the time of the vote, Bosnia consisted of three main ethnic groups: Slavic Muslims (43 percent of the population), Serbs (31 percent), and Croats (17 percent).[23] While these groups are defined on the basis of religion, Bosnia was largely a secular society; a 1985 survey found that only 17 percent of its people considered themselves believers and interfaith marriage was extremely common.[24]

Although the majority of Bosnian Serbs boycotted the poll, independence was the choice of 63 percent of the total electorate. On April 6, the European Community recognized the new independent nation of Bosnia-Herzegovina, with the United States following suit the next day. That same day, the Bosnian Serbs, under the leadership of their self-styled president, Radovan Karadzic, proclaimed the formation of an independent "Republic Srpska" (Serbian Republic of Bosnia and Herzegovina), whose government was located in the city of Pale in southeast Bosnia. The Serbs immediately launched attacks against the Croatian and Muslim populations in northeast and southern Bosnia with the goal of connecting Serb populated regions in north and west Bosnia to Serbia in the east. According to one observer, "The

Bosnian Serbs, with JNA help, seized TV-Sarajevo repeaters around Bosnia and reprogrammed them to carry TV-Belgrade, a key factor in the incitement of ethnic hatred."[25] Assisted by some forty-five thousand JNA troops, the Serb insurgent forces seized control of 70 percent of Bosnia's territory municipality by municipality. By the middle of April, the Muslims were left with control over only a few islands of territory within Bosnia—Sarajevo, Mostar, Bihac, Tuzla, Srebrenica, and Gorazde—and these were shelled relentlessly by JNA and Serb insurgent forces.

The Serbs had planned their attack well in advance. Milosevic had begun to arm and finance local Serb militias more than six months before Bosnia declared its independence.[26] Moreover, according to Borisav Jovic who had been commander of the JNA, in January 1992, Milosevic issued a secret order to start transferring all Serbian JNA officers who had been born in Bosnia back to their native republic.[27] On May 19, 1992, in an unsuccessful attempt to head off the threat of United Nations sanctions for its involvement in the hostilities in Bosnia, Serbia announced the withdrawal of the JNA from Bosnia-Herzegovina. When the JNA pulled out, however, it demobilized 85 percent of the officers and men and left behind most of the army's equipment. The demobilized troops, under the command of former JNA 9th Army Corps Chief of Staff Ratko Mladic, together with local insurgents and Serbia based-militias, became a new army known as the VRS, which continued to receive assistance and instructions from Serbia.[28] Not deceived by this tactic, on May 30 the Security Council adopted Resolution 757 which imposed a sweeping trade embargo on Serbia-Montenegro.

Throughout this period, recurrent efforts by European Community and United Nations mediators to broker a lasting cease fire and a framework for peace met with little success. The United Nations did manage to obtain permission from the warring sides to send in an UNPROFOR contingent to secure the Sarajevo airport in order to open a humanitarian aid pipeline into the besieged city. However, UNPROFOR proved unable to keep the pipeline open on a sustained basis due to frequent attacks on the aircraft bringing in humanitarian aid.[29]

At the same time, international observers, including information-gathering missions under the auspices of the United Nations Human

Rights Commission, the European Community, the Conference on Security and Cooperation in Europe, the International Committee of the Red Cross, Amnesty International, and Helsinki Watch began to document widespread abuses occurring in Bosnia. Through these reports, the world learned of mass forced-population transfers of Muslims, organized massacres, the physical destruction of whole towns, the systematic and repeated rape of thousands of Muslim women and young girls, and the existence of over four hundred Serb-run detention centers. Based on the observations of his own special envoy, Secretary General of the United Nations Boutros Boutros-Ghali reported to the Security Council that the Serbs of Bosnia-Herzegovina, with support from the JNA, were "making a concerted effort...to create ethnically pure regions" in the republic, and that the "techniques used are the seizure of territory by military force and intimidation of the non-Serb population."[30] These methods were as effective as they were brutal. By the end of 1994, the Serbs had expelled, killed or imprisoned 90 percent of the 1.7 million non-Serbs who once lived in Serbian-held areas of Bosnia.[31]

Among the most abhorrent cases of "ethnic cleansing" involved the town of Kozarac, a predominantly Muslim community in the Prijedor region of Bosnia. It was the town which Dusko Tadic had called home. As described by BBC correspondent Misha Glenny, "The Muslims of Kozarac surrendered without a struggle but the Serb forces destroyed the village completely, perpetrating a massacre of hundreds of civilians in the process....Muslims were thrown out of their houses and forced to sign papers handing all their property and worldly goods over to the Serbs."[32]

Muslim women were herded into schools and warehouses and raped repeatedly.[33] Those Muslim men who were not executed on the spot were taken to Serb-run concentration camps, which served as central locations to terrorize individuals and intimidate the entire target population. As a reporter for the *New York Times* recounted: "The men were taken from the village at gunpoint and forced into freight cars. As many as 180 were jammed, standing, into boxcars measuring 39 by 6 feet. They were kept that way for three days, without water or food, as the train moved slowly across the countryside. Nazis transporting Jews in 1942? No, Serbs transporting Muslim Bosnians in 1992."[34] Roy Gutman of *Newsday*, the first journalist to visit the Bosnian Serb concentration camps, wrote on August 2: "The Serb conquerors of northern Bosnia have established two concentration camps in which more than a thousand civilians have been executed or starved and thousands more are being held until they die."[35] Four days later, on August 6, Penny Marshall of International Television News (ITN) filmed conditions at the Omarska concentration camp in Northern Bosnia. She captured startling footage of "men at various stages of human decay and affliction; the bones of their elbows and wrists protrude like pieces of jagged stone from the pencil thin stalks to which their arms have been reduced."[36] The ITN footage resulted in an international outcry to stop the atrocities.

4

MOST EXPERTS AGREE that the Security Council could have acted to stop the atrocities in Bosnia. When Bosnia's president Alija Izetbegovic visited Washington at the end of 1991, he asked for the deployment of preventive peacekeepers in Bosnia. A year later, the United States would employ this very tactic with great success in Macedonia,[37] but the opportunity to prevent the Bosnian war with a trip-wire force was squandered. After the fighting began in 1992, the Bosnian president pleaded for preventive air strikes by NATO, but the United States responded that "no military resolution from outside was possible."[38] Such NATO airstrikes could have been used to disrupt the Bosnian Serb Army's command and control, as well as its crucial supply lines from Serbia.[39] In addition, the main prison camps and associated installations were located in western and northern Bosnia, not in the mountains that covered most of the country, and thus would have made easy targets for surgical air strikes.[40] Finally, NATO aircraft could have lifted the siege of Sarajevo and maintained the safety and integrity of the other "safe areas."[41] But this was not to be. "Had NATO met [the Serb] aggression with airstrikes in the summer of 1992," wrote Warren Zimmermann, the last U.S. ambassador to Yugoslavia, "I believe that a negotiated result would soon have followed. The NATO air campaign [in 1995] came three years and more than a hundred thousand deaths after America's first real opportunity to help end the war."[42] In his memoir on the Balkan conflict, Zimmermann concludes that "the refusal of the Bush administration to commit American [air] power early in the Bosnian war was our greatest mistake of the entire Yugoslav crisis."[43]

After the collapse of the Soviet Union, Yugoslavia had lost its strategic importance to Washington. Preoccupied with the Persian Gulf War and the future of the disintegrating Soviet Union, the United States was satisfied to leave the handling of the Yugoslav conflict to the European Community. In 1989, when Milosevic was consolidating power, an interagency review by the Bush Administration concluded that Yugoslavia held no strategic interests for the United States.[44] When the fighting began in 1991, Secretary of State James Baker bluntly explained the United States' lack of interest by saying, "We don't have a dog in that fight."[45]

Even after receiving reports of Serb-run death camps in Bosnia, Washington was hesitant to act. According to George Kenny, the U.S. State Department official who resigned in protest, the State Department policy at the time amounted to "Let's pretend this is not happening."[46] The day after the ITN footage of Omarska aired worldwide, President Bush told a news conference: "We know there is horror in these detention camps. But in all honesty, I can't confirm to you some of the claims that there is indeed a genocidal process going on there."[47] Thereafter, U.S. officials were instructed to avoid using the "genocide" label with respect to Bosnia so as not to trigger obligations under the Genocide Convention, which obliges parties to prevent and punish acts of genocide.[48]

That policy did not change when the Clinton team took over in 1993. Testifying before Congress in May 1993, Secretary of State Christopher refused to acknowledge that Serbs were committing genocide in Bosnia, asserting instead that "all sides" were responsible for the atrocities there—thus removing the imperative for action.[49] Notwithstanding clear evidence to the contrary, this would remain the party line until two years later, in March 1995, when Clinton Administration officials would leak the finding of a classified CIA study that 90 percent of ethnic cleansing had been carried out by Serbs pursuant to a policy designed to destroy and disperse the non-Serb population.[50]

Britain and France, for their part, insisted on limiting international action in Bosnia to a relief effort assisted by the United Nations Protection Force (UNPROFOR).[51] The British and French governments then argued that the presence of their troops in UNPROFOR made assertive military action, such as airstrikes against the Serbs, impossible because the Serbs would retaliate against the U.N. forces.[52] The United States found it hard to disagree because it was opposed to any deployment of U.S. ground troops in Bosnia. As one political analyst concluded at the time, "Risk avoidance appears to have acquired the force of doctrine at the Pentagon. In the Clinton administration, the concern borders on an obsession with both military and civilian leaders whose view on the use of force was molded by the war in Vietnam."[53]

Britain, moreover, had taken the lead in trying to relaunch the stalled peace process by hosting the International Conference on the Former Yugoslavia in August 1992. The conference participants, with the subsequent endorsement of the Security Council, decided to unify European and United Nations mediation efforts in Bosnia under the cochairmanship of U.N. envoy Cyrus Vance and Lord David Owen of Britain. The Vance-Owen venture came under intense criticism for delinking Serbian abuses from the peace negotiations. "It's fine to argue that human rights and negotiations should be kept separated," said one critic, "but the negotiations should not give the appearance of condoning genocide."[54] In addition, the negotiations were seen as legitimizing the ethnic division of Bosnia and allowing the Serbs to buy time while continuing to push ahead with ethnic cleansing. Asbjorn Eide, the United Nations' Special Rapporteur on the Human Rights of Minorities, said that "the effect of the Vance-Owen plan was to accelerate ethnic purity in the regions controlled by the three ethnic groups, instead of trying to protect minorities or arrange for their harmonious coexistence within the boundaries of Bosnia." "This," he concluded, "had set a dangerous precedent for handling minorities elsewhere in Europe."[55] Despite these criticisms, the British government was firmly committed to the success of the Vance-Owen venture. In its view, the best way to stop the atrocities was to stop the war. Britain was, therefore, reluctant to embrace any actions against the Bosnian Serbs that could potentially disrupt the peace negotiations which limped on without a major breakthrough for four years.

Russia, for its own very different reasons, was also strongly opposed to aggressive actions by the United Nations against the Bosnian Serbs. Russia is linked to Serbia by religion, alphabet, and history, and when the war began in 1991, scores of sympathetic Russians went to fight on the Serb side.[56] Russian hard-liners exploited these links and pressured the Yeltsin government to exercise a de facto veto at the Security Council whenever forceful measures were being considered.[57] Moreover, the Yeltsin government had its own interest in precluding the setting of an interventionist precedent by the international community—a precedent that could be used against Moscow in its dealings with its own minorities.[58] With its human rights record under constant attack in recent years, the fifth permanent member of the Security Council, China, had a similar motivation for opposing forceful action by the U.N. in Bosnia. But, unlike Russia, China had rarely exercised its veto in the Security Council, preferring instead to express dissatisfaction through abstention.

Thus, despite growing public pressure to respond to the Bosnian atrocities, the permanent members of the Security Council—the United States, Britain, France, Russia, and China—remained unwilling to institute vigorous actions to halt the bloodshed and abuses.[59] Instead, they imposed a one-sided arms embargo; they adopted a resolution authorizing the use of military force which was never implemented; they imposed toothless economic sanctions that were so riddled with loopholes as to be completely ineffective; they established a "no-fly zone" which was violated over four hundred times with impunity; and they created "safe areas" which became the sites of the conflict's worst massacres.

After fighting broke out in Slovenia and Croatia in 1991, Belgrade requested that the Security Council impose an arms embargo on Yugoslavia to prevent an escalation of the conflict.[60] Later, the Security Council reaffirmed that its arms embargo would continue to apply to all parts of the former Yugoslavia, "any decisions on the question of the recognition of the independence of certain republics notwithstanding."[61] The only state truly effected by the arms embargo was Bosnia, which was left with no means to defend itself, while Serbia and Croatia had all they needed in terms of military equipment and supplies.[62] President Clinton had campaigned on a pledge to lift the arms embargo on Bosnia, but when he came to office, Russia, Britain, and France made clear that they "would not tolerate a lifting of the arms embargo under any circumstances."[63] Meanwhile, Bosnia was literally pushed to the brink of extinction.

The main thrust of early Security Council action in Bosnia was to provide humanitarian aid. This led to a gradual expansion of the size and mandate of UNPROFOR, which had originally been created to monitor the cease-fire between Serbia and Croatia.[64] In response to frequent Serb attacks on U.N. humanitarian aid convoys, on August 13, 1992, the Security Council adopted Resolution 770 authorizing governments to take "all measures necessary" to ensure the safe delivery of relief aid in Bosnia. This was the same formula that in Resolution 678 authorized the use of massive military force to expel Iraq from Kuwait. International expectations were high for a corresponding response in Bosnia. But, unlike Resolution 678, Resolution 770 led to no military intervention. There was no attempt to launch airstrikes and no plan to send in coalition forces. As U.S. Secretary of State Lawrence Eagleburger explained two weeks after the adoption of the resolution, such action would "not be stomached on either side of the Atlantic."[65] For three years the resolution would remain a dead letter and a monument to the Security Council's lack of will to stop the killing in Bosnia.

Yet the Security Council was not willing to let Serb ethnic cleansing go completely unpunished. The Council decided to impose an economic embargo on Serbia in order to disrupt its economy and thereby "apply pressure on Serbia-Montenegro to meet U.N. demands to cease outside aggression and interference in Bosnia."[66] However, the initial sanctions resolution (Resolution 757) was substantially watered down to satisfy Russian objections. For example, an exception was inserted into the resolution allowing for the transshipment of goods across the territory of Serbia, which were readily diverted to destinations within Serbia itself. Another exception allowed for the shipment of humanitarian items to Serbia, including cigarettes, vodka, clothing, and heating oil, which were freely diverted to the Serb army and paramilitary forces.[67] The embargo, moreover, did not cover shipments to Serb-controlled territories in Bosnia.

In addition, the resolution provided for no enforcement such as maritime interdiction of vessels trading with Serbia-Montenegro or the placement of monitors at Serbia's borders. These loopholes and the lack of enforcement enabled Serbia to successfully circumvent the sanctions.[68] Even after the sanctions were incrementally strengthened through the adoption of Resolution 787 in November 1992 and Resolution 820 in April 1993, they had no perceptible impact on the willingness or ability of the Bosnian Serbs to continue to wage war and commit atrocities.[69]

Another type of sanction pursued was the suspension of Serbia from the General Assembly.[70] When Yugoslavia broke apart in 1992, Croatia, Slovenia, Bosnia, and Macedonia each applied and was accepted as a new member of the United Nations. Serbia knew that the Security Council was unlikely to approve its application any time soon, so Serbia and Montenegro announced that they were the continuation of the old Yugoslavia and were thus entitled to continue its membership at the United Nations. This was, after all, what Russia had been allowed to do after the breakup of the Soviet Union in 1991. The United States, however, did not see that precedent as applicable. In contrast to Russia, Serbia-Montenegro did not comprise a majority of the former Yugoslavia's land, population, or resources, and there had been no agreement between the former Yugoslav republics providing that Serbia-Montenegro should continue Yugoslavia's membership in the United Nations. The United States circulated a draft Security Council resolution that would have denied Serbia-Montenegro's claim and confirm that Yugoslavia's membership in the United Nations had been extinguished with the dissolution of that country. In order to obtain Russian support, however, the resolution was substantially weakened[71] and the U.N. legal counsel interpreted the text as precluding Serbia-Montenegro from participating in the General Assembly, but permitting it to continue to maintain its mission at New York and participate in other U.N. bodies.[72] What was intended to be a legal rejection of Serbia-Montenegro's claim to the Yugoslav seat at the United Nations became, in effect, a new kind of suspension which the International Court of Justice later said was "not free from legal difficulty."[73]

While waiting for the sanctions to take effect, the Security Council found itself faced with a new challenge when Bosnian Serb aircraft began to attack civilian targets from their air base in the Bosnian Serb-controlled city of Banja Luka. The Muslims, who had no airforce, were extremely vulnerable to such "ethnic cleansing by air" and the casualties quickly mounted. In response, on October 9, 1992, the Security Council adopted Resolution 781 imposing a "no-fly zone" over Bosnia. At the urging of the British and French, the clause providing for enforcement of the no-fly zone was omitted from the resolution.

Instead, the resolution called only for monitors to report violations. They had plenty to report. During the next six months there were over 465 documented violations of the no-fly zone.[74] Yet it was not until March 31, 1993, that the Security Council adopted Resolution 816 authorizing NATO to enforce the no-fly zone, and it was not until February 8, 1994, that NATO would finally take action to shoot down Serb aircraft violating the ban.[75] This year-and-a-half delay was not a logistical one; it was purely political.

By far the most controversial of all of the (non)actions taken by the Security Council was the creation of so-called "safe areas" in response to the sustained Serb attacks on the Muslim population centers at the beginning of 1993. In the spring of 1993, the attacks on Srebrenica in eastern Bosnia were particularly ruthless, and by the beginning of April, the city was on the brink of collapse. On April 16, the Security Council adopted Resolution 819 which demanded that all parties treat the city as a "safe area" free from armed attack. A week later, the Council adopted Resolution 824 designating the predominantly Muslim cities of Sarajevo, Tuzla, Zepa, Gorazde, and Bihac as additional safe areas. As a quid pro quo for the withdrawal of Serb forces, UNPROFOR was assigned the task of overseeing the demilitarization of the safe areas. Yet the Council provided no real enforcement component to the safe area concept. While the UNPROFOR commander indicated that it would take 35,000 troops to protect the safe areas, "the Council irresponsibly chose a 'light option' of a 7,500 troop reinforcement to carry out the mandate."[76] When the Serbs attacked the safe areas, the blue helmets retreated, and tens of thousands of defenseless civilians were massacred and carted off to mass graves in the nearby countryside. "Historians will show," wrote the editors of *The New Republic* shortly after the fall of Srebrenica, "that the most important allies of the Bosnian Serbs have been the peacekeeping forces of the United Nations."[77]

Chapter 3

Collecting the Facts

We must establish incredible events by credible evidence.

—Robert H. Jackson
Report to the President
June 7, 1945

1

Having failed to take action to halt the atrocities in Bosnia, the Security Council became determined to at least take steps to hold the violators accountable. The first was in the form of a warning. On July 13, 1992, the Security Council adopted Resolution 764 which stated that persons who committed violations of "international humanitarian law" (a fancy term meaning war crimes) in the former Yugoslavia would be held individually responsible. The second step sought to lay the foundation for future prosecutions of those perpetrators who did not heed the Council's warning. Thus, on August 13, 1992, the Security Council adopted resolution 771 which called upon states and international humanitarian organizations to submit to the Council "substantiated information" in their possession concerning war crimes in the former Yugoslavia.

As Attorney-Adviser for U.N. Affairs at the State Department, I was assigned to prepare the initial draft of Resolution 771. When I came to work the morning of August 7, 1992, the Department of State was in a frenzy over the ITN broadcast of conditions at the Omarska concentration camp. It was clear that some immediate action was required, if only to meet the growing sense of public discomfort as the

Serbs cavalierly pressed on with their campaign of ethnic cleansing in the full glare of the international media. Others felt that wider principles were at stake and that Serbian impunity threatened to subvert emerging norms of international human rights.[1] Thus, I was not surprised to receive a message marked "urgent" from my colleagues in the State Department's International Organizations Bureau, which handles policy concerning the United Nations. "We need a draft resolution to provide a means of documenting these atrocities—ASAP," the note read.

Rather than reinvent the wheel with every new resolution, it is the practice of the Security Council to recycle language found in earlier resolutions. That way, language which was once the product of drawn-out negotiations and careful compromises does not have to be debated anew. In this spirit, I borrowed the language for the main operative clause of Resolution 771 from Resolution 674 concerning Iraq, which had invited member states to "collate substantiated information in their possession or submitted to them on the grave breaches by Iraq. . . . and to make this information available to the [Security] Council." However, only two states—the United States and Kuwait—ever submitted information pursuant to the "invitation" contained in Resolution 674.[2] To avoid falling prey to a repeat of such international apathy, I used somewhat stronger wording for Resolution 771, "calling upon" rather than "requesting" states to submit information and assigning the Secretary General the tasks of collating the information received from states, preparing a report summarizing the information, and recommending additional measures.

I began the draft resolution with a clause which was to become the earliest list of the acts deemed by the Security Council to constitute "violations of international humanitarian law" in the former Yugoslavia.* For maximum deterrent value in the former Yugoslavia, I

---

* The second preambular clause of Resolution 771 provides: "Expressing grave alarm at continuing reports of widespread violations of international humanitarian law occurring within the territory of the former Yugoslavia and especially in Bosnia and Herzegovina including reports of mass forcible expulsion and deportation of civilians, imprisonment and abuse of civilians in detention centres, deliberate attacks on non-combatants, hospitals and ambulances, impeding the delivery of food and medical supplies to the civilian population, and wanton

drafted this list in the language of news reports rather than strictly following the legal terminology of the Geneva Conventions. In light of United Nations' estimates that some 2.8 million Bosnians (more than half the country's entire population) would require food and medical aid to survive[3] and the fact that United Nations' attempts to provide such aid were persistently blocked by Serb paramilitary forces, I specifically included a reference in the list of violations to "impeding the delivery of food and medical supplies to the civilian population." This formulation, which is not contained in the Geneva Convention's list of grave breaches, later reappeared in Security Council Resolution 794 on Somalia and may be the underpinnings of a newly recognized category of war crime carrying individual criminal responsibility.

One thing I regretfully neglected to include in the resolution was a definition of the term "substantiated information." As a consequence, the term was subject to widely divergent interpretations. Canada, for example, reported only information that was "corroborated by other sources.... [through] cross-referencing the information received with other material reporting the same incident, or the same location where a number of allegations took place."[4] The United States, on the other hand, submitted even information contained in newspaper articles, as long as the reporter had indicated "that he/she personally witnessed violations of international humanitarian law."[5] Other countries used the term as an excuse not to submit any information at all, on the ground that it had not been "substantiated" through judicial means.

At the time I was drafting Resolution 771, I was aware of a proposal that had been recently circulated within the Office of the Legal Adviser to establish an international commission to investigate Iraqi war crimes committed during the Persian Gulf War. Although that proposal was never pursued, I thought such language might be appropriate for Resolution 771. In light of the Bush Administration's opposition to the creation of a permanent international criminal court, I recognized that the U.S. government was not ready to entrust the United Nations with the authority to conduct trials of Yugoslav war criminals. But I felt there might nevertheless be support for the creation of a neutral international investigative body that could document

---

devastation and destruction of property." U.N. Security Council Resolution 771 (August 13, 1992).

the facts in a responsible manner. Thus my first draft of the resolution included a clause establishing an international commission to lay the groundwork for future national or international trials, or at least to establish the historic record of atrocities as the recently established U.N. Truth Commission for El Salvador was designed to do. Following standard procedure, after completing the draft resolution I circulated the document to all of the bureaus of the Department of State with a potential interest in the subject matter. In all, I received comments from over two-dozen officials. While several of the Bureaus responded favorably to my proposal to establish an investigative commission, the consensus was to defer the proposal for the time being in favor of the formulation calling on the Secretary General to recommend additional measures.

2

TWO WEEKS LATER, when Tadeusz Mazowiecki, the Human Rights Commission's Special Rapporteur on the Former Yugoslavia, proposed the establishment of such a commission in his first (August 28) report, I was asked to dust off my proposal and draft a new Security Council Resolution which would eventually become Resolution 780. That resolution requested the Secretary General to establish, as a matter of urgency, an impartial commission of experts to assess the information submitted pursuant to Resolution 771 as well as information obtained as a result of its own investigations or efforts, and to provide the Secretary General with its conclusions concerning the evidence of violations of international humanitarian law in the territory of the former Yugoslavia.

The negotiations between the members of the Security Council leading to the adoption of Resolution 780 were particularly acrimonious. My colleagues at the State Department and I had three goals for our draft resolution which we felt were non-negotiable. First, we insisted that the resolution expressly refer to the new body as a "commission," rather than a "committee" as the United Kingdom, France, and Russia desired. We argued that the term "commission" was of historic importance since the investigative body that preceded the Nuremberg Tribunal was known as the United Nations War Crimes Commission. Admittedly, in making this argument, we conveniently overlooked the fact that the World War II commission was largely seen as a failure, as discussed in Chapter 1. Further, we felt the title would be of practical significance since it would suggest a greater degree of independence and authority for the new body. While we would have preferred the title "War Crimes Commission," the United States accepted as a compromise "impartial Commission of Experts," which later came to be referred to simply as the "780 Commission."

Our second goal was that the commission be given authority to undertake its own investigations. The United Kingdom and France, believing that the pursuit of war criminals might damage prospects for a peace settlement, made no secret of their preference that the commission be limited to a passive group that would analyze and collate information that was passed to it.[6] They reluctantly agreed to the commission's investigative authority only after high-level interventions by United States government officials. However, they managed to undermine this authority by insisting that the commission be funded from existing U.N. resources rather than including a specific budget for the commission in the resolution. The United States found it hard to object, having insisted for years on a "zero-growth" U.N. budget. As a result, it would take over a year for the commission to obtain alternative funding to conduct investigations in the field.

Finally, we pressed for a clause in the resolution that would require counties to submit substantiated information in their possession concerning humanitarian violations in the former Yugoslavia. These submissions were to be made to the Commission of Experts within thirty days after the adoption of the resolution and to be periodically updated thereafter. This requirement was seen as important because, in the two months since the passage of Resolution 771, only a small handful of countries had submitted such information to the United Nations. The idea was to ensure some discipline in reporting and also to get a snapshot of what governments had already collected. It was my personal hope that this information would provide a solid basis for a determination as to whether genocide was in fact being committed in Bosnia. While this time limit was included in the final text of the resolution, it was largely ignored. Indeed, with the exception of the

United States, none of the fifteen members of the Security Council complied with the thirty-day deadline.

It is noteworthy that Resolution 780 contained no reference to the creation of an international tribunal. Instead, the resolution requested the Secretary General to take account of the commission's conclusions in "any recommendations for further appropriate steps." While most U.S. officials at the time favored domestic trials, the language deliberately left the door open for an international judicial response. Unfortunately, this creative ambiguity was later exploited by other governments and members of the U.N. Secretariat who argued that the commission was not meant to collect "evidence" of war crimes for use in prosecutions, but to produce a history of war crimes like a truth commission.[7]

3

RESOLUTION 780 WAS ADOPTED UNANIMOUSLY by the members of the Security Council on October 6, 1992. By the end of the month, the Secretary General had appointed five persons on the basis of their "expertise and integrity" to serve on the 780 Commission.[8] Professor Frits Kalshoven, a seventy-year-old Emeritus Professor of International Humanitarian Law at the University of Leiden (the Netherlands) was appointed to chair the new commission. The four other members of the commission were Commander William Fenrick, Director of Law for Operations and Training in the Department of Defense (Canada); Justice Keba M'Baye, former President of the Supreme Court of Senegal and former President of the International Court of Justice (Senegal); Torkel Opsahl, Professor of Human Rights Law at Oslo University and a former member of the European Commission on Human Rights (Norway); and Egyptian-born Cherif Bassiouni, Professor of Law at DePaul University in Chicago.

The composition of the commission quickly brought it under fire. My colleagues at the State Department made no secret about feeling that there was too much emphasis on academic qualifications and too little on investigative or managerial skills. This sentiment was soon publicly voiced by Roy Gutman who wrote that the chairman of the commission, Frits Kalshoven, "tells visitors he does not know why he got the job."[9] The answer to that question was that the commissioners were chosen from a short list of between 10 and 15 names compiled by the U.N.'s Office of Legal Affairs (OLA). OLA vigorously defended Kalshoven's appointment. "We felt we needed an anchor, someone calming," one OLA official is quoted as saying. He added that Kalshoven was chosen because he was known to the U.N. Legal Counsel, Carl-August Fleischhauer, and because of his experience serving on the international committee that monitored the implementation of the Geneva Conventions.[10]

The 780 Commission met for the first of twelve sessions in Geneva in December 1992. Ironically, the commission met in the room next door to where the Conference on the Former Yugoslavia was holding its peace talks and where U.S. Secretary of State Lawrence Eagleburger was dropping a bombshell by announcing that the United States had identified ten suspected war criminals who should be brought to trial. This has become known in government circles as the "naming names speech." The list of persons named by Eagleburger included Borislav Herak, a Bosnian Serb who had confessed to killing more than 230 civilians; "Adil" and "Arif," two members of a Croatian paramilitary force accused of attacking a bus convoy carrying more than 100 Serbian women and children, killing half of them; Zeljko Raznjatovic, leader of the Tigers, a Serbian paramilitary force accused of killing up to 3,000 civilians near the Bosnian town of Brcko; Vojislav Seselj, leader of the Chetniks, a Serbian paramilitary group accused of atrocities in Brcko and other Bosnian towns; Drago Prcac, commander of the Serbian-run Omarska detention camp, where killings and torture had been reported; Adem Delic, commander of the Croatian-run Celebici camp, where at least 15 Serbs were reported to have been beaten to death; Slobodan Milosevic, President of the Federal Republic of Yugoslavia (Serbia and Montenegro); Radovan Karadzic, leader of the self-proclaimed Serbian Republic of Bosnia and Herzegovina; and General Ratko Mladic, commander of the Bosnian Serb military forces.[11]

Eagleburger told the press that the "naming names" speech had been prompted by his recent meeting with Elie Wiesel, the noted author who survived the Nazi death camps. "He persuaded me that these people needed to be named and that this conduct could not go on," Eagleburger said. "It was my last opportunity to do it and I did it on my own."[12] Consequently, the speech was generally assumed to have been largely impromptu and some press reports implied it had not even been cleared with the White House. Nothing could be further from the truth. The "naming names" speech was in fact "cleared" throughout the government in advance, and I, myself, made certain revisions to ensure that the statement contained the requisite legal caveats and qualifiers. Eagleburger did not say the ten named individuals were guilty of war crimes (as was subsequently recounted in the press), but that they "were suspected of war crimes." In addition, he specifically said, "I am not prejudging any trial proceedings that may occur; they must be impartial and conducted in accordance with due process."[13]

Eagleburger's speech evidently rattled Vance and Owen, whose peace plan was dependent upon the cooperation of three of the ten people Eagleburger had just labeled as likely war criminals—Milosevic, Karadzic, and Mladic. One newspaper report put it as follows: "The reaction in the room was dead silence from America's closest allies and subsequent criticism from international negotiator Lord Owen, who, Eagleburger said, 'made it clear that he considered my remarks unhelpful.' "[14] This was to have an effect on the success of the 780 Commission. According to 780 Commission member Cherif Bassiouni, "The last thing [supporters of the Vance-Owen venture] wanted was to have an activist Commission of Experts that could likely prove the accusations made by Secretary Eagleburger. The priority at that time was to achieve a political settlement—and justice was not viewed as an inducement to that end. Indeed, there was then great apprehension that the Commission might be an impediment to a political settlement."[15]

4

In Bassiouni's view, this sentiment was at the root of the funding difficulties that were to plague the commission and cripple its early work. "I'm convinced that U.N. Legal Counsel Fleischhauer and his deputy, Ralph Zacklin, believed, and still do, that the top priority of the Security Council is to achieve a political settlement, and that everything that impedes this goal should be really checked," Bassiouni told one author.[16] "They were fearful of the Commission," he added.[17] As a consequence, the U.N. provided the commission just enough funds to pay the salary of the chairman (the only full-time commissioner); a stipend for the other four commissioners, not to exceed ten days a month; expenses for their travel to meet periodically in Geneva; and the salary of two staff members on loan by the U.N.'s Office of Legal Affairs. Moreover, the U.N. agreed to pay these funds only through August 1993, after which time no U.N. funds were provided whatsoever. Nor did the U.N. ever provide any funds for the investigation or the operating expenses of the commission.[18]

In January 1993, in an effort to secure alternative funding, the commissioners asked the U.N. to set up a trust fund for countries to make voluntary contributions to cover the commission's additional needs. The Office of Legal Affairs opposed this action on the ground that the Security Council had not provided for the creation of such a fund in Resolution 780 and voluntary contributions to the United Nations could not otherwise be earmarked for a specific program.[19] The United States weighed in, however, and in March 1993 a trust fund for the commission was approved by the General Assembly. Soon thereafter, the United States made a $500,000 voluntary contribution to the commission. Yet, due to a series of bureaucratic delays, trust funds were not released to the commission until August 1993—ten months after the commission had been established.[20]

During its first months of operation, the 780 Commission devoted its time to an analysis of the law applicable to the atrocities occurring in the former Yugoslavia, which it presented in the form of an interim report to the Secretary General in February 1993.[21] To many observers, this signaled that the 780 Commission was heading toward the same fate that befell the 1943 United Nations War Crimes Commission which, due to a lack of resources and cooperation from governments, produced nothing more than an academic study of the Nazis' responsibility for war crimes.

The 780 Commission's interim report defined the relatively new term of "ethnic cleansing" in the context of the Yugoslav conflict as "rendering an area wholly homogeneous by using force or intimidation to remove persons of given groups from the area." Based on the submissions of governments and international organizations, the commission determined that ethnic cleansing had been carried out in the former Yugoslavia "by means of murder, torture, arbitrary arrest and detention, extra-judicial executions, rape and sexual assault, confinement of civilians in ghetto areas, forcible removal, displacement and deportation of civilians, deliberate military attacks or threats of attacks on civilians and civilian areas, and wanton destruction of property." The commission concluded that the policy and practices of ethnic cleansing described above constituted crimes against humanity, could be assimilated to specific war crimes, and could constitute the crime of genocide as defined in the Genocide Convention. In its closing remarks, the Commission of Experts discussed the idea of establishing an ad hoc international criminal tribunal in relation to events in the territory of the former Yugoslavia. While expressing the opinion that "it would be for the Security Council or another competent organ of the United Nations to establish such a tribunal," the commission "observe[d] that such a decision would be consistent with the direction of [the Commission's] work."

In September 1993, the chairman of the 780 Commission, Fritz Kalshoven, resigned his post in protest. "The Commission did not have the full political support of major governments," said Kalshoven, charging that the United Kingdom and France in particular had refused to contribute to the trust fund or otherwise cooperate with the commission, thus depriving it of the resources it needed to do its work.[22] "Other major countries haven't given us any support either, but I was very angry about these two because they are permanent members of the U.N. Security Council. If they didn't want us to participate actively, they shouldn't have voted for us," Kalshoven explained.[23] Kalshoven added that when he asked the United Kingdom to supply a combat engineering unit to help with exhumations at a mass grave believed to contain the bodies of two hundred Croatian hospital patients murdered at Vukovar, "Britain simply didn't react to our request."[24]

Kalshoven's resignation was taken as confirmation that the commission would amount to nothing more than a "toothless study," in the words of the *New York Times*.[25] Things became even more bleak when, two weeks later, Commissioner Opsahl died of a heart attack in his Geneva Office, prompting an international headline that read: "U.N. War Crimes Body in Disarray on Anniversary."[26] To the surprise of many, the resulting personnel changes transformed the commission into a more vigorous entity under the leadership of its new chairman, the energetic and resourceful Cherif Bassiouni.

Unlike his predecessor, Bassiouni was not to be deterred by the lack of U.N. support for the commission's activities. With a voluntary staff of fifty attorneys and law students and $800,000 in grants that he obtained from the Soros Foundation, the Open Society Fund, and the John D. and Catherine T. MacArthur Foundation, Bassiouni set about creating the Commission's documentation center and database at DePaul University's International Human Rights Law Institute "with not a penny from the U.N."[27] Bassiouni's efforts were initially opposed by Ralph Zacklin, the British Deputy U.N. Legal Counsel, who drafted a legal opinion stating that an American university could not be entrusted with the sensitive task of collecting and analyzing information for the first-ever war crimes inquiry mandated by the Security Council.[28] The persistent Bassiouni responded by putting in place a series of measures designed to overcome Zacklin's concerns, including locating the center in a guarded room equipped with a security system and alarm, having his personnel sign non-disclosure agreements, and obtaining the protection of the FBI and Chicago police.[29] "Zacklin was unable to come up with a suitable alternative, and he no longer had a legitimate complaint," Bassiouni told me in an interview. "So the members of the Commission agreed that I could run the database from Chicago," he said.[30] By April 1994, the documentation center had systematically catalogued and analyzed over sixty-four thousand documents and had created a computerized archive of over three hundred hours of videotapes containing testimonies of individuals as well as footage capturing the carnage of the Yugoslav conflict.[31]

Once the commission's trust fund was finally established, it enabled the commission to undertake thirty-four field investigations under the direction of Commissioner Fenrick, who had been given the title "Rapporteur for On-site Investigations."[32] Thirteen governments were to contribute a total of $1,320,631 to the commission's trust fund. In addition, several governments provided assistance in kind. The United States, for example, provided over $150,000 to undertake the exhumation of a mass grave. The money was used for materials, transportation of the materials to Vukovar, and the salary and expenses of forensics expert, Clyde Snow. Canada provided three military lawyers and four military police officials to help Commissioner Fenrick with investigations; and Holland made available thirty-five soldiers to help with the exhumation of grave sites.[33]

In addition to several mass grave exhumations, the commission undertook two ambitious investigations based on interviewing refugees. In November 1993, two new members had been appointed to the 780 Commission to replace Kalshoven and Opsahl: Hanne Sophie Greve, a judge from Norway, who had worked in Cambodian refugee camps in Thailand; and Christine Cleiren, a Dutch law professor with expertise in criminal procedure. Commissioner Cleiren took on the task of organizing an investigation into rape and sexual assault. Under her direction, a forty-member all-female team of attorneys, mental health specialists, and interpreters interviewed two hundred twenty-three women in seven cities in Bosnia and Croatia who had been victims of or witnesses to rape.[34] Meanwhile, Commissioner Greve was made "Rapporteur for the Prijedor Project," under which she conducted an in-depth investigation into the ethnic cleansing of the Prijedor region of Bosnia. From some four hundred interviews of witnesses to the destruction there, Greve was able to document how the Serbs in Prijedor had carefully prepared their campaign before Bosnia declared independence on April 6, 1992.

Resolution 780 did not indicate a due date for the completion of the commission's work. Initially, U.N. Deputy Legal Counsel Ralph Zacklin had told the chairman of the commission that he did not expect it to last more than six months.[35] And, as mentioned earlier, no U.N. funds were provided the commission for salaries and travel after August 1993. On December 13, 1993, the commission received a letter from the U.N. Legal Counsel, Carl-August Fleischhauer, saying that the commission would be terminated on April 30, 1994.[36]

This decision was to have serious consequences for the commission's two major investigations. It was to force an early end to Commissioner Cleiren's rape investigation, with two hundred victims from Croatia and Bosnia still scheduled to be interviewed.[37] It also prevented the commission from finishing the exhumation of the Vukovar mass gravesite which had been suspended during the cold Croatian winter.[38] According to Chairman Bassiouni, "The premature termination of the Commission cannot be explained. Could it have been a purposeful political action to prevent the further discovery of the truth, which at the time was not politically propitious? Or was it simply an unwise administrative decision. Or perhaps it is the nature of the U.N. beast—part political, part bureaucratic—that accounts for what I believe to be an unconscionable outcome, no matter what the reason."[39]

At the end of April 1994, the commission submitted its final report, totalling eighty-four pages, along with twenty-two annexes containing 3,300 pages of detailed information and analysis.[40] Upon receipt of the 780 Commission report, Secretary General Boutros Boutros-Ghali stated, "The material and information collected and recorded in the data-base, now transferred to the Tribunal, will not only assist in the prosecution of persons responsible for serious violations of international humanitarian law, but will constitute a permanent documentary record of the crimes committed in the former Yugoslavia, and thus remain the memorial for the hundreds of thousands of its innocent victims."[41] Despite the many hurdles it had to overcome and its premature termination, Bassiouni feels the 780 Commission was an unqualified success. "The fact that the Tribunal's Office of the Prosecutor was able to produce over two-dozen indictments within a few months of the submission of our report indicates how useful the material turned out to be," Bassiouni told me. "More importantly," he added, "our report revealed the large picture—the connection between Belgrade and the policy and tactics of ethnic cleansing."[42]

AP/WIDE WORLD PHOTOS

At the urging of U.S. Ambassador to the United Nations, Madeleine Albright (pictured above), on May 25th, 1993, the U.N. Security Council unanimously voted in favor of Resolution 827 establishing the Yugoslavia War Crimes Tribunal.

Chapter 4

Establishing the Tribunal

This Tribunal, while it is novel and experimental, is not the product of abstract speculations nor is it created to vindicate legalistic theories.

—ROBERT H. JACKSON
Opening Speech for the Prosecution at Nuremberg
21 November 1945

1

IN A DECEMBER 1992 PRESS CONFERENCE following his controversial "naming names" speech, U.S. Secretary of State Lawrence Eagleburger added his voice to a growing international chorus publicly calling for the creation of a Nuremberg-like tribunal to try persons believed to be responsible for atrocities in the former Yugoslavia.* Later

* Elaine Sciolino, "U.S. Names Figures to be Prosecuted Over War Crimes," *New York Times International*, December 17, 1992, p. A-1. Other international experts calling for the creation of an international war crimes tribunal for the Balkans included the rapporteurs appointed by the Conference on Security and Co-operation in Europe under the Moscow Human Dimension Mechanism; the Special Rapporteur appointed by the United Nations Human Rights Commission to investigate the human rights situation in the former Yugoslavia; and Cyrus Vance and Sir David Owen, who were entrusted with conducting the peace talks on Bosnia. See Virginia Morris and Michael P. Scharf, *An Insider's Guide to the International Criminal Tribunal for the Former Yugoslavia*, vol. 1 (1995), p. 29.

that week, I attended a meeting of the U.S. Human Rights Delegation to prepare for the upcoming session of the U.N. Commission on Human Rights scheduled to meet in Geneva from February 1 to March 12, 1993. At the meeting, the head of our delegation, Ambassador Morris Abrahms, asked how we might be able to implement Eagleburger's mandate at the Human Rights Commission. After much discussion, it was agreed that the United States could propose the formation of an expert working group to prepare the statute for an ad hoc international tribunal. Once completed, the statute would be provided to the Security Council for approval.

By the time the U.S. delegation had arrived in Geneva in late January, we had obtained all of the "clearances" necessary to proceed with our war crimes tribunal initiative. Little did we know that France was about to pull the rug out from under us and steal our thunder. At the same time we began consulting our allies on our proposal at the Human Rights Commission, France circulated a draft Security Council resolution in New York calling for the creation of a Yugoslavia war crimes tribunal. The French draft was accompanied by a report prepared by a committee of French jurists containing a detailed analysis of the legal issues involved in the endeavor.[1]

I received a cable from the State Department ordering my early return from Geneva so that I could help craft a response to the French initiative. The cable could not have come at a worse time. I was at that very moment trying to broker a deal between the Islamic countries and the Europeans on a Human Rights Commission resolution entitled the "Rape and Abuse of Women in the Territory of the Former Yugoslavia." The resolution was in response to reports that as many as twenty thousand Muslim women had been systematically raped in Bosnia by Serb forces. Britain had proposed a text which was perceived as too soft by the Islamic countries. They, in turn, circulated a competing resolution which stated that the "systematic practice of rape is being used as a weapon of war against Muslim women and children and as an instrument of ethnic cleansing by the Serbian forces." Their resolution further stated that the rapes in Bosnia constituted genocide—a determination the Europeans were not ready to make. The two sides threatened to vote against each other's resolutions. For our part, the U.S. delegation was not satisfied with either text, since our main objective was the adoption of a resolution that would for the first time in history state that rape in an armed conflict is an international crime.

I requested a meeting of the European and Islamic delegations, at which I argued that it was important that a single resolution on rape in Yugoslavia be adopted by consensus in order to demonstrate to the Serbs that the international community was united in its opposition to the practice of systematic rapes and was willing to act to halt its continuation. To try to bridge the gap, I offered to draft a compromise text, which I would circulate the next day. My compromise text began with a clause stating that rape was a war crime. It also contained some of the strong language contained in the Islamic draft, and at the same time it incorporated the key British clauses requesting a U.N. investigation into the rape and abuse of women in the former Yugoslavia and assistance to the victims of such acts. Finally, it sought to skirt the genocide issue by simply "noting General Assembly Resolution 47/121 of 18 December 1992 in which the Assembly stated, *inter alia*, that the abhorrent policy of ethnic cleansing is a form of genocide."

The negotiations had reached a critical juncture just when I was informed that I would be returning to Washington on the next plane out. The tide was turned when the deputy head of our delegation, Geraldine Ferraro, made a compelling speech urging the two sides to put aside their differences. By describing her experiences working with rape victims as a prosecutor in New York City, the former Democratic vice-presidential candidate was able to transform what had been mainly an academic debate into an emotional appeal that was hard to reject. Minutes before I had to leave, a deal was struck and my compromise text was ultimately adopted without dissent by the Human Rights Commission as Resolution 1993/8.[2]

Upon my return to Washington, I learned that the French draft Security Council resolution proposed an innovative two-step approach to the establishment of a Yugoslavia War Crimes Tribunal under which the Security Council would initially commit itself to the establishment of such a tribunal and later approve the statute for the Tribunal. The process proscribed for drafting the statute was the subject of intense negotiations between the members of the council. During the course of these negotiations, Italy submitted a report prepared by a commission of Italian jurists and Sweden submitted a report prepared by the three distinguished rapporteurs appointed by the Conference on

Security and Co-operation in Europe (CSCE), each containing a draft statute for the Yugoslav War Crimes Tribunal.[3] Two weeks later, on February 22, 1993, the Security Council adopted Resolution 808 in which it decided in principle to establish an international tribunal "for the prosecution of persons responsible for serious violations of international humanitarian law committed in the territory of the former Yugoslavia since 1991."[4] Rather than assign the task of drafting the statute for the Tribunal to a committee of government representatives as the United States had proposed in Geneva, the resolution requested the Secretary General of the United Nations to prepare a report within sixty days "on all aspects of this matter, including specific proposals and where appropriate options for the effective and expeditious implementation of [this decision], taking into account suggestions put forward in this regard by Member States."[5]

At the time of the vote on the resolution, Ambassador Madeleine Albright delivered perhaps her most stirring address ever to the Security Council.[6] "There is an echo in this Chamber today," she began. "The Nuremberg Principles have been reaffirmed. We have preserved the long-neglected compact made by the community of civilized nations forty-eight years ago in San Francisco to create the United Nations and enforce the Nuremberg Principles." Looking each member of the council squarely in the eye, Albright continued, "The lesson that we are all accountable to international law may have finally taken hold in our collective memory." "This will be no victor's tribunal," she concluded. "The only victor that will prevail in this endeavor is the truth."[7]

Resolution 808 was artfully crafted. It reflected a commitment by the Security Council to establish a tribunal, but it did not indicate the shape the Tribunal would take. It guaranteed that the members of the council could have input into the drafting of the Tribunal's statute, but it left the final draft up to the Secretary General, thereby avoiding the prospect of drawn out and contentious negotiations. And the resolution dodged the most potentially explosive issue of all by leaving it to the Secretary General to recommend how the Tribunal would be established.

There were basically two options for establishing the Tribunal. One, advocated by the CSCE Report submitted by Sweden, was to draft a convention that would then be opened to all governments to ratify. Given that governments would need to pass implementing legislation to provide evidence and surrender suspects to the Tribunal, there was a strong argument for allowing states to individually exercise their consent to the Tribunal through ratification of a treaty. On the other hand, it would take time to negotiate a treaty and possibly years before enough governments ratified it. In addition, it was highly unlikely that Serbia would participate, and Serbia's participation was critical.

The other option was for the Security Council to establish the Tribunal itself, as a subsidiary body, acting under the peace enforcement provisions of the United Nations Charter (Chapter VII). This option offered two important advantages. First, it would ensure that the Tribunal was quickly established, since all it would take was a majority vote of the Security Council, including the affirmative vote of the five permanent members. Second, the Security Council's decision to establish the Tribunal under its Chapter VII powers would create binding obligations on all states. But this approach, too, had major drawbacks. There was a real possibility that one of the permanent members of the council, perhaps China or Russia, would veto the draft statute. In addition, the Security Council had never before created a subsidiary judicial body, and there were concerns that such action would be beyond the council's competence.

The United States was one of eighteen governments and international organizations to submit proposals to the Secretary General for the Tribunal's statute.[8] The United States' draft statute was prepared at the Department of State by a team of three lawyers—James O'Brien, Attorney-Adviser for Political-Military Affairs; Robert Kushen, Attorney-Adviser for Law Enforcement and Intelligence; and me. We worked around the clock for two weeks on our proposed statute, which was refined through an extensive interdepartmental and interagency process. Ultimately, our proposals on the general organization of the Tribunal, the rights of the accused, the double jeopardy principle, and the standard for appeals found their way into the Secretary General's draft statute. In addition, our proposal that rape be listed for the first time in the history of humanitarian law as an international crime was also accepted. However, two novel suggestions we made, which were not adopted, are worthy of note.

The first concerned the law that the Tribunal would apply. War crimes are generally viewed as applicable only during international armed conflicts, and it was not clear that the conflict in Bosnia between the Bosnian Serbs and the Bosnian Muslims would necessarily meet that criteria. To ensure that the Tribunal "got it right," we proposed that the Statute stipulate that "for this purpose, the conflict in the former Yugoslavia on or after 25 June 1991 shall be deemed to be of an international character." The Secretary General evidently thought such a clause would be an encroachment on the independence of the Tribunal's judicial function and omitted it from the proposed Statute.

The second suggestion was contained in paragraph 4 of the U.S. proposal, which read: "The Security Council should create a subordinate body, comprised of the members of the Security Council, to be known as the Administrative Council. This body would, among other things, exercise general administrative control over the staffing and operation of the chief prosecutor and the tribunal, and approve recommendations for financing the tribunal's operations." This proposal, which was modeled after the Iraqi Compensation Commission established by Security Council Resolution 687,[9] was meant to ensure some Security Council control over the Tribunal. Moreover, in light of the problems encountered by the 780 Commission, we frankly did not trust the U.N. Secretariat on its own to provide the necessary budget and staff. In hindsight, given the Tribunal's similar administrative problems, our proposal might have made good sense. But at the time it was viewed as "singularly insensitive."[10] Cherif Bassiouni, the chairman of the 780 Commission, described it as a "kneejerk reaction—keep out the General Assembly," and the Secretary General apparently agreed.

2

The report of the Secretary General[11] was prepared by a working group within the United Nations Office of Legal Affairs (OLA), consisting of Larry Johnson, Winston Tubman, Daphna Shraga, and Virginia Morris, working under the direction of the then Legal Counsel, Carl August Fleischhauer, and the Deputy Legal Counsel, Ralph Zacklin. The report, containing a draft statute for the Tribunal, was sent to the Security Council on May 3. For the reader's reference, the statute is reproduced in Appendix B in the back of this book. Under the draft statute, the Yugoslavia Tribunal would be established by a decision of the Security Council under its Chapter VII powers. The Tribunal would be composed of three organs—the chambers (comprising two trial chambers and an appeals chamber), the prosecutor, and the registry—which would be located at The Hague and be funded by the General Assembly. The statute does not establish an office of defense counsel, but it does provide for a right to counsel and for appointment of counsel in the event that the accused lacks "sufficient means" to pay for it.

Under Articles 2 through 5 of the draft statute, the Tribunal would have jurisdiction over four different international crimes committed in the territory of the former Yugoslavia after January 1, 1991:

- *Grave Breaches of the Geneva Conventions of 12 August 1949*—which include the willful killing, torture or inhumane treatment, causing great suffering or serious injury to people protected by the conventions, and the extensive destruction and appropriation of property, not justified by military necessity and carried out unlawfully and wantonly. Grave breaches of the Geneva Convention further include compelling prisoners of war or civilians to serve in the forces of a hostile power, willfully depriving a prisoner of war or a civilian of the rights to a fair and regular trial, the unlawful deportation or transfer or unlawful confinement of civilians, and the taking of civilian hostages.
- *Violations of the laws or customs of war*—which include the employment of weapons calculated to cause unnecessary suffering; the wanton destruction of population centers not justified by military necessity; the attack of undefended population centers; the seizure of, destruction or willful damage done to institutions of religion, charity, education, and the arts and science; historic monuments and works of art and science; and the plunder of public or private property.
- *Genocide*—which is defined as the intentional attempt to destroy, in whole or in part, a national, ethnic, racial or religious group by killing members of the group, causing serious bodily or mental harm to members of the group, deliberately inflicting on its members conditions of life calculated to bring about

the group's physical destruction in whole or in part, imposing measures to prevent births within the group, or forcibly transferring children of the group to another group. Punishable crimes of genocide also include conspiracy to commit genocide, direct and public incitement to commit genocide, attempts to commit genocide, and complicity in genocide.

- *Crimes against humanity*—which include the following acts committed against any civilian population in times of international or internal armed conflict: murder, extermination, enslavement, deportation, imprisonment, torture, rape, persecution on political, racial and religious grounds, and other inhumane acts.

The statute provides for criminal liability of persons who planned, instigated, ordered, committed, or otherwise aided and abetted in these offenses. It expressly incorporates the theory of command responsibility and bans the obedience-to-orders defense. The Tribunal would have primacy over national court proceedings concerning persons indicted of these crimes, and persons tried by the Tribunal could not later be tried before national courts for the same crime. Finally, the statute stipulated that there would be no in absentia trials or imposition of the death penalty.

My colleagues and I at the State Department received the Secretary General's report with mixed impressions. On balance, we thought OLA had done an excellent job, though we were not completely satisfied with every clause of the statute. We were troubled, for example, by the statute's very narrow approach to the applicable law. According to the Secretary General's report, the jurisdiction of the Tribunal was strictly limited to "rules of international humanitarian law which are beyond any doubt part of customary law."[12] Applying this cautious standard, the Secretary General omitted from the Tribunal's jurisdiction the two Additional Protocols to the 1949 Geneva Conventions, which apply the laws of war to "internal conflicts." Having rejected our proposal that the statute stipulate that the war in Bosnia was an international armed conflict, we viewed the inclusion of the protocols as critical to the successful prosecution of atrocities in Bosnia. Although the two protocols had been ratified by well over a hundred governments including the former Yugoslavia, OLA determined that there was not yet sufficient acceptance of them to constitute customary international law. Ironically, the fact that the United States had not yet ratified the protocols was probably the major reason for OLA's position.

We were also concerned about the Secretary General's definition of crimes against humanity contained in Article 5 of the statute. While the Secretary General's report stated that international law now prohibits crimes against humanity "regardless of whether they are committed in an armed conflict,"[13] the proposed statute gave the Tribunal jurisdiction over crimes against humanity only "when committed in armed conflict." This qualification could make it difficult for a prosecutor to win convictions for atrocities committed at Bosnian concentration camps if the prosecutor had to prove such acts were committed in connection with armed conflict. This was a curious limitation given that none of the countries or organizations that submitted proposals suggested that the Tribunal's jurisdiction over crimes against humanity should be so restricted.

In addition, my colleagues at the Pentagon, in particular, had strong objections to the statute's provisions on command responsibility and the defense of superior orders. Article 7(3) of the statute provided that a commander was responsible for the acts committed by a subordinate "if he knew or had reason to know that the subordinate was about to commit such acts or had done so and the superior failed to take the necessary and reasonable measures to prevent such acts or to punish the perpetrators thereof." We had favored a broader formulation, as reflected in the judgment of a military commission under the auspices of the International Military Tribunal for the Far East in the *Yamashita* case.[14] In that case, General Yamashita was found to be criminally liable for atrocities committed by the Japanese forces under his command, not on the ground that he knew or had reason to know of these acts, but on the ground that he condoned a general atmosphere of lawlessness that pervaded the troops under his command. With regard to the statute's prohibition of the defense of superior orders found in Article 7(4), the Department of Defense felt that there should be a limited exception to this rule as recognized in United States law for circumstances in which a subordinate lacks information necessary to adjudge the legality of an act ordered by his superior.[15]

Finally, we were puzzled by the Secretary General's provision on sentencing which stated, "in determining the terms of imprisonment, the trial Chambers shall have recourse to the general practice regarding prison sentences in the courts of the former Yugoslavia." The problem was that the former Yugoslavia had employed the death penalty and its criminal code reflected a policy of "twenty years or death." In other words, since the code favored capital punishment for serious cases, it stipulated that imprisonment for not more than twenty years could be imposed for a capital offense.[16] Since the Secretary General's statute forbade the imposition of capital punishment, we were concerned that it might be read as requiring that twenty years be the maximum penalty—which would be too lenient for the types of crimes committed in Bosnia.

We considered a variety of possible ways to pursue modification of the statute. The most obvious method would be to entertain amendments to the draft on the floor of the Security Council. A second tactic would be to propose certain modifications in an annex to the statute. These could be informally agreed upon by the members of the council in advance. A third strategy would be to specify certain revisions in the Security Council resolution approving the statute. Each of these tactics, however, would have likely resulted in lengthy negotiations and undesirable political compromises.

Our sense of urgency stemmed from the fact that since February 22, when the council had decided in principle to establish the Yugoslavia War Crimes Tribunal, the war in Bosnia had greatly intensified. Fighting had begun between the Bosnian Muslims and Croats, who had been allies against the Serbs in the first year of the war. The same week the Secretary General submitted his proposed statute, we received reports that the Croatian defense forces had rounded up thousands of Muslim men in raids on the city of Mostar and had deported them to detention centers which were little better than the Serb-run concentration camps. Meanwhile, the Bosnian Serbs were conducting a fierce assault on the Muslim towns of Zepa and Srebrenica which had swollen with thousands of refugees from surrounding villages. With these events as a backdrop, the five permanent members of the Security Council agreed during informal meetings that there should be no amendments and no further discussion on the Secretary General's statute for the Tribunal.

In an innovative approach to this dilemma, at the last minute we were able to persuade France, the United Kingdom, and Russia to join us in making similar statements interpreting certain key provisions of the statute when they voted on the resolution.[17] These statements, for example, would express the understanding of the four countries that the jurisdiction of the Tribunal covered the Additional Protocols to the Geneva Conventions and that crimes against humanity under the statute need only be committed "during," rather than "in connection with," armed conflict.

On other matters in which the four countries could not reach quick agreement, we decided to make unilateral "additional clarifications." Thus, on the issues of command responsibility and the defense of obedience to superior orders, Ambassador Albright, reading from a speech I drafted,[18] stated: "It is our understanding that individual liability arises in the case of.... the failure of a superior—whether political or military—to take reasonable steps to prevent or punish such crimes by persons under his or her authority. It is, or course, a defense that the accused was acting pursuant to orders where he or she did not know the orders were unlawful and a person of ordinary sense and understanding would not have known the orders to be unlawful." And on the issue of sentencing, she said, "We also understand that the Tribunal may impose a sentence of life imprisonment or consecutive sentences for multiple offenses, in any appropriate case."

At the time, I was skeptical that our plan would work. I was worried that the international tribunal would not give much weight to the "pre-cooked" interpretive statements since only four of the fifteen members of the Security Council had participated in making similar statements. In addition, the four interpretive statements were not worded identically and, in fact, could be read quite differently. Moreover, Britain, France and Russia limited their interpretive statements to a few select provisions of the statute, while the United States alone made "clarifications" on several other provisions. One of my colleagues has argued that it was significant that none of the members of the council at the time took issue with our "additional clarifications."[19] But this argument ignores the nature of formal proceedings in the council. The representatives are generally not lawyers and for the most part act as mouthpieces for speeches cabled to them from their capitals. No delegate was authorized to jump up and "object" when remarks were made by the United States.[20] Moreover, the statement was given after the delegates had already voted on the resolution, and the delegates had no notice of the United States' additional clarifications until it was too late to vote "no."[21] For added insurance, we later tried to codify our interpretive statements in the Tribunal's Rules of Procedure, but our attempt was rejected by the Tribunal's judges. Ironically, the United States' creative approach to this problem was reminiscent of its unsuccessful attempt to expand the concept of conspiracy in the context of the Nuremberg Tribunal some fifty years earlier, which was discussed in Chapter 1.

Our creative approach also risked alienating the other members of the Security Council. The representative of Venezuela, Diego Arria, said the non-aligned countries felt the resolution "was rammed down our throats."[22] "They said to us: 'If you object, you'll be responsible for damaging the war crimes Tribunal,'" he added.[23] Echoing these sentiments, the representative of Brazil told the council that "We would certainly have preferred that an initiative bearing such far-reaching political and legal implications had received a much deeper examination in a context that allowed a broader participation by all States Members of the United Nations."[24] China, which as permanent member could have vetoed the resolution, told the council that it had serious reservations and that it believed the approach envisaged in the Secretary General's report "is not in compliance with the principle of state judicial sovereignty."[25] Yet with the situation in the former Yugoslavia spinning out of control, no country was willing to be seen as the spoiler.

On May 25, 1993, Resolution 827 approving the Secretary General's statute for the Tribunal was adopted by a unanimous vote of the fifteen members of the Security Council. This resolution, which I had a hand in drafting, contained several other clauses worthy of note. The most important clause provided that all states were required to comply with the orders of the Tribunal. This would obligate countries to provide judicial assistance and arrest and transfer accused persons to the Tribunal. Ambassador Albright warned that noncompliance with this obligation would subject a state to Security Council sanctions or, in the case of Serbia, to continuing or heightened sanctions.[26] Having learned our lesson from the financial difficulties suffered by the 780 Commission, we included a clause authorizing a voluntary fund for the Tribunal and urging states to contribute funds, equipment, and personnel. Since the statute was not particularly detailed as to the investigation, trial, and appeals process, we viewed the Tribunal's Rules of Procedure as critical to the success of the Tribunal. Accordingly, in our draft for the resolution we proposed that the judges should submit the rules to the council for approval. Other members of the council felt such a clause would undermine the independence of the Tribunal, however. As a compromise, Resolution 827 invited states to submit proposals for the Tribunal's rules for the judges' consideration. Finally, because the statute did not give the Tribunal the power to award victim compensation, we included a clause in the resolution declaring that the creation of the Tribunal was without prejudice to the future establishment of a victim compensation program. What we had in mind was a procedure similar to that devised for the victims of the Iraqi invasion of Kuwait, in which frozen Iraqi assets and proceeds from Iraq oil sales would be dispersed to victims through a U.N. Compensation Commission.[27] To date, however, no such institution for Bosnia has been set up by the Security Council.

3

THE FIRST STEP in transforming the Yugoslavia War Crimes Tribunal from a paper court to an operational judicial institution was to appoint the eleven judges that would sit in two three-member trial panels and a five-member appeals chamber. Shortly after the Security Council's decision to establish the international tribunal, the Secretary General initiated the election process by inviting states to submit nominations. The Security Council considered forty-one candidates from thirty-eight countries and came up with a list of twenty-three candidates which was submitted to the General Assembly in late August 1993.[28] In mid-September 1993, in ten contentious rounds of voting over three days, the General Assembly elected eleven judges from this list. Gabrielle Kirk McDonald, a former federal court judge of the United States, garnered the largest number of votes (137) on the assembly's first ballot on which six other judges were chosen. The vote totals for the other six judges were as follows: Italian international law professor Antonio Cassese (123); Egyptian law professor Georges Michel Abi-Saab (116);[29] Chinese Foreign Ministry legal adviser Li

Haopei (111); Germain le Foyer de Costil, presiding judge of the French Court of Major Jurisdiction of Nanterrer (107);[30] and Lal Chand Vohrah, a senior Malaysian high court judge (96). No candidate obtained the required absolute majority of 94 votes needed for election on either the second or the third ballot. On the fourth ballot the assembly elected Sir Ninian Stephen, former governor-general of Australia and judge of the Australian High Court (97 votes). No candidates obtained the required number of votes on the fifth or the sixth ballot. On the seventh ballot, the assembly elected Adolphus Godwin Karibi-Whyte, former Nigerian Supreme Court judge (95 votes). The last two judges, Elizabeth Odio Benito of Costa Rica and Rustam Sidhwa of Pakistan, were selected on the tenth round of balloting. By the time of the Tadic trial, pursuant to a provision in the Tribunal's statute allowing the Secretary General unilaterally to fill vacancies, Judge Sidhwa was replaced by fellow Pakistani Saood Jan, Judge Abi-Saab was replaced by fellow Egyptian Fouad Riad, and Judge de Costil was replaced by fellow Frenchman Claude Jorda.

The nine men and two women elected to the bench were from both civil and common law countries: three from Asia, two from Europe, two from Africa, two from North America and one each from Latin America and Australia. There were several striking characteristics about the composition of the panel selected. The first was the absence of a Muslim on the bench, especially since Muslims constituted by far the largest portion of the victims of atrocities in the former Yugoslavia. "It is absurd that most of the victims are Muslim, yet they have no representatives on the Tribunal," lamented Mohamed Sacirbey, Bosnia's ambassador to the U.N.[31]

On the other hand, four of the eleven judges did come from countries with predominantly Muslim populations—Malaysia, Nigeria, Egypt, and Pakistan—and might therefore be uniquely sympathetic to the Muslim victims. Indeed, an opposite argument could be made—that there was a far greater number of Muslim countries represented on the bench than would be warranted by the percentage of Muslims to the total world population or the percentage of Muslim countries to the total number of countries in the world. In contrast, the nominee for the Tribunal's bench from Russia (the state with the closest historic ties to Serbia), Valentin G. Kisilez, a member of the Presidium of the Kaliningrad Regional Court, was defeated ostensibly to avoid a pro-Serb bias.[32] This drew Russia's ire in light of the unwritten rule that all permanent members of the Security Council are represented on important U.N. institutions.[33]

Also notable was the absence of a British judge. The official British explanation was that they did not put forward a candidate in order not to prejudice the possible selection of Scottish Attorney General John Duncan Lowe, who was then among the leading candidates for the position of the Tribunal's prosecutor. However, it has been suggested by other U.N. diplomats that the real reason was Britain's fear that, like Russia, its candidate might suffer an embarrassing defeat because of Britain's prominent and controversial role in the Bosnian crisis.[34] In fact, at the time of these elections, Bosnia was preparing a submission for the International Court of Justice which would charge Britain with complicity in genocide for having opposed the lifting of the arms embargo on Bosnia and the U.S. proposal for airstrikes against Serb bases.*

The judge who would preside over the panel trying Dusko Tadic was Gabrielle Kirk McDonald, a fifty-three-year-old former federal district judge known for a breezy Texas style that mixed directness with humor. McDonald was born in St. Paul, Minnesota, but grew up just outside Manhattan in Riverside, New York, and in Teaneck, New Jersey, where she was one of two African-American students in her high school class. She attended Boston University and then Howard Law School. After graduation, she joined the NAACP legal defense fund as a staff attorney, where she met Conrad Harper, who would twenty-five years later become State Department Legal Adviser. McDonald made a name for herself as a civil rights lawyer in the 1960s and 1970s, and at age thirty-seven was appointed by President Jimmy Carter to be the third black woman on the federal bench.

She resigned from the judiciary in 1988 to pursue a career in private practice. In 1993 she had accepted an appointment to the faculty of the Thurgood Marshall School of Law in Houston when her old friend Conrad Harper called to see if she would consider being

* On November 24, 1993, the Government of Bosnia sent a letter to the Security Council stating that it planned to institute such proceedings against Britain. The letter was published as Security Council Document S/26806, November 26, 1993. The Bosnian Government dropped its case when Britain threatened to suspend its contribution to the Bosnian relief effort if the case proceeded.

the United States candidate for the Yugoslavia Tribunal. Although she had no prior experience in international law, Harper told one reporter that "McDonald was well qualified as a former federal judge who had heard criminal matters, but she offered more as a woman, an African-American, and someone with a deep interest in civil rights." He added that "the Clinton Administration was interested in nominating a woman for the job on the tribunal because of the use of rape as an instrument of warfare in the Bosnian conflict."[35] A divorced mother with two kids in college, McDonald said it was an offer she could not refuse. "It was an opportunity to participate in something new," she explained. "It was wonderful to be a part of this because I consider myself to be a civil rights lawyer at heart."[36] McDonald compared her new role with her experience working with the newly drafted Civil Rights Act of 1964. "There was little precedent," she said, "so we had to borrow precedent. That is what we're doing at The Hague, we're borrowing precedent from other legal systems."[37]

4

AT THEIR FIRST MEETING at The Hague on November 17, 1993, the judges elected Antonio Cassese from Italy, an authority on international law, as president of the Tribunal. He was to administer the chambers, including assigning judges to cases, and was himself the head of the five-judge appeals chamber. At the time, there were no premises for the Tribunal and no permanent staff. "There was zero!" Cassese says. "Nothing! We had four secretaries, a few computers, and the U.N. had rented a meeting room and three small offices in the Peace Palace. The rent was paid for two weeks."[38] The General Assembly had not yet made a formal decision on the Tribunal's budget, and it would be nearly a year before a prosecutor would take office. A motion was made that the judges adjourn until the General Assembly had provided for "the indispensable minimum infrastructure." But at Cassese's urging, the judges decided instead to begin work immediately on the Rules of Procedure so that they would be ready by the time the office of the prosecution was up and running.[39]

Two months later, on February 11, 1994, the Yugoslavia Tribunal adopted 125 rules, covering some 72 pages.[40] (By way of comparison, it took a committee of American judges and law professors four years to draft the federal Rules of Criminal Procedure in the early 1940s.[41]) The judges decided to embrace a largely adversarial approach to their Rules of Procedure, rather than the inquisitorial system prevailing in continental Europe.[42] Yet there were three significant deviations from the adversarial system. First, as at Nuremberg, there was no rule against hearsay evidence. Second, during a trial, the Tribunal itself could order the production of additional evidence to ensure that it was fully satisfied with the evidence on which its judgments were based and to minimize the possibility of a charge being dismissed for lack of evidence. Third, the practices of plea-bargaining and granting of immunity were not included.

This last departure became a point of heated debate. To induce accused war criminals to testify against higher level officials, the United States proposed a provision for the rules that would have allowed the prosecutor to grant them either full or limited testimonial immunity in exchange for their cooperation.[43] In arguing for its proposal, the United States said, "We recognize that many other legal systems have difficulty with these concepts, but we believe that these tools would be helpful in the war crimes context for leading prosecutors up the chain of command from the foot soldier who directly committed an atrocity to the military or political leader who had knowledge of or commanded it."[44] The president of the Tribunal, Antonio Cassese responded: "The persons appearing before us will be charged with genocide, torture, murder, sexual assault, wanton destruction, persecution and other inhuman acts. After due reflection, we have decided that *no one* should be immune from prosecution for crimes such as these, no matter how useful their testimony may otherwise be."[45] Yet, in a partial concession to the U.S. position, the Tribunal provided that cooperation was a factor to be taken into account in imposing sentence.[46] This provision was to become critical in the case of Drazen Erdemovic who, on May 30, 1996, became the first person to plead guilty before the Tribunal. He admitted to machine-gunning seventy unarmed Muslim civilians at Srebrenica. In return for his testimony against Radovan Karadzic and Ratko Mladic, the prosecutor agreed to ask the court to give Erdemovic a reduced sentence.

Two other important matters addressed in the rules are worth mentioning here. The first has become known as the Rule 61 "super indictment" procedure. Despite the statute's requirement that an accused be present at trial, the judges gave serious consideration to providing for in absentia trial, or "trial by default" as the Tribunal put it, in cases where a state refused to hand over a suspect. As a compromise, the judges crafted Rule 61, which provided for a mini-trial, at which the accused was not present or represented, to enable the prosecutor to introduce in open court (and thus preserve) testimony of witnesses, documentation, physical evidence, and video recordings of witness interviews. The trial chamber would then request the prosecutor to provide an account of the efforts made to arrest the accused. If a majority of the three trial chamber judges determined that the information presented a prima facie case of guilt and that the warrant was not executed due to a refusal to cooperate by the state concerned, it would transmit a certification of this to the Security Council as a basis for possible sanctions. As described below, the Tadic trial was interrupted from June 27–July 14 so that the Tribunal could hold a Rule 61 proceeding concerning Radovan Karadzic and Ratko Mladic.

The second important issue concerned the protection of witnesses. As Judge Cassese remarked, the judges were "very much aware that there may be considerable reluctance on the part of witnesses to come to the Tribunal to testify. One of our overriding concerns has been how to encourage witnesses to do this."[47] To remedy this, the rules provided for the use of depositions (subject to cross-examination of the deponent);[48] measures for shielding the identity of witnesses from the public and even from the defendant "until such time as the witness can be brought under the protection of the Tribunal";[49] the establishment of a "Victims and Witnesses unit" within the registry;[50] and the promulgation of a sweeping rape shield provision.[51]

The purpose of the rape shield provision was to protect a victim of sexual abuse from unreasonable harassment, intimidation, or invasions of privacy by precluding the defendant from raising and trying to prove the defense of consent. Although the provision was applauded by women's groups, it engendered strong criticism from groups worried about safeguarding the rights of defendants. At the insistence of the Australian judge, Sir Ninian Stephen,[52] the judges amended the rape shield provision to allow for the defense of consent if the accused first satisfied the trial chamber *in camera* (in closed proceedings) that the evidence was relevant and credible.[53]

It may prove helpful to the reader at this point to set out the main steps of the proceedings as detailed in the Rules of Procedure. Proceedings are initiated when the prosecutor issues an indictment, which is submitted to the judge who has been designated to review indictments for that particular month. If the judge confirms the indictment, an arrest order or order for the transfer of the accused is sent to the authorities of the state in which the accused is located. After arrest, the accused is transferred to the Tribunal's detention center at The Hague. Immediately upon his arrival, he is brought before a trial chamber and formally charged. Before trial, the prosecution and defense must reciprocally disclose to one another the evidence in their possession.

The trial proceeds as follows: After opening statements by the parties, the prosecutor presents his case. Each witness may be cross-examined by counsel for the defense after he/she has testified and then reexamined by the prosecutor. Next the defense presents its case, and the prosecution cross-examines the defense witnesses, who are then re-examined by the defense. The prosecutor may then present rebuttal evidence. The judges may ask questions of the witnesses at any time during the trial. After the presentation of evidence, the two sides make their closing arguments. Thereafter, the trial chamber deliberates privately and pronounces its findings in public. If two of the three judges determine that the defendant is guilty beyond a reasonable doubt, then sentencing proceedings are initiated. An appeal against the judgment may be lodged within thirty days by either the prosecution or the defense. Finally, the sentence is served in one of the countries that has indicated to the Security Council its willingness to accept convicted persons.

5

THE DRAFTERS OF THE YUGOSLAVIA TRIBUNAL'S statute and rules were determined to prevent the Tribunal from being subjected to the kinds of criticisms that have tarnished the legacy of Nuremberg. The Yugoslavia Tribunal itself acknowledged in its first annual report that "one can discern in the statute and the rules a conscious effort to avoid some of the often-mentioned flaws of Nuremberg and Tokyo."[54] And yet at least one commentator has concluded that the Yugoslavia Tribunal "will likely invite much of the same criticisms that followed the first international war crimes trials."[55]

In some respects, the Yugoslavia Tribunal is a vast improvement over its predecessor. Its detailed Rules of Procedure and Evidence, for example, represent a tremendous advancement over the scant set of rules that were fashioned for the Nuremberg Tribunal. In further contrast to the Nuremberg Tribunal, the Yugoslavia Tribunal prohibits trials in absentia, since these are inherently unfair and are likely to be seen as empty gestures (although the Tribunal's Rule 61 procedure might be susceptible to similar criticisms). In addition, whereas the defense attorneys at Nuremberg were prevented from full access to the Nuremberg Tribunal's evidentiary archives, defendants before the Yugoslavia Tribunal are entitled to any exculpatory evidence in the possession of the prosecutor; and both the prosecution and the defense are reciprocally bound to disclose all documents and witnesses prior to trial. Finally, since the Nuremberg Tribunal has been criticized for compelling defendants to make incriminating statements, the statute of the Yugoslavia Tribunal guarantees every accused the right "not to be compelled to testify against himself or to confess guilt," in addition to a panoply of other rights not recognized under the Nuremberg Charter.

As discussed in Chapter 1, the most often heard criticism of Nuremberg was its perceived application of ex post facto laws, by holding persons responsible for the first time in history for the "crime of aggression" and by applying the concept of conspiracy which had never been recognized in Continental Europe. The creators of the Yugoslavia Tribunal went to great lengths to avoid a similar perception with regard to the international tribunal. The Security Council adopted a series of resolutions that put the people of the former Yugoslavia on notice that they were bound by existing international humanitarian law, in particular the Geneva Conventions. The resolutions enumerated the various types of reported acts that would amount to breaches of this law and warned that persons who committed or ordered the commission of such breaches would be held individually responsible. Moreover, the jurisdiction of the international tribunal was defined on the basis of the highest standard of applicable law, namely rules of law which are beyond any doubt part of customary law to avoid any question of full respect for the principle *nullem crimen sine lege.** It is particularly noteworthy that the crime of waging a war of aggression, which engendered so much criticism after Nuremberg, is not within the Yugoslavia Tribunal's jurisdiction.

In other respects, the Yugoslavia Tribunal may be more susceptible to criticism. Let us begin with the criticism that Nuremberg constituted "victor's justice." In contrast to Nuremberg, the Yugoslavia Tribunal was created neither by the victors nor by the parties involved in the conflict, but rather by the United Nations, representing the international community of states. The judges of the Yugoslavia Tribunal come from all parts of the world and are elected by the General Assembly.

On the other hand, the decision to establish the Yugoslavia Tribunal was made by the U.N. Security Council, which cannot truly be characterized as a neutral third party; rather, it has itself become deeply involved and taken sides in the conflict. As detailed in Chapter 2, the Security Council has imposed sanctions on the side perceived to be most responsible for the conflict, authorized the use of force and airstrikes, and sent in tens of thousands of peacekeeping personnel. Its numerous resolutions have been ignored and many of its peacekeeping troops have been injured or killed; some have even been held hostage. Moreover, throughout the conflict, the Security Council has (justifiably) favored the Bosnian Muslims and Croats over the Serbs. Although it imposed sweeping economic sanctions on Serbia and the Bosnian Serbs, such action was never even proposed when Croatian forces committed similar acts of "ethnic cleansing" in Bosnia in October 1993.† Throughout the conflict, the council had been quite vocal in its condemnation of Serb

---

* A translation of this Latin phrase is: "No one shall be tried for an act which was not forbidden by law at the time when it was committed."

† Cedric Thornberry, the Deputy head of UNPROFOR reported that "the actions of some of the Croats of western Bosnia rivaled in barbarity those of the Serb Chieftains of eastern Bosnia, and what was done to the Muslims of Mostar by Croats was perhaps as bad as the Serb shelling of the mainly Muslim parts of Sarajevo." Cedric Thornberry, "Saving the War Crimes Tribunal," *Foreign Policy* 104 (Fall 1996): 79.

atrocities, but its criticisms of those committed by Muslims and Croats were muted. When the deputy head of UNPROFOR began to raise concerns about the uneven response to violations of international humanitarian law in 1993, he was told by a colleague at U.N. headquarters in New York, "Take cover—the fix is on."[56]

While the Yugoslavia Tribunal is designed to be independent from the Security Council, one cannot ignore the fact that the statute provides that the Tribunal's prosecutor is selected by the Security Council and its judges are selected by the General Assembly from a short list proposed by the Security Council. Indeed, given that the battle for control of Bosnia was in large measure a religious war between Bosnian Muslims and Bosnian Serbs, it is somewhat astonishing that four of the eleven judges elected by the General Assembly upon the nomination of the council come from states with predominantly Muslim populations, while the nominee from the state with the closest historic ties to Serbia (Russia) was defeated to avoid a pro-Serb bias. Not surprisingly, the Tribunal proved unacceptable to the government of Serbia, which sent a letter to the council warning that the Tribunal would not be impartial, given the Security Council's "one sided approach" to the Balkans war.[57]

Another criticism of Nuremberg was that those acquitted by the Tribunal were retried and convicted in subsequent proceedings before national courts. The statute of the Yugoslavia Tribunal, in contrast, expressly protects defendants against double jeopardy by prohibiting national courts from retrying persons who have been tried by the international tribunal.[58] However, by permitting the Tribunal's prosecutor to appeal an acquittal,[59] the Tribunal itself may infringe the accused's interest in finality which underlies the double jeopardy principle.*

* The U.S. Constitutional prohibition of double jeopardy prohibits prosecution appeals of acquittals. The prohibition is not against being twice punished, but against being twice forced to stand trial for the same offense. There are two important rationales for the rule. One rationale is that the trial itself is a great ordeal, and once the defendant has been acquitted, the ordeal must end. See *U.S. v. Ball*, 163 U.S. 662, 669 (1896). The other is based on the increased risk of an erroneous conviction that may occur if the state, with its superior resources, were allowed to retry an individual until it finally obtained a conviction. See *Green v. United States*, 355 U.S. 184, 187-188 (1957) and *United States v. DiFrancesco*, 449 U.S. 117, 130 (1980).

A final criticism of Nuremberg was that it did not provide for the right of appeal. The statute of the Yugoslavia Tribunal has been recognized as constituting a major advancement over Nuremberg by guaranteeing the right of appeal and providing for a separate court of appeal. However, the procedure for the selection of judges by the General Assembly did not differentiate between trial and appellate judges, leaving the decision to be worked out by the judges themselves. When they arrived at The Hague, this became the subject of an acrimonious debate. Nearly all the judges wished to be appointed to the appeals chamber, which was viewed to be the more prestigious assignment. As a compromise, the judges agreed that assignments would be for an initial period of one year and subject to "rotat[ion] on a regular basis" thereafter.[60]

The rotation principle adopted by the judges is at odds with the provisions of the Tribunal's statute intended to maintain a clear distinction between the two levels of jurisdiction. Article 12 provides that there shall be three judges in each trial chamber and five judges in the appeals chamber, and Article 14(3) expressly states that a judge shall serve only in the chamber to which he or she is assigned. These provisions were intended to ensure the right of an accused to have an adverse judgment and sentence in a criminal case reviewed by "a higher tribunal according to law," as required by Article 14 of the International Covenant on Civil and Political Rights. The purpose of the principle of the double degree of jurisdiction under which judges of the same rank do not review each other's decisions is to avoid undermining the integrity of the appeals process. It was feared that judges might be hesitant to reverse decisions in order to avoid a future reversal of their own decisions. The adoption of the rotation rule is not the kind of decision one would expect from a Tribunal keenly aware of the need to be perceived as above reproach. In light of this action, the comment made by my colleague at the State Department about the "water at The Hague" might not have been so far off the mark, after all.

AP/WIDE WORLD PHOTOS

It took the Security Council fourteen months to agree on the Tribunal's prosecutor. Though a surprising choice, Justice Richard Goldstone of South Africa (pictured above) became known as a miracle worker for his successful efforts in building the office of prosecutor and launching the first prosecutions.

Chapter 5

Launching the Prosecution

Despite the magnitude of the task, the world has demanded immediate action. This demand has had to be met, though perhaps at the cost of finished craftsmanship.

—ROBERT H. JACKSON
Opening Speech for the Prosecution at Nuremberg, 21 November 1945

1

THE STATUTE OF THE YUGOSLAVIA TRIBUNAL provides that the prosecutor would be selected by the Security Council. At the time the statute was adopted in May of 1993, no one guessed that it would take the council fourteen months to agree on a candidate for the position. As one of my colleagues at the State Department was quoted as saying, we were confident that the council would "toss around a hat full of names" and that the prosecutor would be at work by July 1993 at the latest.[1] But this was not to be.

The problem began when the Islamic and non-aligned members of the Security Council proposed Cherif Bassiouni, the Egyptian-born DePaul University professor and member of the 780 Commission, for the post. As the author of two-dozen books and over a hundred articles on international criminal law, Bassiouni was arguably the world's leading authority in the field. It did not hurt that he was also a long-time friend of Secretary General Boutros Boutros-Ghali, that he had years of courtroom experience arguing extradition cases, and that he had proven himself to be a creative and effective administrator in establishing the 780 Commission's documentation center at DePaul. On the surface, he seemed to be the perfect person for the job.

Britain did not think so. A senior U.N. official was quoted as saying that "Britain had been vociferous in opposing Bassiouni [on the grounds] that his lack of experience and administrative skills would get in the way of doing the job successfully."[2] But the real reason for the British opposition, wrote the U.N. correspondent to the *London Times*, was that Britain was afraid Bassiouni would "quickly bring charges against Serb leaders" which would disrupt the Vance-Owen peace negotiations.[3] This view was confirmed by Diego Arria, Venezuela's representative to the Security Council, who said: "Bassiouni was seen as a threat to the peace process. He was seen as a fanatic who had too much information. In fact, he is a cautious and careful man. They made a great mistake [in opposing him], and made a mockery out of the Tribunal."[4]

The British campaign against Bassiouni rankled the Secretary General, who told Britain to "put up or shut up."[5] The statute of the Tribunal called for the prosecutor to have "the highest level of competence and experience in the conduct of investigations and prosecutions of criminal cases." Partly to highlight Bassiouni's lack of prosecutorial experience, the British responded by proposing Scottish Attorney General John Duncan Lowe for the post.[6] The Islamic and non-aligned members of the council, who had openly accused Britain of being the main force behind the European refusal to intervene and stop Serbian aggression, lobbied hard to block the appointment of Lowe.[7]

In August 1993, the U.S. government tried to broker a deal in which Bassiouni would be appointed to the post of deputy prosecutor, behind Lowe. But Bassiouni rejected the proposal. As he told me in an interview, "I felt that the number two spot would have no say in deciding the strategy for investigations and prosecutions, and feared that Lowe might follow the British line and subordinate prosecutions to Lord Owen's elusive quest for peace."[8] In informal polling, each candidate received seven votes in favor, seven votes against, with one country, Brazil, abstaining. The United States voted for Bassiouni, but the other four permanent members of the Security Council—France,

Britain, Russia, and China—all opposed him. Part of Bassiouni's problem was that the United States had not aggressively lobbied for him, reportedly because Secretary of State Warren Christopher did not want the Tribunal to be seen "as an American show."[9] Hungary, which had voted against Bassiouni, later let it be known that it would have taken just one letter from the United States to change its vote in his favor, and Brazil, which had abstained, stated that it would have been influenced by a strong U.S. campaign.[10]

When told of the deadlock, Secretary General Boutros Boutros-Ghali tried to force the issue by formally nominating Bassiouni. However, the fate of Bassiouni's candidacy was sealed when, at the United Kingdom's urging, the members of the council informally agreed that the prosecutor should be selected only by consensus—on the grounds that this would ensure that the individual would enjoy the international respect and standing necessary for both the effective performance of his responsibilities vis-à-vis the members of the international community and the undivided support of the Security Council.[11] The decision, which would allow any country to veto a candidate for the post, was more responsible than anything else for the subsequent delays in appointing the prosecutor. This may have been just what Britain had planned, since it gave the Vance-Owen peace process some breathing room before the commencement of prosecutions.

After Britain and France vetoed Bassiouni, the Secretary General nominated former Indian Attorney General Soli Henhangir Soreabjee, who was then vetoed by Pakistan.[12] By now, said one Western diplomat, "frustration was giving way to desperation."[13] Finally, on October 21, 1993, the Secretary General nominated Ramon Escovar Salam, a former Venezuelan attorney general, who drew no objection from any of the fifteen weary Security Council members. Escovar had impressive credentials. As Attorney General of Venezuela, he ran an office of three thousand lawyers, and he demonstrated his independence by spearheading corruption charges against his own country's president, Carlos Andres Perez, who was dismissed from office.[14] However, he was also a man with political ambitions, and just days before he was to have taken up the post in February of 1994, Escovar abandoned the job to become Interior Minister of the new Venezuelan government with the possibility of later assuming the newly created office of Prime Minister.[15]

Within days of Escovar's withdrawal, one of the worst atrocities in the Balkan conflict occurred when the Serbs fired a mortar bomb into the open-air market in the center of Sarajevo, killing forty-nine civilians and seriously wounding over two hundred others.[16] Yet for the next five months, the Security Council proved unable to agree on a replacement for Escovar, with Russia blocking both a Canadian candidate, Christopher Amerasinghe, and an American candidate, Charles Ruff—each of whom had the support of the other fourteen members of the council.[17] Russia made it clear that it would not vote for anyone put forward by a NATO member country, on the ground that a war crimes tribunal headed by a westerner would be biased against the Serbs.[18] As one Security Council member remarked, the search for a prosecutor had turned into "a ghastly nightmare."[19]

The only positive development during this bleak time was the appointment of Graham Blewitt, the former director of the Australian War Crimes Prosecution Unit, as deputy prosecutor on February 15, 1994. Blewitt immediately began the arduous task of building up a team of prosecuting attorneys and investigators. But lacking a sufficient budget, and due to bureaucratic wrangling with the U.N., he was able to hire only eleven persons during this period.

Finally, on July 7, 1994, at the suggestion of Antonio Cassese, the president of the Yugoslavia Tribunal, Secretary General Boutros Boutros-Ghali nominated Richard Goldstone, a justice on the South African Supreme Court. In many ways Goldstone was a surprising candidate. Like Bassiouni, he was vulnerable to the charge that he lacked prior experience as a prosecutor.[20] Moreover, he had received mixed reviews as head of a judicial commission in South Africa whose mandate was to investigate the political violence ravaging the country in the early 1990s. Only one trial resulted from the three-year probe, and critics said Goldstone could have achieved more.[21] In addition, Goldstone was trained in South Africa's version of common law, and some of the members of the Security Council had previously expressed the view that a prosecutor more familiar with civil law was needed since the international tribunal would be employing a combination of the two.[22] Finally, Goldstone made it known that he was being given only a two-year absence from South Africa's new eleven-judge Constitutional Court and, as a consequence, that he could only serve as prosecutor until the summer of 1996.[23]

Goldstone's nomination reflected the recent changes in U.N. politics. The selection of a white South African for the post would have been completely unthinkable even three months earlier, before the election of Nelson Mandela as South Africa's first black president capped the dismantling of apartheid. Also, given that the U.N. had until recently equated "zionism with racism," it was somewhat astounding that the U.N. would select a Jewish man to oversee the prosecution of crimes predominantly against Muslims.[24]

Nevertheless, just one day after his nomination, the Security Council approved Goldstone's appointment by a unanimous 15-0 vote.[25] In the face of charges that "Goldstone's principle qualification is the fact that he doesn't come from a Western country,"[26] U.S. Ambassador to the United Nations Madeleine Albright defended the Tribunal's newly appointed prosecutor as "a seasoned barrister and judge who, at great personal risk, insisted that the truth be known about cruel abuses committed under apartheid in South Africa."[27] In retrospect, Goldstone was perfect for the job. A compact, quietly charismatic man with a resonant voice, the 56-year-old Goldstone effused a sense of deep commitment and had a nose for international politics. Through his unwavering persistence during his two years in the post of prosecutor, Goldstone would expertly navigate the minefields of the U.N. bureaucracy and lead the Yugoslavia Tribunal to international recognition and influence. His greatest challenge, and most notable success, was obtaining funding for the fledgling institution.

2

THE SOURCE OF THE TRIBUNAL'S funding difficulties was a clause in its statute that provided: "The expenses of the International Tribunal shall be borne by the regular budget of the United Nations in accordance with Article 17 of the Charter of the United Nations."[28] This meant that the General Assembly, rather than the Security Council, would control the Tribunal's funding. The argument in favor of this approach was that if the international community was really serious about prosecuting war criminals, then the entire community should be prepared to ensure the necessary funding for the effective functioning of the international tribunal. However, the drawback to this source of funding was that the budget of the International Tribunal would be at the mercy of a little known U.N. body called the "ACABQ"—the Advisory Committee on Administrative and Budgetary Questions.

The sixteen member ACABQ meets behind closed doors and issues no summary records; yet its power within the U.N. is second only to that of the Security Council itself. This is because a decade ago, at the insistence of the United States, the U.N. adopted a procedure that required the members of the ACABQ to reach consensus on the budget of the organization before it could be adopted by the General Assembly.* The intent was to impose greater discipline on U.N. spending and allow the United States more control over the organization's spending priorities. But in the context of the Tribunal, it allowed a group of fiscal zealots to deprive a worthwhile institution of adequate funding.[29]

The mode of funding stipulated in the Tribunal's statute provoked an acrimonious debate among the members of the ACABQ and General Assembly. At the center of the controversy was the constitutional question of competence and authority for the budget and the relationship between the General Assembly and the Security Council concerning the financing of operations approved by the Security Council. Article 17 of the United Nations Charter makes clear that the General Assembly has exclusive control over appropriations of funds. During the ACABQ's consideration of the Tribunal's budget, several members argued that the Security Council had usurped the authority of the General Assembly by requiring it to appropriate funds for the Tribunal out of the general budget.[30] As a consequence, instead of the $32.6 million the Secretary General requested to fund the International Tribunal for its first year of operation,[31] the ACABQ and General As-

* In 1985, the United States enacted the "Kassebaum amendment," which provided that the United States would withhold payments to the United Nations unless it began adopting budgets by consensus instead of the two-thirds vote provided for in Article 18 of the U.N. Charter. Faced with the prospect of bankruptcy, the United Nations made the change, and the U.S. began wielding a de facto U.S. financial veto. See Jose E. Alvarez, "Legal Remedies and the United Nations' A La Carte Problem," *Michigan Journal of International Law* 12 (1991): 229.

sembly granted a provisional budget of one-third that amount in a resolution that "expressed concern that advice given to the Security Council by the Secretariat on the nature of the financing of the International Tribunal did not respect the role of the General Assembly as set out in Article 17 of the Charter."[32]

By the time Goldstone took office a year later, things had improved only slightly. The General Assembly had approved a bare-bones $32 million budget which would cover only the cost of renting the west wing of the Aegon building in The Hague, rental and contracting of equipment and services, and salaries and expenses for a staff of 108 (11 judges, 19 prosecutors, 22 investigators, 10 defense counsel, 10 members of the registry, 12 clerical staff, 12 security guards, and 28 interpreters).[33] In all, 75 percent of the funds budgeted were allocated for the judges, administration, and overhead.[34] Less than 2 percent of the total was budgeted for the critical work of tracking down witnesses, obtaining and translating their accounts, exhuming mass graves and conducting post-mortems, and providing medical and forensic expertise.[35] And no funds at all were budgeted for witness protection, counseling, and security.

In an interview, Tom Warrick, Special Counsel to the Coalition for International Justice, told me that "the Tribunal's first budget was drawn, not on the basis of an actual requirements analysis, but on pure guesswork as to what the Tribunal would need." "But," says Warrick, "it is one thing to design a budget to support an international conference, it is quite another to set up a budget to support a fully functioning international tribunal."[36] Indeed, the first budget betrayed an extraordinary ignorance of the task that faced the prosecution. According to Goldstone's estimates, the average case before the Tribunal would require statements from one hundred victims or witnesses, each averaging between twenty and thirty-five pages; an additional four hundred pages of documents (military maps and charts); over one hundred photographs (autopsies and scene of the crime); between twenty and forty video tapes; twenty audio tapes; physical evidence (weapons; uniforms, etc.); and exhumation examination reports. Between sixty and eighty witnesses might have to attend each actual trial.[37] For the next several months, Goldstone shuttled back-and-forth between The Hague and New York, "ingratiating himself with the various U.N. policy wonks who control funding, working the maze of power and pettiness."[38]

With Goldstone's help, the Secretary General submitted a revised budget of $39 million for 1994–1995, which was approved by the General Assembly. Meanwhile, Goldstone's efforts resulted in the receipt of voluntary contributions of $8.3 million from thirteen countries,* and the loan of fifty-three personnel from six countries and the European Commission at no cost to the U.N.†

Then, in 1995, the United Nations faced a funding crisis that pushed it to the brink of insolvency. U.N. members owed the organization $3.1 billion, with more than half that amount owed by the United States. Under a scale of assessments agreed to in the early years of the organization, the United States is obligated to pay 25 percent of the U.N.'s regular budget and 30 percent of its peacekeeping budget. During the Reagan Administration, the United States began to fall behind in its payments, amassing a huge debt to the U.N. The Bush Administration had adopted a five-year repayment plan, but in 1994 Congress reneged, and by 1995 the United States was $1.6 billion in arrears to the U.N.[39]

With the U.N. literally running out of cash, it was forced to slow the supply of funds to the Tribunal to a trickle. As a consequence, the office of the prosecutor was prevented from spending money to send investigators into the field to investigate the massacre of 8,000 civilians at the U.N. "safe area" of Srebrenica. The office was also precluded from recruiting lawyers, or renewing contracts of current personnel due to restrictions on United Nations agencies imposed by the Secretary General in the face of the fiscal crisis. Evidence already gathered from refugee interviews began to pile up unsifted and untranslated.[40]

---

* According to the *Report of the Secretary-General, Financing of the International Tribunal*, U.N. Doc. A/C.5/49/42, December 5, 1994, p. 35, the voluntary contributions to the Tribunal for 1994-1995 were as follows: Cambodia: $5,000; Canada: $168,280; Hungary: $2,000; Ireland: $6,768; Liechtenstein: $2,985; Malaysia: $2 million; Namibia: $500; New Zealand: $14,660; Norway: $130,000; Pakistan: $1 million; Spain: $13,725; Italy: $1,898,049; United States: $3 million.

† According to the *Report of the Secretary-General, Financing the International Tribunal*, U.N. Doc A/C.5/50/41, December 13, 1995, p. 30, the United States sent twenty-two lawyers and investigators, the United Kingdom five, Sweden and the Netherlands each sent three, and two each were sent from Denmark and Norway.

The Tadic trial, which was scheduled to begin in November 1995, was postponed until May 7, 1996, for want of $78,000 for expenses for defense counsel and investigators.[41] Goldstone, normally the consummate team player, decided the time had come to take his case to the international press. "If these restrictions continue, they will render unconscious the Yugoslav tribunal," Goldstone told a reporter.[42] "The criminal justice system cannot conduct itself if resources are turned on and off," he added.[43] Joining Goldstone's public plea, the Tribunal's president, Antonio Cassese, told the General Assembly, "All these undertakings are costly—of that there is no doubt; but if the United Nations wants to hear the voice of justice speak loudly and clearly, then the Member States must be willing to pay the price."[44]

A solution was reached on August 7, 1995, when the General Assembly approved a resolution deciding that, for now, one-half of the Tribunal's financing would come from the U.N. peacekeeping budget,[45] with member countries assessed at the weighted scale used for U.N. peacekeeping activities. Under this procedure, the Security Council would have a greater degree of influence in determining the budget as compared to the regular budget process.* Moreover, under the weighted scale of assessments used for the peacekeeping budget, the countries with the greatest stake in the international tribunal (the permanent members of the Security Council) would pay the lion's share of its cost.† In addition, a 1954 ruling of the International Court of Justice suggests that the General Assembly would have to honor the Security Council's budget commitments to the Tribunal.[46]

While the peacekeeping budget is barely able to sustain an expanding number of increasingly demanding operations, the costs of the International Tribunal is a mere fraction of what the U.N. spends on a

---

* After the Security Council decides to establish a peacekeeping mission, the U.N.'s Department of Peacekeeping Operations prepares an implementation plan and the U.N.'s Field Operations Division prepares the mission's budget and deployment plan. The mission's budget is then sent to the U.N.'s Advisory Committee on Administrative and Budgetary Questions, the Fifth Committee, and finally the General Assembly for approval. See *U.N. Peacekeeping: Lessons Learned in Managing Recent Missions*, United States General Accounting Office Report, December 1993, p. 16.

† The United States assessment for peacekeeping is 30.4 percent. Its regular budget assessment is 25 percent.

single peacekeeping operation. The U.N. peacekeeping force in the former Yugoslavia, for example, had cost an average of $570 million per year,[47] while the annual cost of the peacekeeping force in Cambodia was $1.6 billion.[48]

3

LOOKING BACK ON THOSE FRANTIC DAYS, Justice Goldstone told me that the challenge of funding was one of the most difficult of all the challenges he faced during his tenure as prosecutor. "The Tribunal has been the child of an insolvent parent, with all the consequences that has," he explained.[49] Having largely overcome the funding obstacles, Goldstone was finally able to proceed with the prosecutions.

By this time, a high-tech courtroom in The Hague had been built, giving the Tribunal a physical home. The courtroom, located in what used to be an executive meeting room used by the Aegon insurance company, was completed in December 1994. The courtroom's special features include three interpreters' booths, a camera control booth, and a public gallery separated from the courtroom by a partition of bulletproof glass. The courtroom employs a range of sophisticated technological equipment. A simultaneous translation system allows viewers in the public gallery to follow proceedings in English, French, or Serbo-Croatian. Electronic stenographic equipment instantly converts the English language into text. Computer monitors on the witness, judges, prosecution, and defense tables allow the trial participants to simultaneously view documents, maps, and videotape exhibits. These can be highlighted and annotated by the witness using the same "magic pen" technology that television football commentators employ to diagram an instant replay. Out of sight is a holding room for the accused, robing rooms for the judges, and a waiting area for witnesses. In addition, a special twenty-four-cell U.N. detention unit has been established at a nearby Dutch prison.

A few floors above the courtroom are the offices of the prosecutor and his 148-person staff, which includes investigators, lawyers, analysts, interpreters, and secretaries.[50] Goldstone organized the office into six sections: the secretariat's office, which includes a number of special advisors with respect to gender-related crimes and political issues; a prosecution section with prosecuting attorneys and legal advisors; an investigation section, made up of investigators, analysts, and interpreters; a special advisory section consisting of advisors on such matters as international law, military organization, and the history of the former Yugoslavia; a computer operation section; and an administration record section. In addition, Goldstone established three-person field offices in Belgrade, Sarajevo, and Zagreb to provide support to investigative teams and to liaise with the local governments.

Now fully staffed, the prosecutor's office launched thirteen investigations. These focused on atrocities that took place at five concentration camps (the Susica camp in eastern Bosnia, and the Omarska camp, the Trnopolje camp, the Keraterm camp, and the Luka camp in northwestern Bosnia); six Bosnian and Croat cities (Bosanski Samac in northeastern Bosnia, Sarajevo and Stupni Do in central Bosnia, Srebrenica in eastern Bosnia, and Zagreb and Vukovar in Croatia); and two areas (the Prijedor district in northwestern Bosnia and the Lasva Valley in central Bosnia). According to Goldstone, "this is the most extensive criminal investigation ever undertaken."[51] As of this writing, the investigation has resulted in the issuance of seventy-five indictments against fifty-five Serbs, seventeen Croats, and three Muslims.

Some of those who have been indicted, such as Radovan Karadzic and Ratko Mladic, are principal civilian and military leaders. In addition, several high-level military officers are on the list, as well as a few notorious concentration camp commanders. But the list also includes relatively minor figures like Dusko Tadic, who had no official rank, and Drazen Erdemovic, who was a foot soldier that confessed to the killing of seventy civilians at Srebrenica. From the description of those indicted, it is hard to divine a clear prosecution strategy. This is because "when we began to work, it was apparent that we could not start, as they did at Nuremberg and Tokyo, with cases against the military and political leaders," Minna Schrag, one of the members of Goldstone's office, explained.[52] According to Goldstone, "Our strategy includes the investigation of lower-level persons directly involved in carrying out the crimes in order to build effective cases against the military and civilian leaders who were party to the overall planning and organization of those crimes."[53]

The most important principle of this prosecution strategy, Goldstone has said, is that "decisions with regard to indictments will be taken solely on a professional basis and without regard to political considerations or consequences."[54] What this meant is that the prosecution would ostensibly be guided by the evidence, not by politics. Yet conspicuously absent from the list of those so far indicted is the name of Slobodan Milosevic, the President of Serbia—the man most responsible for the conflict in Bosnia, and the man most valuable to the United States' 1995 peace initiative.

4

BY AUGUST 1995, THE ETHNIC CLEANSING in Bosnia and Croatia had run its course. Croatia had reclaimed the Krajina territory, which the Serbs had seized in 1991, and driven the Serbs out. With the fall of the "safe areas" of Srebrenica and Zepa to the Bosnian Serbs in the east and the fall of Krajina to the Croats in the west, political boundaries could now be drawn according to ethnic boundaries. "We ought to use it to our advantage," Secretary of State Warren Christopher said of these developments, "or capitalize on it."[55]

Anthony Lake, President Clinton's 55-year-old national security adviser, argued in a confidential memorandum that "the administration's weak, muddle-through strategy in Bosnia was becoming a cancer on Clinton's entire foreign policy—spreading and eating away at its credibility."[56] Vice President Al Gore began to press the President to institute a bolder, proactive policy for the Balkans.[57] President Clinton agreed, telling his foreign policy team, "we've got to change the rules of debate. We can only do it from a position of strength."[58]

After four years of following the lead of the Europeans, Washington was at last ready to take matters into its own hands to compel a peace agreement. "This risks reelection," Clinton told his top advisers, "but we have no choice."[59] Under the long-dormant authority of Security Council Resolution 770, President Clinton approved "Operation Deliberate Force," a massive bombing campaign against Serb targets the purpose of which was to silence the Serb artillery and produce a diplomatic breakthrough. Washington had also indicated that it was willing to provide 20,000 U.S. troops to Bosnia as part of a larger NATO force to make a peace agreement stick. Meanwhile, Serbia-Montenegro, reeling under runaway inflation, was finally beginning to feel the bite of international sanctions. The stage was set for a successful peace initiative, and under the determined energies of U.S. Assistant Secretary of State Richard Holbrooke, the presidents of Croatia, Bosnia, and Serbia (representing both Serbia-Montenegro and the Bosnian Serbs) agreed to meet in Dayton, Ohio, in November 1995, to hammer out a comprehensive peace agreement.

The basic deal underlying the Dayton Accord was known as the "51-49" plan. The Bosnian Serbs would receive nearly half of Bosnia where they would establish a new Serbian republic which would have the right to affiliate with Serbia-Montenegro. The other half of the country would be a Bosnian-Croat federation. Together, these two semi-autonomous republics would comprise a state called Bosnia and Herzegovina led by a three-member collective presidency representing the Bosnian Muslims, Croats, and Serbs. The Bosnian Muslims would receive military assistance to level the playing field and the economic sanctions against the Serbs would be lifted. A 60,000-strong NATO force, known as IFOR would be responsible for implementing the agreement.

On the eve of the Dayton talks, Richard Goldstone formally asked the United States to make the surrender of indicted suspects a condition for any peace accord.[60] The U.S. negotiators responded that they would not make such a condition a "show stopper" to the larger peace settlement.[61] This raised legitimate fears that Dayton would turn into another of the U.N.'s infamous "amnesty-for-peace" deals.

In the five years preceding the Dayton talks, the United Nations had pushed for amnesty-for-peace deals in El Salvador, Cambodia, and South Africa,[62] and in 1993 the Security Council had rescinded the arrest order for Somali warlord Mohamed Aidid in an effort to "foster a political dialogue which can lead to national reconciliation."[63] Throughout the Vance-Owen peace negotiations, there had been suspicions that a similar amnesty deal was in the works for the Serb leadership.[64] In his recently published memoir, Lord David Owen denies that the issue of amnesty or immunity was ever discussed during the peace talks.[65] Yet the rumor was so persistent that U.S. Ambassador Madeleine Albright felt compelled to write an editorial that ran in the

San Francisco Chronicle. She said: "We have made it clear that we will not recognize—and we do not believe the international community will recognize—any deal to immunize the accused from culpability."[66] And Goldstone stressed that even if a Bosnian peace agreement offered immunity to Karadzic and Mladic, "we would not be bound by it." He added that the Tribunal would continue with proceedings against them unless the Tribunal's statute was changed by the United Nations Security Council.[67]

When, in September 1994, the United States and United Nations participated in the negotiation of an amnesty-for-peace swap with the military leaders in Haiti who had been accused of atrocities similar in degree if not scope to those in Bosnia, Richard Goldstone feared the worst. "This is an example of the wrong way to deal with these crimes," he told the press. "It doesn't serve justice and it ignores the victims."[68] "If people look at this as being an avenue for obtaining peace," deputy prosecutor Graham Blewitt added, "it hinders our work."[69]

While Ambassador Albright had ruled out a formal amnesty, Holbrooke did not believe this meant that the peace accord necessarily had to include an agreement to surrender accused war criminals to the Tribunal. However, Bosnian President Alija Izetbegovic felt otherwise. To him, this was the one issue on which there could be no concession. During the first two weeks of the negotiations in Dayton, it appeared that Izetbegovic's stubborn insistence would derail the success of the latest peace initiative.[70]

Then, to just about everybody's surprise, Milosevic consented to the inclusion in the peace accord of five references to the obligations owed the war crimes tribunal. The first reference, contained in the General Framework Agreement, required the parties to "cooperate in the investigation and prosecution of war crimes and other violations of international humanitarian law."[71] The second reference, contained in the Agreement on the Military Aspects of the Peace Settlement (Annex 1 of the Accord), stated that the parties "shall cooperate fully with.... the International Tribunal for the Former Yugoslavia."[72] Also contained in the Agreement on Military Aspects was by far the most explicit reference, which obligated the parties to "comply with any order or request of the International Tribunal for the Former Yugoslavia for the arrest, detention, [and] surrender of" persons who the Tribunal has indicted.[73] The other two references were contained in the new Constitution of Bosnia, which was incorporated as Annex 4 of the Dayton Accord. The first of these provided that "all competent authorities in Bosnia and Herzegovina shall cooperate with and provide unrestricted access to. . . . the International Tribunal for the Former Yugoslavia."[74] The second stated that "no person who is under indictment by the Tribunal and who has failed to comply with an order to appear before the Tribunal, may stand as a candidate or hold any appointive, elective, or other public office in the territory of Bosnia and Herzegovina."[75]

Some believe Milosevic's consent to these provisions was a measure of how badly he wanted peace. During the Croatian offensive, he had refused to lift a finger in the defense of the Croatian Serbs in the Krajina; now he was apparently willing to sell out the Bosnian Serb leadership as well. More likely, Milosevic's acceptance reflected his judgment that the West would not have the stomach to enforce these provisions.

It is significant in this regard that the accord did not stipulate a role for the NATO troops in apprehending wanted Bosnian Serbs. While U.S. Secretary of State Warren Christopher had repeatedly insisted that the troops would arrest any persons they encounter who have been indicted by the Tribunal, the Pentagon was equally resolute that apprehending war criminals was not within NATO's mandate. According to NATO officers, from the beginning of the mission, IFOR gave a "monitor, but don't touch" order to its troops on the ground.[76] Indeed, just two months after the Dayton Accords were formally signed in Paris, NATO troops permitted indicted war criminal Radovan Karadzic to pass unhindered through NATO checkpoints.[77] A few months later when the NATO troops learned that indicted war criminal Ratko Mladic was present in a military installation they were scheduled to inspect, the troops decided not to go inside after all.[78]

Despite his statement that indictments would be issued "without regard to political considerations or consequences," it is hard to believe that Goldstone did not intentionally delay pursuing an indictment of Slobodan Milosevic. Clearly such an indictment would have wrecked any prospect for peace at Dayton. And yet, during the trial of Dusko Tadic and the Rule 61 Hearing for Radovan Karadzic and Ratko Mladic, it would become apparent that the prosecutors saw Milosevic as the mastermind who was ultimately responsible for the war and atrocities in Bosnia. Among the investigators at The Hague, the term "east wind" was often used, in reference to the belief that inquiries were leading inevitably towards Belgrade and Milosevic.

I put the question to Richard Goldstone when I met with him in Brussels in July 1996. "The evidence and references to Milosevic we have so far," he replied, "prove that he was responsible for beginning the war; but that's not a crime within the Tribunal's jurisdiction. While some of the evidence proves assistance and directions coming out of Belgrade, one needs hard evidence of knowledge and intent."[79] His deputy, Graham Blewitt, was even more blunt. "I can state unequivocally that we are not withholding or sitting on any such indictments," he told me. "If we have evidence sufficient to indict senior political or military leaders in Serbia, we would do it, and we would not delay the indictment notwithstanding its effect on the peace."[80]

Peoples and Territories of the Former Yugoslavia, November 1995

AP/WIDE WORLD PHOTOS

A Dustin Hoffman look-alike, 40-year old pub owner and karate instructor Dusko Tadic (pictured above) was the first defendant to be tried by an international criminal tribunal since World War II.

Chapter 6

The First Defendant: The Tale of Dusko Tadic

> What makes this inquest significant is that these prisoners represent sinister influences that will lurk in the world long after their bodies have returned to dust. We will show them to be living symbols of racial hatreds, of terrorism and violence, and of the arrogance and cruelty of power.
>
> —ROBERT H. JACKSON
> *Opening Speech for the Prosecution at Nuremberg, 21 November 1945*

1

IN APPEARANCE, DUSKO TADIC has been described as "a Dustin Hoffman look-alike."[1] He was born on October 1, 1955, in the village of Kozarac, a town nestled at the foot of a mountain in the Prijedor region of Bosnia. Though his family was Serb, they were well respected in the predominantly Muslim town, as his father, two uncles, and grandfather had fought with Tito's partisans for Yugoslav independence from the Nazis in World War II. Growing up, Tadic's friends often called him by the nicknames "Dusan" or "Dule." Like many of his peers, Tadic attended the local primary school and then went off to Belgrade where he studied electrical engineering. At the completion of his studies in 1977, he served his required 14-month stint in the Yugoslav Army (JNA).

When he returned from the Army, he married a petit, dark-haired nurse named Mira and settled in the Bosnian town of Banja Luka where he was employed as a construction worker. But Tadic was not one to hold a job for long, and in 1983 he went to Libya hoping to strike it rich. A year later, he returned to Yugoslavia and found work as a carpenter in Croatia. In 1989, he moved back to his boyhood home town to open a cafe-bar (or pub), which he called "Nippon."

In Kozarac, Tadic, his wife, and their two daughters—Valentina and Saska—lived at Number 36 Masaltiva Street, in the area of town known as the central commune. He kept busy teaching karate and operating his pub. Most of the townspeople remember Tadic from before the war as a failed businessman and somewhat of a bully. "He was a trouble-maker, not very bright, but he was not evil," recalled one of his former neighbors.[2] Though Tadic might not have been born a sadistic torturer and mass murderer, "he was known around Kozarac as gratuitously violent, ready to beat up those who had slighted him," said another neighbor.[3] In addition, he was financially vulnerable. To underwrite the construction of his pub, he had borrowed heavily from Muslim friends. When a burst of building activity in 1990 led his creditors to ask for their money back, Tadic's response was to discover his Serbian identity and to turn against his Muslim friends.

As Ed Vulliamy of *The Guardian* put it, "When the hurricane of violence came, Tadic was in the eye of the storm."[4] While the storm clouds of ethnic tension were approaching in August 1990, Tadic joined the Serbian Democratic Party, known as the SDS. Then, in 1991, he banned Muslims from his pub. At that point, according to Muslim refugees from Kozarac, "Tadic became the big Serb in town. It wasn't very hard because there were hardly any Serbs in Kozarac."[5] But this made him invaluable to the Serb forces during the Serb siege of Kozarac in May 1992.

Kozarac had the misfortune of being one of several predominantly Muslim towns located in the middle of the Prijedor region of Bosnia. The area was of fundamental strategic importance to the Serbs since it straddled the corridor connecting their two-thirds share of Bosnia with their one-third share of Croatia. To claim the Prijedor region, the Serbs had to eliminate its Muslim inhabitants, who accounted for

42 percent of the area's population of 112,000.[6] To accomplish this task, they bombed the villages, massacred thousands of civilians, and set about to terrorize the rest into fleeing the area.

When fighting broke out in the Prijedor region on April 30, 1992, Tadic sent his family to the nearby town of Banja Luka, while he remained behind in Kozarac. A few weeks later, on May 14, the Serbs began their assault on the town. First, they raised roadblocks and cut telephone service, sealing it from the outside world. Ten days later, on May 24, Serb tanks, mortars, and artillery barraged the village at the rate of one shell every four seconds.[7] During the artillery assault, Tadic is said to have played a key role in the selection of useful targets. On May 26, the town signaled its surrender. The Serbs herded the surviving townspeople to a "collection area" at the town's soccer stadium. As townspeople filed toward the collection area, Tadic reportedly helped single out some of the town's intellectuals, civic leaders, police officers, and other prominent Muslims for immediate execution. By one estimate, 90 percent of the town's leaders were killed even before they got to the camps.[8]

Today, Kozarac is a ghost town. One visiting reporter described the scene as "a roadside attraction from hell."[9] Its name has been stricken from Serbian maps. Once a thriving village of well-to-do Muslims, it is now just a collection of burned-out and dynamited houses straddling a highway. But a few of Kozarac's houses have remained miraculously untouched. They are the ones with "Serb House" painted on the side. Among these is Number 36 Masaltiva Street.

Of Kozarac's 15,000 Muslim residents, 2,000 were killed in the artillery barrage. Another 5,000 were summarily executed after the town's surrender. The others were taken to the local concentration camps: Trnopolje, where rape was an evening sport; Keraterm, where several hundred men were machine-gunned in a single night; and Omarska, which became known as a "death camp."[10] There was no one left in Kozarac to frequent Tadic's pub, so Tadic became a traffic cop. But, according to witnesses, he ended up spending much of his time as a "visitor" to the concentration camps, where his brutality stood out even amongst the other atrocities that were being committed.

Recently, Tadic's wife showed a *London Times* reporter a family video of her husband at a party in Kozarac, drinking with his friend

Emir Karabasic—one of the men he is alleged to have tortured and killed at Omarska.[11] "I can't imagine," says deputy prosecutor Graham Blewitt, "sitting there at a barbecue drinking a beer or two with your neighbor one day and then the next day you're murdering or treating that person in the worst way."[12] The fury of the neighbor-on-neighbor violence—perpetrated by the Bosnian Serbs against Muslims as part of a campaign of "ethnic cleansing"—is one of the mysteries of the Bosnian conflict that the Tadic case might be able to answer. "Even the Nazis," Blewitt points out, "killed their victims in a cold, efficient manner; rape and torture were the exception, not the rule. But the atrocities here, this is blood lust."[13]

2

At some point in 1993, things started going badly for Dusko Tadic in Kozarac. According to Steven Ufer, Tadic's German lawyer, Tadic wanted to leave Bosnia because he was about to be drafted into the Bosnian Serb army.[14] Other possible explanations have been suggested for Tadic's departure. With ninety percent of its former population expelled or dead, Kozarac had become a bleak place, with few opportunities for spending money. There are also reports that Tadic insulted senior Serb officials and got involved in a dispute over confiscated Muslim property with Simo Drljac, a powerful local warlord. But whatever the reason, he sent his wife and youngest daughter to Munich in the fall of 1993. A few months later he joined them in the apartment of his older brother, Mladen.[15] "I told him not to come," recalled Mladen, who left Germany for Belgrade after his brother's arrest. "I said to him, 'you may get in trouble here in Germany.' And he told me that he was coming because he wasn't guilty of anything."[16]

Since 1992 Germany had become home to more than three hundred fifty thousand refugees from Bosnian and Croatian war zones. Germany, which allied with the genocidal Croatian Ustasha against the Serbs during World War II, would seem an unlikely destination for Serbs on the run. But for many Serbs, the attractions of Germany's booming economy were enough to forget the past. "In areas of Bosnia where these people took the TVs, the VCRs, the homes, and the land of the Muslims, they calculated they would then be well off," Tilman Zuech, chairman of a German human rights organization explained. "But since then, the Serbian economy has collapsed. They have come to Germany because it has a higher standard of living."[17]

This migration led to scenes on German streets, in cafes, and in train stations, reminiscent of the years following World War II, when a war refugee, haunted by memories of concentration camps, suddenly recognized the face of a tormentor. For Tadic, it happened at a government registration office a few weeks after his arrival. Word immediately went around the exiled Bosnian community in Munich: a man who looked like Dusko Tadic was in town. A television crew caught a few moments of footage of the man believed to be "the Butcher" himself. After that, Tadic seldom went out.

Meanwhile, human rights organizations began to exert pressure on the German government to investigate some of these sightings. Ultimately, the chief federal prosecutor's office opened investigations against thirty-one suspected war criminals from the former Yugoslavia.[18] Under a German law that was passed in the aftermath of the Second World War, thirteen Serb refugees were arrested. One of them was Dusko Tadic.

On the morning of February 12, 1994, Tadic left his brother's dreary flat in Munich where he had been hiding out for several months and walked right into a police trap. An elite German police unit arrested Tadic just one hundred feet from the front door of his brother's flat. Witnesses to the arrest said Tadic drew a pistol, but was disarmed by police and wrestled to the ground before he could shoot.[19] "The suspect is a fanatic supporter of the 'Greater Serbia' idea and sought to make a contribution to ethnic cleansing," a spokesman for the German federal prosecutor's office announced.[20] He was arrested on suspicion of "murder, aiding and abetting genocide, and causing grievous bodily harm."[21] It was the first arrest outside the former Yugoslavia of someone who allegedly took part in "ethnic cleansing" crimes there. Germany is one of the few countries whose law provides for trying people accused of war crimes and genocide, even if the crimes occurred abroad and the suspect is a citizen of a foreign country.[22] The German legal code requires a life prison sentence for those found guilty of carrying out genocide.

3

The Tribunal's deputy prosecutor, Graham Blewitt, had heard of Tadic's arrest long before Richard Goldstone's appointment as prosecutor and had been keeping tabs on the German proceedings. "We were being urged to take the Tadic case by the media and even by some of the Tribunal's judges," Blewitt told me. "But at the time, I felt I lacked the necessary authority, not to mention staff, to rush forward with an indictment."[23] Blewitt added that it made sense to allow Germany to proceed with the Tadic case since they had the necessary evidence and jurisdiction. "Given that we only have one court room at The Hague, national courts are going to have to play a role in the prosecution of these cases when they have the ability and will to do so."[24]

But when Goldstone arrived at The Hague, he realized immediately that this was a high-profile case that could get the prosecution off to a rousing start. In addition, the 780 Commission had just submitted its final report of its investigations of war crimes in Bosnia, concluding that the events which took place in the Prijedor region were unquestionably crimes against humanity and could also legally qualify as genocide. As Goldstone told me in an interview, "I thought it was appropriate to pursue the Tadic case since it impinged so clearly on the Prijedor/Omarska investigation that was already underway in the Office before I came aboard, which began with the work of the Commission of Experts."[25] "During our investigation of Omarska," Graham Blewitt explained, "Tadic's name came up again and again as one of the people who committed the worst crimes."[26] So Goldstone assigned a team of twenty investigators, lawyers, and analysts to the Tadic case.

"Soon it became clear that our investigators and the German authorities were starting to trip all over each other," Blewitt said.[27] Thus, on October 12, 1994, Goldstone requested the Tribunal to order Germany to defer prosecution of Tadic to the Tribunal. A hearing on the matter was held on November 8. This was the first public airing of the allegations against Tadic. As Goldstone told the Tribunal's judges:

> Tadic was involved directly in the events which led to the removal of the majority of the Muslim population of Pri-

> jedor and effectively the destruction of that community.... He helped create what were, in effect, death lists of Muslim intellectuals and other prominent citizens of Prijedor. He was involved in the forced removals of Muslims from the villages of the Prijedor region and the looting and destruction of Muslim houses. I would emphasize that according to eye-witnesses, when he participated in those events, Tadic wore a military uniform and was in command of a group involved in the actions. Again, eye-witnesses are able to testify to Tadic and the group under his command summarily executing unarmed non-Serbs. He was directly involved in directing the transfer of non-Serbs from the villages in the Prijedor region to the camps. He was involved in assaults of prisoners at the camps and at the military barracks in Prijedor. He was seen on numerous occasions in the Trnopolje camp and at Omarska camp. There is an allegation that Tadic was involved in incidents of rape at Omarska.... Among the most widely witnessed events that Tadic was involved in was the murder of Emir Karabasic, Jasmin Hrnjic, and Enver Alic. These three prisoners were brutally beaten and tortured by Tadic and others, using metal rods, truncheons, and knives, to the point of unconsciousness. Tadic then forced a fourth prisoner to drink motor oil from the garage and then bite off the testicles of the unconscious prisoners. The prisoners died as a result of their torture.[28]

Goldstone supported his request with thirteen pieces of documentary evidence—maps, newspapers, and photographs—and nineteen statements from witnesses scattered throughout Germany, the Netherlands, Norway, Sweden, and Switzerland.

Peter Wilkitzi of the German Federal Ministry of Justice appeared at the hearing as *amicus curiae* (meaning friend of the court), to express his government's acceptance of the primacy of the International Tribunal. However, he indicated that Germany was not in a position to surrender Tadic, as the necessary legislation had not yet been passed. This drew a strong rebuke from the judges, who reminded Wilkitzi of "the well-established principle of international law that a State cannot avoid compliance with its international obligations by invoking its municipal law."[29]

The most interesting moment of the deferral proceeding came when Tadic's German lawyer told the court "that the Defense had no objections against the transfer of the proceedings to the Tribunal."[30] Evidently, Tadic felt he faced a better chance of acquittal at The Hague than in Germany. This might have been a miscalculation. Alleged Yugoslav war criminals who had been tried by other European countries had managed quite well in the national courts: Dusko Cvjetkovic, a Bosnian Serb who was tried by Austria for the murder of civilians at Kucice, was acquitted,[31] as was Refic Saric (by reason of insanity), a former Muslim detainee, who was tried in a Danish court for the abuses he inflicted on his fellow prisoners at a Croat-run camp.[32] As the first case to be tried by the Yugoslav Tribunal, much more was at stake, and therefore Tadic faced a greater likelihood of conviction. On the other hand, if convicted by Germany on the charge of genocide, Tadic faced automatic life imprisonment, whereas the Yugoslav Tribunal could hand down a lesser sentence.

With no party objecting to the deferral, it would appear to be an easy decision for the Tribunal. However, the judges were concerned about exercising the Tribunal's primacy over a relatively minor character like Tadic when the government of Germany seemed perfectly capable of prosecuting his case vigorously and fairly. Goldstone replied that "in principle, we have encouraged, and we do encourage, national courts both within the area of the Former Yugoslavia and elsewhere to conduct trials."[33] But, Goldstone explained, "The Tadic case relates to an important investigation which was in any event under way in the Prosecutor's office."[34] Satisfied with Goldstone's explanation, the trial chamber immediately granted the application for deferral.

Four months later, on February 13, 1995, the Tribunal formally indicted Tadic and his Omarska colleagues, including the camp commander, guards, and several freelance torturers/murderers like Tadic. Tadic was charged with thirty-four counts of Breaches of the Geneva Conventions, Violations of the Laws and Customs of War, and Crimes Against Humanity, including murder, rape, and torture of Muslim men and women within and outside the Omarska camp. Specifically, the indictment, which is reproduced in Appendix C of this book, charges that on May 27, 1992, during the surrender of Kozarac, Tadic pulled four named Muslims out of the columns heading for the designated assembly areas, pushed them against a wall, and shot them. According to the indictment, later, during the Serb siege of the villages of Jaskici and Sivci on June 14, 1992, Tadic shot five men in front of their homes and savagely beat others with wooden clubs. Foremost among the charges is Tadic's "participation" on June 18 in the castration and murder of Fikret (Hari) Harambasic and the torture and murder of other Omarska inmates. In addition, the indictment charges that Tadic raped a female prisoner at Omarska identified as victim "F."

Conspicuously absent from the Tribunal's indictment of Tadic is the charge of genocide, especially since it was on the basis of that charge that he had been arrested in Germany. "We were amazed that Germany had no specific evidence on that charge," Graham Blewitt explains. "They were going to attempt to prove it solely on the basis of the testimony of an expert witness. But we thought it would be difficult to establish genocide with respect to Tadic."[35] Genocide is distinguished from ordinary murder or assault by the very specific criminal intent required: the prohibited acts constitute genocide only if they are committed with the "intent to destroy, in whole or in part, a national, ethnic, racial or religious group, as such."[36] It is this specific intent which makes it difficult to prove a charge of genocide, especially against low-level perpetrators. While Goldstone felt he could make a strong case that Tadic committed the alleged rape, murders, and acts of torture, it was not at all clear that his actions were intended to further the Serb policy of ethnic cleansing rather than merely a by-product of it.

Notwithstanding the Tribunal's admonitions to Germany at the deferral proceeding, it was not until March 31, 1995, that Germany finally enacted the necessary legal provisions for extraditing persons to the International Tribunal. Finally, on April 24, Germany turned Tadic over to the Tribunal, where he became the sole occupant of the Tribunal's 21-cell detention center. Two days later, at his arraignment on April 26, Tadic interrupted the proceedings to make his plea: "I do not understand the indictment!" He said in Serbo-Croatian, "I have not participated in any of the alleged crimes."[37]

4

TADIC'S LEAD COUNSEL WAS Michail Wladimiroff, a fifty-one-year-old partner at a high-powered law firm in The Hague and a professor of economic criminal law at the University of Utrecht.[38] After the Dutch Bar Association group that he chaired submitted proposals for the Tribunal's Rules of Procedures, Wladimiroff's name was added to a list of thirty lawyers drawn up by the Tribunal to provide counsel to the defendants. When Tadic was transferred to The Hague, his German lawyer told him that he would have to find other counsel.[39] Although Wladimiroff is Dutch, his was the only Slavic name on the Tribunal's list of defense counsel, and this evidently appealed to Tadic. It turned out to be an excellent choice.

Wladimiroff is the dean of the Dutch criminal defense bar. He is a senior partner at the sixteen-lawyer firm of Wladimiroff and Spong, the largest criminal defense firm in the Netherlands. Although Wladimiroff usually defends large companies involved in tax or environmental disputes, he jumped at the chance to represent Tadic. Asked on the eve of trial to describe his client, Wladimiroff said, "Though not well educated, he's quite intelligent. He's got the memory of a computer and has provided the defense team with names, places, dates—down to the hour."[40] As to why he took the case, Wladimiroff told me, "This is an historic trial. This is the first case that involves discussing a new body of international law. For a jurist, being part of this process is extremely fascinating."[41] So fascinating, it turns out, that Wladimiroff convinced his junior partner, Alfons Orie, to join him and persuaded his firm to contribute resources for the preparation of Tadic's defense. As it turned out, it would be Orie's last case as a litigator. Shortly after the conclusion of Tadic's trial, Orie received a judicial appointment on the Dutch Supreme Court.

Wladimiroff and Orie used their firm's resources to make repeated trips to the Prijedor region of Bosnia where Tadic lived. Wladimiroff speaks Russian and knows a little Serbo-Croatian from his travels to Yugoslavia when he was a young man. This helped him gain the trust of the locals. With the help of one of Tadic's brothers who lived in the area, Wladimiroff found thirty-six people whose testimony, he hoped, would establish Tadic's alibi defense.[42] However, they were afraid to cooperate. Some feared that they would face war crimes charges if they went to The Hague. Others dreaded the local warlord, Prijedor Police Chief Simo Drljac, who made it clear that he did not recognize the legitimacy of the Tribunal. Wladimiroff later overcame these difficulties by convincing the Tribunal to grant temporary immunity to defense witnesses who came to The Hague and to allow others to testify from Bosnia by video-link.

The third member of Tadic's defense team was Steven Kay, a British barrister, who resigned his job as secretary of the Criminal Bar Association in Britain to come to The Hague. Kay was originally brought in on a temporary basis to help Wladimiroff and Orie master the art of cross-examination, which is not employed in the Dutch system. "Two weeks later, they asked me to join the team full time," Kay told me. "And I thought it would be an historic challenge because so much of the process seemed to favor the prosecution: vast resources, a large number of lawyers and investigators, and even the rules of procedure themselves."[43]

Kay was assisted by Sylvia de Bertodano, a twenty-six-year-old British barrister, who joined the defense team just two weeks after returning from her honeymoon. "It was a chance in a lifetime for a young lawyer," she told me. "And I've been able to commute to London to see my husband on weekends."[44]

Two other lawyers were originally part of the defense team: Milan Vujin, a Bosnian Serb attorney with experience defending suspects in courts in the former Yugoslavia; and Nikola Kostich, a Serb-American criminal defense lawyer from Wisconsin. But on April 24, 1996, at Wladimiroff's urging, Tadic dismissed these Serb lawyers because they did not agree with the strategy Wladimiroff wished to pursue for Tadic's defense. Rather than rely on the defense of alibi and mistaken identity, they insisted on a more aggressive frontal assault on all aspects of the prosecution's case.

Meanwhile, Wladimiroff and Orie were busy preparing a series of pre-trial motions which they hoped would prevent Tadic from ever having to stand trial. In these motions, the defense challenged first, the legality of the establishment of the Yugoslav Tribunal; second, its primacy over national courts; and third, its subject matter jurisdiction. The trial court ruled against the motions on August 10, 1995. Because these matters concerned the jurisdiction of the Tribunal, the Tribunal's rules permitted Tadic's lawyers to bring an immediate interlocutory appeal to the appeals chamber, which rendered its decision on October 2, 1995. "This is the first time since the trials at Nuremberg and Tokyo," said the president of the Tribunal, "that an international appellate court has been able to pronounce upon the current status of international criminal law."[45] The Tribunal's decisions on these matters are among the most important developments in the history of international law and are therefore worth exploring in some detail.

Regarding the challenge to the legality of the Tribunal's establishment by the Security Council, the prosecutor took the position that the Tribunal did not have authority to decide the issue. "This International Tribunal is not a constitutional court set up to scrutinize the actions of organs of the United Nations," Goldstone argued. "It is, on the contrary, a criminal tribunal with clearly defined powers, involving a quite specific and limited criminal jurisdiction. If it is to confine its adjudications to those specific limits, it will have no authority to investigate the legality of its creation by the Security Council."[46] The trial chamber agreed, holding that the question was "pre-eminently a matter for the Security Council and for it alone and no judicial body, certainly not this Trial Chamber, can or should review that step."[47] The appeals chamber took issue with the trial chamber conclusion, finding instead that its inherent "incidental" power to determine the propriety of its own jurisdiction (*competence de la competence*) permitted review of the legality of the council's actions in establishing the Tribunal.[48]

This decision came as somewhat of an eye-opener to international law experts across the globe, given that even the International Court of Justice (the World Court) had declared on several occasions that it lacked the power to review the legality of Security Council resolutions. One commentator has said the World Court has treated judicial review like "a contagious disease."[49] Given the World Court's reluctance, "it seems a bit daring for a subsidiary tribunal to exercise such a power, even if couched as an 'incidental' one."[50] In addition, the decision of the Tribunal to confirm the legality of its establishment had important practical consequences. It precluded Tadic's lawyers from arguing the issue during his trial and it ensured that other defendants or government authorities would not be able to raise challenges to the legitimacy of the Tribunal in domestic courts in an effort to resist complying with the Tribunal's orders to surrender an accused or hand over evidence.

Wladimiroff and Orie's second argument was that "to be duly established by law, the International Tribunal should have been created by treaty.... not by resolution of the Security Council."[51] Tadic's lawyers also challenged the legality of the Tribunal on the ground that "the General Assembly, whose participation would at least have guaranteed full representation of the international community, was not involved in its creation."[52] But the heart of their argument was that the Security Council lacked authority to establish a subsidiary organ with judicial powers over criminal matters.[53] The appeals chamber rejected these arguments, finding instead that the establishment of the Tribunal was well within the broad powers of the Security Council under Chapter VII of the U.N. Charter.[54]

As characterized by the appeals chamber, one of the "more forceful arguments" raised by the defense was that the Tribunal was not "established by law" in accordance with Article 14(1) of the International Covenant on Civil and Political Rights—sometimes referred to as the cornerstone of the international bill of rights.[55] That provision states, "[i]n the determination of any criminal charge against him or of his rights and obligations in a suit at law, everyone shall be entitled to a fair and public hearing by a competent, independent and impartial tribunal established by law." A similar provision contained in the European Convention on Human Rights was interpreted by the European Court of Human Rights to require that the establishment of a tribunal must not be dependent on the discretion of the executive, but must be regulated by law emanating from a legislative body.[56]

Since the Yugoslav Tribunal was established by a body with executive powers (the Security Council) which can terminate the Tribunal at any time at its discretion, the defense had solid grounds for arguing that the Tribunal does not meet the requirement of Article 14(1) of the covenant. The appeals chamber nevertheless rejected the argument on three grounds. First, it observed that since there was no legislature, in the technical sense of the term, in the United Nations system, the argument was inapplicable to a Security Council-created judicial institution.[57] Second, it stated that the Security Council was a body which, though not a parliament, has the power to make binding legislative decisions under Chapter VII of the U.N. Charter.[58] Finally, the appeals chamber interpreted the phrase "established by law" as requiring only that the Tribunal be established in accordance with the proper international standards and that it provide all the guarantees of fairness, justice, and even-handedness, in full conformity with internationally recognized human rights instruments.[59]

Next, Tadic's lawyers argued that the Tribunal could not lawfully order Germany to defer its prosecution because among the sovereign powers retained by U.N. members is the right to prosecute in their own courts. The trial chamber ruled that Tadic had no standing to raise the issue of violation of state sovereignty; only Germany could have brought such a claim. The appeals chamber concluded otherwise and considered the merits of Tadic's argument. Relying on precedents established by the Israel Supreme Court in the *Eichmann* case, the *Barbie* case in France, and the *Noriega* case in the United States, the appeals chamber ruled that borders "should not be considered as a shield against the reach of the law and as a protection for those who trample underfoot the most elementary rights of humanity."[60] "State sovereignty," the appeals chamber concluded, "must give way in cases where the nature of the offenses alleged does not affect the interests of one state alone but shocks the very conscience of mankind."[61]

Finally, Tadic's lawyers challenged the lawfulness of his indictment under Article 2 (grave breaches of the Geneva Conventions) and Article 3 (violations of the customs of war) of the Tribunal's statute on the ground that there was no international armed conflict in the region of Prijedor where the crimes he was charged with are said to have been committed. They supported their argument by citing the comments on the Tribunal's statute submitted by the International Committee of the Red Cross (ICRC), the world's leading authority on international humanitarian law. In those comments, the ICRC had "underlined the fact that according to International Humanitarian Law *as it stands today*, the notion of war crimes is limited to situations of international armed conflict."[62]

The Tribunal decided not to follow this conservative view of international humanitarian law. Nor did it skirt the issue by taking judicial notice that the entire conflict in the former Yugoslavia was of an international character. Instead, in what can only be described as a novel interpretation, the appeals chamber ruled (on a four-to-one vote) that, although Article 2 of the Tribunal's statute applied only in international armed conflicts, Article 3 applied to war crimes "regardless of whether they were committed in internal or international armed conflicts."[63] As one commentator has said, this holding "was as bold as it was ill-founded."[64] The Tribunal based its decision on its perception of the trend in international law in which "the distinction between interstate wars and civil wars is losing its value as far as human beings are concerned."[65] In doing so, it referred to the interpretive statement given by the members of the Security Council at the time of voting to establish the Tribunal as evidence that its holding was consistent with the intent of the statute's framers. Asserting that "no delegate contested these declarations," the appeals chamber concluded that they provided an "authoritative interpretation" of Article 3.[66]

Our strategy for the statute, it turned out, had succeeded beyond our wildest hopes. For many, this decision will be the most important legacy of the Tadic trial. For others, the Tribunal's decision will be viewed as raising the specter of ex post facto laws in much the same way Nuremberg did fifty years earlier.

Discouraged but not deterred by its lack of success thus far, the defense submitted two additional pre-trial motions a few months later. In the first of these, the defense argued that at the time of Tadic's transfer to the Tribunal, the proceedings against him in Germany had entered their "final phase." Thus, the defense asserted, trial before the Tribunal would violate the double jeopardy clause contained in the Tribunal's statute. While acknowledging that the German proceedings had passed beyond the purely investigative phase when the German court issued an indictment against Tadic on November 3, 1994, the trial chamber concluded that the double jeopardy provision was not applicable since Tadic "had not been tried in the full sense, i.e., he was neither convicted nor acquitted by the German court."[67]

Wladimiroff and Orie fared better with their second motion, which challenged the form of the indictment. The prosecutor responded to the defense motion by arguing that "the indictment provides the accused with sufficient notice of the nature of the crimes with which he is charged and the facts which support those charges." The prosecutor told the court that its argument was supported by "the statements of Defense Counsel at the initial appearance before the Tribunal that the accused had read a copy of the indictment in his own language and understood the charges. The accused then entered a plea by stating that 'I never took part in any of the crimes with which I am charged.'"[68] While most of the counts of the indictment provide the particulars required by the Tribunal's statute,* the trial chamber agreed that one incident, which gave rise to three counts, was excessively vague.[69] The paragraph in question, which was added when the indictment was amended on September 1, 1995, introduced the charge of deportation and persecution of unnamed Muslims and Croat residents of the Prijedor area during a six-month period. According to the trial chamber, this paragraph "says nothing specific about the accused's conduct, about what was the nature and extent of his participation in the several courses of conduct which are alleged over the months in question."[70] The trial chamber therefore said that the charge must either be dropped or "further amended so as to provide the necessary degree of specificity."[71] In response, Goldstone revised the indictment on December 14, excising the counts in question.

Tadic's lawyers were not the only ones peppering the Tribunal with pre-trial motions. During the pre-trial phase, the prosecutor submitted a controversial motion for the protection of victims and witnesses. Over the strenuous objections of the defense, the chamber ruled that three witnesses who had been victims of sexual assault, known as "H," "J," and "K," could testify anonymously in order to protect them and their families from retribution.[72] The trial chamber subsequently granted a similar motion for witness "L," who had allegedly been a guard at the Trnopolje camp.[73] Such action was seen as necessary because "of the inability of the Tribunal to guarantee the safety of the witness due to the lack of a fully-funded and operational witness protection programme."[74] Afterward, Presiding Judge Gabrielle McDonald said it was one of the toughest rulings she ever had to make in her career because she had to weigh the rights of the witnesses against the rights of the accused.[75]

Even deputy prosecutor Graham Blewitt acknowledged that he was "personally very uncomfortable with the notion of going forward with witnesses whose identity are not disclosed to the accused."[76] In an editorial which appeared in the prestigious *American Journal of International Law*, former Department of State Legal Adviser Monroe

---

* Article 18 of the Tribunal's statute requires "a concise statement of the facts of the case and of the crime with which the suspect is charged."

Leigh argued that McDonald struck the wrong balance. The right to examine or cross-examine witnesses guaranteed by the Tribunal's statute, Leigh argued, cannot be effective without the right to know the identity of adverse witnesses.[77]

McDonald rationalized her decision on the ground that the Tribunal was "comparable to a military Tribunal" which had more "limited rights of due process and more lenient rules of evidence."[78] Her opinion then cited favorably the practice of the Nuremberg Tribunal to admit hearsay evidence and ex parte affidavits with greater frequency than would be appropriate in domestic trials. What McDonald (apparently) failed to realize is that this practice has in fact been a lightning rod for criticism of the Nuremberg Tribunal.[79]

Unlike issues involving the court's jurisdiction, this ruling is not appealable until the end of the trial. Wladimiroff has said that "this is not a normal court, but if the accepted standards of fairness are violated, we will file for a mistrial."[80] This ruling may have given him the ammunition needed for such a motion.

AP/WIDE WORLD PHOTOS

Pictured above, the high-tech courtroom of the Yugoslavia War Crimes Tribunal was located on the second floor of an unassuming insurance building (see below) in The Hague. Judge Gabrielle Kirk McDonald is seated in the second row, far right.

AP/WIDE WORLD PHOTOS

Chapter 7

On Trial

Despite the fact that public opinion already condemns their acts, we agree that here they must be given a presumption of innocence, and we accept the burden of proving criminal acts and the responsibility of these defendants for their commission.

—Robert H. Jackson
Opening Speech for the Prosecution at Nuremberg, 21 November 1945

1

May 7, 1996, was a brilliant, cloudless spring day at The Hague. The famed Dutch tulips, surrounding the reflecting pool in front of the four-story Tribunal building, were in full bloom. To the left of the entrance to the brick building, two bright red tents, serving as trial headquarters for the international press, flapped in the light breeze. Twenty feet away, hundreds of television, radio, and newspaper reporters stood in line to gain entrance to the opening of what they were billing as "the trial of the century."

One reporter described the scene as "a genteel media madhouse, O.J. with accents."[1] Three hundred VIPs and members of the press crowded into the public gallery, separated from the courtroom by floor-to-ceiling panes of two-inch-thick glass. As they filed in, each was handed a sleek black plastic translating device, about the size and shape of a television remote control. Miniature headphones, draped over the back of each seat, could then be plugged into the device, which had separate channels for English, French, and Serbo-Croatian translation, as well as a volume control. Just a little after 10:00 a.m., a hush descended over the throng of observers as the defendant, Dusko Tadic, now forty years old, clean shaven, and somewhat leaner, was led to his seat in the back of the compact courtroom by two blue-uniformed U.N. security guards.

Directly before Tadic, sat his lawyers—the somewhat gaunt but dignified-looking Michail Wladimiroff; Wladimiroff's law partner Alfons Orie, whose bushy grey hair and mustache made him resemble a Dutch version of Captain Kangaroo, the children's television personality; the gangly English barrister Steven Kay, whose powdered wig seemed oddly out of place in the high tech courtroom; and Kay's assistant, Sylvia de Bertodano, at twenty-six, by far the youngest of the lawyers involved in the historic case.

To Tadic's left, dressed in formal red and black robes, sat the three people who would pass judgment on him at the conclusion of the trial: Chief Judge Gabrielle Kirk McDonald of the United States, flanked by sixty-one-year-old Lal Chand Vohrah of Malaysia and seventy-two-year-old Sir Ninian Stephen of Australia. At each end of the judges' bench stood a blue and white United Nations flag—a reminder that this was no ordinary courtroom.

Across from the defense sat the prosecution team led by Australian Grant Niemann, a towering, portly man with slicked back, thinning white hair and half-rimmed glasses worn low on his nose. Seated to Niemann's left were the three American prosecutors who would be assisting him: Lt. Col. Brenda Hollis of the Air Force Judge Advocate General's office; Major Michael Keegan of the Marine Corps Judge Advocate General's office; and Alan Tieger, who had successfully prosecuted the four Los Angeles police officers for the beating of Rodney King. Although the prosecution wanted to avoid the appearance that this was "an American show," the fact that three-fourths of the prosecution team was American was unavoidable, explains Michael Keegan. "The United States was the first country to provide lawyers to the Tribunal, and we were immediately assigned to the Prijedor/Omarska investigation, which was the first investigation undertaken. Since the Tadic case flows out of that investigation, it just made sense that we would be the trial attorneys."[2]

Located in the middle of the courtroom, between the defense and prosecution tables, was the empty witness stand, equipped with a screen to allow certain witnesses to be hidden from the defendant to the left and the public seated behind. Since the witness's back was to the public gallery, an odd consequence of this setup was that observers tended to watch the trial on the large television monitors mounted at the two ends of the gallery, rather than through the clear glass partition in front of them—even though the trial participants were only five feet from the first row of the gallery.

The proceedings began with several surprises worthy of the suspense that had been generated in the weeks leading to the commencement of this historic trial. The first came with the announcement by the prosecution that it would not pursue rape charges contained in the indictment against Tadic (counts 2–4) because the alleged victim, a women identified only as "F," was too frightened to testify.[3] "F" was one of the six witnesses who were placed under a witness protection program in which the Tribunal guaranteed them anonymity for fear of reprisals on their families in Bosnia. The dropping of the rape charge came as a blow to those who hoped the Tadic trial would set a precedent confirming that rape is an international crime. In addition, it was hoped that proving the charge would establish an historical record of how Bosnian Serb commanders used rape as part of an organized campaign to destroy the Muslim and Croat communities.

The next unanticipated revelation was the court's announcement that in addition to issuing summonses and protective measures for defense witnesses, it would also grant "safe conduct" to four of the defense witnesses who feared that they would be arrested and prosecuted for war crimes if they appeared at The Hague to testify on Tadic's behalf. Their concern was well founded given the existence of several sealed indictments which had not been made public and given the experience of Djordje Djukic, the Bosnian Serb general who had been transferred to The Hague as a witness on February 12, 1996, but was then indicted and further detained as an accused.* Under the ruling, the witnesses would be immune from arrest and prosecution during the time they were at The Hague giving testimony. This ruling pro-

* Djukic was later released due to ill health and died of cancer a few weeks later.

voked raised eyebrows since it was so clearly inconsistent with the Tribunal's rationale announced in February 1995 for excluding from its Rules of Procedure the possibility of limited immunity. At that time, the Tribunal had said that "no one should be immune from prosecution for [such grave crimes], no matter how useful their testimony may otherwise be."[4]

Even more astonishing was the court's announcement that it had granted the defense's request to allow seven Bosnian Serbs to testify on Tadic's behalf live from Bosnia via a television link-up—the first such use of this technology by any court in the world.[5] The problem inherent in testimony of this kind is that the judges are unable to ascertain the presence of intimidating or corrupting influences just out of the range of the camera. In addition, the physical presence of a witness at the Tribunal enables the judges to evaluate their credibility and may help discourage the witness from giving false testimony. Yet the judges felt that these concerns were outweighed by the needs of the defendant to produce witnesses in support of his alibi defense. Thus, while such a procedure was not envisioned in the Rules of Procedure, the judges felt "it is in the interest of justice for the Trial Chamber to be flexible and endeavor to provide the Parties with the opportunity to give evidence by video-link."[6] At the same time, the judges made clear in their ruling that they would treat "the evidentiary value of testimony of a witness who is physically present [as] weightier than testimony given by video-link."[7]

Another surprise concerned the court's (non)disposition of the prosecution and defense's request for clarification as to the elements of the charged offenses. On April 10, the prosecution had submitted a sixty-five-page pre-trial brief, elaborating upon the "essential legal elements and requirements of the offenses that have been charged in the case."[8] With certain exceptions, the defense had supported the prosecution's effort to provide clarification as to the proof required for a conviction of crimes that are defined in only the vaguest of terms in the Tribunal's statute.[9] In a questionable ruling that would have far-reaching consequences for the pace and scope of the trial, Judge McDonald said, "The Trial Chamber does not consider that it is appropriate for us at this time to basically formulate an international criminal code; instead, we think it is our responsibility to hear the evidence and to interpret and apply the terms of the Statute of the International Tribunal. So, that is as far as we will go with respect to your request."[10]

A fifth unexpected occurrence came when Judge McDonald decided to begin the trial with an opening statement of her own "to put the trial in context as we see it." She began by acknowledging that "this trial has certain historic dimensions," but she stressed that the accused, who had plead not guilty, "is entitled to a fair trial and to make sure he receives one is our paramount purpose for being here. . . . The lawyers appearing on each side of this case come from different legal systems, as do each of we three Judges, but we all agree on one premise and that is that the rule of law must be upheld and that fairness is a cornerstone of the process of affording justice," she added. Finally, she cautioned the lawyers, saying that counsel would be expected to "discharge their responsibilities in a professional manner." McDonald's no-nonsense opening set the tone for the entire trial. Despite the bright lights, numerous television cameras, the crowded press gallery, and the carnival atmosphere outside the premises, Judge McDonald made it clear that this would be a serious undertaking, conducted with dignity and fairness.

The final surprise of the day was that the opening statement for the prosecution would not be delivered by the chief prosecutor, Richard Goldstone, as had been eagerly anticipated, but rather by his subordinate, Grant Niemann. At Nuremberg, this was thought to be prosecutor Robert Jackson's finest hour and, as quoted throughout this book, his words continue to ring with contemporary relevance. By the opening of the Tadic trial, Goldstone had gained a reputation as a miracle worker for his role in obtaining resources for the Tribunal and successfully launching the prosecution against great odds. But as an orator, Richard Goldstone is no Robert Jackson, and many suspected he did not want to tarnish his place in the history books with a performance that failed to live up to the standard set by Jackson. When I asked Goldstone why he had not delivered the opening, he replied that he "didn't want to politicize the trial." He added that "it would be demeaning to our senior trial attorneys to intervene, and it would raise objections from the defense or the bench since I would not be participating in any other aspect of the trial."[11]

Niemann's opening statement would be a grim two and one-half hour exposition of Tadic's alleged crimes, sparing none of the grisly detail. While it did not lack drama, it had little of the grandeur of Robert Jackson's opening statement at Nuremberg. "I thought a lot about Jackson's opening at Nuremberg, but the Tadic case is different," Niemann recounted. "It is historically important because it would be the first of many, not because it was the big and only one."[12]

2

THE ROBUST, BLACK-ROBED NIEMANN began his presentation by saying: "Through this trial we embark upon an examination of events of unspeakable horror. The evidence of the prosecution will prove beyond reasonable doubt that the accused, Dusko Tadic, committed the crimes with which he has been charged and that it was pursuant to a widespread or systematic attack against the non-Serb population of opstina [meaning, district] Prijedor." The Muslim population of the Prijedor region was reduced in 1992 from 50,000 to about 1,000, he noted.

Niemann then proceeded to sketch a portrait of Tadic before the war, a Serb living in the mainly Muslim town of Kozarac in northern Bosnia. He ran a pub, loved karate enough to earn a black belt, and had many Muslim friends. As Yugoslavia began its painful dissolution, Tadic became active in Serb nationalist politics and joined the local Serb police force, Niemann said. Just before the Serb attack on his town, Tadic moved his wife and children away and turned on his Muslim neighbors. According to Niemann, "Tadic was willingly used by the advancing Serb forces as an important source of intelligence and a person capable of identifying local Muslims. He skillfully performed his task. During 1992 he rose from relative obscurity to a person of influence in the Kozarac area." Niemann asserted that Tadic served as an aide to the Serb military surrounding Kozarac, assisted the artillery attack on the town by firing flares in the air at night over targets he pre-selected, and, after the town's surrender, identified important Muslims for summary execution.

Tadic became so influential that, according to Niemann, he was allowed to visit Serb detention camps nearby and do what he pleased to the defenseless Muslim inmates. Niemann stated that Tadic and men like him "were allowed into the camps in order to commit particularly brutal acts of terror, presumably in furtherance of the policy of ethnic cleansing." Niemann added that such men "either had anti-Muslim political dispositions, which were conducive to the performance of these deeds, or alternatively they were sadistically predisposed towards violence and took pleasure in inflicting tremendous pain and suffering upon the helpless victims, and thus [were] used as a useful agent of the authorities."

Niemann said that the prosecution would present eyewitness testimony linking Tadic to numerous murders and beatings. Niemann then described the infamous incident at the Omarska Camp, in which Tadic ordered a number of Muslim men to appear before him. "These men were then subjected to the most horrific beating and torture. Two other male prisoners were then called out and forced to perform oral sex on Fikret Harambasic and then to sexually mutilate him. And Harambasic died as a result of these assaults," Niemann told the court.

The prosecution planned to call over eighty witnesses in the course of its case. The problem with such a strategy was the likelihood that it would elicit divergent accounts, which could be exploited by the defense. To preempt the defense on the issue of inconsistent witness testimony, Niemann told the court, "The witnesses that will come before you are often bewildered and sometimes angry about the tragic and undeserved fight that is before them. The absolute terror to which they have been subjected in those black days of 1992, and the passage of time since then may have had some effect on their ability to relate all the details of their experiences. But their sincerity and their veracity regarding the crimes they describe which are the responsibility of the accused are, in our observation, beyond question."

In addition to witness testimony, Niemann promised to introduce a number of documents, maps, photographs, and videotapes which would be displayed on the court's high-tech television monitors. But, unlike at Nuremberg, where the prosecution submitted seven million pages of meticulously kept Nazi documents,[13] the Serbs had left a scant paper trail concerning their policy of ethnic cleansing. Therefore, the Tadic case would turn largely on the testimony of witnesses.

Finally, as a reminder of why this case was being tried before an international tribunal, Niemann said, "When an individual commits a crime, the state stands as the bastion of justice, but when the state commits the crime, only the community of nations can protect the individual. Otherwise, evil has no boundary." To ward off criticism that Tadic was a small fry unworthy of such international attention, Niemann sought to portray the defendant as a representative cog in the ethnic cleansing machine. "This is not an isolated affair, but part of a coordinated strategy," Niemann told the Tribunal, adding that Tadic's crimes were committed in pursuance of the goals of the Serbian state. Thus, the trial was not just about "what occurred between the accused and the victims of these crimes," Niemann argued, but about "the tragic destruction of that once proud and beautiful country, Yugoslavia. . . . To have some understanding of why one ethnic group would want to, so cruelly, turn upon another with the intent to bring about their destruction, to have some understanding of the targeted victims of these crimes, then it is necessary to have some understanding of what was Yugoslavia."

Throughout Niemann's presentation, Tadic looked a bit pale but showed no emotion. His expression did not change even as the prosecution denounced him as a "sadist who took pleasure in torturing prisoners." He briefly sighed when Niemann outlined the atrocities he was alleged to have committed, including ordering a prisoner to bite off the testicles of fellow inmates at the Omarska prison camp. From time to time, Tadic took notes on paper placed before him. On that day, he was the only person in court who had to wear an earphone to hear the proceedings translated from English into his native language, Serbo-Croatian; by the end of the trial, his lawyers would later tell me, Tadic had become nearly fluent in English.[14] At one point, he turned to smile at a Serb woman sitting in the gallery, less than ten feet away from him. The woman, who had recently settled in the Netherlands, had often visited Tadic during his year of incarceration in the Dutch detention facility. This woman was apparently Tadic's only friend present at the trial; his wife, two children, and two brothers could not afford the trip from Bosnia.

After a break for lunch, Tadic's chief defense lawyer, Michail Wladimiroff, made his opening statement by countering the attack on his client with an assault on the judicial process itself. "There is a danger of high media exposure and low-quality justice," Wladimiroff began. Wladimiroff suggested that because Tadic was the first person to be tried by the new Tribunal, the judges would be under enormous public pressure to convict him. Wladimiroff said Tadic risked becoming a "symbol" of all that had happened in the former Yugoslavia and the case against him risked being "blown out of all proportion." "The prejudice that exists in this case cannot be underestimated," he added. "Dusko Tadic stands charged as an individual, and the crimes of others cannot and should not be laid at his feet."

Wladimiroff agreed that unspeakable crimes had occurred in the camps, but said that his client was not involved. According to Wladimiroff, Tadic, far from being an agent of genocide, was a traffic policeman, unsympathetic to Serb nationalism, who did his best to provide humanitarian aid for the Muslim refugees who had been his close friends before the bitter conflict. He said Tadic had an alibi for the crucial months of 1992. "The defense case is simply that Dusko Tadic was not involved in the camps in any capacity," Wladimiroff said. Instead, Wladimiroff told the judges, "You will hear how he escaped from his home in Kozarac before the 24th of May with his wife and family to stay in the relative safety of Banja Luka. You will hear how the following month he secured a job in the traffic police in Prijedor." Wladimiroff promised to produce duty rosters and witnesses to support Tadic's alibi.

Wladimiroff then challenged the reliability of the witness testimony which the prosecutor had promised to introduce. The evidence they will give is tainted, Wladimiroff argued, because many of the witnesses had already discussed among themselves the atrocities allegedly committed by Tadic. "Many witnesses have adopted the accounts of fellow prisoners," he said. A composite story emerged. Conditions in the camps "provided the stuff of rumor and the need for a scapegoat," he added. But, he warned, "the thirst for revenge must not be satisfied at the well of polluted justice." "We are standing on the edge of a fair trial," Wladimiroff concluded. "Do not push us over that edge. Help us to stay on the right side and to put forward our case. If you enable us, if you enable our witnesses to testify, you will not convict Dusko Tadic."

The press readily agreed that the defense had won the battle of the opening statements. But Wladimiroff refused to take credit for the majesty and power of his statement. As he recounted, "I developed the themes, but Steven Kay made the language do the work."[15] Yet trials are rarely won on the basis of opening statements, and the defense knew it had an uphill battle ahead of it.

3

DURING ITS CASE, THE PROSECUTION would call three types of witnesses: two "expert witnesses," fourteen "policy witnesses," and fifty-nine "eye witnesses." The prosecution began with an expert witness, Dr. James Gow of the Department of War Studies, Kings College, London—a British military historian and Yugoslav expert.[16] Gow was put on the stand to offer a detailed analysis of the break-up of Yugoslavia, which would relate the charges against Tadic to the wider history of the conflict. Since the Tribunal had ruled before trial that Tadic could not be convicted of grave breaches of the Geneva Conventions under Article 2 of the Tribunal's statute unless the prosecution proved his acts occurred during an "international conflict," Gow's main job was to prove the continuing involvement of Serbia in the conflict in Bosnia *after* Bosnia had been recognized as an independent state in April 1992.

Despite his impressive credentials, the choice of Gow to begin the prosecution's case was a puzzling one. Gow presented himself as anything but the ideal of a distinguished scholarly historian. He was quite young (he looked to be not much over thirty years old), wore his longish dark hair in an unkempt, youthful fashion, and spoke haltingly with a penchant for unnecessary qualifiers and caveats that suggested a lack of confidence. As one press report put it, "Gow's fluency fell well short of his knowledge."[17] To put it another way, he was about as impressive a witness as Kato Kaelin in the O.J. Simpson murder trial. As a result, media attention fell off dramatically during Gow's four-day history lesson. To use another analogy from the O.J. trial, it was as if the prosecution had begun the O.J. case with the DNA experts. People were not tuning in the way the Tribunal had hoped when they decided to authorize gavel-to-gavel television coverage of the proceedings; they were tuning out. In addition, Gow's prolific writings on the Yugoslav conflict gave the defense grounds to challenge his objectivity, if not his credentials. Finally, Gow obviously lacked experience in a judicial setting, which manifested itself in his defensive posture when questioned by the bench and during cross-examination.

Nevertheless, Gow's four days of testimony went a long way toward documenting that what happened in Bosnia was not a local civil war, but part of an international conflict (as required to prove the charge of grave breaches of the Geneva conventions) and that the atrocities were widespread and systematic (as required to prove the charge of crimes against humanity). In addition, his testimony served to establish the historic context for the atrocities that Tadic was alleged to have committed. Through Gow's testimony, the prosecution was able to portray Tadic's acts, not as the isolated abuses of a mad man, but as the calculated deeds of a fifth columnist assisting the broader Serb campaign of "ethnic cleansing" in the Prijedor region of Bosnia.

Relying on excerpts of speeches contained in a British television documentary, entitled "The Death of Yugoslavia," which were introduced into the record, Gow implicated Serbian President Slobodan Milosevic in the war and atrocities in Bosnia. One segment, which Gow told the court was a key to Milosevic's thinking, was recorded in 1990 as the breakup of Yugoslavia loomed. It revealed Milosevic proposing to rewrite the federal constitution to include the right to secede "not just for republics [as Croatia and Slovenia wanted], but also for ethnic groups." Thus, Gow suggested, Milosevic was threatening that if Croatia, Slovenia, and Bosnia seceded, he would support the right of Serb minorities in those territories, in turn, to secede from them and join with Serbia. Another video segment showed a Serbian nationalist leader acknowledging that President Milosevic had armed and supported Serbian paramilitary groups that fought in Croatia and Bosnia. In a third segment, a former Serbian paramilitary leader said his troops fought in Bosnia and Croatia with support from Belgrade. A final extract showed a speech by Radovan Karadzic, leader of the Bosnian Serbs, in which he said, "You Muslims will drag Bosnia down to hell, you could face extinction."

"This series of extracts, I think, shows how the paramilitary groups were operating and cooperating with official bodies of Serbia," Gow told the court. According to Gow, the extracts proved that Serb leaders in Belgrade wanted to create a "Greater Serbia" by taking over these territories where Serbs lived in large numbers of Croatia and Bosnia, cleansing them of non-Serbs, and attaching them to the country calling itself Yugoslavia. To that end, Gow asserted, the Serb-dominated Yugoslav National Army (JNA) teamed up with local Serb militias and waged war against the independent state of Bosnia. It was a land-grab, pure and simple, Gow maintained. Tadic's Muslim neighbors were like the Jews of Poland, liquidated by a foreign power bent on ridding the land of them.

As fate would have it, Steven Kay, the barrister brought aboard the defense team for his expertise in the art of cross-examination, came down with the flu on the last day of Gow's direct examination, so it fell upon Alfons Orie to conduct the first cross-examination of the trial. Orie had never before cross-examined a witness, since the practice is not employed in the Dutch courts. And with the surprise absence of Kay, Orie had very little time to prepare.

I had met and worked closely with Orie at a week-long conference of experts on an international criminal court in Siracusa, Italy, in the summer of 1995. We had co-chaired a group on trial procedures, and I was struck by Orie's keen intellect and his quick wit. (He also had the most impressive lap-top computer I had ever seen!) But most important of all, he possessed the gift of being aggressive without appearing belligerent—a crucial requirement for a successful cross-examination. In addition, Orie told me that he moonlighted as a professional opera singer and was used to performing in the spotlight under pressure. In short, despite his inexperience with the technique, when Alfons Orie stepped to the podium, he was ready to take on Dr. James Gow and to begin building the defense.

Orie started by countering the prosecution's depiction of the large-scale ethnic cleansing of the Muslim population in northern Bosnia, carried out by Bosnian Serbs. He was able to force Gow to acknowledge that Serbs, too, had been chased from their homes, particularly in central and northeastern Bosnia. Next, he coaxed Gow into conceding that the Serb bid for secession from both Bosnia and Croatia may have been motivated as much by a fear of becoming "second-class citizens" in their own country as by a desire to create a "Greater Serbia." In response to Orie's questioning, moreover, Gow admitted that "expansionist ideology" had not been the exclusive province of the Bosnian Serbs and that several ultranationalist Croat and Muslim paramilitary groups had operated in Bosnia and had pushed for their own national ascendancy just as brutally as Serb militias. Orie now had Gow on the defensive, and the witness began to stammer increasingly. At one point, Gow used so many qualifiers in answering one of Orie's questions that the defense counsel commented: "I heard so many 'ifs' and 'if you would look at it this way and that way' that the words of

Shakespeare come into my mind: 'if ifs and ans were pots and pans, there'd be no need for tinkers.'"

But Orie scored the most points when he systematically pinpointed imprecisions in Gow's historic accounts and suggested tersely that the historian's version of events was tainted with an anti-Serb bias. Armed with the full transcripts of the speeches excerpted in the British documentary, Orie cajoled Gow into admitting that he had been mistaken about the date of the Karadzic speech, that some of the other snippets might have been taken out of context, and that some of the translations provided may have been inaccurate and misleading.

Next, Orie read an extract from a 1993 publication by Gow in which the historian referred to Serbia as a "hissing snake spitting its venom." "Doesn't this strong language and disparaging image of the Serbs indicate your anti-Serb prejudice?" Orie inquired. The question seemed to catch Gow momentarily off guard. After stammering for a few seconds, Gow regained his composure and answered that the description did "not indicate prejudice of any kind." He added that his language was "literary" rather than "emotional," but a glance at the judges suggested that they did not find Gow's explanation altogether persuasive.

This exchange reflected an important distinction between the brand of cross-examination practiced in the United States (and often portrayed on American television) and cross-examination under the hybrid system of the War Crimes Tribunal. At The Hague, a witness was not confined to answering with a "yes" or "no." Instead, a witness was given wide latitude to explain and elaborate upon his or her answers. The procedure was intended to make the trial more a search for the truth than a performance carefully choreographed by the lawyers. But as a consequence, the defense counsel had relatively little control of an often unpredictable cross-examination.

Notwithstanding the difficulties inherent in the Tribunal's brand of cross-examination, most observers agreed that Orie got the better of James Gow and that Gow had not been a particularly effective witness for the prosecution. Yet, Mike Keegan of the prosecution team felt Gow accomplished what the prosecution had wanted. "The evidence we were seeking to get before the Court was elicited," Keegan explained. "I think it is very easy for the critics to play armchair quarterback, but the proof of Gow's effectiveness will be in the court's determinations."[18]

4

AT THE CONCLUSION of Gow's testimony, the court interrupted Tadic's trial for a pre-trial hearing for Zejnil Delalic, one of only three Muslims indicted by the Tribunal. With only a single courtroom for the Tribunal's proceedings, such interruptions would be a frequent occurrence throughout the Tadic trial. Delalic was accused of responsibility for murder, torture, and rape committed by troops under his command against Serbian inmates at a prison camp in central Bosnia in 1992. As expected, Delalic pleaded "not guilty." While his trial would have to await the outcome of the Tadic case, it was hoped that his presence at The Hague would demonstrate the Tribunal's neutrality and encourage Serb cooperation.

When Tadic's trial reconvened on the afternoon of May 13, the prosecution called the first of its fourteen "policy witnesses"—thirty-nine-year-old Dragon Lukac, a Bosnian Croat who had been the chief of public security of the Bosnian town of Bosanski Samac before being incarcerated in a nearby Serb-run prison camp. Unlike Gow, Lukac had been an eyewitness to the terrible things that occurred in Bosnia in 1992. However, he had not personally witnessed anything Tadic was alleged to have done. Instead, his role (and that of the other policy witnesses) was to document that similar brutal acts had been committed in other areas of Bosnia, thereby establishing the systematic and widespread nature of the acts. It is a strategy often used in American racketeering and civil rights cases which require a pattern of practice as an element of the crime.

Lukac began with the oath taken by each of the witnesses during the trial: "I solemnly declare that I will speak the truth, the whole truth and nothing but the truth," he repeated. In what would have been a dramatic moment had it not been for the awkward cadence and emotionless voice of the female interpreter, Lukac described his internment and his beatings at the hands of the Serbs. "We were treated very cruelly—we were abused. There was a concrete floor with nothing to sleep on, just two blankets for four of us," Lukac said. He described a starvation diet of one meal a day—"a piece of bread as large as a cigarette box with jam, that's all we had for seventy days"—which caused him to loose sixty-six pounds. After his release under a prisoner exchange, Lukac said he was examined by a doctor who found he had a fractured skull, eight broken teeth, cracked ribs, and a damaged kidney. The prosecution's strategy in calling Lukac was clear. He provided an opportunity to bring in the horrors of the Serb prison camps early in the trial while world public attention was still high.

Yet, after two days of Lukac's testimony, the judges began to get impatient. Judge McDonald pressed Niemann to streamline his case. It had been a week since the trial began, and only two witnesses had testified so far. At this rate, McDonald chided, the case would drag on until December, and the Tribunal had more important cases to try. But Niemann patiently reminded Judge McDonald that with the court's refusal to clarify his legal burden, he had no choice but to "present all the proofs available." The defense, on the other hand, obliged the judges by waiving cross-examination of the witness.

On May 14, Lukac was followed into the witness stand by Sulejman Tihic, a balding, forty-four-year-old Muslim attorney and local politician, also from the town of Bosanski Samac. Lukac said attempts to solve local inter-ethnic strife in the town of thirty-four thousand people would have succeeded "were it not for the JNA." He said that the army mobilized and armed local Serbs, adding that he had been arrested after fighting broke out and the JNA stormed Bosanski Samac with tanks. In detention, Tihic and the other Muslim prisoners were badly beaten and forced to sing "Chetnik" songs. Tihic said he attempted to purchase his freedom for 20,000 Deutsch marks, but the money was taken and he remained a prisoner. He testified that prisoners were forced to beat each other, to engage in oral sex with one another at knife- or gunpoint, and sometimes to kill fellow prisoners. He said that he was persuaded by the use of electronic cattle prods to make propaganda videotapes for the Serbs to give the BBC. But the most powerful moment of Tihic's testimony came when he told how a paramilitary soldier let his girlfriend in Belgrade listen over the phone as the soldier beat Tihic mercilessly.

By May 15, the seventh day of the trial, the prosecution began to speed the pace of the trial. Three witnesses would testify in a single day: Isak Gasi, a world class canoeist and member of the JNA until December 1991; Fadil Redzic, a JNA artillery officer until December 1991; and Ibre Osmonovic, a mechanic who had served in Montenegro as part of a JNA reconnaissance unit in the 1980s. This was the first chance observers would have to see the only female member of the prosecution team in action. Throughout the trial, Col. Brenda Hollis would take the lead when military issues were at the heart of the testimony; and May 15 was to be a military issue day. From the moment Hollis rose to her feet behind the prosecution's table, brushed back her short brown hair, and began to question her first witness, it was clear she had the training and temperament of a military lawyer. Dispassionate and brusk would be the two words most likely used to describe her performance; effective might be the third.

"And what kind of uniforms were they wearing," was the question Hollis repeatedly put to each witness as they described personnel distributing arms to Serbs, manning roadblocks, committing atrocities, or guarding camps. Each of the witnesses had sufficient military experience to be able to identify units by their uniforms, emblems, or weaponry. The descriptions ranged from the plain grayish-green uniforms of the JNA to the multi-colored camouflage fatigues adorned with various insignia of the Serb paramilitary units. The witnesses gave support to the prosecution's theory that the JNA participated directly in the April–May 1992 attacks on Muslims and Croats, and supplied, supported, and guided the actions of the paramilitary units which committed atrocities and manned the internment camps. "What ethnic group did they belong to?" was Hollis's second most frequently asked question. Since all three witnesses had traveled widely in Yugoslavia, Hollis drew upon their ability to identify slogans, accents, and patois. The answer to the question was always the same: "They were Serbs." The third most frequently asked question was whether there was any armed resistance by the Muslims of the area. Gasi and Osmonovic said no. Redzic said there was, but that it was ineffective and meaningless because the Muslims were so badly outgunned.

The final question Hollis put to the witnesses was, of course, "At that time were you or anyone else physically abused?" Gasi, Osmonovic, and Redzic all testified that while interned in the Serb-run camps they saw civilians shot, beaten with sticks and metal objects, and mutilated. At the Luka camp, Redzic said he once went for nine days without any food. Gasi said that he, himself, was beaten with a wrench. He then said a Serb stuck a gun in his mouth, cocked it, and pulled the trigger. The weapon turned out to be unloaded, but his tormentor promised that it would have a bullet for Gasi the next time. Importantly, Gasi testified that the perpetrators of these acts were not the guards but Serbs who visited the camp wearing camouflage uniforms, just as Tadic was alleged to have done at Omarska.

Up until now, the defense strategy had been not to cross-examine the policy witnesses, since Tadic was not contesting that atrocities had occurred throughout Bosnia; only that he, himself, had not committed such acts. But Gasi's assertion that the only weapons the Muslims of Brko (a town in northern Bosnia) had were a few hunting rifles and shotguns seemed to provoke Wladimiroff's ire and Wladimiroff succeeded in demonstrating the absurdity of Gasi's position during a combative cross-examination. When I asked Wladimiroff why he abandoned his strategy to contest that seemingly inconsequential point, he said, "I felt I needed the practice conducting a cross-examination, and it gave me a good opportunity to do so."[19]

May 20 was day eight of the Tadic trial. The prosecution began by calling Elvir Pasic, a twenty-eight-year-old traffic policeman from Rogatica in eastern Bosnia. Pasic testified about the Serb preparations leading up to the outbreak of war, including the creation of a parallel Serb government. He said that he resigned from the police force when the Serbs built a wall down the middle of the police station in the fall of 1991 to separate the Serbs from the Muslim policemen. He then noted the disappearance of TV Sarajevo and its replacement by telecasts filled with nationalist propaganda from Pale and Belgrade in the winter of 1992. Next, he described the Serb shelling and takeover of Rogatica and his subsequent imprisonment in the Batkovic camp where conditions were "appalling." He said that the camp was an "open house" to Serbs from the outside who would roam freely, beating and killing the detainees. When representatives of the International Committee of the Red Cross visited Batkovic, women, children, the aged, and those who had obviously been beaten were removed from the camp, and the remaining inmates were forced to lie about conditions there, he testified. "We were told to say everything was fine, that the food was great, we had cigarettes, there were no beatings and that we were free to move about. None of this was true." "But," he added, "if we didn't say this we were battered."

5

THE NEXT WITNESS WAS Hanne Sophie Greve, the member of the U.N. commission established by Security Council Resolution 780, who had overseen interviews of some four hundred victims and witnesses to ethnic cleansing in the Prijedor region. Like James Gow, she was called as an expert witness since she personally had not seen any of the events to which she would testify. Before the spindly, salt-and-pepper-haired American prosecutor, Alan Tieger, had a chance to ask his first question of the witness, defense counsel Steven Kay was on his feet with an objection to Greve's testimony. "Your honors, this witness's testimony will be hearsay based on second, third, and even fourth-hand testimony," Kay told the court. "And if she is simply summarizing interviews she is not offering any specialized skill to the fact finder." Kay handed the Court a "bundle" (the British term for a brief) supporting his objection.[20]

The defense brief argued that most national systems, even those in which bench trials are used, generally exclude hearsay evidence because it is inherently unreliable in three ways. First, the maker of a statement given in evidence by another person has not taken an oath as to the truth of the statement. Second, such a statement is not subject to cross-examination, which is fundamental in establishing the reliability of a statement. Third, if the person giving evidence of a statement he or she has heard from another has either misheard or misremembered the statement, this would be almost impossible to establish by cross-examination. Further, the brief argued that the use of hearsay statements is contrary to Article 21 of the statute of the Tribunal which affords the accused the right "to examine or have examined the witnesses against him."

Judge McDonald said that the court would reserve decision on Kay's objection, but reminded the barrister that under the Tribunal's rules there was no definition of "expert" and that any relevant evidence which had probative value might be admitted. The rules purposely do not exclude hearsay evidence, she noted. Thus, after the noon recess, Greve was permitted to testify. She would be on the stand for three days.

During her first day of testimony, Greve quantified the number of missing persons in Prijedor in 1992 as 43,000 Muslims and 3,000 Croats. During this time, Greve said, there was a 6,056 person increase in the Serbian population. Next, she explained the strategic significance of Prijedor to the Serbs in the spring of 1992. Prijedor served as a "corridor" which could link the Serb areas in northeast Bosnia adjacent to Serbia with the Krajina Serbian sector in northwest Bosnia and Croatia, she said.

She also highlighted the propaganda used by Serb leaders to frighten and inflame Serbs in northern Bosnia who, Greve claimed, had lived peacefully with their non-Serb neighbors since World War II. She told how the Serbs distributed weapons even to women and small children who could not have been expected to actually use them. She quipped, almost in an aside, that the arming of ordinary people actually makes them more fearful. She then compared the anti-Muslim media blitz to blasting a racist manifesto by David Duke throughout the United States by virtue of the Ku Klux Klan's seizure of U.S. television stations. The day's session ended as Malaysian Judge Lal Vohrah asked prosecutor Alan Tieger, "Who is David Duke?"

The second day of Greve's testimony focused on the Omarska prison camp, where many of Tadic's alleged crimes were said to have occurred. Greve told the court that the camp had the capacity to hold up to 3,300 people at a time between May and August 1992. In response to prosecutor Alan Tieger's question, "How many killings occurred at the camp?" Greve replied, "I would rather suggest thousands, but I'm not in a position to establish numbers." "According to Serb officials," she continued, "there were no large scale releases. Considering the number of people who were taken in, killing must have been on a large scale."

Greve further testified that Serb policemen, regular soldiers, and paramilitaries would arrive at the Omarska camp at night and take prisoners out of the camp. She said that prominent non-Serbs, such as famous athletes or politicians, were especially victimized. Interrogations at the camp were referred to euphemistically by the Serb authorities as "informative talks," Greve said. These invariably involved torture, and death was frequently the result. "According to the head of the Serbian police in the area, six thousand such talks took place in the camps," she added. So-called "confessions" from prisoners were later used by Serb authorities to back claims that non-Serbs had been conspiring to attack and liquidate their neighbors, Greve told the court. Conditions for the thirty-eight women at the camp were only marginally better than for the men, she said. "Women on one level had better conditions than the men but the main problem for them was rapes at nighttime; it happened all the time."

At the end of Greve's testimony, Judge McDonald asked the expert witness to define "ethnic cleansing" for the record. Greve almost apologized for using the term throughout her testimony. "It is a euphemism. It means rounding up an ethnic group by violence or force and taking them to concentration camps like Omarska, or Keraterm, or Trnopolje for torture, murder, or deportation," she answered.

The cross-examination of Greve was conducted by Steven Kay, who repeatedly scuffled with the witness over the accuracy of the census data on which she had relied. The defense strategy with Greve, as it had been with the prior witnesses, was to suggest that events were more complicated than the prosecution's portrait. In particular, Kay sought Greve's admission that the Muslims were well armed, organized, and vigorous in resistance. But Greve would have none of it. In response to Kay's challenge to her version of the bombardment of Kozarac, Greve held fast to her testimony that Muslim life and property took a pounding from Serb artillery on May 24th. When Kay suggested that Serbs, too, were the victims of the attack, Greve rejoined that the Serbs had left town before the 24th. "The only buildings left standing after the attack were the Serb Orthodox Church and houses belonging to Serbs, including the home of Dusko Tadic, which was untouched," she said on redirect. This was the first time since opening statements, two weeks earlier, that the defendant was mentioned during the trial!

The tenth witness of the trial, Muharem Nezirevic, took the stand on May 23.* When the conflict in Bosnia began, the fifty-two-year-old Nezirevic had been a journalist who worked for the newspaper

* Throughout this narrative, reference to minor witnesses whose testimony was merely cumulative has been omitted.

Kovarski Vesnick and its companion entity, Radio Prijedor. He began his testimony with a description of the Serb propaganda offensive. For example, after the Serbs took over the radio station, he recalled, they broadcast an attack on a prominent local Croat physician who was accused of "castrating Serb women and newborn children to prevent the procreation of the Serb people." Soon thereafter, Nezirevic was arrested and sent to Omarska.

Upon arriving at the camp, Nezirevic said that he and other detainees were forced to run a gauntlet of Serbs, who beat them badly. He was taken to the "white house," where he observed prisoners in crowded conditions, stacked on top of one another. The inmates were primarily Muslims, but he also saw abuse heaped upon a Serb, incarcerated as a Muslim sympathizer. He said he would never forget the look of the lost faces of Omarska. "Their eyes were not on the outside, but somewhere deep, deep inside."

Then, verging on tears, Nezirevic told the court how a fifty-year-old Muslim engineer he had known was forced to rape a young girl and was then killed. "They stripped her naked, forced him to undress and beat him. They wanted him to rape her. He was begging, saying 'she could be my child.'" Gulping for breath, Nezirevic said, "I'm sorry for the coarse language, but they said he should try and do it with a finger. It hurt her. She was screaming. They beat him. He had a weak heart." After a long pause, Nezirevic told the court, "In the morning to the left of the White House, I saw his body. He had been beaten to death."

Next, Nezirevic recounted how he had been informed by camp personnel that he was in "Category 1," meaning that he was scheduled for "liquidation." He was told his only hope for reprieve lay in raising 3,000 Deutsch marks (approximately $5,000). He wrote to his wife, requesting that she raise the money, telling her to hurry because, "I may not be alive when you read these words." As he read this letter in court, his voice began to break. Sensing the witness's distress, Judge McDonald called for a luncheon recess.

After the recess, Nezirevic ended his testimony by listing those friends from before the outbreak of the conflict who never returned from Omarska. The defense declined to cross-examine the witness, and the judges posed no questions. As he stepped down from the witness stand, it was clear that Nezirevic would be remembered as one of the most articulate and emotive witnesses of the trial.

The prosecution knew that Nezirevic would be a hard act to follow, but their next witness had an incredible story to tell. In a deadpan monotone, Mevludin Sejmenovic, a boyish-looking thirty-four-year-old Muslim politician who had served in the local assembly, told an unforgettable tale. He spoke of how he had witnessed firsthand the destruction of Kozarac, had observed ethnic cleansing at close range from his hiding place in a septic tank, and had broken into and then escaped from the Trnopolje camp. He later turned himself in to spare his friends from retaliation, after which he was taken to Omarska.

At Omarska, Sejmenovic said he was thrown into a blood-soaked cell. "On the right hand wall above the bed there was an awful bloodstain and the stain of brain as if you took some mud, red in color, and smeared it all around. It was an indication that somebody had recently been shot there at close range." Five guards then came in one by one and beat him until he was unconscious, he recounted. He was beaten this way for six days. "I was completely bloody. I had fractured bones and it was very painful to breath," he said. After the sixth day of his "interrogation," Sejmenovic said he offered to sign any statement put in front of him, if only he could be granted a dignified death.

Apparently moved by this request, his interrogator directed that Sejmenovic be relocated to the "Glass House," where prisoners who had paid money or were favored by the Serbs were housed. Fortune then smiled on Sejmenovic. He was spared further beatings because camp authorities wished to show the Glass House to journalists and decided to stop beating its inhabitants. After eliciting this testimony, the prosecution showed a news clip of Sejmenovic in Omarska. The grey-skinned, walking ghost on the video screen seemed a far cry from the young man in the witness chair. Afterward, Steven Kay offered a token cross-examination, during which he tried to get Sejmenovic to concede that Muslims were armed and organized a month before the Serbian offensive in May 1992. Sejmenovic was not budging, and without any means of impeachment (such as a prior inconsistent statement), Kay promptly ended the cross-examination.

After Sejmenovic came Mirsad Mujadzic, the head of the SDA (the Bosnian Muslim party) in Prijedor before the war. During his two days of testimony, he gave a blow-by-blow description of how the Serbs took over cities in Bosnia by force. He began before the 1990 elections when it became clear that Serb nationalism was rapidly increasing. At first, Serb officials apologized for the misconduct of some who were tearing down opposition placards and spewing nationalist rhetoric, he said. But after the SDS (the Bosnian Serb party) lost most of the elections in Prijedor, the Serb party leaders seemed ready to discard democracy and to take power by force. To ward off such a result, the SDA gave the Serbs control of 50 percent of the government positions in a power-sharing arrangement. But, according to Mujadzic, even that failed to appease the Serbs who set up a parallel government, distributed arms obtained from the JNA, and prepared to seize power. Interestingly, Mujadzic told the court that, having no idea that the Serbs were poised to take control of Prijedor by force, he dined with a Serb colonel and other Serbs the night before they attacked the city.

In his most contentious cross-examination yet, Steven Kay tried to demonstrate that the Muslims were well-financed fighters. In response to Kay's grilling, Mujadzic conceded that the Germans had provided substantial financial support to the Muslim SDA. Kay also attacked Mujadzic's account of an incident in which two Serbs were killed at an SDA checkpoint. Mujadzic had testified that it began when Serb extremists fired on members of the Territorial Defense (TO), the local Bosnian militia. "How on earth," queried Kay, could the witness know who fired the first shot since he had already said that he did not actually see the shooting.

On May 30, the public gallery was cleared, the blinds were lowered, and the court launched into its first closed-door session to protect the identity of a witness, identified only as witness "P." Witness "P" was a Serb turncoat who testified about the military build-up and the actions of the Serb military during the attack on Prijedor.

The next day, the Tadic trial was suspended to allow the court to entertain the plea of twenty-four-year-old Drazen Erdemovic, who was charged with crimes against humanity for shooting as many as one hundred civilian Muslim men outside the safe area of Srebrenica in July of 1995. History was made when Erdemovic became the first person ever to plead guilty before an international tribunal. The small, pimple-faced young man told the court that he was forced under the threat of death to shoot the civilians at a collection site outside of Srebrenica. It was shoot or be shot, he said. "Your, honor, I had to do this. If I refused, I would have been killed together with the victims. They told me, 'if you are sorry for them, stand up, line up with them, and we will kill you too.'"

Under the Tribunal's statute, however, obedience to orders is not a defense, although it can be raised as a "mitigating circumstance" to be considered at sentencing. Erdemovic began to cry uncontrollably as he described how badly he felt for his wife and his child. When his lawyer, Jovan Babic from Serbia, tried to calm him and asked him to quiet down, he said, "No, I cannot be silent any longer." Erdemovic would later be used by the prosecution as the star witness in the Rule 61 proceeding against Bosnian Serb leader Radovan Karadzic and military commander Ratko Mladic. On the last day of the Tadic trial, the Tribunal would sentence Erdemovic to ten years imprisonment.

6

When the Tadic trial reconvened on June 4, the prosecution's inquisitor on military issues, Col. Brenda Hollis, called the prosecution's thirteenth witness, Osman Selak, to the stand. Selak, a Muslim colonel, had been the only high-ranking non-Serb in the JNA until he retired in July 1992. As such, he was in a unique position to give an account of who was calling the shots and who was firing them. He described how in 1991 the Serb-dominated JNA insisted that the TO return all its weapons to the JNA. He said that, at the same time, the JNA forces pulling out of Croatia and Slovenia were relocating to Bosnia. Simultaneously, he testified, all of the Bosnian Serb members of the JNA located in Serbia were transferred to Bosnia.

Next, the former JNA colonel made what was to be the key point of his testimony: After May 18, 1992 (when Milosevic was telling the U.N. that the JNA had been pulled out of Bosnia), the JNA in Bosnia was divided into the army of the Republic Serpska (the VRS) and the Yugoslav army (VJ). Both armies, Selak said, were involved in the attacks on towns in the Prijedor region of Bosnia in May of 1992. And both armies, he added, continued to be controlled and paid for by Belgrade, including his salary! There could be little doubt in the judges' minds after Selak's testimony that the war in Bosnia was an international conflict. Even Steven Kay seemed to recognize the prosecution's final triumph on this point, since he did not try to contest it during his cross-examination of Selak. Instead, he used Selak as a military expert. Kay had him review Tadic's military records including dated stamps which indicated the varying times of service and units. The stamps, Selak conceded, did not show that Tadic had been stationed at Kozarac during its take-over or at the local internment camps thereafter.

Continuing on its military theme, the prosecution's next witness was Col. Ludvik Kranjc, a Slovenian who had been a brigade commander in the JNA. The key moment in Kranjc's testimony came when he said that the paramilitary organizations and the local police forces were under the direct supervision of the JNA in Bosnia. Through the testimony of Selak and Kranjc, the prosecution had successfully linked Tadic's violent activities on the police force in Prijedor to the chain of command going all the way to Belgrade. Next, prosecutor Michael Keegan asked Kranjc the following hypothetical question: "Could a man of military age living near Banja Luka who fled from his commune because he did not want to fight against non-Serbs in his area return three or four weeks after the combat operations to become the head of the local commune and a member of the Serb police force?" "I think it is not possible," the witness responded, thereby putting Tadic's alibi in serious doubt. Finally, Keegan sought to undermine the victory Steven Kay had obtained in his cross-examination of Selak the previous day by asking Kranjc whether all military activities were recorded on those records. The answer, to the prosecution's relief, was "No."

The next witness was Jerko Doko, who had been the former minister of defense for Bosnia. Based on his official position, he would seem to be a very important witness, but his testimony turned out to be merely a reiteration of earlier testimony about the Serb military advances. Given the judges' growing impatience with the rate of the trial, the prosecution wisely cut Doko's testimony short and put the next witness, Edward Vulliamy, a writer for *The Guardian*, on ahead of schedule. Abruptly, the witness was told, "Brace yourself, you're on in five minutes." Vulliamy, who was wearing a faded pair of blue jeans, had to borrow one of prosecutor Mike Keegan's suits. Keegan is a marine who works out. Vulliamy, a journalist who looks very much like the actor Bill Murray, doesn't, and the fit was far from perfect.[21]

Vulliamy was the last of the prosecution's "policy witnesses," but his testimony was remarkable because he provided the judges with their first real look inside the Omarska prison camp. They had heard testimony of the camp earlier, and a seven-foot scale model sat perched on a table in front of the witness stand. However, Vulliamy brought the horrors of the camp alive through videotape of his visit to Omarska in August 1992, when he was one of the first journalists allowed inside the camp. Ultimately, it was this video, aired on Britain's ITN network, and Vulliamy's accompanying press reports that led to the camp's closing a few weeks later. The video displayed on the court's monitors was startling, revealing men who were so emaciated they looked like walking corpses. Now the judges could see for themselves what Muharem Nezirevic, who had testified two weeks earlier, meant when he described the look of the lost faces of Omarska.

With the video in the background, Vulliamy told the court how he had been invited to the camp by Radovan Karadzic, who had said the visit would disprove media reports that Muslim prisoners were being maltreated. At Omarska, Vulliamy watched as groups of detainees, supervised by armed guards, were hustled into a canteen area where they were given sixty seconds to eat a bowl of gruel and a piece of bread. He said that it was immediately apparent that many of the prisoners were in appalling physical condition. "They were very thin, some were skeletal," he said. "And they were eating as if they hadn't eaten for a very long time, as if they hadn't seen food for a while. It was a fairly sobering sight." Under the constant watch of Serb guards, the prisoners were unable to talk freely with the reporters, Vulliamy explained. "They were manifestly scared, scared stiff," he said. "But their physical state told us more than their words." And they communicated with their eyes. "There is something inimitable about somebody staring at you in that way, saying, 'Look at me and try and work out for yourself what I'm trying to say.' "

In addition to the Omarska tape, Vulliamy showed the court video from the Trnopolje camp, which he had visited next. That video showed rail-thin prisoners standing behind barbed wire. Vulliamy testified that the internees had told him Trnopolje was a very bad place, but not as bad as Omarska. Some people, he said, even came there voluntarily to escape the violence in their villages. Vulliamy said the people in charge of Trnopolje camp were proud of that fact, but he drew the opposite conclusion. "If you flee here, what are you fleeing from?"

Vulliamy also testified that he had ridden with a convoy of sixteen hundred Muslims "herded over the mountains by Serbian gunmen." He told how the column of buses, cars, and trucks halted in the town of Skender Vakuf, where drunken Serb soldiers and paramilitaries smashed windows and spat at refugees before taking some women away from the convoy to be raped. When Mike Keegan asked him if the women were returned afterwards, Vulliamy replied, "My impression is no." The refugees were harassed further by a baying mob of Serb civilians. "They literally came streaming across the meadows shouting 'slaughter them, slaughter them,'" said Vulliamy. Eventually, after being thrown off the buses and having their cars commandeered, the refugees were forced to walk towards Bosnian government lines which were engulfed in heavy fighting. "The road was sticky with blood. At one point, I stood on a severed hand," Vulliamy told the court.

He described similar pogroms he had witnessed during his four years in Bosnia at the towns of Bosanska Krupa, Bihac, Jajce, Zepa, Visegrad, and Sarajevo. Judge McDonald interrupted Vulliamy's testimony to ask if all of the refugees had been forced from their homes. She pointed out to the journalist that in time of war, it may be logical to leave your home voluntarily to seek a safer place to live, or because you were not happy with or feared a change in leadership. But Vulliamy said that every refugee with whom he had spoken was forced out, and he said they were all non-Serbs.

Five weeks of the trial had passed without a shred of testimony as to the alleged crimes of the defendant. Indeed, after the opening arguments, his name had been uttered only a single time in the courtroom by a witness. When I interviewed Grant Niemann a few weeks later at The Hague, he explained why the policy-witness phase of the prosecution's case had become so drawn out: "We had asked the judges to determine that the conflict was international and that the abuses were widespread and systematic as a matter of judicial notice on the basis of the pre-trial submissions, and they said these were going to have to be proved in open court during the trial. As a consequence, we took a very cautious approach and elicited a lot of evidence in support of such a determination."[22]

AP/WIDE WORLD PHOTOS

Witnesses during the Tadic trial repeatedly referred to the look of "the lost faces of Omarska." The photo above was taken during a Serb-organized tour of the camp on August 9, 1992.

Chapter 8

Eyewitnesses

You will find it difficult, as I do, to look into the faces of these defendants and believe that in this Twentieth Century human beings could inflict such sufferings as will be proved here, on their own countrymen as well as upon their so-called "inferior" enemies.

—Robert H. Jackson
Opening Speech for the Prosecution at Nuremberg, 21 November 1945

1

On June 12, the prosecution finally began its parade of eyewitnesses who could allegedly point the finger of blame directly at Tadic.[1] Grant Niemann told the court that he had been forced to pare down the number of such witnesses because several had become unwilling to testify. Judge McDonald, purposely looking directly into the television camera, reiterated that anyone found intimidating or interfering with witnesses could face six months in jail or a $10,000 fine.

After five weeks with almost no mention of the defendant, the media hoped the trial would soon turn interesting. However, their hopes were temporarily dashed when the Tribunal announced that the first eyewitness, identified only as "Q," had requested anonymity and the session would take place behind closed doors. It was not until the closing arguments in November that the world would learn that witness "Q" had testified that he had seen Tadic using flares to mark Muslim targets during the Serb siege of Kozarac. After witness "Q," the court heard from Azra Blazevic, the eighteenth witness of the trial. The few journalists sitting among the rows of empty seats in the gallery finally got what they wanted. Blazevic's entrance into the courtroom has been described as "an electrifying moment," as she aimed a forthright stare at Dusko Tadic, who in turn met her gaze, blinked, and then lowered his eyes toward his desk.[2]

Blazevic, a Muslim, was a veterinarian who lived in Kozarac, the home of Dusko Tadic. She was very thin, had frizzy brown hair, extremely pale skin, and dark-ringed sullen eyes, which made her look at least twenty years older than her thirty-six years. Without knowing it, the court had actually been introduced to Dr. Blazevic two days earlier, as her visage was caught for a moment in the video of Trnopolje which had been shown during Ed Vulliamy's testimony. With Dr. Blazevic, Col. Brenda Hollis would be given a new role: in addition to inquisitor on military issues, the prosecution wisely assigned her to handle some of the most anguished female witnesses.

In response to Hollis's gentle questioning, Blazevic testified that before the attack on Kozarac she had seen Tadic "maybe every day, or even a few times a day," as his pub was located just two hundred yards from her house and veterinary practice. She then described with chilling matter-of-factness the chaotic events of late May 1992, when Serb forces cut off Kozarac from the outside world by erecting roadblocks and severing telephone lines. She told the court how the Serb forces allowed their fellow Serbs to leave Kozarac before unleashing a ferocious artillery barrage. "The attack started suddenly with terrible shelling," she said. "It was as if thousands of shells were landing at the same time."

In the midst of the tumult, Blazevic said she offered her services to the Kozarac medical center, working around the clock with barely any supplies to treat civilians of all ages wounded by the shelling. "Mostly people had very serious wounds, either amputations of limbs, parts of their bodies were missing or they had completely shattered parts of the body," she said. She then described how the shelling forced her and a team of doctors to retreat to a motel from the local medical center where they had been treating the wounded. She said it appeared that the medical facility was a specific target of the barrage. As she testified, the prosecution displayed a video of Kozarac, showing almost every house gutted by shellfire. The witness trembled slightly as she identified the ruined buildings near her former home, including the charred mosque. A few structures, she pointed out, remained miraculously untouched, including Dusko Tadic's pub. She said Tadic's house was undamaged as well and that it had a sign on it, which read, "Serb House. Do Not Touch."

Then, Dr. Blazevic described her final minutes in Kozarac before she and others were taken away to the camps. She said the Serbs took her and other medical personnel to an intersection in Kozarac. While she was there, she heard someone whisper, "There's Dule"—Dusko Tadic's nickname. She looked up and saw Tadic walking across the street. She said he was wearing a uniform and had a weapon in one hand. "Can you identify the man in the courtroom who you saw that day?" asked Col. Hollis. You could have heard a pin drop in the gallery as Dr. Blazevic looked around the courtroom. "It is the individual sitting between the two policemen in the back row," Blazevic calmly answered. Thus, the witness, whose credibility seemed beyond question, had gone a long way toward proving count 1 of the indictment, which charged Tadic with participating in the Serb attack on Kozarac and in assisting in the seizure, collection, segregation, and forced transfer to detention centers of the majority of the non-Serb population in the area.

Next, Dr. Blazevic described her internment at Trnopolje. She said conditions there were impossible. They had no running water, no regular meals, and not enough sleeping room. Many people contracted diarrhea, lice, and scabies from the unclean conditions. She narrated a second video of Trnopolje showing where the inmates lived and where the beatings took place. She said that rapes were commonplace at the camp and that she had talked with many of the victims and their mothers. Sometimes girls as young as thirteen were brought in to the makeshift infirmary which she ran. Once, she said, eight mothers brought in their daughters at one time. They had all been raped by Serbs and they were requesting tranquilizers because they were hysterical. She noted that Serbs from outside the camps often frequented the camps and participated in the beatings and rapes—a theme the prosecution was developing nicely.

Defense counsel Michail Wladimiroff knew the witness had to be handled carefully. He decided it was best to target the reliability of her sighting of Tadic in Kozarac, rather than to challenge her credibility as a witness. When he pressed her on how long she had seen the person identified as "Dule," she admitted it was for "just a few seconds." "Isn't it possible," Wladimiroff asked, "that when you heard someone whisper, 'there's Dule,' that you just assumed it would be Dule Tadic?" Blazevic replied that she was sure it was Tadic, whom she had known since she moved to Kozarac in 1986. Wladimiroff then suggested that Tadic may have been living abroad from 1986 to 1992, the time period during which the witness had said she saw him as often as twice a day. Blazevic backpeddled slightly, saying it was possible that he might have been out of the country and she would not have realized it. Seeing a possible opening, Wladimiroff pushed the point further, suggesting that Blazevic was only able to identify Tadic in court because he was sitting in the logical place for a defendant to be sitting in a courtroom. "I know him and it doesn't matter to me where he sits, I can recognize him," Blazevic answered convincingly.

The second eyewitness to place Tadic in Kozarac during the Serb takeover was Nasima Klipic, the wife of a Muslim policeman who had been stationed in the town until he disappeared during the violence in May 1992. Klipic's identification of the defendant would be even more difficult for the defense to impeach since she testified that she had known Tadic "all of my life." They had many common friends, and her brother even gave Tadic lumber for the construction of his pub, she said.

Clutching a white tissue and speaking emotionally, Klipic said she had not seen her husband, two brothers, and thirty-two other family members since Kozarac was taken over by the Serbs in May 1992. As for the defendant, she said she saw Tadic twice on May 27, 1992. The first time, she said, Tadic was patrolling the column of Muslim civilians in a police car. The second time she saw him he was slightly unkempt, dressed in a camouflage uniform, and carrying an automatic rifle and pistol. She said he was standing with a group of Serbs who were separating the thousands of surviving residents of Kozarac into three groups destined for the three detention camps in the area—Omarska, Keraterm and Trnopolje. She added that she heard Tadic ask a fellow Serb, "Where do I take these?" Klipic testified that she saw Tadic again with Serbian police in June outside the Trnopolje camp. When asked to identify Tadic in court—something that would become a sort of ritual for each of the eyewitnesses—Klipic pointed to the defendant and scolded him for the way he looked. "He never was so smartly dressed like this," she said. "Shame on you." Then, in an effort to thwart the defense contention that a man who looked like Tadic committed the crimes for which he stood accused, the prosecution asked Klipic if there was anyone who looked a bit like Tadic in the Prijedor area. "I don't know anyone who looks like him," she replied.

Defense counsel Steven Kay skillfully used a prior statement Klipic had given to a Tribunal investigator to cast doubt on the reliability of Klipic's testimony. "Why hadn't you mentioned seeing Tadic twice on May 27 in that prior statement?" Kay pressed. She said she had forgotten the first sighting. Nor could she explain why in the prior statement she had said Tadic was "deciding" where Muslims would be sent, while in her in-court testimony she said she heard him say, "Where do I take these?"—a comment which painted him in a much more benign role. In addition, she could not explain why she said in the statement that Tadic was "clean-shaven" when she saw him, but she said on the stand that he was "unkempt." But Klipic managed to get the last word, insisting that she did not make up the sighting as Kay suggested. "I spoke the truth," she said. "I would be happier if I was lying to you and if my family was alive."

The next witness, Nihad Seferovic, would turn out to be among the most important of the entire trial. He was one of only two of the seventy-five prosecution witnesses to testify that he saw Tadic commit murder with his own eyes. The forty-six-year-old Seferovic stared frostily at Tadic as he entered the Tribunal's courtroom to give evidence at the end of the sixth week of the trial. He said that he grew up only a few houses away from the Tadic family and was a childhood friend of the defendant and his brothers. When the attack began on Kozarac in May 1992, Seferovic said that he fled to the hills seeking safety. Two days later, he snuck back into town to feed his pet pigeons, he said. As he was hiding in an orchard across the street from the Serbian Orthodox Church near his brother's house, he saw Tadic and other Serb paramilitaries line up a group of captured Muslim policemen, he testified. He added that he recognized four of the Muslims. Then, he said, he saw Tadic drag two of the men—who Seferovic identified as Osman (no last name given) and Edin Besic—away from the others and slit their throats. "I did not see the knife, just the gush of blood, then gunfire from the Serbs, as if they were applauding the event," he said, adding that he then "retreated in despair." A few days later, Seferovic was picked up by Serbs and taken to the Omarska detention camp where he suffered various forms of maltreatment, which he described for the court. When asked to identify Tadic in court, Seferovic gestured towards the dock. Tadic returned Seferovic's gaze, cocking one eyebrow and throwing a defiant smirk at his former friend.

If there was ever a challenge for barrister Steven Kay, this witness was it. Not only did Seferovic testify that he had known the defendant for some forty years, but at the time of the incident, the witness was close enough to be able to identify Tadic and his victims and to see the method of killing. Kay began by suggesting that Seferovic could not have had a clear view of the church where the killings allegedly occurred because he was hiding in brush. Seferovic denied that the brush had obscured his line of sight, saying that his view of the church was "all too clear." Stating that he was finding it hard to believe that Seferovic would really sneak back into enemy hands just to feed his pigeons, Kay suggested that the witness had invented the entire incident. An indignant Seferovic answered, "I saw it with my own eyes."

Next, Kay asked a series of questions calculated to lock Seferovic into his story about the identity of the victims and the manner of their death. This point was important since the only persons that the indictment alleged that Tadic killed in Kozarac were Ekrem Karabasic, Ismet Karabasic, Seido Karabasic, and Redo Foric, who he allegedly pulled from a column and shot. Although the indictment had been amended twice prior to the trial, the prosecution never included any reference to the incident Seferovic described. Thus, the defense hoped that even if Seferovic's account was believed, it would not form a basis for a conviction.

After the court recessed for the day, the prosecution announced that one of the seven people in the Tribunal's custody, Goran Lajic, would be set free because investigators had concluded that he had been detained as a result of mistaken identity. When he was arrested near Nuremberg, Germany, in March 1996, he had said, "I am not this man. There would be many Goran Lajics in Bosnia-Herzegovina." He added that he had "never set eyes on the camp Keraterm. I have never been there and I do not even know where that camp is in that town." Prosecutors later conducted a photo spread, showing his picture to ten witnesses on June 12, 1996. Although his name and date of birth were identical with those of a wanted camp commandant, nine out of the ten witnesses from the camp did not recognize him as the man who ran the Keraterm prison camp. Three of the witnesses said they knew that Lajic before the war and that they were "100 percent certain the Lajic in custody was not the Lajic who was at the camp."

The next day, two Bosnian Muslims accused of war crimes were arraigned before the Tribunal. One of the men, Hazim Delic, was accused of being the commander of the Muslim-run Celebici camp in 1992—a camp whose conditions were reminiscent of Omarska. Among other things, Delic and his co-defendant, Esad Landzo, were accused of four murders, two rapes, and five acts of torture. These acts included helping to nail a badge into an elderly Serb's head before the Serb died, burning a cross into another man's hand, and carving a fleur-de-lis on another man's palm. Both men pleaded not guilty and their attorneys told the court that the Muslims were acting only in self-defense to protect themselves from the aggression of the Bosnian Serbs. "It is common knowledge in the tribunal and in the world that the aggressor was Serbia," the attorney for Landzo said. "It was not an attack, it was self-defense. It was the only way to save the city from the same fate as Prijedor and Kozarac."

When the Tadic trial resumed on June 18, Ferid Mujcic, a Muslim survivor of Omarska, was called to the stand. Mujcic's battered face and broken nose were physical reminders of the ordeal he had endured at the camp. Mujcic's testimony was important in two respects. First, he said that after the Serb takeover of Kozarac he saw Tadic, whom he had known since childhood, armed and wearing a camouflage uniform. Tadic was standing next to the four men named as Tadic's victims in counts 24–28 of the indictment—Ekrem Karabasic, Ismet Karabasic, Seido Karabasic and Redo Foric. Although Mujcic did not witness their deaths, he was able to corroborate that Tadic was present when they had been pulled from the column of Muslims. Such special treatment could only mean one thing, he suggested.

Second, Mujcic said that at Omarska on June 18, 1992, he had glimpsed Tadic, again armed and wearing a camouflage uniform. Mujcic testified that he saw Tadic as guards opened and shut the door to the hangar after calling out the names of the five men who were later named as Tadic's victims in counts 5–11 of the indictment—Emir Karabasic, Jasmin Hrnic, Enver Alic, Fikret Harambasic, and Emir

Beganovic. Thus, Mujcic was the first witness to indirectly testify about the infamous castration incident. As the doors shut, a terrified silence fell upon the remaining prisoners, only to be shattered by shouts and obscenities referring to rape and oral sex, he said. "After that there were very loud screams and they were saying pull, pull harder and even now I can hear those words sounding in my ears," Mujcic recounted. "The screams reflected great pain, there were deathly moans. . . . after that everything went silent," he said. Then, asked by the prosecution to identify Tadic, Mujcic stretched his arm out toward the defendant and said, "Yes, he is sitting between two policemen and he's dressed in a greenish colored suit, he has a tie and he is looking directly at me."

On cross-examination, Mujcic firmly denied the defense contention that he was mistaken about seeing Tadic during the Serb takeover of Kozarac and later at Omarska. "It can't be that I did not see him," Mujcic replied. "I'd guarantee my testimony with my life." Steven Kay pressed Mujcic to explain how it was that he could not remember the date he was captured in Kozarac but could be positive the incident with the men named in the indictment occurred on June 18. "Did you have a calendar or some other way of keeping track of time when you were in the camp?" Kay inquired incredulously. Kay, it seemed, did not hold to the rule that a wise lawyer will only ask questions when he knows in advance what the answer will be. This turned out to be a particularly ill-advised question because Mujcic had a solid answer, which Kay had not anticipated. Mujcic said that Jasmin Hrnic, one of the inmates allegedly killed by Tadic on June 18, had handed out biscuits on June 16 in honor of the birthday of his son. He said the event stuck in his mind because "I'd never had food that tasted as delicious as that biscuit tasted." He said he was sure of the date of the castration incident because it was two days after he ate the biscuit.

The next witness, Salko Karabasic, a fifty-one-year-old Muslim laborer, was the twenty-second of the trial. His testimony would be critical in proving counts 24-28 of the indictment. These counts alleged that after the Serb takeover of Kozarac, as Muslims marched in columns to assembly points, Tadic ordered four men out of the column and shot and killed them. Karabasic said that he and his family were among the hundreds of Muslims ordered to assemble in Kozarac for transfer to the camps. As the column filed into town, Karabasic said he noticed his brother Ismet and another man, Redo Foric, standing to one side. Tadic, wearing a camouflage uniform and carrying a pistol in his belt and an automatic rifle in his hands, was standing beside the men, Karabasic said. Tadic then ordered a fellow Serb, Goran Borovnica, to pull another of Karabasic's brothers, Ekrem, and Karabasic's son, Seido, from the column. "Dule Tadic was issuing orders and Borovnica was implementing them," he said. "I tried to pull my son toward me," Karabasic told the court. "But he snatched him from me and said, 'Do you want to come, too?'" Although Karabasic did not witness their deaths, he testified that the four men Tadic had pulled out of the column were never again seen after that day.

Karabasic then identified Tadic in court and said he was "1,000 percent sure" the defendant was the same man who singled his brothers and son out of the column that day. Karabasic said that he grew up in Kozarac and knew Dusko Tadic "very well." He not only saw Tadic that day, but heard his voice, which he recognized. Although on cross-examination, Steven Kay highlighted some minor inconsistencies between Karabasic's testimony and an earlier statement given to the Tribunal's investigators, he was unable to shake Karabasic's quiet confidence. Finally, a despairing Kay said, "I suggest to you that you did not see Dusan Tadic pick anybody out of the column because he wasn't there." Karabasic did not respond to Kay's statement, other than to glare at Tadic, who sat impassively throughout the testimony.

The next witness, thirty-three-year-old Uzier Besic, would be the first to testify to actually seeing Tadic abuse prisoners at Omarska. He said that he and other prisoners were ordered to lie face down in the courtyard but that he looked up several times and saw Tadic and other Serbs mistreating prisoners. "Tadic was beating them and jumping on them. One prisoner was shouting, 'Please kill me.' I think his backbone was broken," Besic told the court—thereby providing evidence in support of counts 18–20 of the indictment. Asked to point out the man he had seen that day abusing prisoners, Besic rose from his chair and pointed at the defendant, saying: "There he is. He's nicely dressed. Cleanly shaven. His hair is in order." Besic said he was sure this was the same man he had seen because he had known Tadic since he was a boy.

On cross-examination, Steven Kay suggested that Besic made up the alleged Tadic sighting because he had seen Tadic on television and in the news. An increasingly desperate-sounding Kay accused Besic and other inmates of comparing stories so they could all come to court and testify about basically the same thing. Kay also suggested that if Besic were telling the truth about the severity of the beatings, he would have been too frightened or in too much pain to look at Tadic, as he claimed he did. It was unclear whether Kay was making any points with the judges in his attempt to undermine the credibility of the witness. "With testimony coming in largely through interpreters, many of the traditional cues to judging witness veracity—voice inflection, the presence of a stutter or hesitation—are absent from this proceeding," he would later tell me in an interview.[3]

On June 20, the twenty-sixth day of the trial, two survivors of the Omarska camp testified about the horrors there, but neither offered particularly incriminating testimony against the defendant. The first, Nihad Haskic, said he saw Tadic twice at Omarska, but that he didn't see him doing anything other than standing with other Serbs wearing camouflage uniforms. The second, Saud Hrnic, said Tadic had once beat him up, but that had occurred more than twenty years before. And yet, this date saw one of the most memorable incidents of the trial. It happened when Haskic was asked to identify Tadic in court, as each of the preceding eyewitnesses had done. Unexpectedly, Tadic stood up and shouted impatiently, "I'm Dusan Tadic." A clearly unamused Judge McDonald immediately told the lawyers that she wanted to see them in closed session. After an uncomfortable session with the judges, the defense team cautioned Tadic that such outbursts could seriously undermine his case.[4]

At the end of the seventh week of the trial, Sulejman Besic, a 46-year-old former lumberjack, took the judges on a tour of some of the most shocking acts of savagery described during the entire trial. Up until then, Omarska had received most of the attention. Besic made it clear that the Trnopolje camp was in some ways even worse. He said that there was "constant shooting" of prisoners at the camp. "They were shooting for fun," he said. "It was like music to them. They couldn't do without it." Speaking in low, even tones, Besic recalled seeing a boy shot after being ordered to have sex with his mother's corpse, a pile of twenty dead bodies with their heads caved in, and a Muslim professor murdered by a vengeful Serb soldier to whom he had once given bad marks. Judge McDonald visibly shuddered when Besic described how the stench from a fellow inmate's gaping maggot-infested wounds—crosses carved on his front and back—prevented other prisoners from treating him. "When we looked on his back where they had cut him there were worms, live worms wriggling around and we tried to take them out, but the stench was so horrible you could not get near him," he told the court. But throughout, there was not a single mention of the defendant, and Judge McDonald told prosecutor Niemann she was growing increasingly concerned about the slow pace of the trial.

Besic had been saving his most important testimony for a closed session of the Tribunal, during which he provided detailed corroboration of the testimony of Salko Karabasic about Tadic's role in the killing of Ismet, Ekrem, and Seido Karabasic and Redo Foric during the Serb takeover of Kozarac. According to the transcript of the closed proceedings,[5] Besic told the court he saw "Tadic and Goran Borovnic standing about one and a half meters behind the men with their weapons pointed toward the men who were lined up, facing the wall with their legs apart and their arms stretched in front of them." When the witness was looking in the opposite direction, he heard a burst of machine-gun fire. When he turned, he saw the bodies of the four men, riddled with bullets. Though he did not see Tadic or Borovnic fire the shots, Besic said there were no other armed men in the immediate vicinity.

The next four witnesses—Hamdija Kahrimanovic, Zijad Jakupovic, Demal Deomic and Kemal Susic—were all survivors of Omarska, who had known Tadic well before the war. Each told his own tale of horror of his experience at the camp, with Kemal Susic describing Omarska as "evil itself." More importantly, all said they were sure that they had repeatedly seen Tadic at the camp, dressed in camouflage and carrying a weapon. By this time, it was becoming increasingly clear that Tadic would not prevail on his alibi defense. Too many believable witnesses who knew Tadic well had testified that he had been at Omarska. But it would take far more than mere proof that he was present at the camp to convict him of the specific charges.

Of these four witnesses, the only new insight about Tadic came during the testimony of Hamdija Kahrimanovic, a grey-haired Muslim who had been the principal at the Kozarac school before the Serb takeover of Kozarac. Kahrimanovic said that prior to the war, Kozarac had been the picture of tranquility. He said Serb and Muslim children went to his school together, married one another, and lived side by side without ethnic tension. He even pointed out that he had exchanged keys with his next door neighbor, a Serb, because they had become such close friends. At the close of his testimony, Judge McDonald asked Kahrimanovic a question that went to the very core of the trial: she wanted to know how things had gotten so bad in the once peaceful Kozarac that friends turned on life-long friends. She asked how people who were once neighbors could be so cruel to one another in time of war. Kahrimanovic replied that he could not really answer that question and said only that people seemed to have succumbed to a kind of madness during the war.

For Dusko Tadic, that madness might have begun in 1990. It was then, according to Kahrimanovic, that a Belgrade newspaper reported that Tadic had received an anonymous letter from Muslim nationalists saying he and his family would be "liquidated" in three months if they did not move out of Kozarac. Kahrimanovic described the report as "thunder" in the area because nothing like that had ever happened in Kozarac before. He stressed that there were no such "Muslim hate groups" in Kozarac who would write such a thing to Tadic. "We were not like that, we the people of Kozarac," he said. Whether the letter was real or not, afterward Tadic began to associate with politically active Serbs, Kahrimanovic said.

2

ON JUNE 26, THE TADIC TRIAL went into a two-week recess so that the Tribunal's single courtroom could be used for the Rule 61 hearing in the case against Bosnian Serb leader, Radovan Karadzic, and the commander of the Bosnian Serb Army, General Ratko Mladic. The two men had been charged with genocide, crimes against humanity, and grave breaches of the Geneva Conventions and violations of the laws and customs of war for atrocities committed against the civilian population of Bosnia. The alleged acts included persecution of Muslims; internment of civilians in prison camps; shelling of civilian centers; a sniping campaign against the civilian population of Sarajevo between May 5, 1992 and May 31, 1995; taking U.N. peacekeepers hostage and using them as human shields between May 26 and June 2, 1995; and the summary execution of thousands of the inhabitants of the U.N. "safe area" of Srebrenica in July 1995. The need for a Rule 61 hearing became apparent because Serb authorities had refused to arrest Mladic when he was present at a funeral in Belgrade and because the NATO-led IFOR force had shied away from arresting the two men for fear of a confrontation which would disrupt implementation of the peace accord.

A Rule 61 hearing is like a televised grand jury proceeding in that only the prosecution is permitted to participate and present its case. The purpose of the hearing is to allow prosecutors to convince the Tribunal judges to issue an international arrest warrant when an accused has eluded justice and when the authorities in the area where the initial arrest warrant was issued have refused to cooperate with the Tribunal. According to prosecutor Richard Goldstone, the Rule 61 hearing would serve two important purposes: "Firstly, it will mean something for the victims in Bosnia. It will be the first time that there's proof in a formal setting of a court as to what happened in Srebrenica and Sarajevo and other places. It will also increase the pressure on the international community to do something about getting Karadzic and Mladic to The Hague."[6]

The three judges presiding over the Rule 61 hearing were Claude Jorda from France (who had replaced Judge Le Foyer de Costil), Fouad Riad from Egypt (who had replaced Judge Abi-Saab), and Elizabeth Odio Benito from Costa Rica. The prosecution's team was composed of sixty-eight-year-old Eric Ostberg of Sweden and two Americans—Mark Harmon from the Department of Justice in Washington and Teree Bowers, an Assistant U.S. Attorney in Los Angeles. Fifteen witnesses, including victims, U.N. peacekeeping personnel, Tribunal investigators, the mayor of Sarajevo, and even one of the perpetrators of the Srebrenica massacre, testified against Karadzic and Mladic over seven days.

Before the hearing could get underway, however, a dispute arose when Karadzic's attorney, Igor Pantelic, appeared and asked to be allowed to be present in the courtroom during the presentation of evidence against his client "with a view to preparing a possible defense." Rather than promptly deny the request on the ground that the Tribunal's rules do not permit defense counsel to attend Rule 61 hearings, the judges foundered into confusion. It turned out to be a cunning propaganda coup for Karadzic. If the judges barred his lawyer from the courtroom, it would only confirm the one-sided nature of the proceedings against Karadzic. And yet, if the judges were to allow Pantelic to participate in the Rule 61 hearing, they ran the risk of turning the proceeding into a full blown trial in absentia, something forbidden under the Tribunal's statute. And who knew what Karadzic's astute counsel would do once allowed in. After several hours of off-the-record discussion, the judges decided to allow Pantelic to be present in the courtroom for the reading of the indictment against his client and then to sit in the public gallery during the remainder of the proceeding. Pantelic promptly withdrew his application to represent Karadzic at the proceeding and returned to Bosnia.

Afterward, prosecutor Eric Ostberg attempted to put a positive spin on the Pantelic affair, suggesting that through Pantelic's request Karadzic had formally recognized the legitimacy of the Tribunal after spitting defiance at it for more than two years. There was even some speculation that Karadzic had hired foreign counsel to advise him about both the pros and cons of surrendering to the Tribunal and the possibility of a plea bargain.[7]

The Rule 61 hearing finally got underway at a little after 4:00 p.m. on June 26, when Ostberg presented his opening statement. He noted that the crimes charged were among the most horrendous in history and that Srebrenica had joined the ranks of Katyn, Ladice, and Babi Yar as history's most notorious massacres. Ostberg said that ten thousand Srebrenica residents remained unaccounted for since the Serb take-over on July 11, 1995. He then showed a videotape of Mladic directing the attack on the U.N. "safe area." As for the responsibility of Karadzic, Ostberg showed a videotaped interview in which the Bosnian Serb president had said, "I am absolutely fully involved. Everything concerning the Serb Republic is in my hands." In another video, Karadzic was shown with the Russian poet Limonov on a mountain overlooking Sarajevo. Karadzic invited the poet to fire a high-powered sniper weapon into the besieged city, which Karadzic treated as his personal plaything. "Perhaps it was one of his shots," the prosecutor suggested, "which killed one of the victims named in the indictment."

One of the highlights of the Rule 61 hearing was the testimony of Captain Patrick Rechner of the Canadian Army. Rechner, a U.N. military observer, was taken hostage the day after the first NATO bombing raid on the bunkers on the outskirts of Pale on May 25, 1995. He said that he and other U.N. observers were brought to the bunkers, handcuffed at strategic locations, and used as human shields to prevent further NATO bombing. His captors told him that one U.N. observer would be killed for every bomb that was dropped, he told the court.

Another unforgettable moment came during the testimony of witness "A," an elderly Muslim resident of Srebrenica, who had been forced with thousands of others into buses bound for a killing field on the edge of the city. He said that he was taken to a clearing where he saw piles and piles of corpses. The Muslim men were lined up in four rows with their backs to the Serb soldiers, he said. When General Mladic gave the order, the soldiers opened fire with their machine guns, the witness told the court. Miraculously, witness "A" survived the spray of bullets when he fell and was covered by other bodies. He said that he waited until nightfall to claw his way out from the pit of bloody cadavers and make his way to the safety of Muslim-held territory.

By far the most remarkable witness of the Rule 61 hearing was twenty-four-year-old Drazen Erdemovic, who, on May 31, 1996, had become the first person in history to plead guilty before an international tribunal. Although the Tribunal had postponed Erdemovic's sentencing hearing until November because he was suffering from post-traumatic stress disorder, he was permitted to participate in the Rule 61 hearing as the prosecution's star witness. Erdemovic began by telling the court that in July 1995 he was with the 10th Sabotage Unit of the Bosnian Serb Army. On July 16, he said, his unit was assigned to join others to act as execution squads at a farm in Pilice, near Srebrenica. There, from 9:30 a.m. to about 3:30 p.m., he witnessed the arrival of twenty busloads of men, aged sixteen to seventy. He testified that groups of ten Muslims at a time were brought to the field where the execution squad waited for them. When Erdemovic initially resisted the order to shoot, his commanding officer told him that he should line up with the Muslims if he felt sorry for them, he told the court. Erdemovic obeyed the order. He said that he would rather not know how many deaths he was personally responsible for, but that more than one thousand Muslims were killed that day, based on the number of buses that arrived.

On the morning of July 8, 1996, Mark Harmon presented the Rule 61 hearing's closing argument. "We are repelled by notions of collective guilt," he said. "By our two indictments of Dr. Karadzic and General Mladic, we accuse, in unequivocal terms, two individuals who we allege are two of the persons who instigated, planned and ordered the genocide and the ethnic cleansing in Bosnia, crimes which have shocked the conscience of the world." After summarizing the evidence that had been presented, Harmon said: "Today, both Dr. Karadzic and General Mladic remain fugitives from international justice. As we approach the first anniversary of these tragic massacres, massacres that annihilated a generation of Srebrenicians and left thousands of widows and orphans, the resulting toll of human misery is felt not only today but will be felt for generations to come. In the Balkans, a part of the world where history is never forgotten, where the pain of centuries old battles is still palpable, Dr. Karadzic's and General Mladic's perfidious and cowardly deeds will long be remembered. What should not be remembered as well is that the world had the ability to bring these two alleged architects of genocide to justice and did nothing. It will haunt the victims and it will shame us all."

Not surprisingly, on July 11, 1996, the trial chamber decided unanimously to issue the international arrest warrant for Karadzic and Mladic.[8] In addition, it certified to the Security Council that the failure to arrest the two men "may be ascribed to the refusal of Republika Srpska and to the Federal Republic of Yugoslavia (Serbia-Montenegro) to cooperate with the Tribunal."[9] What was surprising, however, was the court's call for an investigation to determine whether President Slobodan Milosevic of Serbia shared responsibility for war crimes in the former Yugoslavia.

According to Presiding Judge Claude Jorda, based on the evidence presented, the court had no choice but to ask the prosecution "to investigate decision-making responsibility at the same, or higher level."[10] Jorda explained that the documents and testimony suggested "that a plan existed, designed at the highest Serbian political and military level, to set up a new state through the use of violence" in Bosnia.[11] Subsequently, a court official confirmed that the Tribunal was now looking into the Serbian president's possible responsibility for war crimes.[12] But deputy prosecutor Graham Blewitt told me in an interview that he was not altogether comfortable with Judge Jorda's comments about Milosevic. "It's just not appropriate for the judges to make public comments about ongoing investigations or cases," he said.[13]

3

THE TRIAL OF DUSKO TADIC resumed on Tuesday, July 16, with the testimony of two more survivors of the Omarska camp. One of the men, twenty-three-year-old Sead Halvadzic, would be the first of several witnesses to testify that he had personally been beaten by the defendant. The incident occurred when Halvadzic had been detained at a military barracks in Prijedor on June 8, 1992, before being transferred to Omarska. Halvadzic said that he was beaten by two military policemen who were wearing camouflage uniforms. He said one of the two was called "Tadic." While his face was to a wall, one of the policeman administered a disabling karate blow, he testified—something, Tadic, as a black belt in karate, might be likely to do. Although Halvadzic had never before met Tadic, in June 1996, he was able to identify the defendant from a photo lineup as one of his assailants that day. After the fourteen photos Halvadzic had looked at were introduced into evidence, Steven Kay began his cross-examination by accusing the witness of selecting Tadic's photo because he had seen Tadic's image on television and in the newspapers in recent months. When Halvadzic responded that he did not watch the news or have time to read the paper, Kay tried a different tack. He grilled Halvadzic about whether he knew how many people were named Tadic in Prijedor and about whether he knew there was a village called Tadica—driving home the point that the name "Tadic" the witness heard just before he was beaten could have been any number of people.

The second witness of the day, fifty-two-year-old Kasim Mesic, told the court about a gruesome murder he witnessed from the courtyard in Omarska known as the "pista." A young man asked a guard for bread, and the guard pushed him away. Then, according to Mesic, the guard fired an entire round of bullets into the young man. Immediately after the incident, a soldier in camouflage walked up to the guard, he said. Mesic told the court that some prisoners standing with him then said, "Here's Tadic," referring to the man who approached the guard. Tadic then smiled at the guard, said hello, and shook the man's hand, Mesic testified. What the prosecution hoped to gain by putting Mesic on the stand to tell this story was unclear. Though the incident painted Tadic in a bad light, it proved nothing upon which he could be convicted. The witness did not say that Tadic witnessed the murder, let alone ordered it, and it is no criminal offense merely to smile at, say hello to, or shake hands with someone who has just committed a senseless murder.

The next witness, identified only as "R," was a thirty-two-year-old Muslim survivor of Omarska. "R," hidden from the public gallery by screens, testified that, while he was on the "pista" at Omarska, one of the prisoners nearby said, "That's Dusko," and pointed to a man coming out of the white house where interrogations and beatings took place. "R" said he immediately recognized Tadic from newspaper photos related to karate that he had seen before the war. "R" then said he saw Tadic go behind the white house, where dead bodies were usually piled for disposal the following morning. This testimony suggested that Tadic was not only present at Omarska, but that he knew of the killings committed there, so Steven Kay used his cross-examination to attack the veracity of the witness's testimony. In a heated exchange, Kay asked "R" if his hatred of Serbs had caused "R" to manufacture his testimony after reading about Tadic in the news. "I do not hate anyone. I'm telling you again that the horror of Omarska is something I do not wish to follow in the news. It is worse than any Alfred Hitchcock film," the witness replied.

Witness "R" was followed to the stand by Mehmedalija Huskic, another survivor of Omarska, who told the court that he was pistol-whipped by Tadic, whom he had known for twenty years. The forty-nine-year-old Huskic was a dead ringer for Groucho Marx, with a loud green and blue plaid shirt, thick glasses, a prominent nose, and an oversized mustache. His story was anything but funny, however. Huskic testified that on June 20, 1992, he was taken to a large room in Omarska which housed about two hundred other Muslim men. Shortly after Huskic arrived there, he was ordered to stand at attention as Tadic and another Serb entered the room. The prisoners were made to form two lines as Tadic yelled verbally abusive things to the men, Huskic said. Huskic told the court that the defendant, sporting about a week's worth of growth on his face, carrying a pistol, and wearing a camouflage uniform with a submachine gun strapped to his back, then proceeded to go down the rows of men, pistol-whipping about every other man, including Huskic. He said that he was only a few feet away from Tadic when Tadic struck him on the head. Defense counsel Michail Wladimiroff attempted to discredit Huskic's story by pointing out some inconsistencies with a statement Huskic had given to investigators a year earlier. In the statement, Huskic had said Tadic was clean-shaven and that he entered the room with three or four other Serbs. But after four years, these types of minor inconsistencies were to be expected, and Huskic turned out to be a hard witness for the defense to shake.

The third person to testify about personally being beaten by Tadic was twenty-four-year-old Edin Mrkalj, a round-faced Muslim policeman from Prijedor with feathery hair. Mrkalj told the court that Emir Karabasic had introduced him to Tadic in early 1991. Afterwards, Mrkalj saw Tadic several times in Prijedor; he also saw him once in Omarska, when Mrkalj was interned there, he said. Mrkalj said that on June 16, 1992, he was ordered to the administration building at Omarska to remove a dead body. He testified that once inside the building he had to stand with his head bowed next to a man who was being beaten severely with a rubber baton. The man wielding the baton then jammed the weapon under Mrkalj's throat and jerked his head upright. "At that moment I saw and recognized Dusko Tadic," Mrkalj told the court. "I saw the cynicism in his face, the smile, the grin on his face, his look as if he was enjoying himself," Mrkalj said. "At one point the rubber baton fell on the floor then Dusko Tadic said to me: 'Pick up the baton and say, Here you are, mister Serb,' " Mrkalj said. After Mrkalj stooped to pick up the weapon, Tadic rammed the barrel of a submachine gun into his mouth and launched into a beating in tandem with another man, he recalled. "There was this barrel in my mouth, then I started receiving blows on my head. I was receiving double blows with the baton and with a metal spring. My head was bursting, blood was bursting, my teeth were breaking, everything was breaking," he said, describing how his head was whipped backwards and forwards by the alternating blows. Mrkalj said that Tadic took a step back and then delivered a blow that knocked him unconscious.

Mrkalj told the court that until three months ago, he suffered from pain in his hand as a result of that beating and that he had to undergo three operations to correct the injuries to his mouth. At the end of his direct examination, prosecuting attorney Hollis asked Mrkalj to make an in-court identification. The witness rose from his seat, pointed to Tadic and said, "That is the garbage over there." This drew a harsh rebuke from Judge McDonald. On cross-examination, Steven Kay repeated his earlier mistake of asking the witness how he could be so sure the date of the beating was June 16, 1992. Mrkalj calmly explained that, as a police officer, it was part of his job to note the date and times of criminal events. He added that the beating had occurred at about 2:00 p.m. Mrkalj also said he was wearing a watch at the time, which displayed the day of the month. The watch was seized shortly after the incident, he said.

On July 19, 1996, the prosecution presented yet another witness who testified that he had been assaulted by Tadic at Omarska. Unlike the previous witnesses, Emir Beganovic was specifically named as one of Tadic's beating victims in the indictment (counts 5–11). The forty-one-year-old Beganovic had been a successful Muslim businessman in Prijedor, owning three restaurants and a flower shop. Beganovic, wearing a khaki jacket over a lime green t-shirt, told the court that he had known Tadic for about ten years before the war. Beganovic described the defendant as somewhat of a bully. Tadic and his friends, the witness said, would come to Prijedor to start trouble and pick fights.

At Omarska, at about the time the castration incident was alleged to have occurred, Beganovic was called out to the hangar, where he said a half-dozen uniformed Serbs beat him with their boots, metal rods, and cables. He said that he suffered multiple skull fractures, a broken nose, spine and kidney injuries, and lost most of the use of his left hand (which he held up for the court to inspect). When Beganovic identified the defendant as one of his assailants, he called Tadic "Serb garbage," drawing another sharp rebuke from the bench. Beganovic's testimony placed the defendant at the hangar of Omarska in mid-June 1992 and established that he was a participant in severe beatings that occurred there. This would help lay the foundation for the castration charge, which occurred in the same building at about the same time.

When Steven Kay suggested on cross-examination that the severity of the beating might have affected Beganovic's ability to make a reliable identification of Tadic among his several assailants, Beganovic replied that "the other faces meant nothing to me because I did not recognize them, only Tadic." Finally, in response to a question from Judge Stephen about the role of alcohol consumption in these atrocities, Beganovic said the Serbs were almost always drunk when they committed acts of savagery.

The next witness, Senad Muslimovic, said that he was also beaten by Tadic at Omarska. Muslimovic, a thirty-three-year-old Muslim from Prijedor, is the brother of a famous Yugoslav folk singer. Although he did not know Tadic before Omarska, Muslimovic said that he saw him often at the camp and that on one occasion Tadic beat him into unconsciousness. Tadic's karate kicks were some of the most painful blows he received at the camp, the witness said. During another occasion, Muslimovic said, he was ordered to kneel on the floor of the camp's hangar building while Tadic held his head and put a knife to his throat and threatened to cut off his ear. The witness also testified that he saw Tadic attack another inmate with a knife, while the man pleaded, "I've done nothing, Dule, cross my heart." "He was being sliced as one slices chops," Muslimovic said.

Muslimovic had made a photo identification of Tadic, and the prosecution introduced the book of photos shown to the witness into evidence. On cross-examination, Steven Kay suggested that Muslimovic was familiar with Tadic's appearance only from news accounts on television and was determined to place blame on Tadic because he was a Bosnian Serb. Kay was beginning to sound like a broken record, and he had not succeeded in making a single witness, including Muslimovic, recant. "You really have no idea what he looked like," Kay posited. But Muslimovic shot back, "If you went through the same thing I did, you'd remember." Perry Mason would not have been impressed.

The prosecution was now ready to build its case against Tadic on the grizzliest charges of the trial—counts 5–11 of the indictment—the torture-murder of Emir Karabasic, Jasmin Hrnic, Enver Alic, Emir Beganovic, and the castration of Fikret Harambasic. The prosecution began with the testimony of Armin Kenjar, a policeman in Kozarac who had known Tadic for most of his life. Like many other witnesses, Kenjar said he had seen Tadic at Omarska. He then told the court how Emir Karabasic, who had shared a room at Omarska with Kenjar, was called out for the last time. Kenjar testified that he heard "screams, wailing, cries of pain. It was really horrible, a nightmare. It must have been a massacre in the worst way possible." Kenjar said that some time after the screaming had stopped, he was ordered to go to the toilet with cleaning materials, where he found a prisoner identified in court as "G" and asked him what happened. "He answered, 'don't ask,' and he was scared stiff, he looked terrible," Kenjar recalled. In one of his rare cross-examinations, lead defense counsel Michail Wladimiroff emphasized the point that Kenjar had only allegedly heard the castration incident; he did not actually witness the assault and did not know who the perpetrators were.

Next, the prosecution called Mehmed Alic, an elderly Muslim man from Prijedor, who said he had known the Tadic family for his entire life. Like Kenjar, Alic said he had seen Tadic twice inside Omarska. On the afternoon of the alleged castration incident, Alic said he was ordered to fetch his son Enver from his cell and bring him to Serb soldiers waiting downstairs. As the Serbs dragged Enver around the corner, Alic said he heard his son shouting, "Dule, brother, how have I wronged you; why do you beat me?" Alic told the judges that shortly thereafter, he heard the wails of his son and then heard a guard say, "This one is finished." Alic never saw his son again.

The key witness for the castration charge was thirty-one-year-old Halid Mujkanovic, another of Tadic's lifelong acquaintances from Kozarac. Speaking from behind a screen in the courtroom in order to conceal his face from the public gallery, Mujkanovic told the court how two prisoners in his cell, identified as "G" and "H," were summoned from the room by Serb guards. His voice breaking with emotion, Mujkanovic testified that as he looked through the glass door to the hangar, he saw several Serbs force "G" into a pit containing engine oil. They made him say, "I am a pig and I like pigs," Mujkanovic told the court. (For Muslims, who don't eat pork and believe that pigs are unclean, this treatment would be perceived as especially demeaning and degrading.) "Then 'H' had to pick someone and 'G' was forced to bend down, to put his head between the man's legs and then was ordered to bite off his testicles," he said. Mujkanovic said that he then looked away. "When I looked up the second time, there were screams, and 'G' got up with his mouth full, he was covered with blood and oil." Mujkanovic said the group then turned on his friend Jasmin Hrnic. "A soldier beat him with a metal, iron bar. He fell, he showed no sign of life." Throughout, said Mujkanovic, the Serbs who oversaw this barbarity "looked as though they were attending a sports match, supporting a team." At the same time, a tape recorder was insidiously blasting the popular song, "Let Me Live, Don't Take Away My Happiness," he said. "I escaped, I don't know how, to go to the toilets on the floor above to be sick, but I had nothing to vomit because they gave us nothing to eat," he said.

Prosecutor Alan Tieger then asked Mujkanovic if during this incident he saw anyone he recognized. "Yes, Dule Tadic," the witness answered, adding that he had known the defendant since primary school. "I saw him with my own eyes, I know him well," Mujkanovic stated adamantly when defense lawyer Stephen Kay suggested he had wrongly identified the defendant. However, following the brief cross-examination, Judge McDonald asked Mujkanovic, "Did you see Tadic himself involved at all in the incident, taking an active part?" Mujkanovic answered, "I did not see those moments." "So you did not see Tadic require 'G' to commit the act you described?" the judge pressed. "No, I did not," Mujkanovic replied.

The next witness, identified as "H," was to be the icing on the cake for the prosecution. Their witnesses so far had convincingly proven that Tadic had been present during the castration incident. According to plan, the next witness, who was actually in the hangar during the incident, would tell the court the roll Tadic played. But the best laid plans. . . .*

"H" testified in closed session on July 24. According to the transcript[14] (purged of any references that might suggest the identity of the witness), "H" told the court that he was a twenty-eight-year-old Muslim, who had been taught karate by Tadic before the war. Corroborating Mujkanovic's story, "H" said that he and "G" were summoned to the hangar. When they arrived, the Serbs ordered them to lie in a pit and drink oily water, he said. According to witness "H," a third prisoner, Fikret Harambasic, was then ordered to jump naked into the pit. "Were you ordered to lick his arse?" asked prosecutor Michael Keegan. "Yes," "H" replied. "Was 'G' ordered to suck Harambasic's penis?" Keegan pressed. "Yes," the witness answered. Keegan then inquired, "Was the

---

* Ihara Saikaku, *The Japanese Family Storehouse; or, the Millionaires' Gospel*, bk. II, p. 2 ("There is always something to upset the most careful of human calculations."); Robert Burns, "To a Mouse" (1785), st. 7 ("The best laid schemes o' mice and men Gang aft a-gley.").

next order for 'G' to bite his testicles?" Again, the witness responded, "Yes." "H" then elaborated, telling the court that "a knife was put against my eye, and I was ordered to hold Harambasic's hands and if they heard his voice they would gouge both my eyes." He said that the Serbs were yelling, "Bite, harder, harder" as "G" bit off one of Harambasic's testicles. "He spit it out and that ball had fallen through the grate that served for sewage and a vein or something got stuck in the grate," "H" said.

Then, prosecutor Michael Keegan asked the question the prosecution hoped would nail the lid on the case: "Was the defendant there during this incident?" The answer, to everyone's surprise, was a simple "No." Conventional wisdom among defense attorneys when presented with an unexpected gift of this type is to leave well enough alone, lest the witness be given another chance to explain his answer in a way that undermines its apparent significance. But throughout the trial, defense counsel Steven Kay had shown a penchant for taking risks. While most had not paid off, this time he got exactly what he wanted. Kay asked witness "H" whether anyone in the hangar that day even resembled the defendant. "H" answered that a bearded man in uniform had ordered "G" and him to clear away bodies, but that he did not think it was Tadic. Kay pressed on, "Did you ever see Tadic at the camp?" "I did not see him," "H" replied.

We will perhaps never know how the prosecution could have been caught so off guard by the testimony of witness "H." In an interview with me the next morning, Michael Keegan said, "These witnesses from Bosnia don't think or describe events in the same way that we do in English. In our system we are used to eliciting very specific descriptions. Bosnians aren't use to being questioned the way we are about events." He added, "There is no such thing as literal translation from Serbo-Croatian into English. You cannot expect that through an interpreter an English speaker will understand exactly what the witness is saying."[15] Whether the prosecution's investigators had simply misunderstood "H," or that "H" had been influenced to change his story by money or threats as members of the press were hypothesizing, it was clear that this was a turning point in the trial.

I went out to dinner with the defense team the night after witness "H" had testified. Their mood was jubilant. "We'll file for a dismissal of the castration charge," Steven Kay told me.[16] Before the trial,

Michail Wladimiroff had described defending Tadic as "the ultimate challenge." Leaning back, puffing on his favorite brand of Cuban cigar, Wladimiroff confided that the challenge had become a whole lot more manageable.[17] But, Wladimiroff acknowledged, with several months of trial left to go, there was plenty of time for the prosecution to regroup from its first setback.

4

ON JULY 25, THE PROSECUTION would call two more witnesses in an attempt to bolster the case against Tadic on the castration charge. The first, Muharem Besic, a Muslim who had known Tadic most of his life, testified that he saw Tadic at Omarska the day of the castration incident. While Besic was not an eyewitness to the incident, he said he was one of many ear-witnesses. "You could hear screams from pain, like animal screams, like horses being castrated," Besic testified. He said he could hear words like, "Bite, suck, hit him." When asked by prosecutor Alan Tieger if he remembered this incident accurately, Besic said, "I don't think there is a man at Omarska who doesn't remember this incident. This is the first thing people think of when they think of Omarska." On cross-examination, Steven Kay countered, "You've made up the story that you saw Tadic, didn't you?" "Not true," Besic answered. "I have a moral obligation to my people and my state to tell the truth."

With the second witness, Hussein Hodzic, the prosecution made up some of the ground it had lost with witness "H." Hodzic, a former employee of the Omarska complex, described the last moments of Emir Karabasic, one of the internees allegedly killed during the castration incident. Hodzic, who shared a sleeping area with Karabasic, said Karabasic had repeatedly insisted that his one-time friend, Dusko Tadic, would kill him because he had seen something he "was not supposed to have seen." According to Hodzic, on the day of the castration incident, Karabasic saw Tadic and said to his cellmate, "Dule has arrived, I'm finished." At this, Steven Kay jumped to his feet and blurted out, "I object, this is highly prejudicial hearsay." Judge McDonald overruled the objection, saying that given the hybrid common law/civil law nature of the Tribunal's loosely structured rules of evidence, the judges would only exclude such a statement if "the statement precludes a fair trial." Then, like other witnesses, Hodzic described the sounds he heard coming from the hangar shortly after Karabasic was summoned from their room. He said he heard, "'Bite, pull, grab, tear,' to that effect, each command referred to the genitals. I heard 'bite off his balls' and a painful scream. I prayed to God not to be there, it was difficult for a normal man to endure those sounds. If I had to go through that again—just listening to it—I couldn't survive. It's the worst thing I've ever experienced." At the end of his direct examination of the witness, Alan Tieger introduced into evidence a photograph from before the war of Karabasic and Tadic together, arms around each other's shoulders in a friendly pose.

Steven Kay made two points during his cross-examination of Hodzic. First, he succeeded in getting the witness to admit that he did not see any of the alleged castration incident, and thus did not know if Tadic was actually involved—Karabasic's fears notwithstanding. Next, Kay confronted Hodzic with a statement that he had given investigators a year after he was released from Omarska. Kay pointed out that nowhere in the statement did Hodzic say that he heard Emir Karabasic say the prophetic words, "Dule has arrived, I'm finished." Hodzic merely shrugged, saying, "If I told everything that I heard and saw, it would last a very long time; it would be more than one volume of a book."

Although doubts still lingered after Hodzic's testimony, by July 26 the prosecution had run out of witnesses who could implicate Tadic in the castration incident. With little fanfare, the prosecution moved on to counts 18–20 of the indictment—known as the fire-extinguisher charge. To prove the charge, prosecutor Brenda Hollis called Elvir Grozdanic to the stand. Grozdanic said that he had taken karate lessons from the defendant and recognized him immediately when he saw him at Omarska. According to the witness, the third time he saw Tadic at the camp, Tadic was carrying a fire extinguisher and "shoved the hose into the mouth of a prisoner" who was lying in a wheelbarrow.

On cross-examination, Grozdanic admitted that he did not see whether Tadic had actually discharged the contents of the fire extinguisher into the prisoner's mouth as the indictment alleged, or even if the prisoner had been alive when Tadic placed the hose into his mouth. The latter point was particularly important since it is not a crime to torture a corpse. In a fashion strikingly similar to that of her colleague Steven Kay, Sylvia de Bertodano then said to the witness: "What I'm suggesting is this, that you didn't see Dusko Tadic at all on that day, that you heard afterward, from other prisoners and reports in the media about what had happened in that camp, on that day, and you made up this story that you yourself had seen Dusko Tadic." To this, Grozdanic replied, "I am quite ready to take Dusko Tadic's place, and for him to sit here, if I have said a single lie."

The prosecution quickly moved on to counts 21–23 of the indictment, which concerned the torture of Hase Icic. Like many of the other witnesses, Icic began by telling the court that he had known Tadic for most of his life. Icic said that one day in July, while he was incarcerated at Omarska, Serb guards pulled him into a torture room. One of the Serbs in the room was his old acquaintance, Dusko Tadic. Then, Icic said, one of the Serbs put a noose around his neck, which was pulled tight. According to Icic, the Serbs then beat him into unconsciousness.

The next witness, Hakija Elezovic, offered some of the most persuasive testimony of the trial. Testifying about the events alleged in counts 15–17 of the indictment, the elderly Muslim told the court how he had been twice beaten by Tadic, and how the defendant had assaulted and presumably killed his son. Elezovic also said he had known Tadic from before the war and that his son had known him quite well. He said that while interned in the Keraterm camp, he encountered Tadic, who beat him and savagely administered "a master's kick." Later he was transferred to Omarska, where he said he was taken to the white house in which the Serbs tortured inmates. According to Elezovic, when he entered the building, he saw Tadic among a group of Serbs beating prisoners, including Elezovic's son, Salih. He said that Tadic began to kick him and then "went after my son with a pistol." Elezovic was then hit on the back of the head and fell unconscious, he told the court. When he awoke an hour later, he found himself behind the white house, where he saw his son's body among many others being loaded onto a truck, he said. In an aside which was later to prove an unexpected boon to the defense, Elezovic added that his cellmate, Samir Hodzic, was ordered to turn over the bodies and asked Elezovic if he could have Salih's shoes before his body was taken away.

Elezovic would be one of the last of the witnesses to testify about Tadic's role in the horrors of Omarska. Including Elezovic, the prosecution had produced twenty witnesses who testified that they saw Tadic at the Omarska prison camp at the times alleged by the prosecution. Four of those had said that they observed Tadic abusing other prisoners, and five testified that they had themselves been beaten by the defendant at Omarska. But not one professed that they had seen Tadic commit a murder at the camp, and after the testimony of witness "H," it was left unclear whether he was even present during the infamous castration incident.

5

ON JULY 31, THE PROSECUTION SHIFTED ITS FOCUS to counts 29–34 of the indictment, under which Tadic was charged with killing five Muslim men and beating eight others in two villages near Kozarac. Specifically, that portion of the indictment reads: "About 14 June 1992, armed Serbs, including Dusko Tadic, entered the area of Jaskici and Sivci in opstina Prijedor and went from house to house calling out residents and separating men from the women and children." After leaving the gloom of Omarska, the pace of the trial began to noticeably quicken, with as many as five witnesses testifying in a day and generally little or no cross-examination.

The prosecution began with Sakib Sivac, who testified that he had known Tadic most of his life and had seen him at the town of Sivci the day it was attacked by the Serbs—June 14, 1992. Sivac said that Tadic was wearing a camouflage uniform and holding a rifle, a pistol, a knife, and handcuffs. According to Sivac, Tadic pushed him and other Muslim prisoners onto a packed bus to be taken to Keraterm camp. "I saw every wrinkle of his face," said Sivac. "When Tadic pushed me in the back, I turned around and looked him in the eyes: there was just the barrel of his gun between us."

Next, two sisters—Drajuni Jaskic and Subha Mujic—recounted how the defendant had abused several members of their family later that day during the Serb takeover of the village of Jaskici. Both had known Tadic from before the war. When prosecutor Brenda Hollis asked the first of the sisters, forty-one-year-old Drajuni Jaskic, to describe what she had seen out the window as the Serbs marched from house to house, the curly haired witness responded, "I saw Dule Tadic beat my father, my brother-in-law, my husband, all my family and some friends." "They were forced to lie on the floor, face in the sand, hands behind the neck, and Tadic beat them with a big club," her elder sister, Subha Mujic, testified a few moments later. "Dule Tadic... beat them until they fell unconscious," she said. According to the two women, who claimed they were positive about their identification of the accused, Tadic then ordered Serb soldiers who were with him to force the victims to an unknown destination by beating them with sticks. The sisters said they had not seen any of their relatives since that day, despite efforts to locate them.

The next day, the prosecution called two more witnesses, Zamha Sahbaz and Senija Elasovic, who testified that they had seen Tadic wearing a camouflage uniform in the village of Jaskici on the day of the Serb invasion. Sahbaz said that Tadic ordered her family out of the house and was giving orders to other uniformed Serbs to beat Muslim residents. At the end of that awful day, Elasovic later told the court, "only three Muslim men remained in the Jaskici village." Those three helped to carry the bodies of the many slain Jaskici residents to the forest so that "their mothers wouldn't see them," she added.

From the towns of Jaskici and Sivci, the prosecution next took the judges to the hellhole that was the Trnopolje prison camp. The defendant's alleged crimes at Trnopolje, according to count 1 of the indictment, eclipsed his brutality at Omarska. According to paragraph 4.3 of the indictment: "Tadic physically took part or otherwise participated in the killing of more than 30 detainees, including groups of male detainees executed near a white house adjacent to the camp and a group of male detainees executed in a plum orchard adjacent to the camp." It goes on to say that "Tadic also physically took part or otherwise participated in the torture of more than 12 female detainees, including several gang rapes, which occurred both in the camp and at a white house adjacent to the camp during the period between September, 1992 and December, 1992."

The first witness of the trial to identify the defendant as being at Trnopolje was Vasif Gutic, a twenty-six-year-old Muslim doctor, who had set up a makeshift clinic when he was detained at the camp. While the prosecution played a videotape of the camp, Gutic gave a lengthy description of life in Trnopolje. In a soft voice, Gutic explained that the majority of detainees inside the camp were women and that rape was a common occurrence. The women were led in the evening to nearby houses where they were sexually abused, he said. "When the rapes started, everyone lost hope." He told the court that the youngest rape victim he treated was only twelve years old. "I still remember that case. The girl was still a child. She had not yet had her first period at that time." Gutic's eyes misted as he told the court, "Her expressionless stare had nothing in it. Her beautiful eyes I remembered from our previous meeting were gone." Next, Gutic said that women detainees were subjected to frequent gang rapes. One woman, he recounted, had suffered severe hemorrhaging after being raped by seven men at one time. Then Gutic placed Tadic at Trnopolje. He said he saw the defendant, who he knew from before the war, talking to the deputy commander of the camp, Slavko Puhalic. The two men were examining a piece of paper which Gutic believed to be a list of Muslims from Kozarac being sought by the Serbs.

On cross-examination, Steven Kay challenged Gutic's identification of the piece of paper. Gutic conceded that he was some distance away from Tadic and Puhalic at the time, but said that he could clearly see that it was a white piece of paper with writing only on the left-hand side.

Several witnesses that followed would also testify that they saw Tadic at Trnopolje. Forty-four-year-old Sefik Kesic testified that he had been beaten by Tadic at the camp, but he admitted on cross-examination that he did not know the defendant well. The prosecution then called to the stand Adil Jakupovic, who had lived next door to the defendant in Kozarac. Jakupovic testified that he had never given Tadic permission to take his driver's license, which had been found in Tadic's possession when he was arrested in Germany. Jakupovic also said that he had seen Tadic at Trnopolje—and who would better be able to recognize the defendant than his own next-door neighbor? Later, six other witnesses—Mustofa Mujkanovic, Misrad Blazevic, Jusuf Arifagic, Mesud Arifagic, Eniz Besic, and witness "P"—would provide further corroboration that Tadic frequented the Trnopolje camp, but it would not be until the seventy-third witness of the trial that the story of Tadic's brutal acts there would be told.

6

On August 5, 1996, with the trial more than two-thirds over, the judges finally handed down their written ruling on the defense motion to exclude hearsay evidence elicited during the trial. The judges rejected the motion on the grounds that the Tribunal's rules do not specifically exclude hearsay evidence. Instead, as the court noted in its ruling, Rule 89 (C) provides that a trial chamber may hear any evidence deemed to have probative value. The court explained that, while perhaps appropriate in the context of a jury trial, a rule against hearsay is not warranted during bench trials, where the judges are able "by virtue of their training and experience to hear the evidence in the context in which it was obtained and accord it appropriate weight. Thereafter, they may make a determination as to the relevance and the probative value of the evidence."[18]

On the next day of trial, August 7, the prosecution focused on two themes—Tadic's status in the Serb paramilitary hierarchy and Tadic's motives for abusing his former Muslim neighbors. As to the first, Misrad Blazevic, a forty-year-old Muslim plumber, told the court that Tadic was a senior officer in the police force of Kozarac, not a reserve policeman as his lawyer suggested in his opening statement. In the middle of September, the thin, white-haired, pointed-nosed witness said he was taken from the Trnopolje camp to act as forced labor in Kozarac. According to Blazevic, when he and the reserve policeman who was guarding him encountered Tadic, the defendant "immediately jumped into action" and told the policeman how to handle the prisoners. Another soldier then told the policeman to obey Tadic because he "is the chief commander of the special police force here," Blazevic said. Blazevic said he later heard Tadic tell three Serb soldiers who were attempting to take furniture out of the town, "Nothing can leave Kozarac. I liberated Kozarac and nothing can leave Kozarac, not over my dead body."

According to the prosecution's theory of the case, sometime before the war Tadic, who once had many Muslim friends, had become infected with a cruel brand of Serb nationalism that swept across Bosnia. The next witness, Zihad Badnjevic, a former policeman with the Prijedor police department, provided corroboration for the earlier testimony of Hamdija Kahrimanovic about the time in which Tadic's transformation had first manifested itself. Badnjevic said that in 1990, Tadic had made a formal complaint to the Prijedor police after allegedly receiving a letter threatening him and his family. The letter, written in Arabic, had been translated by an official at the local mosque, who mentioned his doubts about its authenticity, Badnjevic said. Badnjevic added that examination of the script carried out by a police graphologist had cleared the three Muslim suspects fingered by Tadic, and the case had been closed.

But Badnjevic suggested that Tadic's transformation might have begun six months earlier, in 1989, when Tadic had reported to the Prijedor police that several Muslim men had raped his niece. The witness said Tadic told the police that upon discovery of the rape, he beat the attackers. Badnjevic then told the court that after police investigated the alleged rape, they discovered that Tadic had made the whole thing up, seemingly to justify his beating of the Muslim men. After medical examinations revealed no trace of rape, Tadic's niece, the witness said, told police her uncle had invented the story.

Like the story of the threatening letter Tadic said he received from anonymous Muslims in 1990, there are several possible ways to read this incident, all of which show the defendant in a bad light. One interpretation is that Tadic was prone to violence and quick to lie. Another is that he was succumbing to the growing anti-Muslim propaganda and beginning to sever his ties to Kozarac's Muslim community. A final interpretation is that he was attempting to endear himself to the Serb nationalists. As a consequence, the defense team knew that this was a damaging story which had to be debunked. Thus, on cross-examination Steven Kay badgered the witness about the thoroughness of the investigation into the rape incident, suggesting that it was more likely that the police botched the investigation than that the defendant had made up the story.

On August 9, after several weeks without mention of the dreaded Omarska death camp, the prosecution returned to that subject with Samir Hodzic, the seventieth witness of the trial. Like so many of the other witnesses, Hodzic said he had known Tadic since "he came out of primary school." After the fall of Kozarac, Hodzic said he was taken to Omarska, where he was held in the white house with Hakija Elezovic, who had testified two weeks earlier. Hodzic said that Elezovic had, in fact, been called out of the room in which they were detained and beaten. A few hours later, Hodzic said, he was outside the white house when he saw a group of Serb guards wearing camouflage uniforms, including the defendant. The Serbs ordered him to turn over a pile of bodies lying face down near the white house. He told the court that he recognized the bodies of Sejad Sivac and Hakija Elezovic's son, Salih—both listed among Tadic's alleged beating victims in counts 15–17 of the indictment. Hodzic's testimony was bolstering the prosecution's case nicely, until he added that he had not seen Hakija Elezovic behind the white house with the other dead men.

The defense did not hesitate to pounce on this key inconsistency. Hakija Elezovic, who had been one of the prosecution's most important witnesses, had testified that he was left for dead behind the white house when his son was attacked and presumably killed by Tadic. He said he was there when Hodzic turned over the bodies and even described Hodzic taking Salih's shoes after first asking Elezovic's permission. Now, Hodzic had testified that Elezovic was never there. On cross-examination, Steven Kay aggressively pressed the point. Hodzic, not comprehending the significance of the moment, stuck to his story that he did not see Elezovic behind the white house that day. Next, Kay pointed out that in January 1996, Hodzic gave a statement to the Tribunal's investigators in which he described the man he said was Tadic as having a high forehead and short-cut light hair. (Tadic, in fact, has a low hairline and dark brown hair.) Kay then suggested that Hodzic told Hakija Elezovic that he saw Tadic kill Salih Elezovic, but that Hodzic was mistaken about Tadic's identity—given the evidence, a perfectly plausible conclusion. Kay could not suppress his smile as he returned to his seat, for he knew this was the stuff of which "reasonable doubt" is made.

The prosecution was running out of witnesses and it was determined to end its four-month case on a strong note. On August 13, Grant Niemann paraded out his star witness: witness "L," whose real name we would later learn was Drago Opacic. Witness "L" would testify against Tadic anonymously and without the presence of reporters and other observers in order to protect him and his family from possible reprisals. "L's past position in Trnopolje camp and his present willingness to testify against the accused make him a traitor in the eyes of his co-perpetrators," the prosecution said in its application for measures to protect the identity of the witness. According to an edited transcript of the witness's testimony,[19] "L" was a guard at the Trnopolje camp. He said that Tadic had a position of authority at the camp. Recalling a day in November 1992, "L" told the court that Tadic ordered him to kill ten Muslim inmates at Trnopolje. When "L" failed to carry out the order, Tadic "approached two of those prisoners, took out a pistol from the holster, and killed those two prisoners right into the head," "L" told the court. "Then he came to me and ordered me to kill the remaining eight." Fearing for his life, "L" shot the men, he said. Tadic had forced him to shoot or cut the throats of many other prisoners, he added. "L" also told of an incident in December 1992, in which he observed Tadic raping a young female prisoner who was tied to a bed in a house just outside the camp. "L" said that he had deserted from Trnopolje while on leave at the end of December 1992, joined the Bosnian Serb forces, and was captured by the Muslim-led Bosnian army. Two months later, the prosecution would seriously regret having called this witness, for witness "L" would turn out to be the Mark Fuhrman of the Tadic trial—to draw a parallel to the discredited star prosecution witness of the O.J. Simpson case.

The prosecution ended its case on August 15, 1996 with the testimony of Tribunal investigator Robert Reid. The prosecution used Reid to introduce the documents that German police seized from Tadic's brother's flat in Germany when Tadic was arrested in 1994. Those documents included Tadic's statement to German police, in which Tadic claimed, "I never set foot" in Omarska, and the driver's license of Adil Jakupovic, who had earlier testified that he had never given Tadic permission to take his driver's license. Two other key documents suggested that Tadic was no minor player in Serbian politics. The first, bearing the seal of the Republika Srpska, recognized him as the president of the local board of the SDS (Serb party). The other was a decision signed by him regarding the "relocation of residents of the local Kozarac commune"—most likely referring to the forced deportation of Muslims.

After the last witness had departed from the courtroom, Grant Niemann stood to proclaim that the prosecution had at last concluded its case. As the prosecution team collected their notes and documents, it was hard to tell whether the expressions on their faces reflected relief or concern. The defense team, on the other hand, seemed genuinely pleased with the way things were going, and immediately announced to the press that they would be filing a motion for dismissal of the charges that the prosecution had failed to prove. At the defense's request, the Tribunal declared an adjournment until September 10 to give the defense time to line up its witnesses and to give the court time to rule on the defense motion.

AP/WIDE WORLD PHOTOS

Pictured above, lead prosecutor Grant Niemann of Australia (right) converses with the defense team (from left to right), Steven Kay, Michael Wladimiroff, Alfons Orie, and Sylvia de Bertodano.

Chapter 9

The Defense Case

> We must never forget that the record on which we judge these defendants today is the record on which history will judge us tomorrow. To pass these defendants a poisoned chalice is to put it to our lips as well. We must summon such detachment and intellectual integrity to our task that this trial will commend itself to posterity as fulfilling humanity's aspirations to do justice.
>
> —Robert H. Jackson
> *Opening Speech for the Prosecution at Nuremberg, 21 November 1945*

1

During the intermission in the trial, the defense team traveled to Prijedor, Banja Luka, and Kozarac to find witnesses in support of Tadic's alibi. "We've spoken to about 120 people and about 40 will be relevant for our case," defense counsel Michail Wladimiroff told Court TV.[1] "Because the time-frame of the charges begins on May 3 and ends on December 31, 1992, it is impossible to build an airtight alibi for that entire period of time. So what we do is locate people who worked with him so we can tell the court where he was during the day. We've also talked to people who were working in the camps, who will give evidence that Tadic was not there." According to the defense theory of the case, Tadic moved to the town of Banja Luka prior to the Serb takeover of Kozarac in mid-May 1992; from June to August, he worked as a traffic policeman outside of the town of Prijedor; during the months of August and September, he served as a reserve police officer in Kozarac; and in October and December, he worked for the Kozarac Housing Commission.

The defense told the court that it planned to call thirty-five or thirty-six alibi witnesses to the stand. The plan was for ten of them to give evidence via satellite link from Bosnia, while the others would travel to The Hague under temporary immunity. The defense team was not optimistic, however, that all of its witnesses would make themselves available. According to co-counsel Steven Kay, "We're asking these witnesses to leave a country that's not recognized and where they don't have passports, and travel a thousand miles to Holland, and give evidence before the world cameras on TV. I think that fairly simple, unsophisticated people will find that a challenge." Further complicating the defense efforts was the ever-present threat of the local Serb warlord, Simo Drljac, who had made it clear that he was not interested in cooperating with the Tribunal.

After a three-week break in the proceedings, Michail Wladimiroff began the defense of Dusko Tadic by arguing the motion to dismiss twenty-one of the thirty-four charges.[2] The only charges that were not included in the motion to dismiss were count 1 (the persecution charge), counts 21–23 (the beating of Hase Icic and other prisoners at Omarska), and counts 29–30 (the beating and killing of men at the towns of Jaskici and Sivci). Wladimiroff contended that dismissal of the other twenty-one charges was warranted because there were major inconsistencies between the testimony of the key witnesses and because there had been discrepancies between what many of the witnesses told investigators in statements before trial and what they told the court under oath. Most importantly, he argued, on some of the counts the witnesses' testimony only placed the defendant at the scene of the crime and did not establish that he was an active participant. "It is not enough," he contended, "to show that Tadic was there; prosecutors must show that he did something."

This last argument did not, however, mean that the defense was changing its theory of the case from alibi to bystander. "You walk on two legs," Wladimiroff said in an interview broadcast that day on Court TV. "Alibi is our main defense but just in case the judges don't buy our alibi, we're also telling them that the prosecution witnesses do not prove Tadic actually participated in many of the acts charged even if he was there." In sum, it was the defense's position that the prosecution had not established a prima facie case on most of the charges because the evidence presented was insufficient for a conviction.

In response, the prosecution argued that the rules only permit the judges to consider the evidence once, at the end of the trial. Prosecutor Grant Niemann pointed to Rule 87(A), which provides: "When both parties have completed their presentation of the case, the Presiding Judge shall declare the hearing closed, and the Trial Chamber shall deliberate in private." But Wladimiroff countered that fundamental justice demanded that an accused be cleared of baseless charges as soon as possible in a trial. "The Rule does not state that the Trial Chamber may only deliberate after both sides have presented their case," he said. "On the whole the Rules are clearly marked by the American experience. Many of the Rules are counterparts to the American Rules. In common law countries, the Judge may during the trial be called on to decide whether the condition of the evidence is such that the case may be disposed of without running the full course."

Judge Stephen pointed out a problem with the defense reference to the traditional common law approach. Most motions to dismiss seek to stop a charge from going to the jury on the basis of law in order to protect a defendant from the jury. "But there's no need for that here," Judge Stephen said, since the Tribunal judges were both arbiters of law and finders of fact. He suggested that there was no difference between determining that the prosecution had not carried their burden now—at the motion to dismiss stage—and later, at the final determination.

In the end, Judge Stephen's view carried the day. In a short statement, Presiding Judge McDonald said the defense motion was denied and the rest of the trial would proceed as planned. She said the court felt this was not the appropriate time to weigh the evidence, but that it would make such a decision at the end of the trial when it decided whether the prosecution had proven the charges against Tadic beyond a reasonable doubt.

2

FOR FOUR MONTHS, THE JUDGES HAD LISTENED to story after story of the defendant's sadistic treatment of his former Muslim neighbors. Now, it was the defense's opportunity to prove that Dusko Tadic had been wrongly accused. The defense began its case by calling Dr. Robert M. Hayden to the stand. Hayden was a professor of anthropology at the University of Pittsburgh in the United States. The purpose of Hayden's testimony was to refute the prosecution expert, Dr. James Gow, on the subject of why and how the war in Bosnia was fought. Gow watched Hayden's testimony from the prosecutor's table in the courtroom, where he feverishly scribbled notes for the prosecutors.

Hayden could have been Gow's polar opposite. Where Gow was young, clean shaven, and had unkempt hair, Hayden was a distinguished-looking, middle-aged scholar with a nearly bald head and a full beard. Where Gow spoke haltingly, Hayden spoke with an easy-to-follow cadence. Where Gow was quick to draw broad conclusions, Hayden's theory was that the conflict, like life itself, was a bit more complicated. The war in Bosnia, he testified, was not a planned operation from Belgrade (as Gow had asserted), but an inevitable by-product of the break up of Yugoslavia.

Hayden told the court how, after the death of Tito, the people of Yugoslavia chose—fairly and freely—to partition themselves into ethnically exclusive cantons. When Bosnia's turn to decide came, the people of that multi-ethnic land made the same choice—with tragic results. The Serbs, the Croats, the Slovenes, and the Muslims all, he said, embarked on the path of destruction. In his words:

> This nationalism is based on the premise that these people cannot in fact co-exist and when that succeeded in regard to the breakup of the former Yugoslavia, the logic of the equation is if there cannot be a common state of Serbs, Croats, Muslims and others called Yugoslavia how then can there be a common state of Serbs, Croats, and Muslims called Bosnia and Herzegovina? . . . In the situation that was produced by this very brief stab at democracy at the end of communism in 1990 the political constructions that won

> on all sides led to a situation where civil war was inevitable in Bosnia.

At one point, one of the judges interrupted Hayden to tell him that the last twenty minutes of his testimony were meaningless. Defense lawyer Alfons Orie responded, "The main conclusion of Dr. Gow is that this nationalistic movement mainly arose in Serbia. We want to see whether it's also the opinion of Professor Hayden"—which it clearly was not.

Yet, in one crucial respect, Robert Hayden turned out to be very much like James Gow: both had been chosen as expert witnesses because of their scholarly writings about the breakup of Yugoslavia. And like Gow's, Hayden's writings provided the opposing side ammunition to impeach him. On cross-examination, prosecutor Grant Niemann inquired, "Isn't it true that in your article 'Yugoslav Collapse, National Suicide, and Foreign Assistance,' you wrote that, quote, with the recognition of the independence of Croatia, Slovenia, and Bosnia, and their acceptance into the United Nations, the European Community and the United States legally transformed the civil war into an international armed conflict, end quote?" Hayden conceded the point, saying that "I believe I wrote that in May of 1992, and since then I have rethought my position." Score one for the prosecution!

The second witness for the defense, identified only as witness "U," testified from behind a screen that he knew nothing of allegations that Tadic had murdered, tortured, or raped Muslims in 1992. The witness, a Bosnian Croat postal worker in Kozarac who was married to a Serb, told the judges that he attended a residents meeting at the end of September 1992, at which Tadic was elected secretary of the local council. "It was because he was the greatest supporter of bringing Kozarac back to life," the witness said, adding that Tadic had told him of his hopes to rebuild the town he loved. Asked by defense counsel if Tadic's election had anything to do with politics, the witness replied, "No, it was the people who elected him because he championed the return to Kozarac." Under cross-examination from prosecutor Michael Keegan, "U" acknowledged that one of the functions of the council to which Tadic had been elected was to decide who could come back to Kozarac and where they could live. Currently, there were virtually no Muslims to be found in Kozarac, the witness conceded.

At the end of the testimony by witness "U," Michail Wladimiroff told the court that his planned schedule for defense witnesses would be disrupted by Bosnia's first post-war elections, scheduled to be held that weekend—on September 17. Incredibly, the election took place with no bloodshed and little fraud, and the results provided a glimmer of hope that Bosnia would survive as a unified nation. The international body supervising the elections certified the results, giving Bosnia a three-member national presidency, a national House of Representatives, separate Muslim-Croat and Serb parliaments, a Serb republic president, and ten cantonal assemblies.[3]

Bosnian Muslim Alija Izetbegovic won the most votes for the three-person presidency and thus the right to serve as chairman and head of state pursuant to the Dayton Accord.[4] The Bosnian Serb candidate, Momcilo Krajisnik, came in second and pledged to honor the Dayton treaty's commitment to peace and democracy. "I think that we will bring the Bosnian crisis to an end in the next two years," said Croatian Kresimir Zubak, who was elected to the third spot on the three-person presidency.[5]

A week later, in his address before the United Nations General Assembly, Izetbegovic underscored the continuing importance of the work of the War Crimes Tribunal to the peace process, stating: "For the road to reconciliation to be opened, the criminals must be punished."[6] The next day, the Security Council voted to lift the economic sanctions it had imposed on Serbia in accordance with the Dayton Accord.[7] A day later, Izetbegovic and Serbian President Slobodan Milosevic, meeting in Paris, agreed to establish full diplomatic relations and work toward restoring trade and economic ties between Bosnia and Serbia.[8]

Meanwhile, back at The Hague, the Tadic case ran into another procedural wrangle, as the prosecution demanded access to witness statements made to defense lawyers. When Judge McDonald ruled in closed session that the prosecution was entitled to the statements of defense witness "W," Michail Wladimiroff vowed not to call any additional witnesses until the court had a full hearing on the matter.

The prosecution argued that they needed access to the witness statements in order to prepare their cross-examination, but the defense team claimed disclosure would be tantamount to asking Tadic to incriminate himself. At the heart of the argument was the interpretation of Rules 66 and 67 of the Tribunal's Rules of Procedure. Rule 66(B) stated that "the Prosecutor shall, on request, permit the defense to inspect any... documents in his custody or control, which are material to the preparation of the defense, or are intended for use by the Prosecutor as evidence at trial." Rule 67(C), entitled "Reciprocal Disclosure," states that "if the defense makes a request pursuant to Sub-rule 66(B), the Prosecutor shall be entitled to inspect any... documents, which are within the custody or control of the defence and which it intends to use as evidence at trial."

Prosecutor Grant Niemann began his argument by reading from a pre-trial brief filed by the defense in which it had stated that "the right to a fair trial requires equality of arms between the prosecution and the defense." "In our submission," Niemann told the judges, "when dealing with this question, there is no doubt that the Court would not allow the Prosecution to refuse to disclose statements of its witnesses to the Defense, so that the Defense could conduct an effective cross-examination." He continued, "Since that is the approach to be taken with prosecution witnesses, then the principle of equality of arms would require that approach to be applied to the defense."

Steven Kay, arguing for the defense, pointed out that Rule 67(C) was worded differently than Rule 66(B) and did not require disclosure of documents material to the preparation of the prosecution, but only documents which the defense intended to actually use as evidence at trial. Moreover, Kay argued, the privilege against self-incrimination recognized in Article 21 of the Tribunal's statute (reproduced in Appendix B of this book) was broad enough to protect statements of defense witnesses. He told the court that the defense witnesses feared arrest and prosecution by the Tribunal and spoke only after defense attorneys promised that they would not disclose the statements, as consistent with a pre-trial ruling by the Tribunal. Finally, Kay warned that the defense would refuse to call additional witnesses rather than disclose the witness statements if the court ordered disclosure of the statements.

It was the last point that probably decided the issue. The judges were keenly aware that if the proceedings came to an abrupt end as threatened by the defense, it would forever be questioned whether the defendant had received a fair trial. Thus, after a ten-minute deliberation, the trial chamber ruled 2–1 for the defense, with Judge McDonald dissenting. As presiding judge, McDonald ironically had to read the decision in open court. "The Trial Chamber has reconsidered its ruling that the prior statement of defense witness 'W' was not privileged and was subject to disclosure to the prosecution for impeachment purposes," she announced. "The Trial Chamber now reverses that ruling and finds that such statements are privileged and not subject to the disclosure of the Prosecution." The result was to cripple the ability of the prosecution to discredit many of the remaining defense witnesses.

3

THE TADIC CASE WAS AGAIN DELAYED until October 2 to allow the defense to assemble another group of witnesses from Bosnia. When the trial resumed, the defense felt that it finally had the ammunition it needed to begin to prove Tadic's alibi. The defense started with Dragolje Balta, a chubby Bosnian Serb locksmith with bushy eyebrows and receding hair, who told the court that Dusko Tadic had moved into the house next door to his in the town of Banja Luka the day before Kozarac fell to the Bosnian Serbs. Three other defense witnesses—witness "X," Nikola Petrovic, and Borka Rakic—would later corroborate Balta's testimony that Tadic had moved to Banja Luka before the Serb takeover of Kozarac. The testimony was meant to contradict that of prosecution witnesses who said Tadic was in Kozarac during the Serb attack, that he helped herd a column of Muslims to Serb detention camps, and that he murdered several Muslims during the takeover of the town. Yet Balta admitted during cross-examination that Banja Luka is only about 25 kilometers (15.5 miles) from both the town of Kozarac and the Keraterm, Omarska, and Trnopolje camps. The prosecution had made its point: the fact that Tadic moved to Banja Luka in May of 1992 would not prevent him from making frequent visits to nearby Kozarac or to the camps.

The next witness, Miroslav Brdar, would turn out to be the most important of all the defense witnesses. Brdar, a Serb reserve policeman with a slight build and greasy hair, told the court that he and Dusko Tadic manned the Orlovci checkpoint in northwest Bosnia in June and July 1992—the months in which Tadic is alleged to have committed an orgy of torture and murder at the Omarska detention camp and in the towns of Jaskici and Sivci. Defense lawyer Steven Kay used Brdar to introduce a copy of Tadic's duty rosters from June 16 to August 1. Brdar confirmed that the rosters were part of the official records held at the Prijedor police station. The rosters were drawn up by the station commander, who, Brdar stressed "was quite conscientious in keeping an accurate record of duty shifts." The rosters detailed Tadic's shifts at the checkpoint, which varied from six-hour day shifts to twelve-hour nights, suggesting that Tadic had no time to be at the Omarska camp during the dozens of incidents prosecution witnesses reported. Most importantly, for June 18—the date of the castration incident—the roster indicated that Tadic had worked from 9:00 p.m. until 7:00 a.m. Asked by Kay whether it was possible for anyone manning the checkpoint to be absent for a significant amount of time, Brdar replied: "Something like that could not happen given the circumstances," adding that the posts were subject to surprise checks up to three times a day. As for Tadic's off-hours, Brdar said: "You had to be on call when you were off-duty. No one could go anywhere without permission."

Prosecutor Alan Tieger began his cross-examination of Brdar by challenging the authenticity of the duty rosters, noting that they were all written in the same hand, covering all shifts, twenty-four hours a day. "So if the person was recording them as the shifts were being completed or begun as you say, then that person would need to be present twenty-four hours a day, every day," Tieger pressed.

Tieger also managed to obtain several incriminating pieces of information from the witness. First, Brdar admitted that the checkpoint Tadic and he manned was located only four kilometers (two and a half miles) from Omarska. This indicated that Tadic would have had easy access and ample opportunity to visit Omarska while on duty or after hours. Next, Brdar acknowledged that the same police department in charge of the checkpoint also manned the detention camps, suggesting that Tadic might have been authorized—or even ordered—to visit the camps. In response to Tieger's next question, Brdar conceded that the chief of the police was none other than Simo Drljac—the same man that Michael Wladimiroff had earlier told the court was a powerful warlord who was hindering his efforts at obtaining defense witnesses. Finally, Tieger asked Brdar what he knew of the ethnic cleansing going on in the nearby towns and camps while he manned the checkpoint—a question he would put to each of the subsequent defense witnesses. Brdar's credibility imploded when he implausibly answered that he was not aware that fifty-thousand Muslims were cleansed from the area. Judge McDonald interposed by asking the witness about the purpose of the checkpoint; was it to check ethnic identities? With a straight face, Brdar answered that it was set up simply to watch for stolen cars. None of the judges seemed to be accepting that one. Thus, the prosecution had made its point: while a police officer would normally be the best possible alibi witness, this was not necessarily the case with an officer who was a fellow Serb during an ethnic conflict.

The defense may have scored some points with a story told by the next witness, Nikola Petrovic. Petrovic, a policeman stationed in Banja Luka, told the court that he was with Tadic one day when Tadic opened a newspaper and read a headline that said "Dusko Tadic War Criminal." Petrovic recalled how the news story made them laugh because it was "so incredible. It was just a big lie." This is not the way one would expect the real "Butcher of Omarska" to react to such news, the defense suggested. The story also suggested how extensive and therefore prejudicial was the media coverage of the accusations against Tadic.

Next, the defense called Rajko Karanovic, a Serb truck driver who delivered food to the Serb troops in Kozarac for forty days from the end of May through the beginning of July 1992. Karanovic said he passed through the Orlovci checkpoint three or four times a day and frequently saw Tadic on duty. Karanovic, a large man with a square jaw and high forehead, told the court that he never saw Tadic at Kozarac. He also said he delivered food to the guards at the Trnopolje detention camp and that he never saw Tadic at the camp or heard that he was a guard there.

On cross-examination, prosecutor Grant Niemann tried to discredit the witness by suggesting that he, too, had taken part in ethnic cleansing. Although the witness's testimony did not go very far in proving that Tadic had not committed atrocities at Kozarac or the camps, Niemann used his cross-examination to remind the judges once again of the horrors of ethnic cleansing. Niemann focused his questions on an incident in which Karanovic allegedly violently evicted a Muslim woman and her child from an apartment, which he then appropriated for his own use. Reciting the story as if he heard it from the Muslim woman herself, Niemann suggested that Karanovic, armed with a knife and a machine gun, burst into the apartment where the woman was alone with her daughter. According to Niemann, Karanovic then held the machine gun to the ten-year-old girl's head and said if they did not leave for good they would be killed. Karanovic denied the story, saying that he had permission from the local board to take the apartment; but judging by the way that the witness squirmed on the witness chair, Niemann's tale seemed to ring with more than a little bit of truth.

The last of the defense witnesses to testify at The Hague as to Tadic's whereabouts in June and August 1992 were two women who lived near the Orlovci checkpoint—Slavica Lukic and Nada Vacina. Each told the court that they had seen Tadic at the checkpoint frequently during the time in question. Lukic added that she often chatted with Tadic and that he never expressed extreme nationalist views or intimated that he hated Muslims.

Next, the defense began to build Tadic's alibi for the period of time during which, according to witness "L," Tadic had been a guard at the Trnopolje camp. The defense called Tomislav Dasic, a wiry man with a mop of gray hair, who told the court that he was part of the three-member commission that was charged with inspecting abandoned houses in the Kozarac area. The purpose of these inspections, he said, was to determine which dwellings could be used to house incoming Serb refugees. According to the witness, Dusko Tadic and a female surveyor made up the other two members of the commission. Dasic said that their work was done during the period between October 1, 1992, and December 15 of that year. During this period, Dasic said, both he and Tadic lived in Prijedor and returned to their homes every night. Dasic also claimed that he never heard Tadic express any extreme nationalist views, even though he admitted that he felt Tadic would be entitled to such views, due to the turbulent times. Finally, the witness attempted to downplay Tadic's importance in Kozarac, asserting that the defendant was made a member of the commission primarily because he was a local person who knew the area. Dasic stressed that the commission only examined abandoned homes for suitability and did not have the power to allocate them.

During cross-examination, Dasic confirmed earlier testimony that the Tadic family home in Kozarac had the notation "Serb House, Do Not Touch" painted on it when he first saw it. But he said similar markings were seen on other houses as well and that there was no way to know when this "graffiti" might have been painted. When pressed by prosecutor Alan Tieger, Dasic admitted that no compensation was ever paid to the Muslim owners of the homes being confiscated and turned over to the refugees, but he insisted that the Serb authorities proclaimed the homes for temporary use only.

Jumping back two months in the chronology of Tadic's alibi, the defense next called witness "Y" to the stand. The witness, testifying behind a screen to protect his identity, said he was a Serb mechanical engineer. He told the court that he and his family had been forced to flee from their predominantly Muslim region of Bosnia in June 1992 after his father's house had been burned down by Muslims. He said that the seventy Serb families from his village made their way to the Prijedor region in August 1992 and were assigned vacant homes in Kozarac. This testimony corroborated the view expressed by the defense's expert witness, Dr. Robert Hayden, that large numbers of people on all sides of the conflict were forced to flee their homes, not as part of ethnic cleansing, but as a natural byproduct of civil war. Witness "Y" then told the court that he obtained a job as a reserve police officer in Kozarac. He added that he saw Dusko Tadic, who was then also employed as a reserve policeman, every day at the police station in Kozarac in August and September of 1992. Most importantly, he testified that he was sure that Tadic never spent time at the Trnopolje camp because that area "was not within our jurisdiction."

The next witness, Dusan Vajagic, was meant to corroborate the testimony of witness "Y," but he ended up providing far more incriminating than exculpatory information. Vajagic, a professional fireman, claimed that his family and other Serbs were driven from their homes by Muslims in late July 1992. On August 2, he was part of a group of some one hundred families who arrived in the Kozarac area, where he was assigned an abandoned house. Vajagic also joined the Kozarac reserve police force and said he saw Tadic frequently at the police station in August and September. He described Tadic as "a family man, willing and eager to help people, a good man, never involved in conflict or clashes."

During Vajagic's cross-examination, for the first time in the trial, the world learned that Tadic was not such a bit player, after all. Vajagic admitted to prosecutor Grant Niemann that Tadic had been elected president of the local Serb party (the SDS) and that Tadic organized SDS meetings and coordinated with higher SDS authorities in Prijedor. But Vajagic denied that the local SDS was involved in ethnic cleansing, insisting that under Tadic's leadership "the party was only trying to establish a free life for its people, a fatherland"—a phrase eerily similar to that used by the Nazis in the 1930s.

4

THE MOST RIVETING MOMENT of many criminal trials occurs when the defendant takes the stand, looks each member of the jury in the eye, and asserts his innocence. Tadic's attorneys, however, initially felt the risks of exposing Tadic to a lengthy and combative cross-examination outweighed any potential benefit of putting him on the stand. Besides, they believed they had a better alternative—the defendant's wife, Mira. Through her testimony, the defense could both humanize the defendant and prove his alibi. Moreover, as a nurse and working mother with two girls, the defense hoped the attractive, dark-haired woman with the pageboy haircut would be a sympathetic witness whom the prosecution would be forced to treat gently.

Thus, on October 9, 1996, one of the most eagerly awaited witnesses of the trial was called to the stand. As she entered the courtroom, Mira Tadic smiled nervously at the defendant sitting in the dock only a few feet away from her. It was the first time the two had been in the same room since his arrest in Munich two years earlier. Appearing tense as she gripped the arms of the chair in the witness stand, Mira began to recount for the court her life with Dusko Tadic.

She told the judges how she and Dusko had fallen in love and married in 1979. She painted a rosy picture of their early life together. Dusko was a loving father to their two girls and a devoted husband, she said. They had many friends in the Muslim community in those years. As she continued to humanize the defendant, it was becoming increasingly difficult to view Tadic as the sadistic monster that prosecutor Grant Niemann had made him out to be in his opening speech back in May. But then again, the prosecution witnesses had revealed that in Bosnia atrocities were committed not by monsters, but by ordinary individuals caught up in ethnic conflict.

However, the testimony of Mira Tadic soon took an unexpected turn. The witness told the court that in 1986 she and Dusko had gone to Libya where she had found a nursing job. Perhaps the defense hoped the trip to Libya would show that Tadic was willing to live among Muslims, but that country's reputation for extremism could not possibly reflect well on the defendant. Next, Mira testified that on their return to Bosnia in 1987, the couple was divorced to make it easier for her to apply for a nursing post in Switzerland. Mira said that, although she did not get the job, she and Dusko had never remarried. Though she insisted that they continued to live together, a seed of doubt began to take root as to whether Mira could really account for the defendant's whereabouts during the summer of 1992—a theme the prosecution would later hammer in its cross-examination of the witness.

Finally, the witness provided the prosecution its best evidence yet of Tadic's motives for committing the heinous crimes of which he was charged. Mira said that Dusko had been close friends with many in the Muslim community before war broke out in the region in May 1992, describing how Muslims had even lent the Tadic family money to set up their pub. She said that one of Dusko's best friends was Emir Karabasic—one of the men the defendant was alleged to have murdered at Omarska—"but that they didn't remain close friends after 1991." She explained that at the end of 1991 relations between the ethnic groups began rapidly to deteriorate because "the Serbs wanted to remain in Yugoslavia the way it was at that time. The Muslims wanted their own state, Bosnia, and the Croats wanted a state of their own. Everyone was turning to follow their own leaders."

According to Mira Tadic, the tensions became more personal when the windows of the Tadic pub were smashed twice, the pub was burglarized and vandalized, and the couple received death threats. Mira also testified that she faced hostility from her Muslim co-workers at the Kozarac hospital. "We got a letter saying that we should leave Kozarac, that if we didn't leave within three months we would be killed. It was signed by the Muslim party—the SDA," she said. Mira unwittingly was making the same point the prosecution had tried to prove with several of its witnesses. With this background, the judges could now understand why the defendant might have turned on his Muslim neighbors in such a vicious way.

"At that time in Kozarac it was not safe anymore. We were the minority. The Muslim people became organized, they had their barracks, their uniforms, their guns—I was afraid," the witness recounted in an effort to explain why the Tadic family moved out of Kozarac in April 1992. When asked by Steven Kay if Dusko Tadic had spent protracted periods away from the family during the spring and summer of 1992, Mira replied, "No," adding that he spent most nights at home with his family. But this did not correspond with the testimony of Miroslav Brdar, who a few days earlier had told the court that Tadic worked several nights a week at the Orlovci checkpoint. Given this testimony, it would not be hard for the judges to picture Dusko Tadic telling Mira that he was off to Orlovci, when in fact he was really headed to the nearby detention camps to torment the Muslim prisoners held there. She even admitted that Dusko had told her he had gone once to the Trnopolje camp, though she said it was "to help a friend find his sister."

Addressing the prosecution's allegations that the defendant was often to be seen armed and in camouflage uniform after the war broke out, Mira said that it had been impossible to move around the region without either of those trappings. However, what was important in the eyes of the judges was that the witness had confirmed that Tadic carried a handgun and a rifle and that he normally wore a summer camouflage uniform. Suddenly, the reason became clear for all that testimony Col. Brenda Hollis had elicited early in the trial from Isak Gasi, Fadil Redzic, and Ibre Osmonovic about the uniforms of the Serb paramilitary forces. It would seem that Dusko Tadic was no ordinary traffic cop.

Later, Mira Tadic provided an answer to another mystery surrounding the Tadic case when she explained why the couple had fled Bosnia for Germany in 1993. Once again the name Simo Drljac emerged like a shadowy apparition haunting the defense. Mira said that a vendetta had erupted between the defendant and the police chief cum warlord, who wanted premises which the Tadics had been promised for a cafe in Prijedor. What was amazing was that all of this came out on direct examination by defense counsel Steven Kay.

It is true that on direct examination, lawyers will try to anticipate and blunt the opposing side's damaging evidence by putting such facts in a positive light for their client. Yet, in this case, one is reminded of Marlene Dietrich's performance in the classic film, "Witness for the Prosecution," in which she conspired with the opposing side to fix the outcome of the trial. Here, the star defense witness, Mira Tadic, for reasons one can only guess, had all but sealed her former husband's fate.

In one respect, the defense strategy had succeeded; there was little left for the prosecution to raise during its cross-examination of Mira Tadic. Yet prosecutor Michael Keegan had a few cards that remained to be played. He began by reading from a letter Dusko Tadic had allegedly written to Mira from prison in Germany, in which the defendant stated:

> We have been divorced from 1985 and have only been seeing each other once in a while. Remember that we spent each night together from 15-20 June, 1992. I worked for the Traffic police in Prijedor. I hope that you will be able to testify.

The witness was clearly caught off guard with this revelation. After a long pause, she replied with an awkward smile, "I don't recall that, really." When shown a copy of the letter, however, Mira confirmed that it was in Dusko Tadic's handwriting. The letter, which the prosecution suggested was a script to guide Mira Tadic's testimony, was promptly admitted into evidence. Before he was finished with the witness, Keegan elicited one other key admission. In response to Keegan's question about the loans for the establishment of Tadic's pub, Mira Tadic conceded that the defendant was in substantial debt to Muslims before the war—debts he never repaid. As the key alibi witness, Mira Tadic turned out to be not only unreliable, she was poison. It was beginning to look like the defense would have to put Dusko Tadic on the stand after all.

5

No one would ever claim that the trial of Dusko Tadic was a classically choreographed proceeding. Throughout the trial, the testimony of prosecution and defense witnesses jumped back and forth concerning the chronology of events during the summer of 1992, providing a confusing montage rather than a seamless narrative of the defendant's alleged whereabouts and actions. This was largely due to the fact that, in the absence of an effective international subpoena power, both sides were forced to schedule their witnesses according to their availability, rather than their particular relevance to the case. Thus, the defense was not yet ready to rest its case even after the testimony of its key witness, Mira Tadic. Given some of the incriminating statements she made, perhaps this was for the best.

With the end of the trial approaching, the defense had been anxiously waiting for the Tribunal to establish a satellite video-link to enable some of its most important witnesses to testify live from Bosnia. Although the judges had ruled that such testimony would not weigh as heavily as evidence given in court, the defense felt that this testimony would be critical to its case.[9] On October 15, after ninety-six witnesses had appeared before the judges in The Hague, modern technology brought the testimony of some of the final witnesses of the trial from Banja Luka, Bosnia.

The Tribunal's deputy-clerk Dominique Marro, defense counsel Michail Wladimiroff, and prosecutor Michael Keegan traveled to the northern Bosnian city to serve as silent observers of the testimony, while the other lawyers, the interpreters, and the judges remained in the Tribunal's courtroom in The Hague.[10] Although the set-up had a hefty price tag—$120,000 for use of the U.N.'s global satellite system for four days—the system was far from perfect.[11] The picture was grainy and produced a strobe effect that made the movements of the witnesses appear spasmodic—sort of like the television broadcast of Neil Armstrong's first steps on the moon back in 1969.

In addition, the sound quality was poor and the transmission was cut off on several occasions. The ability of the judges to assess the credibility of the Serbo-Croatian-speaking witnesses was already impaired by the use of interpreters, which masked such things as voice inflection, pauses, or a stammer. With the video-link, the judges were further disadvantaged because they could not see clearly such signs of untruthfulness as facial ticks, awkward smiles, or even a sweaty brow. However, it was important that the defense be given the opportunity to call witnesses who would not have voluntarily come to The Hague.

Thus, on October 16, the judges were introduced to Duro Prpos, Tadic's shift commander in the Prijedor traffic police. Testifying from a small, dimly lit room with a United Nations flag as a backdrop, Prpos, a grim figure in a dark suit, told the court more about the police records introduced by the defense during the testimony of Miroslav Brdar two weeks earlier. Prpos confirmed that Tadic had worked at the Orlovci checkpoint at the times and dates in June and July 1992 indicated in the duty rosters, which he was responsible for certifying. He said that he inspected the four checkpoints under his authority at random times of the day and night, and sometimes several times a day. Tadic was always at his post, Prpos added.

If Prpos and the duty rosters he maintained were to be believed, it is unlikely the defendant would have had time to frequent the Omarska camp in the summer of 1992 as the prosecution witnesses had testified. However, in what was perhaps the most important cross-examination of the entire trial, prosecutor Brenda Hollis ensured that Prpos was unlikely to be believed. The following tense exchange between prosecutor and witness gives a sense of how this was accomplished:

> Hollis: Sir, in fact you knew about the plan for the takeover of opstina Prijedor, and you participated in it, and you profited from it, didn't you?
>
> Prpos: No, that is not true.
>
> Hollis: On the 29th of April 1992, Serbs took over positions of authority in opstina Prijedor, did they not?
>
> Prpos: Yes.
>
> Hollis: When did you first learn that Serbs were going to take that action?
>
> Prpos: On the evening of April 29th.
>
> Hollis: Who promoted you to your position in the Prijedor Traffic police?
>
> Prpos: Simo Drljac.

Hollis: After the Serb take-over in the end of April 1992, how many Muslims continued to work in the Prijedor police?

Prpos: None of them remained.

Hollis: Did you take part in any killings or beatings of any non-Serb civilians in opstina Prijedor?

Prpos: No, my authority was to control traffic, and myself and my policemen did nothing beyond that.

Hollis: Were you aware that such beatings and killings were occurring?

Prpos: No.

Hollis: You would have been told when convoys of Muslims were being removed from the opstina, would you not?

Prpos: As far as I know, they were not forcibly removed, they went of their own free will.

Hollis: Is it your testimony that the thousands of Muslims who left opstina Prijedor between April and December 1992, did so purely voluntarily?

Prpos: That is true.

Here was a man appointed to his position by a notorious Serb warlord (Simo Drljac), who claimed not only that the men under his supervision did not engage in brutalities against Muslims, but that he was completely unaware such brutalities had occurred in the nearby towns and internment camps. Here was a man whose job was to monitor the traffic on the roads leading to Kozarac and Prijedor, yet who claimed he did not know of the convoys of trucks forcibly removing the Muslims from these towns to the concentration camps. Here was a man, aware that the judges watching him had listened to months of testimony about ethnic cleansing, who claimed that all the Muslims who left the area did so voluntarily. Here was a man whose testimony was not likely to be trusted.

The next to testify via satellite-link was Mirko Vujanovic, the officer in charge of maintaining records at the Prijedor police station. Vujanovic identified documents, which he said showed that Dusko Tadic worked long hours as a reserve policeman in the town of Prijedor virtually every day between August 7 and September 9, 1992. According to the records, which the defense would later submit into evidence, Tadic's regular tour of duty was patrolling the bus and railway station in the center of town. Vujanovic said that on September 9, Tadic was transferred to the police station in the town of Kozarac.

On cross-examination, Vujanovic admitted that he maintained the records in question based on documents supplied to him by other police supervisors, and therefore he did not have personal knowledge that the defendant actually worked on the days and at the times reflected. But he steadfastly maintained that the records were accurate and insisted that if an officer left his post for even a brief time it would be duly indicated. No such indication appears in the documents concerning Tadic's shifts. Later, the prosecution confronted Vujanovic with a discrepancy concerning the daily schedule of the Prijedor police for August 21, 1992. The daily schedule showed that Tadic worked a shift between the hours of 2:00 p.m. and 9:00 p.m. while the official work list for that day indicated that the defendant had worked a shift from 6:00 a.m. to 2:00 p.m. The prosecution suggested that these records were at best unreliable and at worst tampered with.

But Vujanovic suggested something much less sinister. He told the court the discrepancy was most likely just a typing error and suggested that the date recorded on the official work list should actually be August 12, a day on which the daily schedule had Tadic working from 6:00 a.m. to 2:00 p.m. Although Vujanovic was among the most persuasive of the defense witnesses, his testimony only provided Tadic an alibi from August 7 to September 9, 1992. Most of the prosecution witnesses testified to acts that occurred in May through July of 1992, and witness "L" had placed Tadic at Trnopolje later in the fall of that year.

The next three video-link witnesses testified about Tadic's whereabouts immediately prior to the Serb takeover of Kozarac on May 24, 1992. First, one of Tadic's neighbors, Trivo Reljic, testified that he, his wife, and their two sons took Dusko Tadic with them when they left Kozarac in their car (a Fiat 850 Feature) at 6:40 a.m. on May 23, 1992—the day before the Serb takeover of the town. According to Reljic, they dropped Tadic off in Prijedor at 7:00 a.m. Then Jelena Gajic, the thirty-nine-year-old sister of Mira Tadic, testified that the defendant showed up at her flat in Prijedor later that same morning at about 9:30 a.m. She told the judges that Tadic visited with her for about two hours and then he went "to the railway station to take a train to Banja Luka to be with his family." Finally, Dragoljub Savic, an employee of the Bosnian railroad, introduced timetables showing that there was a train from Prijedor to Banja Luka on the afternoon of May 23, 1992, and that the trip took approximately an hour and a half. While these witnesses may have proved that the defendant left Kozarac on May 23, it was still possible that he returned to Kozarac during the next few days and played a role in the murder and forced expulsion of the town's Muslim population as the prosecution witnesses had suggested. Before Savic was excused, Judge McDonald asked him whether the trains traveling between Prijedor and Banja Luka would pass through Omarska. Savic answered in the affirmative and added that the trip from Prijedor to Omarska took only about twenty minutes—reinforcing how easy it would be for Tadic to have frequented the camp from his post in Prijedor.

The next video-link witness turned out to be a more effective character witness for the defendant than Mira Tadic. Stojan Smoljic, a Serb refugee with gray hair and a large mustache who settled with his family in Kozarac in October 1992, told the judges how Tadic (as secretary of the local commune) helped to find a dwelling for him and his family. Smoljic also said that Tadic was in charge of distributing humanitarian aid to the refugees in the area and that the defendant handed out this aid regardless of a person's ethnic origin. In fact, the witness insisted, Tadic gave even more aid to non-Serbs in an effort to avoid any appearance of favoritism. Smoljic repeatedly described Tadic as humane and said he was extremely surprised to hear of Tadic's arrest and subsequent trial.

Smoljic was followed into the witness stand at the other end of the video-link by Jovo Samardija, a man with large sagging jowls, a bulbous nose, and sullen eyes. When Mira Tadic had testified a week earlier, she told the judges how the defendant had accompanied an elderly man to the Trnopolje camp to help him search for his missing sister. Samardija was that man. He was also the last witness to testify from Banja Luka. Looking into a television camera, from hundreds of miles away he told the judges that he had served with the defendant's father during World War II and came to Kozarac to visit his sister and the Tadic family three or four times a year. He said that in the days immediately after the surrender of Muslims in Kozarac in May 1992, he learned that his sister (a Serb) had been rounded up along with the Muslims and taken to the Trnopolje camp. As Samardija lived in Banja Luka near the home where Tadic and his family were staying, he asked Tadic to accompany him to Trnopolje to look for his sister, who remains missing to this day.

While the defense sought to use Samardija's testimony to offer a benign explanation for Tadic's presence at Trnopolje, the witness also provided some very incriminating information. Samardija said, for instance, that he felt safer traveling to Trnopolje with the defendant because Tadic wore a uniform and carried a semi-automatic rifle. He said that when they arrived at the camp, Tadic spoke to guards that he appeared to know. When asked if he saw Tadic engage in mistreatment of the inmates, Samardija answered in the negative, but he put it an odd way, saying: "No, no, no, he wouldn't dare in front of me. Because I know those people, I would never let him do anything. I can tell you for sure that he didn't." This seemed to suggest that if it was not for Samardija's presence, Tadic would have felt free to brutalize the inmates. Needless to say, this was something far less than the ringing character endorsement the defense was looking for.

6

ON OCTOBER 22, THE TADIC TRIAL shifted back to the Netherlands for what was scheduled to be the last week of defense testimony. The defense began by calling Joso Popovic who had been the vice president of the SDS party while Dusko Tadic served as president. Wearing a fashionable leather jacket while he testified, the tanned Popovic looked like a politician. Popovic testified that Tadic was very involved in trying to bring the town of Kozarac back to life in the autumn of 1992 and that he spent all his free time working very hard toward that aim. When asked by Steven Kay to describe the work of the SDS party under Tadic's leadership, the witness said it engaged in political activity and was not at all involved in planning for the cleansing of non-Serbs from the Kozarac region. However, the benevolent picture of Tadic's leadership in the SDS was fractured somewhat when Popovic was forced to admit during the cross-examination by prosecutor Michael Keegan that his own son worked as a guard at the Trnopolje detention camp.

The next witness, Drago Jankovic, was the defendant's thirty-five-year-old cousin, who had been part of a Serb army unit stationed between Kozarac and Prijedor. A large man with wavy brown hair and a burly mustache, Jankovic made some remarks that were probably a bit hard for the judges to swallow. For one thing, he maintained that the shelling of Kozarac—which other witnesses had described as a constant barrage over a period of four days—consisted only of brief periods of shelling over just three-quarters of a single day. For another, Jankovic told the judges that his unit was only there to protect civilians—to help Serbs and non-Serbs alike escape injury. The shelling, he claimed, was done only in self-defense. Finally, Jankovic insisted that there was no forced deportation of Muslims; rather, all civilians—men, women, and children—were given safe passage to Prijedor. It is unlikely that the judges found Jankovic to be a compelling witness, and it is not clear what the defense hoped to gain with his testimony.

The judges were then introduced to another member of the Tadic family—Ljubomir, the defendant's forty-three-year-old brother. A bulky, balding man with a round face, Ljubomir Tadic told the judges that his little brother, Dusko, had never showed much interest in politics, even though they both joined the SDS in 1991. "He joined for the simple reason to protect himself because he was living in an environment in which ninety-five percent of the inhabitants were Muslims and they were all members of the SDA," Ljubomir rationalized. Later, Ljubomir provided further corroboration to the testimony of other defense witnesses who had said that during the Serb takeover of Kozarac and its immediate aftermath the defendant was with his family in Banja Luka, some twenty-four kilometers away. Ljubomir also explained how a month later Tadic ended up being posted at the Orlovci checkpoint as a traffic cop. "On June 16, there was a general mobilization," Ljubomir said. "Dusko had to report to the military staff and then he got a war time assignment. He told me that he didn't want to join a military unit. He had no experience, he had no will, and I think he was afraid to go to the front, so they assigned him to the traffic police," the witness told the court.

On cross-examination, prosecutor Brenda Hollis focused her assault on Tadic's alibi for late May 1992. "During the several days that this attack on Kozarac lasted, were you with your brother every hour of every one of those days," she pressed. Ljubomir answered, "No." "Were you with your brother every hour of every evening during those days?" Hollis shot back. Again, the answer was "no." "And did you spend the night with him when he slept?" Hollis inquired sarcastically. The point was made that Ljubomir could not completely vouch for Tadic's whereabouts in late May 1992, although the witness maintained that he saw his brother regularly in Banja Luka during that time.

Dr. Willem Wagenaar, a professor of psychology at the University of Leiden, Netherlands, was expected to be the final witness called by the defense. Wagenaar, who is the spitting image of the white-haired actor, Hal Holbrook, is one of the leading experts in the field of criminal identification, or, as he put it, "human perception and the functioning of memory." Resting his thumb and forefinger on his bushy white mustache, Wagenaar told the court that he had testified many times in the past in both Dutch and international cases, including the infamous Ivan the Terrible case in Israel, in which a Polish-born American retired autoworker was accused of being a brutal World War II concentration camp guard.

During the prosecution's case, some forty-eight witnesses had identified Dusko Tadic in the courtroom as the man they had seen either at the site of war crimes in Bosnia or actually committing these crimes. Many of those said they had known Tadic for years before the war. Another four witnesses did not know the defendant before the conflict but identified him through use of a photo lineup prior to the trial. Wagenaar explained why neither type of identification could be relied upon in the context of this case.

Wagenaar told the judges that it is common for witnesses who have known a suspect before a crime to confuse him with someone whom they subsequently see commit that crime. As far as the photo identifications were concerned, Wagenaar suggested that the prosecution may not have strictly followed the traditional rules for a valid photo lineup. Among the rules Wagenaar mentioned were: investigators who administer a lineup should not know which photo represents the accused; witnesses should have to make an identification quickly and not be given a lot of time to think about it; witnesses should be told that it is possible there is no photo of the accused in the lineup; and witnesses who have been shown a photo lineup should not be allowed to interact with other witnesses who have yet to take it.

In addition, Wagenaar said the photo identifications were corrupted since it was likely that the witnesses had seen Tadic's picture in newspapers or on television before being shown the photo lineup. Later, the defense would establish through the testimony of Thomas Deichmann, a German journalist and media expert, that Tadic's photo had appeared in hundreds of papers and television reports throughout Europe and Bosnia between the time of his arrest and his trial. While the judges seemed impressed with the testimony of Wagenaar and Deichmann, it's hard to understand how someone who grew up, went to school, and lived down the street from the defendant prior to the conflict and was then assaulted by Tadic at point-blank range could possibly be mistaken about the identification.

Just when it looked as though the defense would rest its case, the prosecution dropped an unexpected bombshell. Grant Niemann found himself with the most unpleasant task of having to inform the judges that one of the prosecution's most important witnesses, witness "L," had lied when he told them that Tadic had committed atrocities at the Trnopolje camp in the fall of 1992. Tribunal investigator Robert Reid explained to the court that the prosecutor's office had doubts about Opacic's testimony after he appeared in closed session in August and that it had been investigating the witness over the past several weeks. After being confronted, the witness, whose real name was Drago Opacic, eventually admitted that he was ordered by Bosnian Muslim authorities to give that testimony "or be executed, and I took this to mean murder," Reid told the court. According to Reid, Opacic said the Bosnian authorities showed him videos of Tadic and of the Trnopolje camp "as training" before they sent him to The Hague with his phony story about Tadic's crimes. Opacic told Reid that the first time he saw Dusko Tadic was on a video in Sarajevo. As a consequence of the revelations, Grant Neimann told the court that "the prosecution feels we can no longer support him as a witness of truth. We invite the chamber to disregard his testimony entirely, and in relation to those matters the defendant has no case to answer."

The Tribunal has the power to impose a maximum $10,000 fine and/or a one-year imprisonment on Opacic for perjury. However, the witness may have been gambling that his new story would help him avoid a much longer sentence for war crimes in Bosnia. Bosnia's ambassador to the U.N. appeared on Dutch television that evening to refute the charge that Bosnian authorities had manipulated Opacic's testimony. "To believe that it is in the interest of the Bosnian government to falsify the trial of Tadic means ignoring how important it is to ensure that the Yugoslav War Crimes Tribunal and the Bosnian government retain their credibility and that justice is rendered to victims," he said.[12] Whether Opacic was lying now rather than earlier, the effect on the prosecution's case was the same.

"Very serious allegations have been made which may have an impact beyond the facts of the Tadic case, including on the prosecutor's relationship with the Bosnian government," a representative of the prosecutor's office told the press.[13] Lead defense attorney Michail Wladimiroff put it more directly: "If the tribunal has been manipulated by Sarajevo authorities it is clear that the tribunal is being used as an instrument in a propaganda war," he stated.[14] As to the effect on his client's trial, Wladimiroff suggested, "Without today's events, Tadic would likely have been convicted on the strength of Opacic's statement."[15] What he did not add, but must have been thinking, was that *with* the day's events, there was actually a chance now for an outright acquittal. Meanwhile, the prosecutor's office tried to put a positive spin on the development, saying "The exposition of the untruthfulness of a witness does not undermine the process: it vindicates it."[16]

From a legal viewpoint, Opacic's admission should have had little effect on the outcome of the trial since his testimony was used only to support count 1—the general persecution count—rather than any of the specific charges of rape and murder contained in the indictment, and there was plenty of other evidence on the persecution count. Yet this incident would certainly tarnish the general credibility of the prosecution's case. The opportunistic defense decided to try to take advantage of this development. It was time to call the defendant, Dusko Tadic, to the stand.

7

AT 3:05 P.M. (NETHERLANDS TIME) on Friday, October 25, 1996, Dusko Tadic began what was to be the most important dialogue of his life. Other than an outbreak of acne on one side of his face, Tadic showed no overt signs of stress as he calmly answered the questions put to him by his attorney, Steven Kay. He masterfully took advantage of the same ploy that Hermann Goering had used at Nuremberg in 1946[17]: Although by now Tadic understood English fairly well, the questions were still being translated into Serbo-Croatian, giving him additional time to improvise his answers.

Tadic began by describing his background and experiences prior to the fall of Kozarac in 1992. He said that most of his friends as he was growing up in Kozarac had been Muslims or Croats and that he never thought anything about this because that was the way his father had raised him. In particular, he described his lifelong friendship with Emir Karabasic, whom he was charged with murdering. He said that he and Karabasic were as close as brothers and often vacationed together. And though others had testified that this relationship appeared to cool in late 1991 and early 1992, Tadic insisted they remained as close as ever during that time, but simply could not see each other as often as they had in the past because of personal problems Karabasic was having. Tadic also testified that 98 percent of the customers at his pub had been Muslims and added that he had employed a Muslim as a waiter. "It wasn't a Serb cafe. It was for all communities," he said.

Tadic did, however, acknowledge a change in Kozarac as the conflict drew closer. He described the threatening letter he allegedly received in 1990 from radical Muslims in Kozarac and said he and his family also received threatening phone calls during this time. By April 1992, Tadic said that desperation began to grip the town. "There were many groups of people who were spreading lies," he explained. "Everybody was acquiring weapons. You no longer knew who to trust. There was a general feeling of insecurity," he added. He told the court that both Serbs and non-Serbs in Kozarac who had friends or relatives elsewhere were leaving town, which is why he sent Mira and their two daughters to stay with a friend in Banja Luka while he stayed behind to continue to operate their pub. Next, he explained why he decided to leave town himself on May 23, 1992:

> I remember a very serious incident on the twenty-second of May. My neighbors told me to shut off the lights, there would be shelling. When I came out of my house, I saw women and children heading for shelters and I saw many people in uniform carrying weapons.... That evening, I said to myself, I should flee because if there was a conflict I'd have no chance to flee. The next morning, I saw my neighbor, Trivo Reljic, packing up to leave and I asked if I could go with him and he said O.K.

"During this period had you taken part in any of the 'cleansing' activities as they are called in the area?" Steven Kay asked his client, who simply answered, "No." Tadic told the court that he was settling his family into their flat in Banja Luka, about forty kilometers (twenty-five miles) south of Kozarac at the time he is accused of guiding Serb artillery onto his hometown and helping to round up Muslims for deportation to the detention camps.

Echoing the testimony of Mira Tadic, the defendant said that he wore a pair of camouflage overalls, which his brother had given him, when he traveled because it was impossible at that time to move around the area without military trappings. As for his one visit to Trnopolje, Tadic said that Jovo Samardija first asked Tadic's brother and then asked him to go to Trnopolje to look for Samardija's missing sister. "He was an old man who needed help; that's why I accepted." According to Tadic, when he got to the camp, "I saw my old neighbors there, we kissed each other, and they asked me what was going on on the outside." This last point was Tadic's first misstep, since it was unlikely that the judges would believe that the Trnopolje inmates would embrace their uniformed former Serb neighbor after what they were enduring at the hands of the Serbs.

Mobilized into a prized job in the reserve police force on June 16, 1992, Tadic said he had never taken unexplained absences from work because he feared losing his job and being sent to fight on the front lines. Following his reassignment to guard the bus and railway station in Prijedor in August, he was finally transferred to the Kozarac police in September of 1992, he said. When asked if he had ever visited the Omarska camp, Tadic replied: "In all my life I have never been to the Omarska ore mine before, during, or after the war. I never set foot there. I was never there officially or privately. I was not forced to go there. I had no business there so I never went there." Here, a simple "no" might have been a preferable response, for as Shakespeare would say, "The [witness] doth protest too much, methinks."[18]

As to why he moved to Germany, Tadic offered an intriguing explanation which differed from what Mira Tadic had suggested a few weeks earlier. He explained that the military authorities tried to draft him despite a certificate from the civil authorities in Prijedor which said that his post exempted him from military conscription. He added that in June 1993 he was finally picked up and taken directly to a front line area to fight. According to the defendant, this was illegal, so he ran away with the help of a sympathetic driver who hid him in his truck. From that point on, the military viewed him as a deserter, Tadic said.

Although he began to speak a little more quickly, Tadic outwardly seemed quite composed during the cross-examination by prosecutor Alan Tieger, at one point saying, "I've nothing to hide." Tieger began by asking the defendant about his attitude towards the non-Serbs living in Kozarac at the time. "You have spoken of the good people of Kozarac. But those Muslims are not there any more," Tieger said. "They have been driven from their homes. Many were rounded up by Serb forces and put into camps," he continued. Tadic firmly replied, "I did not take part in such activities. I do not know what happened to them." Tieger then asked the defendant if he had seen busloads of Muslim prisoners being transported to camps at Omarska and Keraterm in July 1992 while he was stationed at the Orlovci checkpoint. "Maybe I saw a couple of buses but I don't know where they came from or where they were going," Tadic calmly answered.

As the cross-examination continued, however, the questions became increasingly more difficult for Tadic to evade, and his answers began to sound a bit too inventive to be believed. Tieger began by asking the defendant about a certificate, dated from before the fall of Kozarac in May 1992, permitting Tadic to have possession of a semiautomatic rifle. The certificate was issued by the Bosnian Serb authorities in Banja Luka. Tadic answered that the certificate was a fake that had been given to him by his brother, Ljubomir, and that he had been given the weapon from a deserter from Slovenia sometime after the Serb attack on Kozarac. Next, Tieger asked the defendant about the uniforms he owned during 1992, and which he actually wore. At first,

Tadic said that he wore only a blue police uniform while he was working at the Orlovci checkpoint, but later he was forced to concede that he may also have worn a camouflage uniform there. He claimed, however, that he would only have worn the camouflage uniform when his regular uniform was being laundered. Finally, Tieger tried to discredit the defendant by pointing out that he had lied when he told the German authorities who arrested him in 1994 that he never wore a camouflage uniform. Tadic did not deny the accusation, but dismissed its significance, responding, "I don't know, it's possible."

As he neared the end of his cross-examination, Tieger's questions became increasingly strident, but Tadic refused to lose his cool. "You have spoken about 'we simple ordinary people,' but the fact is you were not only a member of the SDS, but an earnest member who before the conflict tried to obtain weapons for Serbs, organized assignments and obtained information about Muslim weapons," Tieger pressed. "That's your opinion," Tadic answered. To prove the point, Tieger confronted Tadic with letters he had written to Serb authorities making such claims and denouncing other Serbs in Kozarac because they were married to Muslims. Tadic responded that he wrote the letters in his capacity as local secretary of the SDS, not as a private individual. "They do not reflect my views," he said. "I don't think I participated in any denunciation." Tieger pressed on. "But the cook and the carpenter and the florist and the homemaker and the businessman and the school teacher and dozens and dozens and dozens of others from Kozarac, from Prijedor, from Jaskici and Sivci, they're all gone," Tieger said, his voice growing shrill. Tadic answered that he and his family, who were forced to move to Banja Luka, were just as much the victims of ethnic cleansing as anybody.

With that, Dusko Tadic's cross-examination came to a close. "You are now excused as a witness, Mr. Tadic," said Judge McDonald. "But you will still be with us." After his Academy Award-quality performance, Tadic hoped she meant only until the end of the trial. On October 30, 1996, the defense rested its case.

The final act in this judicial drama was the rebuttal by the prosecution. The prosecution called a total of ten rebuttal witnesses over a two-day period. Each was called to discredit a specific defense witness. For example, Fikret Kadiric, the Muslim traffic police commander in Prijedor prior to the Serb takeover, testified that at the end of May

1992 he saw his successor, Duro Prpos, participating in the loading of Muslim men into buses bound for the concentration camps. Kadiric's testimony contradicted Prpos's claim that he was completely unaware of such acts of ethnic cleansing. But by far the most unforgettable of the rebuttal witnesses was Sofia Tadic, the defendant's ex-sister-in-law.

Brushing her long, wavy brown hair out of her eyes, Sofia Tadic told the court that she had been married to the defendant's brother Mladen from 1978 until 1991. A Croat by birth, Sofia Tadic had lived in Munich with her husband, but said they visited the Tadic family in Kozarac regularly, sometimes for up to two months a year. Sofia Tadic contradicted several things the defendant and Mira Tadic had said when they had testified. She claimed, for example, that Dusko and Mira showed an increasing interest in Serb nationalism by the late 1980s. She told the court that Dusko and Mira were planning to name their second child "Slobodan" if it was a boy, after Serb leader Slobodan Milosevic. She also said that Dusko and Mira's relationship had been rocky and added that Mira told her in 1993 that she was leaving Dusko because she had caught him with a lover.

Yet Sofia Tadic's most important testimony concerned the defendant's character. Like several other prosecution witnesses, she testified that Dusko Tadic had a hot temper. She called him "violent" and said one had to be careful not to set him off. She described an incident in which Dusko apparently beat Mira. "We heard yelling and arguing from the next room where Mira and Dule lived, and I saw Mira the next day with black and blue marks on her face," the witness recounted. She then described another incident in Germany in which the defendant got into a heated argument with another man. According to the witness, the argument escalated and came to blows in the back seat of Sofia and Mladen Tadic's car: "The argument turned into a fight. As I turned around I saw Dule hitting the man in the face and then grabbing him by the genitals and squeezing." When Steven Kay accused Sofia Tadic of fabricating this story to bolster the castration charge of the indictment, Sofia held her ground, saying, "I saw it with my own eyes." This would be one more eyewitness whose credibility would bedevil the judges.

The defense did not believe the rebuttal witnesses had done any real damage to their case and chose not to follow with any rebuttal witnesses of their own. In all, the trial chamber had heard the testimony of 125 witnesses, amounting to more than 6,000 pages of transcripts.

WAR CRIMINALS INDICTED BY THE INTERNATIONAL CRIMINAL TRIBUNAL FOR THE FORMER YUGOSLAVIA

WARRANTS FOR THEIR ARREST ARE HELD BY THEIR RESPECTIVE CAPITALS

ZLATKO ALEKSOVSKI
DOB: 08/01/60
NATIONALITY: CROATIAN
DESCRIPTION: NOT AVAILABLE
ADDRESS: MOSTAR, BiH

TIHOFOL BLASKIĆ
DOB: 02/11/60
NATIONALITY: CROATIAN
DESCRIPTION: NOT AVAILABLE
ADDRESS: MOSTAR, BiH

RANKO CESIĆ
DOB: 01/01/64
NATIONALITY: BOSNIAN SERB
DESCRIPTION: MEDIUM HEIGHT AND BUILD; BROWN HAIR AND EYES
ADDRESS: BIJELJINA, POSSIBLY BRCKO, BiH

RADOVAN KARADŽIĆ
DOB: 19/06/45
NATIONALITY: BOSNIAN SERB
DESCRIPTION: 185 CM; BROWNISH-GRAY HAIR; FLAMBOYANT
ADDRESS: PALE, BiH

DARIO KORDIĆ
DOB: 14/12/60
NATIONALITY: CROATIAN
DESCRIPTION: 173 CM; DARK, CROPPED HAIR; GLASSES
ADDRESS: PRESIDENT OF CROATIAN COMMUNITY OF HERCEG-BOSNA

MILAN MARTIĆ
DOB: 18/11/54
NATIONALITY: SERBIAN
DESCRIPTION: 172-180 CM; 85-90 KG; DARK BROWN HAIR; GREEN-BROWN EYES
ADDRESS: UNKNOWN

ŽELJKO MEAKIĆ
DOB: 02/08/64
NATIONALITY: BOSNIAN SERB
DESCRIPTION: 175 CM; 65 KG; BROWN HAIR; BLUE EYES
ADDRESS: PETROV GAJ

SLOBODAN MILJKOVIĆ
DOB: 01/01/53
NATIONALITY: SERBIAN
DESCRIPTION: 180 CM; DARK BROWN HAIR; SCAR ON SIDE OF NOSE; TATOOS ON BOTH ARMS
ADDRESS: UNKNOWN

RATKO MLADIĆ
DOB: 12/03/43
NATIONALITY: BOSNIAN SERB
DESCRIPTION: SHORT, STOCKY; RED-FACED
ADDRESS: BELGRADE, SERBIA

MILAN MRKSIĆ
DOB: 20/07/47
NATIONALITY: SERBIAN
DESCRIPTION: 180 CM; GRAY, WAVY HAIR
ADDRESS: CDR, RSKA ARMY

DRAGAN NIKOLIĆ
DOB: 01/01/57
NATIONALITY: BOSNIAN SERB
DESCRIPTION: 190-200 CM; BLOND HAIR
ADDRESS: UNKNOWN

DRAŽENKO PREDOJIVIĆ
DOB: 02/04/70
NATIONALITY: BOSNIAN SERB
DESCRIPTION: 175 CM; BLACK HAIR; MISSING FRONT TOOTH
ADDRESS: GRADINA, BiH

MIRSOLAV RADIĆ
DOB: 01/01/61
NATIONALITY: SERBIAN
DESCRIPTION: 180 CM; DARK, STRAIGHT HAIR; PROPORTIONAL BUILD
ADDRESS: UNKNOWN

MLADEN RADIĆ
DOB: 15/05/52
NATIONALITY: BOSNIAN SERB
DESCRIPTION: 170 CM; 100 KG; LIGHT BROWN HAIR; FAT BUILD
ADDRESS: OMARSKA, BiH

VESELIN ŠLJIVANČANIN
DOB: 01/01/53
NATIONALITY: SERBIAN
DESCRIPTION: 190 CM; DARK EYES; DARK, GRAYING, SHORT, THINNING HAIR
ADDRESS: UNKNOWN

STEVAN TODOROVIČ
DOB: 01/01/57
NATIONALITY: UNKNOWN
DESCRIPTION: 180-185 CM; 100 KG; BROWN HAIR, BALDING
ADDRESS: BOSANSKI SAMAC, BiH

ZORAN ŽIGIĆ
DOB: 20/09/58
NATIONALITY: BOSNIAN SERB
DESCRIPTION: 175 CM; 80 KG; DARK BROWN HAIR
ADDRESS: FORMER TAXI DRIVER IN PRIJEDOR, BiH

PHOTOS NOT AVAILABLE FOR THE FOLLOWING:

MIRKO BABIĆ
DOB: UNKNOWN
NATIONALITY: BOSNIAN SERB
DESCRIPTION: 175 CM; GINGER HAIR
ADDRESS: GUARD AT OMARSKA, BiH

NEDELJKO/NENAD BANOVIĆ
DOB: 28/10/69
NATIONALITY: BOSNIAN SERB
DESCRIPTION: 150 CM; BLACK HAIR; LOOKS LIKE BROTHER
ADDRESS: SKENDAR KULENOVIC STR 31; PRIJEDOR, BiH

PREDRAG BANOVIĆ
DOB: 28/10/69
NATIONALITY: BOSNIAN SERB
DESCRIPTION: 160-165 CM; BLACK HAIR; WORE GOLD
ADDRESS: SKENDAR KULENOVIC STR 31; PRIJEDOR, BiH

GORAN BOROVNICA
DOB: 15/08/65
NATIONALITY: BOSNIAN SERB
DESCRIPTION: 175 CM; BROWN HAIR; CROSS-EYED; HAD BEARD; POSSIBLE BURN SCAR ON FACE
ADDRESS: KOZARAC, BiH

MARIO CERKEZ
DOB: 27/03/59
NATIONALITY: CROATIAN
DESCRIPTION: NOT AVAILABLE
ADDRESS: ZRTAVA FASIZMA; VITEZ, BiH

DAMIR DOSEN
DOB: 07/04/67
NATIONALITY: BOSNIAN SERB
DESCRIPTION: 190 CM; LIGHT BROWN HAIR
ADDRESS: FIRST CAMP COMD. AT KERATERM, BiH

DRAGAN FUSTAR
DOB: 28/03/56
NATIONALITY: BOSNIAN SERB
DESCRIPTION: 170-180 CM; 100 KG
ADDRESS: 1 MAY STR 41; PRIJEDOR, BiH

ZDRAVKO GOVEDARICA
DOB: 02/01/63
NATIONALITY: BOSNIAN SERB
DESCRIPTION: 180 CM; DARK COMPLEXION; POSSIBLE MOUSTACHE
ADDRESS: UNKNOWN

MOMČILO GRUBAN
DOB: 19/06/61
NATIONALITY: BOSNIAN SERB
DESCRIPTION: 185 CM; BLACK HAIR; BLUE EYES
ADDRESS: UNKNOWN

GRUBAN
DOB: UNKNOWN
NATIONALITY: UNKNOWN
DESCRIPTION: UNKNOWN
ADDRESS: UNKNOWN

NIKICA JANJIĆ
DOB: 06/04/72
NATIONALITY: BOSNIAN SERB
DESCRIPTION: 190 CM; BLACK HAIR; OLIVE COMPLEXION, CLEAN SHAVEN
ADDRESS: ISTARSKA ST, PRIJEDOR, BiH

GORAN JELIŠIĆ
DOB: 07/06/68
NATIONALITY: BOSNIAN SERB
DESCRIPTION: MEDIUM HEIGHT; SLENDER; LIGHT BROWN HAIR; BROWN EYES
ADDRESS: BIJELJINA, BiH

DUŠAN KNEŽEVIĆ
DOB: 01/01/55
NATIONALITY: BOSNIAN SERB
DESCRIPTION: 170 CM; BLACK HAIR; OBESE; OLIVE COMPLEXION
ADDRESS: FORMER MP LEADER OF GD SHIFT AT KERATERN

DRAGAN KONDIĆ
DOB: 08/12/64
NATIONALITY: BOSNIAN SERB
DESCRIPTION: 190 CM; LIGHT BROWN HAIR
ADDRESS: JNA STREET; JARUGE; BiH

MILOJICA KOS
DOB: 01/04/63
NATIONALITY: BOSNIAN SERB
DESCRIPTION: 175 CM; 85 KG
ADDRESS: OWNED RESTAURANT IN OMARSKA, BiH

PREDRAG KOSTIĆ
DOB: OOA 01/01/66
NATIONALITY: UNKNOWN
DESCRIPTION: 180-185 CM; DARK BROWN HAIR (MILITARY CUT); BLUE EYES
ADDRESS: UNKNOWN

DRAGAN KULUNDŽIJA
DOB: 31/07/66
NATIONALITY: BOSNIAN SERB
DESCRIPTION: NOT AVAILABLE
ADDRESS: JNA STREET; PRIJEDOR, BiH

MIROSLAV KVOČKA
DOB: 01/01/57
NATIONALITY: BOSNIAN SERB
DESCRIPTION: 180 CM; 75 KG; BLACK HAIR
ADDRESS: UNKNOWN

GORAN LAJIĆ
DOB: 25/09/67
NATIONALITY: BOSNIAN SERB
DESCRIPTION: NOT AVAILABLE
ADDRESS: KERATERM GUARD

NEDJELJKO PASPALJ
DOB: 22/01/61
NATIONALITY: BOSNIAN SERB
DESCRIPTION: 175 CM; BLOND HAIR
ADDRESS: 348 BISTRICA, BiH

MILAN PAVLIĆ
DOB: UNKNOWN
NATIONALITY: BOSNIAN SERB
DESCRIPTION: 180 CM; 100 KG; BLACK, CURLY HAIR ON ONE SIDE, ORANGE ON OTHER
ADDRESS: GUARD AT OMARSKA

MILUTIN POPOVIĆ
DOB: 20/09/55
NATIONALITY: BOSNIAN SERB
DESCRIPTION: 180 CM; 80 KG; BLACK HAIR
ADDRESS: GUARD AT OMARSKA

DRAGOLJUB PRČAC
DOB: 18/07/37
NATIONALITY: BOSNIAN SERB
DESCRIPTION: 175 CM; GRAY HAIR; BROWN EYES
ADDRESS: RADKA VUJOVICA COCE 11; OMARSKA, BiH

IVICA RAJIĆ
DOB: 05/05/58
NATIONALITY: BOSNIAN CROAT
DESCRIPTION: 170 CM; 80 KG; GRAYING HAIR; BROWN EYES, MOUSTACHE, HEAVY-SET
ADDRESS: MOSTAR, BiH

IVAN ŠANTIĆ
DOB: 01/01/42
NATIONALITY: CROATIAN
DESCRIPTION: NOT AVAILABLE
ADDRESS: HVO VITEZ

DRAGOMIR SAPONJA
DOB: 08/06/65
NATIONALITY: BOSNIAN SERB
DESCRIPTION: 180 CM; BLOND HAIR
ADDRESS: MARSALA TITA 56, PRIJEDOR, BiH

ŽELJKO SAVIĆ
DOB: 01/01/70
NATIONALITY: BOSNIAN SERB
DESCRIPTION: NOT AVAILABLE
ADDRESS: UNKNOWN

BLAGOJE ŠIMIĆ
DOB: 01/01/60
NATIONALITY: BOSNIAN SERB
DESCRIPTION: 180-185 CM; 100 KG; DARK BROWN HAIR
ADDRESS: BOSANSKI SAMAC, BiH

MILAN ŠIMIĆ
DOB: 01/01/58
NATIONALITY: BOSNIAN SERB
DESCRIPTION: 185-190 CM; 85 KG; BLACK HAIR; DARK EYES
ADDRESS: BOSANSKI SAMAC, BiH

DUŠKO SIKIRICA
DOB: 23/03/64
NATIONALITY: BOSNIAN SERB
DESCRIPTION: 180 CM; DARK BROWN HAIR
ADDRESS: CIRKIN POLJE, BiH

PERO SKOPLJAK
DOB: 05/06/43
NATIONALITY: CROATIAN
DESCRIPTION: NOT AVAILABLE

MIROSLAV TADIĆ
DOB: 12/05/37
NATIONALITY: BOSNIAN SERB
DESCRIPTION: 160-170 CM;

NEDJELJKO TIMARAC
DOB: 18/04/54
NATIONALITY: BOSNIAN SERB
DESCRIPTION: 180 CM; BLACK

SIMO ZARIĆ
DOB: 25/07/48
NATIONALITY: BOSNIAN SERB
DESCRIPTION: 178 CM; 80 KG;

Chapter 10

Epilogue and Assessment

> Civilization asks whether law is so laggard as to be utterly helpless to deal with crimes of this magnitude by criminals of this order of importance. It does not expect that you can make war impossible. It does expect that your juridical action will put the forces of International Law, its precepts, its prohibitions and, most of all, its sanctions, on the side of peace, so that men and women of good will, in all countries, may have "leave to live by no man's leave, underneath the law."
>
> —ROBERT H. JACKSON
> *Opening Speech for the Prosecution at Nuremberg, November 21, 1945*

1

THE STORY THAT I SET OUT TO RECOUNT in this book ends with the case going to the judges. The trial chamber's verdict and sentence, and the appeal that is certain to follow, will undoubtedly be the subject of countless other scholarly articles and books. Yet to understand fully the challenge that confronted Judges McDonald, Vohrah, and Stephen on that cold November day in 1996 when the Tadic trial finally came to an end, it seems appropriate to conclude this book with an assessment of the evidence that was elicited by the 125 witnesses during the seven-month trial, followed by an assessment of the broader ramifications of the case.

In determining Tadic's fate, the judges had to decide three issues:

1. Was the war in Bosnia an international armed conflict or a civil war? The requirement of an international armed conflict is a prerequisite for conviction on all charges relating to grave breaches of the Geneva Conventions.
2. Did there exist widespread and systematic abuses against non-Serbs? This is a prerequisite for conviction of the persecution count (count 1) and all charges relating to crimes against humanity.
3. Did Tadic himself engage in acts of persecution against non-Serbs during the war (count 1 of the indictment), or commit any of the thirty crimes with which he is specifically charged in counts 5–34. (The prosecution had dropped counts 2–4 prior to the trial).

The first of these questions seemed to be answered by the videotape evidence presented during the testimony of Dr. James Gow, as well as the testimony of the two former JNA colonels—Osman Selak and Ludvik Kranjc. Based on this evidence, the judges could conclude that the takeover of the Prijedor region of Bosnia in the spring of 1992 was accomplished by Bosnian Serb paramilitary forces acting with the assistance of the reconstituted Yugoslav National army (the VRS), that both the paramilitary forces and the VRS continued to be controlled and paid for by Belgrade, and that the detention camps were operated by the police who were under the supervision of the VRS. Moreover, the prosecution presented uncontested evidence of the important role television and radio propaganda originating in Belgrade played in the events in Bosnia. Because of this outside involvement, the prosecution argued in its closing, atrocities committed in the Prijedor region could be found to be part of an international armed conflict. Even the defense expert, Dr. Robert Hayden, had acknowledged this fact in an article he wrote in 1992, although he told the court that he had since "rethought" his earlier position.

Nor did the defense ever really attempt to dispute the second question. Its strategy was to acknowledge that atrocities occurred throughout Bosnia, but to deny that Tadic had any involvement in them. Thus, the defense rarely challenged the testimony of the fourteen policy witnesses presented by the prosecution who described the widespread and systematic abuses committed by the Serbs against the Bosnian Muslims and Croats in the summer of 1992. Particularly persuasive were the videos of Omarska and Trnopolje shown during the testimony of Edward Vulliamy, Mevludin Sejmenovic, and Vasif Gutic. Instead, the defense sought to turn this liability into an asset by suggesting that the evidence given by prosecution witnesses was unreliable because in many cases it was prejudiced testimony of Muslim victims who saw all Serbs as their oppressors. "These ingredients are a perfect recipe for a miscarriage of justice," Michail Wladimiroff warned in his closing argument.

As to the third question, the persecution count of the indictment (count 1) charged Tadic with facilitating the Serb attack on Kozarac on May 24, 1992; assisting in the forced transfer of the town's Muslim population May 24–27; taking part in the beating, torture, and killing of detainees at the Omarska camp between May 25 and August 8; and raping, torturing, and killing detainees at the Trnopolje camp between September and December 1992. After the debacle with witness "L," the prosecution withdrew the allegations concerning Trnopolje. In addition to the persecution count, Tadic was specifically charged with killing four Muslims during the Serb takeover of Kozarac on May 27, 1992 (counts 24–28); beating and killing residents of the towns of Jaskici and Sivci on June 14 (counts 29–34); participating in the castration incident at Omarska on June 16 (counts 5–11); and beating other Omarska inmates at various times in July of 1992 (counts 12–23).

For the prosecution, the key to proving the charges was establishing motive and opportunity. As to motive, the prosecution claimed that Tadic turned on his Muslim neighbors because he had become infected by Serb nationalism. The defense countered that some of the alleged victims were in fact Tadic's very best friends, whom he would never harm. The evidence elicited during the trial suggested that Tadic did in fact have various motives to participate in violent acts against the Muslims of Kozarac. Both the defendant and Mira Tadic testified that in the months leading up to the conflict in Bosnia Tadic had amassed a substantial financial debt to his Muslim neighbors (which he never repaid); that they had received threatening letters and phone calls from Muslims; that Muslims had repeatedly vandalized and burglarized their pub; and that Mira's Muslim co-workers had become openly hostile to her. They also admitted that Tadic joined the Serb party (the SDS) in 1990 and that during the summer of 1992 he was elected president of the SDS in Kozarac. Curiously, most of this evidence was introduced by the defense, not the prosecution. What emerged from the testimony was a composite picture of the defendant as a small-town bully with a grudge—and with the physical skills of a karate instructor, such a person could be very dangerous indeed.

Regardless of any possible motive, the defense argued that Tadic would not have had the opportunity to commit the alleged acts. The defense witnesses established that Tadic was living in Banja Luka from May 23 until June 16, 1992. Consequently, the defense argued that Tadic could not have been involved in the attack on Kozarac, the forced transfer of its population, the incidents at the towns of Jaskici and Sivci, or the acts that had occurred at the Omarska camp during that time. But the defense witnesses conceded that Banja Luka was just a short drive or train ride from Kozarac and was even closer to the Omarska camp. Although several witnesses said they saw Tadic in Banja Luka during that time, even his wife and brother were forced to admit that they could not account for all of his time during those days.

According to the defense, from June 16 until August 1, 1992, Tadic served as a traffic cop at the Orlovci checkpoint outside of Prijedor. The most persuasive evidence for the defense was the duty rosters showing that Tadic had worked six- and twelve-hour shifts at the Orlovci checkpoint during the time he was alleged to have been frequenting the Omarska camp as a visiting sadist. But the prosecution demonstrated that the same police department that ran the checkpoint also ran the Omarska camp two and a half miles away and that the chief of police had been none other than the dreaded Serb warlord, Simo Drljac. The evidence proved that Tadic would have had easy access and ample opportunity to visit Omarska while on duty or after hours and that he was likely authorized and possibly ordered to visit the camps by his superiors.

In its closing argument, the prosecution compared Tadic's alibi to a person who was working for the Ku Klux Klan in the 1950s saying that he could not have been responsible for acts against blacks because "I was working at my job at the time." As prosecutor Brenda Hollis explained to the judges, "Just as history shows that the Ku Klux Klan were bound up inextricably with mistreating blacks during the '50s, the police in Prijedor were bound up inextricably with the persecution that was going on there."

Perhaps the most incriminating testimony against Tadic was Mira Tadic's statement, and his own later admission, that during May and June of 1992 he was often armed and dressed in a summer camouflage uniform. This was precisely the description given by so many of the prosecution witnesses who said they had seen the defendant at Kozarac, Jaskici, Sivci, and Omarska. Moreover, according to the former JNA members who testified for the prosecution, this was the official uniform of the Bosnian Serb paramilitary force.

Thus, notwithstanding his attempt at an alibi, Tadic was clearly at the wrong places at the wrong times—and literally dressed to kill. But this did not mean that the prosecution had proven that he actually did kill. Only two prosecution witnesses had testified that they had seen him do so, and one of them, witness "L" (Dragon Opacic), later recanted. The other witness was Nihad Seferovic who had told the unlikely story that he had seen the defendant slit the throats of two Muslim policemen when he snuck back into Kozarac after the Serb takeover to feed his pigeons.

As for the castration charge, the insistence of witness "H" that Dusko Tadic was not in the room at the time and Halid Mujkanovic's testimony that Tadic was there but was not involved provided the very definition of reasonable doubt. The prosecution seemed to fare no better with the second most grizzly count of the indictment—the fire extinguisher charge. Since there was no evidence that the person in the wheelbarrow was alive when Tadic placed the hose of the fire extinguisher in his mouth, Michail Wladimiroff argued convincingly that "the significant character of crimes against humanity is that only human life is protected, not dead bodies." There was some circumstantial evidence relating to the killing of Ekrem Karabasic, Ismet Karabasic, Seido Karabasic, and Redo Foric in Kozarac, but most of the evidence introduced during the trial merely related to beatings perpetrated by the defendant.

In its closing argument, the prosecution suggested that Tadic should be convicted of the murder charges even if the evidence proved only that he was present when such acts were committed. "With all of these Serbs around, cheering, yelling, firing guns into the air, victims would be less likely to flee, to try to escape their fate, even if it was only momentarily. The accused's presence as well as the presence of other members of the groups, assisted in creating an intimidating, terrorizing situation that rendered these victims completely helpless," prosecutor Brenda Hollis told the court. This is essentially the same argument that the prosecution successfully made in the "Big Dan" rape trial in Bedford, Massachusetts, which was the subject of the Academy Award winning movie, "The Accused," starring Jody Foster.[1] But Michail Wladimiroff countered in his closing that "participation in the context of the Tribunal's Statute is, contrary to the assertions of the Prosecution, not an almost unrestricted notion." He added that "it is way beyond its limits" to say that mere presence in a group of armed Serbs that committed crimes constitutes aiding and abetting in planning, preparation, or execution of a crime as required by the Tribunal's statute.

The Tadic case presented an extraordinary conflict in testimony. The portrayal of events by each side was diametrically opposed. Like many cases, this one would come down to the question of credibility: Who would the judges believe? What made this case so unique, however, was that most of the testimony on both sides was inherently biased. The prosecution eyewitnesses were Muslims who were victims of abuse at the hands of Serbs during an armed conflict; the defense witnesses were all Serbs, many of whom might well be guilty of their own war crimes.

At Nuremberg, prosecutor Robert Jackson told the judges, "We will not ask you to convict these men on the testimony of their foes. There is no count in the Indictment that cannot be proved by books and records."[2] But in the Tadic trial that is exactly what the prosecution was asking. The prosecution's task became all the more difficult when its most important witness—witness "L"—later told the court that he had falsely testified about Tadic's involvement in crimes at the Trnopolje camp. In his closing argument, lead defense counsel Michail Wladimiroff said the prosecution had been "one-sided" and was built on a "shaky and incomplete investigation." "The testimony of witness 'L' helped the prosecution draw the perfect picture of a perfect and stereotypical criminal," Wladimiroff said. But the prosecution did not check if his statements were true and therefore left reasonable doubt about the credibility of other witnesses, he suggested.

The prosecution tried to overcome the credibility problem through sheer numbers: over forty prosecution witnesses testified that they saw Dusko Tadic commit war crimes or placed him in locations where war crimes were committed. The prosecution strategy was to make the judges ask themselves: How could so many people be so wrong about Tadic's participation?

In the prosecution's closing argument, Brenda Hollis said of Tadic: "This is not the common man, the refugee, he would have you believe he was. This is the Serb nationalist who saw the persecution there as an opportunity to contribute to the Serb aim of ethnic dominance in the region and at the same time, to enhance his own status in the area, particularly in Kozarac. He is also a man who is willing to use violence to get what he wants and to pay back those with whom he disagrees. This is the man who committed the crimes named in the charge sheet." In response, defense counsel Michail Wladimiroff reminded the judges that the purpose of the trial was "not to satisfy the victims of crimes but to see if the prosecution has met its burden of proof. We submit that the evidence of the prosecution witnesses is insufficiently reliable to provide the basis of a conviction."

It took the judges over five months to render their judgment in the Tadic case. As the pressure mounted in the weeks leading up to the verdict, Tadic got into a fight with a prison guard,* fired his able defense team, and reinstated Belgrade attorney Milan Vujin as his counsel at the urging of Serb authorities.† Finally, at 11:00 a.m. on May 7,

---

* *Agence France Presse*, April 23, 1997. According to the spokesman for the Yugoslavia Tribunal, Tadic was treated for a bloody forehead resulting from the incident and the guard was transferred from the U.N detention center.

† According to an April 22, 1997 Press Statement made by the Dutch law firm of Wladimiroff & Spong: "Tadic, on the advice of authorities of the former Yugoslavia, wishes to instruct additional parties [Milan Vujin] to act on his behalf with those previously instructed and this is not a situation Professor Wladimiroff and his team are willing to accept."

1997, exactly a year from the day the historic trial began, the Tribunal announced its decision.* Dusko Tadic was found guilty of 11 of the 34 counts in the indictment, including the persecution charge, but was acquitted of the castration charge, the fire extinguisher charge, and all of the specific murder charges.†[3] Perhaps the biggest surprise was his acquittal of the charges relating to grave breaches of the Geneva Conventions, based on the conclusion of two of the three judges that Serbia had not been directly involved in these acts, and therefore that they were not committed in an international armed conflict. "Although this is the first trial conducted by the international tribunal and thus has some historic dimension, the goal of the trial chamber was always first and foremost to provide the accused with the fair trial to which he was entitled," Judge McDonald said after pronouncing the verdict and summarizing the Tribunal's 301-page decision. "This, we believe, has been done."[4]

2

DESPITE THE MIXED VERDICT, historians are likely to rank the trial of Dusko Tadic among the most important trials of the century.[5] Unlike other renowned criminal trials such as the treason trials of Esther and Julius Rosenberg, the Chicago Seven trial, the Watergate trials, the Rodney King case, and the O.J. Simpson trial, the importance of the Tadic case lies not in the status of the defendant or even the nature of his alleged crimes, but in the fact that the proceedings constituted an historic turning point for the world community. Just as the Nuremberg trials following World War II launched the era of human

* The official summary of the Tribunal's Opinion is reproduced in Appendix D of this book.

† By a unanimous decision, the three judges found Tadic guilty of counts 1, 10, 11, 13, 14, 16, 17, 22, 23, and in part counts 33 and 34. By unanimous decision, he was found not guilty of counts 6, 7, 19, 20, 25, 26, 28, 30, 31, and in part counts 33 and 34. A majority, with Judge McDonald dissenting, found that the accusations of grave breaches of the Geneva Conventions were not applicable and that Tadic was therefore not guilty of counts 5, 8, 9, 12, 15, 18, 21, 24, 27, 29, and 32.

rights promulgation fifty years ago, the Tadic trial has inaugurated a new age of human rights enforcement.

As the Yugoslav Tribunal itself reflected in its first annual report: "The United Nations, which over the years has accumulated an impressive corpus of international standards enjoining States and individuals to conduct themselves humanely, has now set up an institution to put those standards to the test, to transform them into living reality. A whole body of lofty, if remote, United Nations ideals will be brought to bear upon human beings. Through the Tribunal, those imperatives will be turned from abstract tenets into inescapable commands."[6]

At the opening session of the Yugoslav Tribunal in November 1993, U.N. Under-Secretary General for Legal Affairs Carl-August Fleischhauer said that in setting up the Tribunal, the Security Council had demonstrated a determination to achieve three aims: "First, to put an end to the crimes being committed in the former Yugoslavia; second, to take effective measures to bring to justice the persons who are responsible for those crimes; and, third, to break the seemingly endless cycle of ethnic violence and retribution."[7] It is no overstatement to suggest that the success or failure of the Yugoslav Tribunal in meeting these goals of deterrence, justice, and peace will decide the direction of human rights enforcement into the next century.

With respect to the first of these goals, the trial of Dusko Tadic should be seen as an effort not merely to bring an individual to justice but to understand the most barbarous butchery to blight Europe in fifty years—and perhaps prevent a repetition of recent history. The record of the trial provides an authoritative and impartial account to which future historians may turn for truth, and future leaders for warning. While there are various means to achieve an historic record of abuses after a war, the most authoritative rendering is possible only through the crucible of a trial that accords full due process.*

---

* One means of establishing an historic record of atrocities which is in vogue these days is through the establishment of a "Truth Commission." See generally, Priscilla B. Hayner, "Fifteen Truth Commissions—1974 to 1994: A Comparative Study," in N. Kritz, ed., *Transnational Justice: How Emerging Democracies Reckon with Former Regimes* 1, (1995), p. 223. Yet, truth commissions are a poor substitute for prosecutions. They do not have prosecutory powers such as the power to subpoena witnesses or punish perjury, and they are viewed as one-

If, to paraphrase American writer and philosopher George Santayana, we are condemned to repeat our mistakes if we have not learned the lessons of the past, then we must establish a reliable record of those mistakes if we wish to prevent their recurrence. The chief prosecutor at Nuremberg, Robert Jackson, underscored the logic of this proposition when he reported to President Truman that one of the most important legacies of the Nuremberg trials was that they documented the Nazi atrocities "with such authenticity and in such detail that there can be no responsible denial of these crimes in the future and no tradition of martyrdom of the Nazi leaders can arise among informed people."[8] Similarly, the Tadic trial has generated a comprehensive record of the nature and extent of international crimes in the Balkans, how they were planned and executed, the fate of individual victims, who gave the orders, and who carried them out. By carefully establishing these facts one witness at a time in the face of vigilant cross-examination by distinguished defense counsel, the Tadic trial produced a definitive account that can endure the test of time and resist the forces of revisionism.

A half century after Nuremberg, historians like Daniel Jonah Goldhagen continue to address the question of how so many ordinary people could be so readily enlisted to participate in atrocities. Goldhagen's recent work, *Hitler's Willing Executioners*, hypothesizes that the Holocaust was a product of the German people's unique cultural predisposition to "eliminationist antisemitism."[9] But the Tadic case suggests a different answer. Lead prosecutor Grant Niemann believes the trial proved that "human beings are universally capable of doing the things Tadic has done."[10] The most extraordinary hallmark of the Yugoslav carnage was its intimacy. Torturers knew their victims and had often grown up alongside them as neighbors and friends. Perhaps the real lesson of the Tadic trial is that given the right set of circumstances, many of us can become willing executioners. It is what the American historian Hannah Arendt, in her classic account of the Eichman trial, referred to as the "banality of evil."* Four centuries earlier,

---

sided since they do not provide those accused of abuses with the panoply of rights available to a criminal defendant.

* Hannah Arendt, *Eichman in Jerusalem: A Report on the Banality of Evil* (1964), p. 252. Arendt concluded that Adolf Eichman, who stood trial in Jeru-

the philosopher Thomas Hobbes hypothesized that there is everywhere a thin line between civilization and barbarism.[11]

What are the circumstances that can lure out this dark side of human nature and push us across that thin line? "That is one of the mysteries of the Yugoslav conflict," says deputy prosecutor Graham Blewitt. "What transforms ordinary people into savages? The Tadic case gave us a glimpse of how provocation, incitement, and propaganda can raise hatred and fear to such an extent that ordinary people turn on their neighbors in a bloodthirsty way," he added.[12] Throw in official sanction, a bit of coercion by persons in authority, pressure from assenting comrades, and opportunities for personal gain. Then add a long history of ethnic tension and you have the active ingredients of ethnic cleansing—Bosnian style.

What is most shocking about the Balkan conflict is not that atrocities were committed, but that the rest of the world did so little to prevent them or bring them to an end. As the Court TV anchor, Terry Moran, observed during the trial, "The Tadic trial proved once again how very difficult it is for people to care about evil in countries and places that are far from their personal experiences. Whether we are humankind in fact as well as in name is an open question in light of what happened in Bosnia and the international community's continuing inadequate response."[13]

Unfortunately, worldwide ethnic nationalism has not likely reached its peak with events in the former Yugoslavia. As Senator Daniel Patrick Moynihan recently observed, "Of the next fifty states which will come into being in the next fifty years, ethnic conflict will almost [always] be the defining characteristic by which that process will take place."[14] Consequently, the questions raised by the savagery in the Balkans—how to preserve minority rights, when to recognize claims to self-determination, how to apply preventive strategies, and when to use force—are likely to confront us again and again in the coming years.[15] More than anything else, the record of the Balkan

---

salem in the summer of 1962 as "the engineer of Hitler's Final Solution," was no monster nor a "perverted sadist" as the prosecution had described him. Rather, Arendt believed that "the trouble with Eichman was precisely that so many were like him, and that the many were neither perverted nor sadistic, that they were, and still are, terribly and terrifyingly normal." (p. 276).

hostilities generated by the Tadic trial should stand as a reminder to the international community of the perils of unchecked ethnic conflict.

If the fate of the victims of Bosnia stands as a lesson to the international community, the image of Dusko Tadic in the dock, transmitted throughout the world by satellite, sends a message to would-be war criminals and human rights abusers around the globe that in the future those who commit such acts may be held accountable for their actions. As Judge McDonald, who presided over the Tadic trial, succinctly put it: "We are here to tell people that the rule of law has to be respected."[16]

The vehicle of a televised trial is an especially potent one both for attaining respect for the rule of law and for deterring future violations. Throughout the summer of 1996, live television coverage of the Tadic trial was carried throughout Bosnia, while private cable TV transmission in Belgrade made the trial accessible to at least a limited Serbian audience. As chief prosecutor Richard Goldstone told me in an interview, "People don't relate to statistics, to generalizations. People can only relate and feel when they hear somebody that they can identify with telling what happened to them. That's why the public broadcasts of the Tadic case can have a strong deterrent effect."[17]

While Nuremberg came too late to help the Nazis' victims, the Tadic trial and the subsequent trials before the Yugoslav Tribunal at least have a chance of deterring Serbs and others from continuing to commit atrocities.[18] There is particular benefit to exposing the unscathed Serbian population in Belgrade to the ghastly consequences of blood-curdling nationalistic rhetoric. Even for those who support Karadzic and Milosevic, "it will be much more difficult to dismiss live testimony given under oath than simple newspaper reports," Graham Blewitt points out. "The testimony will send a reminder in a very dramatic way that these crimes were horrendous."[19]

Although there is ongoing debate about the general deterrent value of criminal punishment,* prosecutor Grant Niemann believes

---

* J. Andenaes, *Punishment and Deterrence* (1974), pp. 45–46, concludes that those who commit crimes under emotional stress (such as murder in the heat of passion) or who have become expert criminals (such as professional safecrackers

"deterrence has a better chance of working with these kinds of crimes than it does with ordinary domestic crimes because the people who commit these acts are not hardened criminals; they're politicians or leaders of the community that have up until now been law abiding people."[20] Richard Goldstone adds, "If people in leadership positions know there's an international court out there, that there's an international prosecutor, and that the international community is going to act as an international police force, I just cannot believe that they aren't going to think twice as to the consequences. Until now, they haven't had to. There's been no enforcement mechanism at all."[21]

Indeed, Richard Goldstone believes the existence of the Tribunal may have already deterred human rights violations in the former Yugoslavia during the Croatian army offensive against Serb rebels in August 1995. "Fear of prosecution in The Hague," he said, "prompted Croat authorities to issue orders to their soldiers to protect Serb civilian rights when Croatia took control of the Krajina and Western Slavonia regions of the country."[22] Unfortunately, it did not have a similar deterrent effect when the Serbs massacred over ten thousand civilians in the "safe area" of Srebrenica the previous month. Perhaps this was because, at the time, the Bosnian Serb leaders responsible for the Srebrenica atrocities (Radovan Karadzic and General Ratko Mladic) had no reason to believe there was a real possibility that they would be brought to trial before the Tribunal.

The Tribunal's deterrent value may ultimately be linked to the eventual fate of these two men. "The international community, acting through the Security Council, has raised the victims' expectations that war criminals would be brought to account for the terrible atrocities they have suffered," Goldstone has said. "If the accused are left free to continue to flout international agreements and international law, is there really less likelihood of further violence in the former Yugoslavia?"[23] He adds, "The failure to make arrests also risks destroying the broader deterrent value of the Tribunal. Future tyrants will be given notice that they also have nothing to fear from international justice for as long as they are surrounded by armed guards."[24]

---

and pickpockets) are less likely than others to be deterred by the threat of criminal punishment.

3

In a sense, four trials were simultaneously held in that compact, high-tech courtroom at The Hague from May through November 1996. First, and most obviously, there was the trial of Dusko Tadic, whose fate was in the hands of the Tribunal. Second, there was the trial of the Bosnian Serb leadership and even the authorities in Belgrade, who were implicitly in the dock with Tadic. In fact, during the first six weeks of the trial, there was nearly as much evidence introduced into the record of Slobodan Milosevic's responsibility for ethnic cleansing as about the particular crimes Tadic had committed. Third, there was the trial of the international community, which had failed to prevent or halt the bloodshed in the former Yugoslavia. The trial made clear that the fate of Bosnia could have been avoided if only the major powers had possessed the political will and judgment to take vigorous actions when the time was right. And fourth, perhaps most importantly, the Tribunal was itself on trial. For in assessing the Tadic trial one must ask, did the Tribunal discharge its duty in a way that will create confidence and faith that guilt and innocence can be adjudicated by an international war crimes tribunal?

"Whatever amounts from this Tribunal," deputy prosecutor Graham Blewitt told me, "there will always be debates about whether it has been successful or not. It's difficult to quantify success. It's not just a matter of looking at the number of indictments, the number of persons tried, and the number of convictions. To me, the best measure of success is if it can achieve the prosecution of individuals fairly, regardless of whether they are convicted or acquitted."[25] Clearly, this international tribunal, with its detailed rules of procedure, represents an advance on its Nuremberg predecessor—notably by forswearing in absentia trials, by making better provisions for the defense, and by providing a right of appeal. Still, at times, the Tribunal tread dangerously close to denying Tadic a fair trial, most conspicuously by its decision to allow certain prosecution witnesses to testify anonymously and by permitting the prosecution to base so much of its case on hearsay. "For those who would respond to criticisms of the Tribunal by saying you have to start somewhere," Tadic's lawyer Michail Wladimiroff told me, "I say that's not good enough when you're dealing with a person whose life and liberty are at stake."[26]

In contrast to most televised trials, the Tadic proceedings were marked by a great deal of substance and very little sensationalism. The rhetoric was restrained, objections were few, and the cross-examination was forceful but seldom insulting. Perhaps this is one of the inherent benefits of a jury-less trial. Then again, the effort to ensure an absolutely fair trial may have cut against the goal of deterrence, for the world media (and viewers) soon lost interest in the orderly, unenthralling proceedings. Reflecting this development, over the course of the trial, the number of print journalists covering the case dwindled from over a hundred to less then a handful. When I visited the Tribunal in July, the only other person in the entire three hundred-seat public gallery was Ed Vulliamy from *The Guardian*. While prosecutor Goldstone repeatedly extolled the educational benefits of the worldwide coverage of the trial and its potential deterrent value, Grant Niemann told me that "the popular appeal and educational aspect of the trial was not part of our consideration at all. Our prosecution strategy, including the order of our witnesses, was designed to secure a conviction, not boost the ratings of Court TV."[27] But, as Fred Graham, the chief anchor and managing editor of Court TV, pointed out, "The prosecutors should have realized that if they presented an airtight case at the cost of boring the world into tuning them out, they had failed to accomplish an important part of their mission."[28]

In addition to deterrence and justice, there is the issue of peace and reconciliation. The Yugoslav Tribunal was created, in the words of Security Council Resolution 827, "to contribute to the restoration and maintenance of peace." As with Nuremberg, the sight of leading war crimes suspects—from all sides of the ethnic divide—standing trial and receiving sentences is supposed to enable a population scarred by the war to apportion blame on individuals and not on the collective. "Avoiding collective guilt will greatly strengthen the peace process in Bosnia," says the Tribunal's press spokesman, Christian Chartier.[29] "We have an obligation to carry forward the lessons of Nuremberg," President Clinton stated. "Those accused of war crimes, crimes against humanity, and genocide must be brought to justice. There must be peace for justice to prevail, but there must be justice when peace prevails," he added.[30] In a similar vein, on the day the Dayton Peace Agreement was signed, the president of the Tribunal, Judge Antonio Cassese, said: "Justice is an indispensable ingredient of the process of national reconciliation. It is essential to the restoration of peaceful and normal relations especially for people who have had to live under a reign of terror. It breaks the cycle of violence, hatred and extrajudicial retribution. Thus peace and justice go hand-in-hand."[31]

If it achieves its aims, the Tribunal will do far more to secure lasting peace in Bosnia than the sixty thousand NATO troops stationed there as part of the Dayton Accords. "If the trials fail," Justice Goldstone warns, "so will any attempt at peace."[32] "It is nonsensical to expect that hundreds of thousands of victims could forgive or forget. And if there is a peace treaty in former Yugoslavia or anywhere else in which the architects of atrocities are left unpunished in leading positions, then all it will be is an interval between cycles of violence," he adds.[33] For this reason, Goldstone insists, the arrest of the indicted Bosnian Serb leader Radovan Karadzic, "is not only in the interests of justice but in the interests of peace."[34]

To some extent, the Dayton Accords transformed the role of the Tribunal. After Dayton, its function was not just to punish the guilty, but through the issuance of indictments, to identify persons who, under the agreement, were prohibited from being elected or appointed members of government in Bosnia. In this way, official accusation became a means of removing from the political scene men like Karadzic who were viewed as the greatest impediment to peace.

4

DUSKO TADIC STOOD TRIAL FOR THE MURDER of thirteen people and the torture of nineteen others. In the United States, he would have been considered among the nation's worst mass murderers, rivaling the likes of Charles Manson, Albert DeSalvo ("the Boston Strangler"), Kenneth Bianchi ("the Hillside Strangler"), David Berkowitz ("Son of Sam"), Ted Bundy, and Jeffrey Dahmer.[35] And yet, in the context of the former Yugoslavia, he is persistently referred to as just a bit player.

A number of critics have even questioned whether the Tribunal was right to focus on such a minor sadist for its first case, whereas Nuremberg tried the key Nazi leaders themselves. If, as one newspaper put it,

"Mr. Tadic was no more than a monstrous tadpole in a pool of sharks,"[36] why should he have been the subject of the Tribunal's first prosecution? Hanne Sophie Greve, the Norwegian judge who served on the 780 Commission, remarked that "he is not the level of person I would like to see at The Hague. I think they should have aimed higher up."[37]

There are several reasons, however, why Dusko Tadic turned out to be an ideal subject for the first trial. First, Tadic fell into the hands of the international community when he was arrested in Germany in 1994. Given the nature of his alleged offenses and the evidence pointing to his guilt, the Tribunal could not turn a blind eye to the allegations. Second, through the Tadic case, the Tribunal has begun to build a pyramid of evidence leading to the principals ultimately responsible for the horrors in Bosnia. Third, to the victims of Dusko Tadic and his colleagues, to those who suffered as a result of the actions of ordinary prison guards and police officials, it is very important that some of their torturers be brought to justice. Only by prosecuting individuals at all levels of responsibility can the victims see that justice has been done. Finally, the Tadic case has provided an opportunity for the Tribunal to work out the kinks in its procedures before turning to more important and more difficult cases.

Asked whether the Tadic case was a good one to begin with, Richard Goldstone replied, "If one had a choice, clearly not. Instead one would have wanted to start with a higher profile defendant. It is highly unsatisfactory that someone at the level of Dusko Tadic should face trial and that those who incited and facilitated his conduct should escape justice and remain unaccountable. But it's really an academic question because we had no choice; Tadic was the only accused available to bring before the Tribunal at a time when the judges, the media, and the international community were clamoring for us to begin prosecutions."[38]

At the time of the Tadic trial, there were just six other indicted Yugoslav war criminals in custody at The Hague: Croatian General Tihomir Blaskic, Bosnian Croat Zdravko Mucic, Serbian Army member Drazen Erdemovic, and three Bosnian Muslims—Zejnil Delalic, Hazim Delic, and Esad Landzo. (The number in custody was at one time eight, but Bosnian Serb general Djordje Djukic had been released for medical reasons prior to his death and Bosnian Serb Goran Lajic was released when it was determined by the prosecution that he was the wrong Goran Lajic.) "If we don't get more arrests for the Tribunal in the fairly near future," laments Richard Goldstone, "then I think people with justification will be able to conclude that we've been effectively prevented from doing the work that we've been set up to do. What worries me about the failure to effect arrests," Goldstone continues, "is that the public perception of the success of the Tribunal is inextricably linked to the resources we are given. The politicians won't want to spend scarce dollars on what the public regards as a failure." Tadic's trial alone cost the Tribunal some twenty million dollars. "Ultimately," Goldstone adds, "credibility is going to depend on whether we are able to put on trial in The Hague the major people who have been indicted."[39]

The challenge for the Tribunal is to work backwards from the likes of Tadic to those who fanned the flames of hatred. Goldstone did not hesitate to indict Karadzic and Mladic, despite criticism at the time that such indictments would derail the peace process. But will the Tribunal's prosecutor have the fortitude to indict Slobodan Milosevic if the mounting evidence establishes his culpability? From a political point of view, such action in the near future would seem to be folly. But from the point of view of justice, it might be indispensable. Despite Goldstone's insistence that the indictment process is immune from politics, there is reason to believe that global diplomacy, for better or worse, affects the Tribunal's policies.

Even bringing Karadzic and Mladic to justice has turned into an uphill battle for the Tribunal. In its resolution conditionally lifting the trade sanctions on Serbia and Republika Srpska (Resolution 1022), the Security Council reiterated that compliance with the orders of the Tribunal was integral to the obligations of Serbia and Republika Srpska under the Dayton agreement. Under the resolution, if either the commander of IFOR, Admiral Leighton Smith of the United States, or United Nations High Representative Carl Bildt of Sweden, had reported that those governments had significantly failed to carry out their obligations, then the sanctions were to be automatically reimposed within five days. However, in another indication of the relationship between international politics and the functioning of the Tribunal, no action was taken when General Ratko Mladic boasted of his freedom in front of television cameras on a ski slope and then appeared in public in Belgrade at the funeral of indicted war criminal,

Djordje Djukic.[40] In May 1996, Tribunal president Antonio Cassese called for the re-imposition of sanctions against Serbia for failing to execute arrest warrants.[41] That request was elevated to a demand in June following the Rule 61 hearing on Karadzic and Mladic. The Security Council responded by stating that it "deplores the failure to date of the Federal Republic of Yugoslavia (Serbia and Montenegro) to execute the arrest warrants," but it neither threatened nor took any further action.[42]

Goldstone places much of the blame on the NATO-led IFOR for Karadzic and Mladic's evasion of justice. "There is no moral, legal or political justification for a military authority to grant effective immunity to persons whom the prosecutor, on behalf of the Security Council, has determined should be brought to trial," he says.[43] "That IFOR, with its force of 60,000 troops, its sophisticated weaponry and intelligence capability, is able to effect such arrests must be beyond question. From a political point of view, can IFOR's men in uniform legitimately argue that they can avoid certain duties because they are potentially dangerous? On a national level, policemen are not infrequently obliged to arrest people who are armed and dangerous. Yet, it is inconceivable that an attorney general would call off the arrests because of the risks to the lives of the arresting officers."[44] Expressing a similar sentiment, Chief Judge Cassese threatened that the Tribunal judges would resign en masse in the summer of 1997 unless the attempt was made to bring Karadzic and Mladic to justice.[45]

Others felt that dispatching NATO troops to hunt down Serbs would be a tragic mistake. They feared it would fuel the conflict by handing the two sides more scores to settle when NATO was scheduled to depart at the end of the year. General Mladic, himself, has said that NATO-led military forces would pay heavily if they tried to arrest him. "They have to understand one thing, that I am very expensive and that my people support me," Mladic told an interviewer.[46] Serbian President Slobodan Milosevic has similarly warned that Bosnia "could blow up" if top Bosnian Serb indicted war criminals were arrested.[47]

The U.S. Joint Chiefs of Staff have told Congress that even if IFOR had orders to arrest the indicted war criminals who are at large in Bosnia, the NATO force just does not have enough intelligence information on their whereabouts.[48] Yet, based on the addresses printed on the Tribunal's "Most Wanted" poster and other leads, a Washington-based group called the Coalition for International Justice easily located thirty-six of the seventy-five indicted war criminals.[49]

According to Richard Goldstone, the trials before the Tribunal are likely to continue for at least the next three to four years.[50] Whether men like Karadzic and Mladic will ever face justice before the Tribunal remains to be seen. Even if they do, however, Goldstone will not have the satisfaction of overseeing their prosecution. At the end of the Tadic trial, the Tribunal's venerated prosecutor resigned from his post to resume his position on South Africa's Constitutional Court. He was succeeded by Justice Louise Arbour, a rising star in the Canadian court system who has presided over some of her country's most politically charged civil rights and war crimes cases. Like Goldstone, Arbour had no previous prosecutorial experience. Yet Goldstone's strengths were his vision and his diplomatic acumen, rather than his administrative or trial skills. Arbour is relatively unknown in legal or human-rights circles outside Canada, but I had the opportunity to speak with her at an international conference in Brussels the week before she was to move her family and belongings to The Hague. Where Goldstone had been tenacious in his quest to launch the prosecutions and obtain resources for the Tribunal, Arbour struck me as somewhat more cautious in her approach, though no less personally committed to the success of the Tribunal. Only time will tell whether she will be able to insure that the Tribunal maintains momentum at a critical period in its history.

5

THE YUGOSLAVIA TRIBUNAL WAS MEANT as a one-time-only ad hoc institution. But soon after the Tribunal had been established, the Security Council found itself faced with an even greater genocide when over half a million Tutsis were massacred by the Hutus in Rwanda during a one hundred-day period in the spring of 1994. Comparing the scale of the crimes committed in Rwanda to Nazi Germany and Bosnia, Rwanda's Prime Minister-designate queried the United Nations Security Council, "Is it because we're Africans that a [similar] court has not been set up?"[51] With the justifiable charge of Eurocentricity ringing through the Security Council, the Council was compelled to establish a Rwanda Tribunal, which has its own trial chambers but shares the appeals chamber and the office of the prosecutor of the Yugoslavia Tribunal.[52]

The creation of the Rwanda Tribunal showed that the machinery designed for the Yugoslavia Tribunal could be employed for other specific circumstances and offenses, thereby avoiding the need to reinvent the wheel in response to each global humanitarian crisis. Why then, one might inquire, has a Tribunal not been set up for the Iraqi violations of international humanitarian law committed during the Gulf War? These violations included the taking of civilian hostages, the use of hostages as human shields, rape and willful killing of civilians, torture of prisoners of war, pillage of Kuwaiti hospitals, indiscriminate Scud missile attacks against civilians in Saudi Arabia and Israel, intentional release of oil into the Persian Gulf, igniting oil fields in Kuwait, and the use of poisonous gas against the Kurds in Northern Iraq. After all, the Security Council has condemned these violations, warned that individuals, as well as the government of Iraq, would be liable for them, and called on member states to submit information on Iraqi atrocities to the council for further action.[53]

There would seem to be a moral imperative to make the attempt to bring such persons to justice before an international Tribunal in light of the scale, brutality, and depravity of their violations of international humanitarian law (which followed the Security Council's warning that individuals would be held accountable). At the very least, an international tribunal for Iraqi war crimes could help develop and preserve the historical record and express international outrage by issuing indictments. And yet, the Security Council shows no signs of taking such action. Nor is there serious consideration of setting up a tribunal for the genocide in Cambodia, the terrorism committed by Libya, or the crimes against humanity recently committed in El Salvador, Haiti, East Timor, or Burundi.

There are several reasons why the Security Council has proven unwilling or unable to continue with the ad hoc approach that was employed for Yugoslavia and Rwanda. The first reason, which is sometimes referred to as "tribunal fatigue," is that the process of reaching a consensus on the tribunal's statute, electing judges, selecting a prosecutor, and appropriating funds has turned out to be extremely time-consuming and politically exhausting for the members of the Security Council. At least one permanent member of the Security Council—China—has openly expressed concern about using the Yugoslavia Tribunal as a precedent for the creation of other ad hoc criminal tribunals,[54] perhaps out of fear that its own human rights record might subject it to the proposed jurisdiction of such future international criminal courts. In addition, the creation of ad hoc tribunals by the council is viewed as inherently unfair by the vast majority of countries of the world that do not possess permanent membership and a veto on the council because the permanent members are able to shield themselves and their allies from the jurisdiction of such tribunals, notwithstanding atrocities that may be committed within their borders. The final reason for hesitance in creating additional ad hoc tribunals is purely economic; that is, the expense of establishing tribunals is simply seen as too much for an organization whose budget is already stretched too thin.

A permanent international criminal court established by treaty is hailed by the majority of countries in the United Nations as the solution to the problems that afflict the ad hoc approach. The U.N. General Assembly has set up a preparatory conference to hammer out a statute for a permanent international criminal court based on the draft completed in 1994 by the International Law Commission.[55] This time, even the United States is giving its support to the endeavor.[56] "Perhaps the real yardstick for assessing the success of the Yugoslavia Tribunal," says prosecutor Goldstone, "is whether it leads to the establishment of a permanent international criminal court."[57] For, there could be no greater contribution to a new world order than to provide the necessary legal machinery to deter and, if necessary, to respond to the most serious violations of international law wherever they occur. Conscious of the risk of failure, Goldstone asks, "What are the alternatives? It seems to me that if you don't have international tribunals, you might as well not have international law."[58] But the experience of the Yugoslavia War Crimes Tribunal suggests that the emerging international criminal justice system might require more than just a court and a prosecutor. To function effectively, it may also need a constabulary.

Appendix A

Chronology of the Yugoslav Conflict

1389

- Ottoman Turks defeat Serbian forces at the battle of Kosovo Polje, beginning a 200-year Ottoman subjugation of Croatia and 400-year Ottoman subjugation of Bosnia and Serbia.

1918

- Creation of the Kingdom of Serbs, Croats and Slovenes, under the crown of Peter I.

1941

- Axis powers invade Yugoslavia and create the Ustasha Independent state of Croatia, which includes Bosnia-Herzegovina. The regime persecutes both Serbs and Jews.
- Josip Broz ("Tito") emerges as leader of partisan resistance.

1944

- With support from the Allies, the Communists, under Tito's leadership, secure control over the territory of Yugoslavia. Tito creates a federal state of six republics (Slovenia, Croatia, Bosnia-Herzegovina, Macedonia, Serbia, and Montenegro) and two autonomous provinces (Kosovo and Vojvodina, both in Serbia).

1948

- Soviet Premier Joseph Stalin breaks relations with Tito's government. With support from the West, Yugoslavia prospers, and Tito becomes one of the leaders of the non-aligned bloc.

1980

- Tito dies.

1986

- Memorandum of the Serb Academy of Arts and Sciences is published, becoming the manifesto of the Serb nationalist movement.

1990

- First multiparty elections held in the six republics of Yugoslavia. Serbian Communist leader Slobodan Milosevic elected Serbian President.

1991

January

- The leaders of the six Yugoslav republics hold a series of meetings in order to find a compromise over the redefinition of the Yugoslav federation. Slovenia and Croatia, strongly pushing for a decentralization of power, threaten to dissociate from the federation unless an agreement is reached by the end of June.

June

- Slovenia and Croatia declare their independence from Yugoslavia. Milan Kucan and Franjo Tudjman, respectively, elected presidents.
- The Yugoslav National army (JNA) invades Slovenia to prevent secession.
- Slovene forces resist JNA in a ten-day war. European Community negotiates a settlement, and JNA forces withdraw from Slovenia.
- Ethnic Serbs in Croatia, with support from JNA, begin war and quickly seize one-third of Croatia. Systematic "ethnic cleansing" by Serbians against Croats is first reported.
- Ethnic Albanians in the Serbian province of Kosovo vote for independence from Serbia. Serbia vows to crush any attempt at secession.

September

- Macedonia votes for independence from Yugoslavia and seeks international recognition.
- The U.N. Security Council adopts Resolution 713 imposing an arms embargo on the territory of Yugoslavia at the request of the Yugoslav government.

November

- Serb soldiers massacre 200 Croatian patients of the hospital in the town of Vukovar, Croatia.

December

- Germany recognizes Slovenia and Croatia as independent states. Other members of the European Community follow suit shortly thereafter.
- Bosnian Serbs declare Serb Republic of Krajina in Bosnian Serb enclave. Rodovan Karadzic elected president of the Bosnian Serb Republic.

1992

January

- U.N. envoy Cyrus Vance negotiates a cease-fire between Croatian and Serbian forces in Croatia. Both sides agree to the deployment of 14,000 U.N. peacekeepers in the Serb-held territories.

February

- The Security Council adopts Resolution 743, establishing a United Nations Protection Force (UNPROFOR) for deployment in the Serb-held territories of Croatia to be known as U.N. Protected Areas (UNPAs).

March

- Bosnia declares its independence. Alija Izetbegovic elected president of Bosnia.
- War between Bosnian government and Bosnian Serb paramilitary troops and JNA forces begins.
- European Community and United States recognize Bosnia as an independent state.

- Bosnian Serbs declare independence and form Serbian Republic of Bosnia.

April

- Serbia and Montenegro agree to establish the Federal Republic of Yugoslavia as successor to the former Yugoslavia.
- Bosnian Serbs, aided by the JNA, seize two-thirds of Bosnia. The Serbian siege of Sarajevo and other Muslim population centers is initiated and Serbian "ethnic cleansing" begins in Bosnia.

May

- The United Nations admits Croatia, Slovenia, and Bosnia-Herzegovina as new members of the U.N.
- Serbia-Montenegro demobilize JNA forces in Bosnia leaving behind heavy weapons and 40,000 troops to form a new Serb paramilitary force.
- The Security Council adopts Resolution 757, imposing economic sanctions on Serbia for its involvement in the conflict in Bosnia.

June

- The Security Council adopts Resolution 761 and deploys 1,000 UNPROFOR troops to secure Sarajevo airport in Bosnia for delivery of humanitarian aid. International aid airlift begins soon thereafter.

July

- War breaks out between Bosnian government and Bosnian Croat forces seeking to unify a portion of Bosnia with Croatia.
- First reports of Serb-run detention camps in Bosnia.

August

- Britain's Independent Television News (ITN) broadcasts film of emaciated detainees at the Omarska camp.
- The U.N. Human Rights Commission meets in the first emergency session in its forty-five-year history to consider the situation in the former Yugoslavia. Former Polish Prime Minister Tadeusz Mazowiecki is appointed special rapporteur on the former Yugoslavia with a mandate to collect evidence

of human rights abuses and war crimes and report back to the commission.

- The Conference on Security and Cooperation in Europe (CSCE) appoints three rapporteurs to investigate the reported atrocities and to make recommendations regarding the feasibility of attributing personal responsibility therefor.
- The Security Council adopts Resolution 770, authorizing member states to take "all necessary measures" to ensure the delivery of relief supplies throughout Bosnia.
- The Security Council adopts Resolution 771, condemning violations of international humanitarian law, demanding that the International Committee of the Red Cross be granted access to all detention centers, and requesting states to submit information in their possession about atrocities in the former Yugoslavia to the United Nations.
- The International Conference on the Former Yugoslavia is convened, chaired by U.N. envoy Cyrus Vance and E.C. envoy Lord David Owen.

September

- The Security Council adopts Resolution 776, enlarging the size and mandate of UNPROFOR to enable it to provide protection to humanitarian relief convoys in Bosnia.

October

- The Security Council adopts Resolution 780, establishing a War Crimes Commission to investigate atrocities in the former Yugoslavia.
- The Security Council adopts Resolution 786, establishing a no-fly-zone over Bosnia. However, no enforcement for the no-fly-zone is authorized.

November

- The Security Council adopts Resolution 787, strengthening the embargo on Serbia-Montenegro and authorizing member States to enforce the embargo on the high seas.

December

- U.S. Secretary of State Lawrence Eagleburger publicly identifies persons suspected of war crimes in the former Yugoslavia, including Serbian President Slobodan Milosevic; Vojislav Seselj, leader of the Serbian Radical Party; Serbian member of parliament Zaljko Raznjatovic (Commander Arkan); Radovan Karadzic, the leader of the Bosnian Serbs; and General Ratko Mladic, commander of the Bosnian Serb military forces.

1993

January

- The Vance-Owen peace plan is presented to divide Bosnia into ten autonomous provinces under a decentralized federal government. Bosnian Croat forces accept the plan, but it is rejected by the Bosnian government and Bosnian Serb forces.

February

- CSCE rapporteurs issue their report, proposing establishment of a war crimes tribunal for the Former Yugoslavia.
- U.N. War Crimes Commission established by Security Council Resolution 780 issues a preliminary report, concluding that war crimes and crimes against humanity had been committed in the former Yugoslavia and recommending the establishment of a war crimes tribunal.
- The Security Council adopts Resolution 808, deciding to establish a war crimes tribunal and requesting the Secretary-General to submit options for the tribunal's statute for the Council's consideration.

March

- Bosnian government and Bosnian Croats agree to modification of the Vance-Owen plan and signal acceptance, but Bosnian Serbs maintain their opposition to the accord.
- The Security Council adopts Resolution 816, authorizing enforcement of the no-fly-zone over Bosnia through NATO airstrikes in close coordination with the United Nations Secretary General.

April

- Bosnian Croats step up their offensive, precipitating renewed wave of Croat "ethnic cleansing" in Bosnia.

- The Security Council adopts Resolution 819 designating the Muslim enclave of Srebrenica a "safe area."
- The Security Council adopts Resolution 820, further strengthening the economic embargo against Serbia-Montenegro and Serb-held territory in Bosnia.
- Serbian President Milosevic agrees to support Vance-Owen peace plan, but the Bosnian Serb parliament continues to reject plan.
- The United States proposes lift-and-strike option: lift arms embargo against Bosnian government and support its ground forces with airpower. The European Union rejects the proposal.
- The Security Council and General Assembly adopt resolutions deciding that Serbia-Montenegro is not entitled to continue Yugoslavia's membership in the United Nations.
- The Security Council adopts Resolution 827 establishing a War Crimes Tribunal.

May

- Serbian President Milosevic's government condemns the Bosnian Serb rejection of the Vance-Owen plan and vows to cut off all military assistance to the Bosnian Serbs.
- The Security Council designates five additional Bosnian cities (Sarajevo, Bihac, Tuzla, Gorazde, and Zepa) as safe areas, but attacks against these areas continue.

June

- Thorvald Stoltenberg of Norway replaces Cyrus Vance as U.N. mediator. A new peace proposal providing for the division of Bosnia into three ethnic entities is accepted by Croatia and Serbia-Montenegro, but rejected by the Bosnian government.

August

- The Security Council adopts Resolution 857, nominating twenty-three candidates for the judges of the War Crimes Tribunal, and the General Assembly elects the Tribunal's eleven judges in ten contentious rounds of voting.

October

- Croatian nationalist army of Bosnia massacres Muslim population of the Bosnian city of Stupni Do. The U.N. threatens sanctions against Croatia.
- The Security Council adopts Resolution 877, appointing Ramon Escovar-Salam as prosecutor for the War Crimes Tribunal. He subsequently resigns from the position before even being sworn in.

November

- The judges of the War Crimes Tribunal are sworn in and begin to draft the Rules of Procedure and Evidence.

1994

February

- Sixty-eight civilians are killed and two hundred others are wounded in Sarajevo marketplace massacre when Bosnian Serbs launch mortar strike into bread lines.
- NATO shoots down four Bosnian Serb aircraft for violating the no-fly-zone, marking the first offensive action by NATO in its history.
- Bosnian Serbs begin shelling U.N. safe areas.
- Bosnian government and Bosnian Croats end hostilities and announce the formation of a federation.
- Graham Blewitt of Australia is appointed deputy prosecutor of the War Crimes Tribunal and begins to assemble staff.
- Dusko Tadic is arrested in Germany after refugees identify him as the "Butcher of Omarska."

April

- Safe area of Gorazde falls to Bosnian Serbs.

May

- U.S. Senate votes to unilaterally lift arms embargo against Bosnian government despite opposition from permanent members of the Security Council. France threatens to withdraw its U.N. peacekeeping troops if the embargo is unilaterally lifted.

July

- The Security Council adopts Resolution 936 appointing South African judge Richard Goldstone to the position of prosecutor of the War Crimes Tribunal.
- Contact Group (United States, France, Germany, Great Britain, and Russia) proposes new peace plan based on a territory division of 51% Bosnian Confederation, 49% Bosnian Serbs. The proposal is accepted by Croatia, Serbia-Montenegro, and the government of Bosnia, but the Bosnian Serbs reject the plan.

August

- Serbian President Slobodan Milosevic criticizes Bosnian Serb rejection of the peace proposal and announces that Serbia-Montenegro will close its borders to Bosnian Serbs for all purposes except the delivery of humanitarian goods.

November

- Bosnian government and Bosnian Croat forces launch a coordinated assault on Bosnian Serb positions.
- The U.N. authorizes NATO airstrikes on any aircraft launched from either Bosnian or Croatian territory.
- The United States announces that it will no longer enforce the arms embargo with its ships.
- The War Crimes Tribunal issues its first indictment against Dragan Nikolic, the Serb commander of the Susica concentration camp in Bosnia.
- The War Crimes Tribunal conducts its first hearing concerning a request that Germany defer to the competence of the Tribunal in the Tadic case.

1995

February

- Dusko Tadic is indicted by the War Crimes Tribunal.

April

- Dusko Tadic is transferred from Germany to the War Crimes Tribunal. Pre-trial proceedings begin in the Tadic case.

May

- Croatian government forces recapture portions of western Slavonia from Croatian Serb forces. Croatian Serbs launch missile attacks on Croatian capital.
- NATO launches airstrikes against Serb heavy weapons which are attacking Sarajevo.
- Bosnian Serb forces launch attack on five of the six U.N. safe areas. They take U.N. peacekeepers hostage, chaining them to military targets to prevent NATO airstrikes.

July

- Bosnian Serb forces capture Srebrenica and Zepa. Survivors witness Bosnian Serb General Mladic personally participating in mass execution of Muslim men and boys there.
- Rodovan Karadzic, the leader of the Bosnian Serbs, and Ratko Mladic, the commander of the Bosnian Serb army are indicted by the War Crimes Tribunal.

August

- Croatian army recaptures all remaining territory of western Slavonia from Croatian Serb forces.
- Bosnian Serbs shell the Sarajevo marketplace. In response, NATO launches Operation Deliberate Force, bombing numerous Bosnian Serb targets.
- Bosnian Serbs authorize Serbian president Milosevic to negotiate a peace agreement on their behalf.
- War Crimes Tribunal's trial chamber issues decisions on the jurisdiction of the Tribunal and protective measures for witnesses in the Tadic case.

October

- War Crimes Tribunal's appeals chamber issues decision on question of the jurisdiction of the Tribunal.

November

- Peace talks held in Dayton, Ohio, attended by the presidents of Croatia, Bosnia, and Serbia. Peace accord is initialed, and is later accepted by Bosnian Serbs.
- NATO pledges 60,000 troops, including 20,000 from the United States, to implement the Dayton accord.

- The Security Council adopts Resolution 1022, conditionally lifting the sanctions imposed on Serbia and the Bosnian Serbs.

1996

February

- The Security Council adopts Resolution 1047, appointing Judge Louise Arbour of Canada to replace Richard Goldstone as the chief prosecutor of the War Crimes Tribunal, effective October 1996.
- Siege of Sarajevo officially ends.

May

- The trial of Dusko Tadic begins.

June

- Drazen Erdemovic becomes the first indicted Yugoslav war criminal to plead guilty.
- The Tadic trial is interrupted for a ten-day Rule 61 hearing for Radovan Karadzic and Ratko Mladic. At the conclusion of the hearing, the Tribunal issues international arrest warrants for Karadzic and Mladic.
- Radovan Karadzic agrees to leave Bosnian Serb politics.

August

- The prosecution rests its case in the Tadic trial.
- The defense files a motion to dismiss most of the charges against Tadic.

September

- The defense motion to dismiss is denied and the defense begins to call its witnesses.
- Nationwide elections held pursuant to the Dayton plan. Muslim leader Alija Izetbegovic, the former president of Bosnia, garners the most votes and is elected chairman of the three-person presidency. Momcilo Krajisnik was elected to represent the Bosnian Serbs, and Kresimir Zubak is elected to represent the Bosnian Croats.

October

- The Security Council adopts Resolution 1074, permanently lifting the sanctions imposed on Serbia and the Bosnian Serbs.

November

- The defense rests its case and the prosecution presents rebuttal testimony in the Tadic case.
- Drazen Erdemovic, a Croat foot soldier who confessed to taking part in the execution of more than 1,000 Muslim civilians outside the "safe area" of Srebrenica, is sentenced by the Yugoslavia Tribunal to ten years imprisonment.
- The prosecution and defense present closing arguments in the Tadic case.

1997

April

- Dusko Tadic fires his defense counsel and retains Milan Vujin to handle the remainder of his case.

May

- The Tribunal announces its verdict in the Tadic case. Tadic is found guilty of eleven of the thirty-four counts in the indictment. Attorney Milan Vujin files an appeal.

Appendix B

Statute of the Yugoslavia Tribunal

S/RES 827 (1993)
25 May 1993
ENGLISH
ORIGINAL: ENGLISH AND FRENCH

France, New Zealand, Russian Federation, Spain, United Kingdom of Great Britain and Northern Ireland and United States of America

The Security Council,

Reaffirming its resolution 713 (1991) of 25 September 1991 and all subsequent relevant resolutions,

Having considered the report of the Secretary-General (S/25704 and Add.1) pursuant to paragraph 2 of resolution 808 (1993),

Expressing once again its grave alarm at continuing reports of widespread and flagrant violations of international humanitarian law occurring within the territory of the former Yugoslavia, and especially in the Republic of Bosnia and Herzegovina, including reports of mass killings, massive, organized and systematic detention and rape of women, and the continuance of the practice of "ethnic cleansing", including for the acquisition and the holding of territory,

Determining that this situation continues to constitute a threat to international peace and security,

Determined to put an end to such crimes and to take effective measures to bring to justice the persons who are responsible for them,

Convinced that in the particular circumstances of the former Yugoslavia the establishment as an ad hoc measure by the Council of an international tribunal and the prosecution of persons responsible for serious violations of international humanitarian law would enable this aim to be achieved and would contribute to the restoration and maintenance of peace,

Believing that the establishment of an international tribunal and the prosecution of persons responsible for the above-mentioned violations of international humanitarian law will contribute to ensuring that such violations are halted and effectively redressed,

Noting in this regard the recommendation by the Co-Chairman of the Steering Committee of the International Conference on the Former Yugoslavia for the establishment of such a tribunal (S/25221),

Reaffirming in this regard its decision in resolution 808 (1993) that an international tribunal shall be established for the prosecution of persons responsible for serious violations of international humanitarian law committed in the territory of the former Yugoslavia since 1991,

Considering that, pending the appointment of the Prosecutor of the International Tribunal, the Commission of Experts established pursuant to resolution 780 (1992) should continue on an urgent basis the collection of information relating to evidence of grave breaches of the Geneva Conventions and other violations of international humanitarian law as proposed in its interim report (S/25274),

Acting under Chapter VII of the Charter of the United Nations,

1. *Approves* the report of the Secretary-General;

2. *Decides* hereby to establish an international tribunal for the sole purpose of prosecuting persons responsible for serious violations of international humanitarian law committed in the territory of the former Yugoslavia between 1 January 1991 and a date to be determined by the Security Council upon the restoration of peace and to this end to adopt the Statute of the International Tribunal annexed to the above-mentioned report;

3. *Requests* the Secretary-General to submit to the judges of the International Tribunal, upon their election, any suggestions received from States for the rules of procedure and evidence called for in Article 15 of the statute of the International Tribunal;

4. *Decides* that all states shall cooperate fully with the International Tribunal and its organs in accordance with the present resolution and

the statute of the International Tribunal and that consequently all states shall take any measures necessary under their domestic law to implement the provisions of the present resolution and the Statute, including the obligation of states to comply with requests for assistance or orders issued by a Trial Chamber under Article 29 of the Statute;

5. *Urges* States and intergovernmental and non-governmental organizations to contribute funds, equipment and services to the International Tribunal, including the offer of expert personnel;

6. *Decides* that the determination of the seat of the International Tribunal is subject to the conclusion of appropriate arrangements between the United Nations and the Netherlands acceptable to the Council, and that the International Tribunal may sit elsewhere when it considers it necessary for the efficient exercise of its functions;

7. *Decides* also that the work of the International Tribunal shall be carried out without prejudice to the right of the victims to seek, through appropriate means, compensation for damages incurred as a result of violations of international humanitarian law;

8. *Requests* the Secretary-General to implement urgently the present resolution and in particular to make practical arrangements for the effective functioning of the International Tribunal at the earliest time and to report periodically to the Council;

9. *Decides* to remain actively seized of the matter.

Annex
Statute of the International Tribunal

Having been established by the Security Council acting under Chapter VII of the Charter of the United Nations, the International Tribunal for the Prosecution of Persons Responsible for Serious Violations of International Humanitarian Law Committed in the Territory of the Former Yugoslavia since 1991 (hereinafter referred to as "the International Tribunal") shall function in accordance with the provisions of the present Statute.

Article 1
Competence of the International Tribunal

The International Tribunal shall have the power to prosecute persons responsible for serious violations of international humanitarian law committed in the territory of the former Yugoslavia since 1991 in accordance with the provisions of the present Statute.

Article 2

Grave breaches of the Geneva Conventions of 1949

The International Tribunal shall have the power to prosecute persons committing or ordering to be committed grave breaches of the Geneva Conventions of 12 August 1949, namely the following acts against persons or property protected under the provisions of the relevant Geneva Convention:

(a) wilful killing;
(b) torture or inhuman treatment, including biological experiments;
(c) wilfully causing great suffering or serious injury to body or health;
(d) extensive destruction and appropriation of property, not justified by military necessity and carried out unlawfully and wantonly;
(e) compelling a prisoner of war or a civilian to serve in the forces of a hostile power;
(f) wilfully depriving a prisoner of war or a civilian of the rights of fair and regular trial;
(g) unlawful deportation or transfer or unlawful confinement of a civilian;
(h) taking civilians as hostages.

Article 3

Violations of the laws or customs of war

The International Tribunal shall have the power to prosecute persons violating the laws or customs of war. Such violations shall include, but not be limited to:

(a) employment of poisonous weapons or other weapons calculated to cause unnecessary suffering;
(b) wanton destruction of cities, towns or villages, or devastation not justified by military necessity;
(c) attack, or bombardment, by whatever means, of undefended towns, villages, dwellings, or buildings;

(d) seizure of, destruction or wilful damage done to institutions dedicated to religion, charity and education, the arts and sciences, historic monuments and works of art and science;
(e) plunder of public or private property.

Article 4
Genocide

1. The International Tribunal shall have the power to prosecute persons committing genocide as defined in paragraph 2 of this article or of committing any of the other acts enumerated in paragraph 3 of this article.

2. Genocide means any of the following acts committed with intent to destroy, in whole or in part, a national, ethnic, racial or religious group, as such:

(a) killing members of the group;
(b) causing serious bodily or mental harm to members of the group;
(c) deliberately inflicting on the group conditions of life calculated to bring about its physical destruction in whole or in part;
(d) imposing measures intended to prevent births within the group;
(e) forcibly transferring children of the group to another group.

3. The following acts shall be punishable:

(a) genocide;
(b) conspiracy to commit genocide;
(c) direct and public incitement to commit genocide;
(d) attempt to commit genocide;
(e) complicity in genocide.

Article 5
Crimes against humanity

The International Tribunal shall have the power to prosecute persons responsible for the following crimes when committed in armed conflict, whether international or internal in character, and directed against any civilian population:

(a) murder;
(b) extermination;

(c) enslavement;
(d) deportation;
(e) imprisonment;
(f) torture;
(g) rape;
(h) persecutions on political, racial and religious grounds;
(i) other inhumane acts.

Article 6
Personal jurisdiction

The International Tribunal shall have jurisdiction over natural persons pursuant to the provisions of the present statute.

Article 7
Individual criminal responsibility

1. A person who planned, instigated, ordered, committed or otherwise aided and abetted in the planning, preparation or execution of a crime referred to in articles 2 to 5 of the present Statute, shall be individually responsible for the crime.

2. The official position of any accused person, whether as head of State or Government or as a responsible Government official, shall not relieve such person of criminal responsibility nor mitigate punishment.

3. The fact that any of the acts referred to in articles 2 to 5 of the present statute was committed by a subordinate does not relieve his superior of criminal responsibility if he knew or had reason to know that the subordinate was about to commit such acts or had done so and the superior failed to take the necessary and reasonable measures to prevent such acts or to punish the perpetrators thereof.

4. The fact that an accused person acted pursuant to an order of a Government or of a superior shall not relieve him of criminal responsibility, but may be considered in mitigation of punishment if the International Tribunal determines that justice so requires.

Article 8
Territorial and temporal jurisdiction

The territorial jurisdiction of the International Tribunal shall extend to the territory of the former Socialist Federal Republic of Yugoslavia, including its land surface, airspace and territorial waters. The temporal jurisdiction of the International Tribunal shall extend to a period beginning on 1 January 1991.

Article 9

Concurrent jurisdiction

1. The International Tribunal and national courts shall have concurrent jurisdiction to prosecute persons for serious violations of international humanitarian law committed in the territory of the former Yugoslavia since 1 January 1991.

2. The International Tribunal shall have primacy over national courts. At any stage of the procedure, the International Tribunal may formally request national courts to defer to the competence of the International Tribunal in accordance with the present Statute and the Rules of Procedure and Evidence of the International Tribunal.

Article 10

Non-bis-in-idem

1. No person shall be tried before a national court for acts constituting serious violations of international humanitarian law under the present Statute, for which he or she has already been tried by the International Tribunal.

2. A person who has been tried by a national court for acts constituting serious violations of international humanitarian law may be subsequently tried by the International Tribunal only if:

(a) the act for which he or she was tried was characterized as an ordinary crime; or

(b) the national court proceedings were not impartial or independent, were designed to shield the accused from international criminal responsibility, or the case was not diligently prosecuted.

3. In considering the penalty to be imposed on a person convicted of a crime under the present Statute, the International Tribunal shall take into account the extent to which any penalty imposed by a national court on the same person for the same act has already been served.

Article 11

Organization of the International Tribunal

The International Tribunal shall consist of the following organs:

(a) The Chambers, comprising two Trial Chambers and an Appeals Chamber;

(b) The Prosecutor, and

(c) A Registry, servicing both the Chambers and the Prosecutor.

Article 12

Composition of the Chambers

The Chambers shall be composed of eleven independent judges, no two of whom may be nationals of the same State, who shall serve as follows:

(a) Three judges shall serve in each of the Trial Chambers;

(b) Five judges shall serve in the Appeals Chamber.

Article 13

Qualifications and election of judges

1. The judges shall be persons of high moral character, impartiality and integrity who possess the qualifications required in their respective countries for appointment to the highest judicial offices. In the overall composition of the Chambers due account shall be taken of the experience of the judges in criminal law, international law, including international humanitarian law and human rights law.

2. The judges of the International Tribunal shall be elected by the General Assembly from a list submitted by the Security Council, in the following manner:

(a) The Secretary-General shall invite nominations for judges of the International Tribunal from States Members of the United Nations and non-member States maintaining permanent observer missions at United Nations Headquarters;

(b) Within sixty days of the date of the invitation of the Secretary-General, each State may nominate up to two candidates meeting the qualifications set out in paragraph 1 above, no two of whom shall be of the same nationality;

(c) The Secretary-General shall forward the nominations received to the Security Council. From the nominations received the Security Council shall establish a list of not less than twenty-two and not more than thirty-three candidates, taking due account of the adequate representation of the principal legal systems of the world;

(d) The President of the Security Council shall transmit the list of candidates to the President of the General Assembly. From that list the General Assembly shall elect the eleven judges of the International Tribunal. The candidates who receive an absolute majority of the votes of the States Members of the United Nations and of the non-member States maintaining permanent observer missions at United Nations Headquarters, shall be declared elected. Should two candidates of the same nationality obtain the required majority vote, the one who received the higher number of votes shall be considered elected.

3. In the event of a vacancy in the Chambers, after consultation with the Presidents of the Security Council and of the General Assembly, the Secretary-General shall appoint a person meeting the qualifications of paragraph 1 above, for the remainder of the term of office concerned.

4. The judges shall be elected for a term of four years. The terms and conditions of service shall be those of the judges of the International Court of Justice. They shall be eligible for re-election.

Article 14

Officers and members of the Chambers

1. The judges of the International Tribunal shall elect a President.

2. The President of the International Tribunal shall be a member of the Appeals Chamber and shall preside over its proceedings.

3. After consultation with the judges of the International Tribunal, the President shall assign the judges to the Appeals Chamber and to the Trial Chambers. A judge shall serve only in the Chamber to which he or she was assigned.

4. The judges of each Trial Chamber shall elect a Presiding Judge, who shall conduct all of the proceedings of the Trial Chamber as a whole.

Article 15

Rules of procedure and evidence

The judges of the International Tribunal shall adopt rules of procedure and evidence for the conduct of the pre-trial phase of the proceedings, trials and appeals, the admission of evidence, the protection of victims and witnesses and other appropriate matters.

Article 16
The Prosecutor

1. The Prosecutor shall be responsible for the investigation and prosecution of persons responsible for serious violations of international humanitarian law committed in the territory of the former Yugoslavia since 1 January 1991.

2. The Prosecutor shall act independently as a separate organ of the International Tribunal. He or she shall not seek or receive instructions from any Government or from any other source.

3. The Office of the Prosecutor shall be composed of a Prosecutor and such other qualified staff as may be required.

4. The Prosecutor shall be appointed by the Security Council on nomination by the Secretary-General. He or she shall be of high moral character and possess the highest level of competence and experience in the conduct of investigations and prosecutions of criminal cases. The Prosecutor shall serve for a four-year term and be eligible for reappointment. The terms and conditions of service of the Prosecutor shall be those of an Under-Secretary-General of the United Nations.

5. The staff of the Office of the Prosecutor shall be appointed by the Secretary-General on the recommendation of the Prosecutor.

Article 17
The Registry

1. The Registry shall be responsible for the administration and servicing of the International Tribunal.

2. The Registry shall consist of a Registrar and such other staff as may be required.

3. The Registrar shall be appointed by the Secretary-General after consultation with the President of the International Tribunal. He or she shall serve for a four-year term and be eligible for reappointment. The terms and conditions of service of the Registrar shall be those of an Assistant Secretary-General of the United Nations.

4. The staff of the Registry shall be appointed by the Secretary-General on the recommendation of the Registrar.

Article 18

Investigation and preparation of indictment

1. The Prosecutor shall initiate investigations ex-officio or on the basis of information obtained from any source, particularly from Governments, United Nations organs, intergovernmental and non-governmental organizations. The prosecutor shall assess the information received or obtained and decide whether there is sufficient basis to proceed.

2. The Prosecutor shall have the power to question suspects, victims and witnesses, to collect evidence and to conduct on-site investigations. In carrying out these tasks, the Prosecutor may, as appropriate, seek the assistance of the State authorities concerned.

3. If questioned, the suspect shall be entitled to be assisted by counsel of his own choice, including the right to have legal assistance assigned to him without payment by him in any such case if he does not have sufficient means to pay for it, as well as to necessary translation into and from a language he speaks and understands.

4. Upon a determination that a prima facie case exists, the Prosecutor shall prepare an indictment containing a concise statement of the facts and the crime or crimes with which the accused is charged under the Statute. The indictment shall be transmitted to a judge of the Trial Chamber.

Article 19

Review of the indictment

1. The judge of the Trial Chamber to whom the indictment has been transmitted shall review it. If satisfied that a prima facie case has been established by the prosecutor, he shall confirm the indictment. If not so satisfied, the indictment shall be dismissed.

2. Upon confirmation of an indictment, the judge may, at the request of the Prosecutor, issue such orders and warrants for the arrest, detention, surrender or transfer of persons, and any other orders as may be required for the conduct of the trial.

Article 20

Commencement and conduct of trial proceedings

1. The Trial Chambers shall ensure that a trial is fair and expeditious and that proceedings are conducted in accordance with the rules

of procedure and evidence, with full respect for the rights of the accused and due regard for the protection of victims and witnesses.

2. A person against whom an indictment has been confirmed shall, pursuant to an order or an arrest warrant of the International Tribunal, be taken into custody, immediately informed of the charges against him and transferred to the International Tribunal.

3. The Trial Chamber shall read the indictment, satisfy itself that the rights of the accused are respected, confirm that the accused understands the indictment, and instruct the accused to enter a plea. The Trial Chamber shall then set the date for trial.

4. The hearings shall be public unless the Trial Chamber decides to close the proceedings in accordance with its rules of procedure and evidence.

Article 21
Rights of the accused

1. All persons shall be equal before the International Tribunal.

2. In the determination of charges against him, the accused shall be entitled to a fair and public hearing, subject to article 22 of the Statute.

3. The accused shall be presumed innocent until proved guilty according to the provisions of the present Statute.

4. In the determination of any charge against the accused pursuant to the present Statute, the accused shall be entitled to the following minimum guarantees, in full equality:

(a) to be informed promptly and in detail in a language which he understands of the nature and cause of the charge against him;

(b) to have adequate time and facilities for the preparation of his defense and to communicate with counsel of his own choosing;

(c) to be tried without undue delay;

(d) to be tried in his presence, and to defend himself in person or through legal assistance of his own choosing; to be informed, if he does not have legal assistance, of this right; and to have legal assistance assigned to him, in any case where the interests of justice so require, and without payment by him in any such case if he does not have sufficient means to pay for it;

(e) to examine, or have examined, the witnesses against him and to obtain the attendance and examination of witnesses on his behalf under the same conditions as witnesses against him;

(f) to have the free assistance of an interpreter if he cannot understand or speak the language used in the International Tribunal;

(g) not to be compelled to testify against himself or to confess guilt.

Article 22

Protection of victims and witnesses

The International Tribunal shall provide in its rules of procedure and evidence for the protection of victims and witnesses. Such protection measures shall include, but shall not be limited to, the conduct of *in camera* proceedings and the protection of the victim's identity.

Article 23

Judgement

1. The Trial Chambers shall pronounce judgements and impose sentences and penalties on persons convicted of serious violations of international humanitarian law.

2. The judgement shall be rendered by a majority of the judges of the Trial Chamber, and shall be delivered by the Trial Chamber in public. It shall be accompanied by a reasoned opinion in writing, to which separate or dissenting opinions may be appended.

Article 24

Penalties

1. The penalty imposed by the Trial chamber shall be limited to imprisonment. In determining the terms of imprisonment, the Trial Chambers shall have recourse to the general practice regarding prison sentences in the courts of the former Yugoslavia.

2. In imposing the sentences, the Trial Chambers should take into account such factors as the gravity of the offense and the individual circumstances of the convicted person.

3. In addition to imprisonment, the Trial Chambers may order the return of any property and proceeds acquired by criminal conduct, including by means of duress, to their rightful owners.

Article 25
Appellate proceedings

1. The Appeals Chamber shall hear appeals from persons convicted by the Trial Chambers or from the Prosecutor on the following grounds:

(a) an error on a question of law invalidating the decision; or

(b) an error of fact which has occasioned a miscarriage of justice.

2. The Appeals Chamber may affirm, reverse or revise the decisions taken by the Trial chambers.

Article 26
Review proceedings

Where a new fact has been discovered which was not known at the time of the proceedings before the Trial chambers or the Appeals Chamber and which could have been a decisive factor in reaching the decision, the convicted person or the Prosecutor may submit to the International Tribunal an application for review of the judgement.

Article 27
Enforcement of sentences

Imprisonment shall be served in a State designated by the International Tribunal from a list of States which have indicated to the Security Council their willingness to accept convicted persons. Such imprisonment shall be in accordance with the applicable law of the State concerned, subject to the supervision of the International Tribunal.

Article 28
Pardon or commutation of sentences

If, pursuant to the applicable law of the State in which the convicted person is imprisoned, he or she is eligible for pardon or commutation of sentence, the State concerned shall notify the International Tribunal accordingly. The President of the International Tribunal, in consultation with the judges, shall decide the matter on the basis of the interests of justice and the general principles of law.

Article 29
Cooperation and judicial assistance

1. States shall cooperate with the International Tribunal in the investigation and prosecution of persons accused of committing serious violations of international humanitarian law.

2. States shall comply without undue delay with any request for assistance or an order issued by a Trial Chamber, including, but not limited to:

(a) the identification and location of persons;
(b) the taking of testimony and the production of evidence;
(c) the service of documents;
(d) the arrest or detention of persons;
(e) the surrender or the transfer of the accused to the International Tribunal.

Article 30
The status, privileges and immunities of the International Tribunal

1. The Convention on the Privileges and Immunities of the United Nations of 13 February 1946 shall apply to the International Tribunal, the judges, the Prosecutor and his staff, and the Registrar and his staff.

2. The judges, the Prosecutor and the Registrar shall enjoy the privileges and immunities, exemptions and facilities accorded to diplomatic envoys, in accordance with international law.

3. The staff of the Prosecutor and of the Registrar shall enjoy the privileges and immunities accorded to officials of the United Nations under articles V and VII of the Convention referred to in paragraph 1 of this article.

4. Other persons, including the accused, required at the seat of the International Tribunal shall be accorded such treatment as is necessary for the proper functioning of the International Tribunal.

Article 31
Seat of the International Tribunal

The International Tribunal shall have its seat at The Hague.

Article 32

Expenses of the International Tribunal

The expenses of the International Tribunal shall be borne by the regular budget of the United Nations in accordance with Article 17 of the Charter of the United Nations.

Article 33

Working languages

The working languages of the International Tribunal shall be English and French.

Article 34

Annual report

The President of the International Tribunal shall submit an annual report of the International Tribunal to the Security Council and to the General Assembly.

Appendix C

Indictment of Dusko Tadic

THE INTERNATIONAL CRIMINAL TRIBUNAL
FOR THE FORMER YUGOSLAVIA

CASE NO: IT-94-1-T

THE PROSECUTOR OF
THE TRIBUNAL
AGAINST
DUŠAN TADIĆ a/k/a "DULE" a/k/a "DUŠAN"
GORAN BORVONICA

INDICTMENT (AMENDED)

Richard J. Goldstone, Prosecutor of the International Criminal Tribunal for the former Yugoslavia, pursuant to his authority under Article 18 of the Statute of the International Criminal Tribunal for the former Yugoslavia ("The Statute of the Tribunal") and Rule 50 of the Rules of Procedure and Evidence of the Tribunal, charges:

1. Beginning on about 23 May 1992, Serb forces, supported by artillery and heavy weapons, attacked Bosnian Muslim and Croat population centres in opština Prijedor, Bosnia-Herzegovina. In the following days, most of the Muslims and Croats were forced from their homes and seized by the Serb forces. The Serb forces then unlawfully confined thousands of Muslims and Croats in the Omarska, Keraterm and Trnopolje camps. The accused, **Dušan TADIĆ a/k/a "Dule" a/k/a "Dušan"**, participated in the attack on, seizure, murder and maltreatment of Bosnian Muslims and Croats in opština Prijedor both within the camps and outside the camps, between the period begin-

ning about 23 May 1992 and ending about 31 December 1992. The accused, **Goran BOROVNICA**, participated with **Duško TADIĆ** in the killing of Bosnian Muslims in the Kozarac area, as set forth below:

Background

2.1 About 23 May 1992, approximately three weeks after Serbs forcibly took control of governmental authority in opština Prijedor, intensive shelling by Serb forces of Bosnian Muslim and Croat areas in opština Prijedor caused Muslim and Croat residents to flee their homes. The majority of them were seized by Serb forces. As the Serb forces rounded up the Muslim and Croat residents, they forced the Muslims and Croats to march in columns bound for one or another of the prison camps that the Serb authorities had established in the opština. The Serb forces pulled many of the Muslims and Croats from the columns and shot or beat them on the spot.

2.2 On about 25 May 1992, shortly after the start of large scale military attacks on Muslim population centres, the Serb forces began taking prisoners to the Omarska, Keraterm and Trnopolje camps.

2.3 During the next several weeks, the Serb forces continued to round up Muslims and Croats from Kozarac, Prijedor town, and other places in the opština and interned them in the camps. Many of Prijedor's Muslim and Croat intellectuals, professional and political leaders were sent to Omarska. There were approximately 40 women in the camp, and all the other prisoners in the camp, were men.

2.4 Within the area of the Omarska mining complex that the Serb authorities used for the camp, the camp authorities generally confined the prisoners in three different buildings: the administration building, where interrogations took place and most of the women were confined; the garage or hangar building; the "white house," a small building where particularly severe beatings were administered; and on a cement courtyard area between the buildings known as the "pista". There was another small building, known as the "red house", where prisoners were sometimes taken but most often did not emerge alive.

2.5 Living conditions at Omarska were brutal. Prisoners were crowded together with little or no facilities for personal hygiene. They were fed starvation rations once a day and given only three minutes to get into the canteen area, eat, and get out. The little water they received was ordinarily foul. Prisoner had no changes of clothing and no bedding. They received no medical care.

2.6 Severe beatings were commonplace. The camp guards, and others who came to the camp and physically abused the prisoners, used all manner of weapons during these beatings, including wooden batons, metal rods and tools, lengths of thick industrial cable that had metal balls affixed to the end, rifle butts, and knives. Both female and male prisoners were beaten, tortured, raped, sexually assaulted, and humiliated. Many, whose identities are known and unknown, did to survive the camp. After the initial collection of thousands of Bosnian Muslims and Croats in late May, 1992, groups of Serbs, including the accused, continued to enter the villages in which Muslims and Croats remained, killing some villagers and driving others from their homes and into the camps.

2.7 Keraterm camp was located at a former ceramics factory in Prijedor. Conditions for prisoners were similar to those in Omarska camp; physical and psychological abuse, including assaults and killings, were common. Trnopolje camp was established at the site of a former school in Trnopolje village. Men, women and children were detained in Trnopolje camp; the majority of those detained were then expelled from opština Prijedor. In Trnopolje, female detainees were sexually abused, and detainees were murdered and otherwise physically and psychologically abused.

General Allegations

3.1 At all times relevant to this indictment, a state of armed conflict and partial occupation existed in the territory of Bosnia-Herzegovina.

3.2 All acts or omissions set forth as grave breaches recognized by Article 2 of the Statute of the Tribunal occurred during that armed conflict and partial occupation.

3.3 All of the prisoners at the Omarska, Keraterm and Trnopolje camps, and the Bosnian Muslims and Croats of opština Prijedor referred to in this indictment were, at all relevant times, persons protected by the Geneva Conventions of 1949.

3.4 The accused in this indictment were required to abide by the laws and customs governing the conduct of war, including the Geneva Conventions of 1949.

3.5 Unless otherwise set forth below, all acts and omissions set forth in this indictment took place between about 23 May and about 31 December 1992.

3.6 In each paragraph charging torture, the acts were committed by, or at the instigation of, or with the consent or acquiescence of, an official or person acting in an official capacity, and for one or more of the following purposes: to obtain information or a confession from the victim or a third person; to punish the victim for an act the victim or a third person committed or was suspected of having committed; to intimidate or coerce the victim or a third person; and/or for any reason based upon discrimination of any kind.

3.7 In each paragraph charging crimes against humanity, a crime recognized by Article 5 of the Statute of the Tribunal, the alleged acts or omissions were part of a widespread or large-scale or systematic attack directed against a civilian population, specifically the Muslim and Croat population of opština Prijedor.

3.8 The term "Serb" refers either to Bosnian citizens of Serbian descent or to individuals of Serbian descent whose citizenship in the former Yugoslavia is unknown.

3.9 Paragraphs 3.1 through 3.8 are realleged and incorporated into each of the charges described below.

CHARGES:

PERSECUTION
(Count 1)

4. Between about 23 May 1992 and about 31 December 1992, **Duško TADIĆ** participated with Serb forces in the attack, destruction and plunder of Bosnian Muslim and Croat residential areas, the seizure and imprisonment of thousands of Muslim and Croats under brutal conditions in camps located in Omarska, Keraterm and Trnopolje, and the deportation and/or expulsion of the majority of Muslim and Croat residents of opština Prijedor by force or threat of force. During

this time, Serb forces, including **Dušan TADIĆ**, subjected Muslims and Croats inside and outside the camps to a campaign of terror which included killings, torture, sexual assaults, and other physical and psychological abuse.

4.1 Between the dates of 24 to 27 May 1992, Serb forces attacked the village of Kozarac and other villages and hamlets in the surrounding area. **Duško TADIĆ** was actively involved in the attack. His participation included firing flares to illuminate the village at night for the artillery and tank guns as the village was being shelled, and physically assisting in the seizure collection, segregation, and forced transfer to detention centres of the majority of the non-Serb population of the area during those first days. **Duško TADIĆ** also took part in the killing and beating of a number of the seized persons, including: the killing of an elderly man and woman near the cemetery in the area of "old" Kozarac, the acts described in paragraphs 11 and 12 below, the beatings of at least two former policemen from Kozarac at a road junction in the village of Kozarac, and the beating of a number of Muslim males who had been seized and detained at the Prijedor military barracks.

4.2 **Duško TADIĆ** was also seen on numerous occasions in the three main camps operating within opština Prijedor: Omarska, Keraterm and Trnopolje. During the period between 25 May 1992 and 8 August 1992, **TADIĆ** physically took part or otherwise participated in the killing, torture, sexual assault, and beating of many detainees at Omarska camp, including: those acts set forth in paragraphs 5 through 10 below and other instances of torture and beating prisoners in the "white house", the "administration building", the "pista" and the main garage area. During the same period, in Keraterm camp, **Duško TADIĆ** physically took part or otherwise participated in the beating of detainees and looting of their personal property and valuables, including, on more than one occasion, the mass beating of a number of detainees from Kozarac being confined in "Room 2".

4.3 During the period between 25 May 1992 and 31 December 1992, **Duško TADIĆ** physically participated and otherwise assisted in the transfer to and unlawful confinement in Trnopolje camp of non-Serb persons from the Kozarac area. Additionally, during the period between September, 1992 and December, 1992, in Trnopolje camp or in the adjacent area, **TADIĆ** physically took part or otherwise participated in the killing of more than 30 detainees, including groups of male detainees executed near a white house adjacent to the camp and a group of male detainees executed in a plum orchard adjacent to the camp. **TADIĆ** also physically took part or otherwise participated in the torture of more than 12 female detainees, including several gang rapes, which occurred both in the camp and at a white house adjacent to the camp during the period between September, 1992 and December, 1992.

4.4 Between 25 May and 31 December 1992, **TADIĆ** physically participated in the seizure and selection of individuals for detention in the camps and transported Muslims and Croats who had been seized, to the camps for detention. During the time he was engaged in this seizure, selection, and transfer of non-Serbs to various detention centres, **Duško TADIĆ** was aware that the majority of those detainees who survived detention would be deported from the territory of Bosnia-Herzegovina.

4.5 Concurrent with the attack and seizure of the non-Serb population of Kozarac and the surrounding area, the Serb forces plundered and destroyed the homes, businesses, and other property of non-Serbs. The seizure, transfer and detention of the non-Serb population and the plundering and destruction of their property continued for a number of weeks. During the period between 23 May and 31 August 1992, **Duško TADIĆ** was aware of the widespread nature of the plunder and destruction of personal and real property from non-Serbs and was physically involved and otherwise participated in that plunder and destruction, including the plunder of homes in Kozarac and the looting of valuables from non-Serbs as they were seized and upon their arrival at the camps and detention centres.

By his participation in these acts, **Duško TADIĆ** committed:

Count 1:

a **CRIME AGAINST HUMANITY** recognized by Articles 5(h) (persecution on political, racial and/or religious grounds) and 7(1) of the Statute of the Tribunal.

FORCIBLE SEXUAL INTERCOURSE WITH "F"
(Counts 2-4)

5. "**F**" was taken to the Omarska camp as a prisoner in early June 1992. Sometime between early June and 3 August 1992, "**F**" was

taken to the Separacija building at the entrance to the Omarska camp and placed in a room where **Duško TADIĆ** subjected "**F**" to forcible sexual intercourse. By these acts, **Duško TADIĆ** committed:

Count 2:

a **GRAVE BREACH** recognized by Articles 2(b) (inhuman treatment) and 7(1) of the Statute of the Tribunal; and

Count 3:

a **VIOLATION OF THE LAWS OR CUSTOMS OF WAR** recognized by Articles 3 and 7(1) of the Statute of the Tribunal and Article 3(1)(a) (cruel treatment) of the Geneva Conventions of 1949; and,

Count 4:

a **CRIME AGAINST HUMANITY** recognized by Article 5(g) (rape) and 7(1) of the Statute of the Tribunal.

KILLING OF EMIR KARABAŠIĆ, JASMIN HRNIĆ, ENVER ALIĆ, AND FIKRET HARAMBAŠIĆ, BEATING OF EMIR BEGANOVIC AND INHUMANE ACTS AGAINST "G" AND "H" IN OMARSKA CAMP
(Counts 5-11)

6. During the period between 1 June and 31 July 1992, a group of Serbs, including **Duško TADIĆ**, severely beat numerous prisoners, including Emir KARABAŠIĆ, Jasmin HRNIĆ, Enver ALIĆ, Fikret HARAMBAŠIĆ, and Emir BEGANOVIC, in the large garage building or hangar of Omarska camp. The group forced two other prisoners, "G" and "H", to commit oral sexual acts on HARAMBAŠIĆ and "G" to sexually mutilate him. KARABAŠIĆ, HRNIĆ, ALIĆ, and HARAMBAŠIĆ died as a result of the assaults. By his participation in these acts, **Duško TADIĆ** committed:

Count 5:

a **GRAVE BREACH** recognized by Articles 2(a) (wilful killing) and 7(1) of the Statute of the Tribunal; and,

Count 6:

a **VIOLATION OF THE LAWS OR CUSTOMS OF WAR** recognized by Articles 3 and 7(1) of the Statute of the Tribunal and Article 3(1)(a) (murder) of the Geneva Conventions; and,

Count 7:

a **CRIME AGAINST HUMANITY** recognized by Articles 5(a) (murder) and 7(1) of the Statute of the Tribunal; and,

Count 8:

a **GRAVE BREACH** recognised by Articles 2(b) (torture or inhuman treatment) and 7(1) of the Statute of the Tribunal; and,

Count 9:

a **GRAVE BREACH** recognised by Articles 2(c) (wilfully causing great suffering or serious injury to body and health) and 7(1) of the Statute of the Tribunal; and,

Count 10:

a **VIOLATION OF THE LAWS OR CUSTOMS OF WAR** recognised by Articles 3 and 7(1) of the Statute of the Tribunal and Article 3(1)(a) (cruel treatment) of the Geneva conventions; and,

Count 11:

a **CRIME AGAINST HUMANITY** recognised by Articles 5(i) (inhumane acts) and 7(1) of the Statute of the Tribunal.

BEATING OF ŠEFIK SIVAC IN OMARSKA CAMP
(Counts 12-14)

7. Around July 10, 1992, in the building known as the "white house" in Omarska camp, a group of Serbs from outside the camp, including **Duško TADIĆ,** severely beat ŠEFIK SIVAC, threw him onto the floor of a room and left him there, where he died. By his participation in these acts, **Duško TADIĆ** committed:

Count 12:

a **GRAVE BREACH** recognised by Articles 2(c) (wilfully causing great suffering or serious injury to body or health) and 7(1) of the Statute of the Tribunal; and,

Count 13:

a **VIOLATION OF THE LAWS AND CUSTOMS OF**

WAR recognised by Articles 3 and 7(1) of the Statute of the Tribunal and Article 3(1)(a) (cruel treatment) of the Geneva Conventions; and,

Count 14:

a **CRIME AGAINST HUMANITY** recognised by Article 5(i) (inhumane acts) and 7(1) of the Statute of the Tribunal.

BEATINGS OF SALIH ELEZOVIĆ, SEJAD SIVAC, HAKIJA ELEZOVIĆ AND OTHER UNNAMED PRISONERS IN OMARSKA CAMP
(Counts 15-17)

8. Around late July, 1992, behind the building known as the "white house" in Omarska camp, a group of Serbs from outside the camp, including **Duško TADIĆ**, severely beat and kicked Hakija ELEZOVIĆ, Sejad SIVAC and other prisoners. Hakija ELEZOVIĆ survived the beating. Salih ELEZOVIĆ, Sajad SIVAC, and other prisoners were found dead in the same spot later that day. By his participation in these acts, **Duško TADIĆ** committed:

Count 15:

a **GRAVE BREACH** recognised by Articles 2(c) (wilfully causing great suffering or serious injury to body or health) and 7(1) of the Statute of the Tribunal; and,

Count 16:

a **VIOLATION OF THE LAWS AND CUSTOMS OF WAR** recognised by Articles 3 and 7(1) of the Statute of the Tribunal and Article 3(1)(a) (cruel treatment) of the Geneva Conventions; and,

Count 17:

a **CRIME AGAINST HUMANITY** recognised by Articles 5(i) (inhumane acts) and 7(1) of the Statute of the Tribunal.

ABUSE OF UNKNOWN PRISONERS IN OMARSKA CAMP
(Counts 18-20)

9. Around the latter part of June or first part of July, 1992, near the building known as the "white house," a group of Serbs from outside the camp, including **Duško TADIĆ**, ordered prisoners, whose names

are not known, to drink water like animals from puddles on the ground, jumped on their backs and beat them until they were unable to move. As the victims were removed in a wheelbarrow, **TADIĆ** discharged the contents of a fire extinguisher into the mouth of one of the victims. By his participation in these acts, **Duško TADIĆ** committed:

Count 18:

a **GRAVE BREACH** recognised by Articles 2(c) (wilfully causing great suffering or serious injury to body or health) and 7(1) of the Statute of the Tribunal; and,

Count 19:

a **VIOLATION OF THE LAWS OR CUSTOMS OF WAR** recognised by Articles 3 and 7(1) of the Statute of the Tribunal and Article 3(1)(a) (cruel treatment) of the Geneva Conventions; and,

Count 20:

a **CRIME AGAINST HUMANITY** recognised by Articles 5(i) (inhumane acts) and 7(1) of the Statute of the Tribunal.

BEATING AND ABUSE OF HASE ICIĆ AND OTHER UNNAMED PRISONERS IN OMARSKA CAMP (Counts 21-23)

10. About 8 July 1992, in the building known as the "white house," a group of persons from outside the camp, including **Duško TADIĆ**, called prisoners individually from one room in the "white house" to another, where they were beaten. After a number of prisoners were called out, Hase ICIĆ was taken into the room where members of the group, including **Duško TADIĆ**, beat and kicked him until he was unconscious. By his participation in these acts, **Duško TADIĆ** committed:

Count 21:

a **GRAVE BREACH** recognize by Articles 2(c) (wilfully causing great suffering or serious injury to body or health) and 7(1) of the Statute of the Tribunal; and,

Count 22:

a **VIOLATION OF THE LAWS OR CUSTOMS OF**

WAR recognised by Articles 3 and 7(1) of the Statute of the Tribunal and Article 3(1)(a) (cruel treatment) of the Geneva Conventions; and,

Count 23:

a **CRIME AGAINST HUMANITY** recognised by Articles 5(i) (inhumane acts) and 7(1) of the Statute of the Tribunal.

KILLING OF EKREM KARABAŠIĆ, ISMET KARABAŠIĆ, SEIDO KARABAŠIĆ AND REDO FORIĆ IN KOZARAC
(Counts 24-28)

11. About 27 May 1992, Serb forces seized the majority of Bosnian Muslim and Bosnian Croat people of the Kozarac area. As Muslims and Croats marched in columns to assembly points in Kozarac for transfer to camps, Serb forces, including **Duško TADIĆ** and **Goran BOROVNICA**, ordered Ekrem KARABAŠIĆ, Ismet KARABAŠIĆ, Seido KARABAŠIĆ and REDO FORIĆ from the column and shot and killed them. By their participation in these acts, **Duško TADIC** and **Goran BOROVNICA** committed:

Count 24:

a **GRAVE BREACH** recognized by Articles 2(a) (wilful killing) and 7(1) of the Statute of the Tribunal; and,

Count 25:

a **VIOLATION OF THE LAWS OR CUSTOMS OF WAR** recognised by Articles 3 and 7(1) of the Statute of the Tribunal and Article 3(1)(a) (murder) of the Geneva Conventions; and,

Count 26:

a **CRIME AGAINST HUMANITY** recognised by Articles 5(a) (murder) and 7(1) of the Statute of the Tribunal; or,

Count 27:

Alternatively, a **GRAVE BREACH** recognised by Articles 2(c) (wilfully causing great suffering or serious injury to body or health) and 7(12) of the Statute of the Tribunal' and,

Count 28:

Alternatively, a **CRIME AGAINST HUMANITY** recognised by Articles 5(i) (inhumane acts) and 7(1) of the Statute of the Tribunal.

KILLING OF SAKIB ELKAŠEVIĆ, OSME ELKAŠEVIĆ, ALIJA JAVOR, ABAZ JASKIĆ AND NIJAZ JASKIĆ AND BEATING OF MEHO KENJAR, ADAM JAKUPOVIĆ, SALKO JASKIĆ, ISMET JASKIĆ, BEIDO BALIĆ, SEFIK BALIĆ, NIJAS ELKAŠEVIĆ AND ILIJAS ELKASIVIC IN AREA OF JASKIĆI AND SIVCI
(Counts 29-34)

12. About 14 June 1992, armed Serbs, including **Duško TADIĆ**, entered the area of Jaskići and Sivci in opština Prijedor and went from house to house calling out residents and separating men from the women and children. The armed Serbs killed Sakib ELKAŠEVIĆ, Osme ELKAŠEVIĆ, Alija JAVOR, Abas JASKIĆ and Nijaz JASKIĆ in front of their homes. They also beat Meho KENJAR, Adam JAKUPOVIĆ, Salko JASKIĆ, Ismet JASKIĆ, Beido BALIĆ, SEFIK BALIĆ, Nijas ELKAŠEVIĆ and Ilijas ELKAŠEVIĆ and then took them from the area to an unknown location. By his participation in these acts, **Duško TADIĆ** committed:

Count 29:

a **GRAVE BREACH** recognised by Articles 2(a) (wilful killing) and 7(1) of the Statute of the Tribunal; and,

Count 30:

a **VIOLATION OF THE LAWS OR CUSTOMS OF WAR** recognised by Articles 3 and 7(1) of the Statute of the tribunal and Article 3(1)(a) (murder) of the Geneva Conventions; and,

Count 31:

a **CRIME AGAINST HUMANITY** recognised by Articles 5(a) (murder) and 7(1) of the Statute of the Tribunal; and,

Count 32:

a **GRAVE BREACH** recognised by Articles 2(c) (wilfully causing great suffering or serious injury to body or health) and 7(1) of the Statute of the Tribunal; and,

Count 33:

a **VIOLATION OF THE LAWS OR CUSTOMS OF WAR** recognised by Articles 3 and 7(1) of the Statute of the Tribunal and Article 3(1)(a) (cruel treatment) of the Geneva Conventions; and,

Count 34:

a **CRIME AGAINST HUMANITY** recognised by Articles 5(i) (inhumane acts) and 7(1) of the Statute of the Tribunal.

[signed]
Richard J. Goldstone
Prosecutor

Appendix D

Summary of the Tadic Verdict

Press Release—7 May 1997
CC/PIO/190-E
The Hague, 7 May 1997

TADIC CASE: THE VERDICT

Today, one year to the day after the beginning of the trial of the Accused Dusko TADIĆ, Trial Chamber II (composed of Judge Gabrielle Kirk McDonald, Presiding, Judge Ninian Stephen and Judge Lal Chand Vohrah) has handed down its *"Opinion and Judgment"*.

Out of 31 counts, the Accused has been found:

- not guilty on 20 counts (9 murder counts because of insufficient evidence and 11 counts declared inapplicable) and
- guilty on 11 counts (persecution and beatings).

As pointed out by the Chamber itself, this judgement is *"the first determination of individual guilt or innocence in connection with serious violations of international humanitarian law by an international tribunal (. . .). The international military tribunals at Nuremberg and Tokyo, . . . , were multinational in nature, representing only part of the world community"*.

More broadly, and in particular for the victims of the armed conflict in the Prijedor area, the verdict represents the first ever judicial condemnation of the "ethnic cleansing" policy.

It is the result of a thorough and meticulous consideration of a voluminous quantity of testimonial and written evidence: during the six month-long trial of the Accused, 125 witnesses were called and 473 exhibits were tendered by the Prosecution and the Defence. It also reflects a detailed exploration of legal issues raised for the first time before a Trial Chamber of the International Tribunal.

The written Opinion and Judgement is a sizable document, amounting to 301 pages, with one Separate and Dissenting Opinion of 19 pages and a further 30 pages or so of annexes (the indictment; a map of Bosnia and Herzegovina; photos of the model of Omarska camp; photos of Keraterm and Trnopolje camps; photos of a hangar, of an inscription on a wall and of the model of the "white house" at Omarska camp).... This press release is merely intended as a "reader's guide" of the verdict.

THE VERDICT READS AS FOLLOWS:

The Accused is *"a citizen of the former Yugoslavia, of Serb ethnic descent, and a resident of the Republic of Bosnia and Herzegovina at the time of the alleged crimes"*.

The Accused was charged with 31 individual counts of persecution, murder, beatings and other offences alleged to have been committed in 1992 in the Prijedor district (northwestern part of the Republic of Bosnia and Herzegovina) and more specifically at the Omarska, Keraterm and Trnopolje camps, in Kozarac and in the area of Jaskici and Sivci.

In all cases the Accused was charged with individual criminal responsibility.

The Accused pleaded not guilty and *"raised a defence of alibi"* saying *"that he was elsewhere when each of those acts* [referred to in the counts] *is said to have occurred . . ."*

The Chamber finds:

1. By a majority, the Presiding-Judge dissenting, that the accusations of "Grave breaches of the 1949 Geneva Conventions" were NOT APPLICABLE and that the Accused is NOT GUILTY on the 11 relevant counts (being 5, 8, 9, 12, 15, 18, 21, 24, 27, 29, 32) running throughout all the charges in the indictment.

2. Unanimously, that the Accused is NOT GUILTY on 11 counts, (6, 7, 19, 20, 25, 26, 28, 30, 31, and in part 33 and 34) charging him with 13 murders, 5 beatings, 2 inhumane acts and one case of abuse of pris-

oners. The Prosecutor has failed either to establish beyond reasonable doubt the elements of the offences, or to present conclusive evidence linking the accused to the related acts or to satisfy the Judges beyond reasonable doubt that victims named were murdered.

3. Unanimously, that the Accused IS GUILTY on 11 counts, (1, 10, 11, 13, 14, 16, 17, 22, 23 and in part 33 and 34) charging him with persecution and 14 beatings. The Chamber has found the Accused *"untruthful"* as to his whereabouts at the time of the alleged offences and has been satisfied beyond reasonable doubt by the Prosecution's evidence that the accused either was present at the scene of, or did participate into, the alleged offences.

II. FACTUAL AND LEGAL FINDINGS COUNT BY COUNT

11 counts inapplicable

As previously stated, 11 counts charging Grave Breaches of the Geneva Convention of 1949 have been declared inapplicable by a majority of Judges. These counts are counts 5, 8, 9, 12, 15, 18, 21, 24, 27, 29 and 32.

Count 1 : Persecution

Accused guilty of persecution

1. As to the events alleged to have taken place during and subsequent to the attack on Kozarac and its outlying villages, the Trial Chamber is satisfied beyond reasonable doubt that the Accused:

- *"participated in the attack on Kozarac and the surroundings areas and in the collection and forced transfer of civilians to detention camp;*
- *participated in the calling-out of four Muslim men from a column of civilians (. . .) and the beatings, calling-out, separation and forced transfer of non-Serb civilians;*
- *participated in the beating of a Muslim policeman in Kozarac;*
- *kicked one Muslim prisoner and beat another while they were held at the Prijedor military barracks;*
- *and killed two Muslim policemen in Kozarac.*

2. As to the events alleged to have taken place at the Omarska and Keraterm camps, the Trial Chamber has found that the Accused:

- *"took part in the beating of Edin Mrkalj and Senad Muslimovic in the administration building and the hangar building respectively* (Omarska camp);
- *took part in the beatings of the prisoners and took part in one mass-beating of prisoners from room 2* (Keraterm).

3. As to the events alleged to have taken place in the Trnopolje camp:

- the Trial Chamber notes that most of the allegations were supported only by the testimony of Dragan Opacic, whose testimony under the pseudonym of Witness L was later withdrawn.
- The only remaining portion of the initial charge deals with alleged incidents of transfer and unlawful confinement in the Trnopolje camp. The Trial Chamber *"finds beyond reasonable doubt that the accused participated in the transfer to and in the initial confinement of non-Serbs in camps generally, and in the Trnopolje camp in particular. However, the Trial Chamber finds that the accused did not take an active role in the continued confinement of non-Serbs in the Trnopolje camp".*

4. As to the alleged participation of the accused in the seizure, selection and transportation of individuals for detention, the Trial Chamber *"is satisfied beyond reasonable doubt that the accused participated (. . .) and was aware that the majority of surviving prisoners would be deported from Bosnia and Herzegovina".*

5. As to the allegations of plunder and destruction of personal and real property of non-Serbs, the Trial Chamber states that *"evidence regarding the accused's role in the destruction, plunder and looting is non-existent".*

6. **"The acts of the accused constitute persecution".**

The Trial Chamber notes *"the horrendous treatment inflicted on the non-Serb population of opstina Prijedor on the basis of religion and politics (. . .) A policy to terrorize the non-Serb civilian population of opstina Prijedor on discriminatory grounds is evident and that its implementation was widespread and systematic throughout, at the minimum, opstina Prijedor is apparent. The events described in paragraph 4 of the indictment [Count 1] occurred within this context of discrimination."*

With regard to the accused, the Trial Chamber notes that *"he was one of the first SDS member in opstina Prijedor and, in his own estimation, a trusted SDS member who was asked to run a crucial plebiscite in the Kozarac area . . . As organizer of the plebiscite in Kozarac and President of the local SDS, the accused had knowledge and supported the plan for a Greater Serbia . . . He himself admits this knowledge and support for the plan when he describes himself as an enthusiastic supporter of the creation of* Republika Srpska."

The Trial Chamber concludes: *"The accused's role in, inter alia, the attack on Kozarac and the surrounding areas, as well as the seizure, collection, segregation and forced transfer of civilians to camps, calling-out of civilians, beatings and killings described above clearly constituted an infringement of the victims' enjoyment of their fundamental rights and these acts were taken against non-Serbs on the basis of religious and political discrimination. Further, these acts occurred during an armed conflict, were taken against civilians as part of a widespread or systematic attack on the civilian population in furtherance of a policy to commit these acts, and the accused had knowledge of the wider context in which his acts occurred".*

The accused is thus guilty of a Crime against Humanity.

Counts 2 to 4: Forcible sexual intercourse with "F"

Counts withdrawn at the Prosecutor's request.

Counts 6, 7, 10, and 11: Killings, beatings and sexual mutilation in Omarska

Accused not guilty of murder
Accused not guilty of sexual mutilation
Accused guilty of beatings

1. As to the beating of Emir Beganovic and Senad Muslimovic, the Trial Chamber *"is satisfied beyond reasonable doubt that the accused was one of the men who severely beat them."*

2. As to the beatings of the Emir Karabasic, Jasmin Hrnic and Enver Alic, the Trial Chamber is *"further so satisfied that the accused was present on the hangar floor when the three victims were called out and attacked . . . , that the accused attacked Jasmin Hrnic with a knife . . . , took part in the at-*

tack upon and the beating of Emir Karabasic... and took part in the beating of Jasmin Hrnic".

3. As to the assault upon and the sexual mutilation of Fikret Harambasic, the Trial Chamber *"is satisfied beyond reasonable doubt that the accused was on the hangar floor on this occasion... but is not satisfied that he took any active part in the assault and the mutilation".*

4. As to the alleged deaths of Fikret Harambasic, Emir Karabasic, Jasmin Hrnic and Enver Alic *"which it is said resulted from the assaults upon them"*, the Trial Chamber notes that *"the Prosecutor failed to elicit clear and definitive evidence from witnesses about the condition of the four prisoners after they had been assaulted (...) and to establish beyond reasonable doubt that any of these four prisoners died from injuries received in the assaults made on them in the hangar...".*

5. The Trial Chamber finds the accused guilty of a violation of the laws and customs of war for his participation in the beatings and other grievous acts of violence inflicted on Enver Alic, Emir Karabasic, Jasko Hrnic, Senad Muslimovic, Fikret Harambasic and Ermir Beganovic, none of whom were taking part in the hostilities. Further, it finds the accused guilty of a crime against humanity: the beatings and other acts of violence which were suffered by the six victims were committed during an armed conflict as part of a widespread or systematic attack on a civilian population. *"The accused intended for discriminatory reasons to inflict severe damage to the victims' physical and human dignity".*

Counts 13 and 14: Beating of Sefik Sivac in Omarska

Accused guilty

1. The Chamber finds beyond reasonable doubt that *"Sefik Sivac was beaten and that the accused was part of the group that threw Sefik Sivac onto the floor... after he had been beaten and that Sefik Sivac later died from these injuries".*

2. However, *"there is no direct testimony that the accused was present during the beating of Sefik Sivac"*. But the Trial Chamber finds that there is evidence that *"the accused intentionally assisted directly and substantially*

in the common purpose of the group to inflict severe suffering upon Sefik Sivac".

3. The Trial Chamber finds the accused guilty of a violation of the laws and customs of war (cruel treatment on a prisoner who did not take active part in the hostilities) and of a crime against humanity (inhumane act committed during an armed conflict as part of a widespread and systematic attack on a civilian population and intended for discriminatory reasons to inflict severe damage to the victim's physical integrity and human dignity).

Counts 16 and 17: Beatings at Omarska

Accused guilty

1. The Trial Chamber is satisfied beyond reasonable doubt that the accused *"severely beat and kicked Hakija Elezovic and severely beat Salih Elezovic."*

2. The Trial Chamber finds the accused guilty of a violation of the laws and customs of war (cruel treatment of two Muslims neither of whom were taking active part in the hostilities) and of a crime against humanity (inhumane act committed during an armed conflict as part of a widespread [or systematic attack on the civilian population]).

Counts 19 and 20: Abuse of prisoners in Omarska

Accused not guilty

1. As to the allegations that the accused was a member of a group of Serbs beating prisoners and forcing them to drink water from the ground like animals, the accused was not named by the Prosecution's witness as part of the group.

2. As to the allegation that the accused discharged the contents of a fire extinguisher into the mouth of a man in a barrow, *"two factual deficiencies in the Prosecution case have been exposed:... no evidence has been furnished of such discharge, and.... the Prosecution has failed to establish that the man* [in the barrow] *was alive."*

3. The Trial Chamber finds the accused not guilty: *"no conclusive evidence has been presented linking the accused with the related acts."*

Counts 22 and 23: Beating and abuse of Hase Icic in Omarska

Accused guilty

1. The Trial Chamber finds beyond reasonable doubt that the accused *"was part of a group of Serbs who beat and kicked Hase Icic until he was unconscious."*

2. For these acts committed in the context of the armed conflict, the Trial Chamber finds the accused guilty of a violation of the laws and customs of war (cruel treatment of a Muslim not taking active part in the hostilities) and of a crime against humanity (inhumane act committed during an armed conflict as part of a widespread [or systematic attack on the civilian population]).

Counts 25, 26, and 28: 4 killings in Kozarac

Accused not guilty

1. The Trial Chamber is not satisfied beyond reasonable doubt that the shooting and killing by the accused of the individuals at a kiosk at the corner of Marsala Tita Street and the road to Kalate in Kozarac occurred as alleged, or in fact that the shooting did take place.

2. The Trial Chamber however is satisfied that the accused participated in the calling-out of people from the moving column.

3. The Trial Chamber finds the accused not guilty of murder (violation of the laws and customs of war): *"the Chamber is not satisfied beyond reasonable doubt that the four persons named were murdered"*. Further it finds the accused not guilty of an inhumane act (crime against humanity): *"although this Trial Chamber is convinced of the accused's participation in the calling-out of people, such participation per se, in the Trial Chamber's view, cannot patently constitute an inhumane act within the meaning of Article 5 of the Statute [Crimes against humanity]"*.

Counts 30, 31, 33 and 34: 5 killings and 8 beatings in Jaskici and Sivci

Accused not guilty of killing
Accused not guilty of 4 beatings
Accused guilty of 4 beatings

1. As to the alleged killing of 5 men taken from their homes, the Trial Chamber is satisfied beyond reasonable doubt that the accused was part of the group of Serbs who rounded up the men in the village. But *"it cannot be satisfied beyond reasonable doubt that the accused had any part in the killing of the five men or any of them . . . Nothing is known as to who shot them or in what circumstances."*

2. As to the beatings of Beido Balic, Sefik Balic, Ismet Jaskic and Salko Jaskic, the Trial Chamber is satisfied beyond reasonable doubt that the accused *"took part in the brutal and violent beating."*

3. As to the beating of Ilijas Elkasovic, Nijas Elkasovic, Meho Kenjar and Adam Jakupovic *"there is no evidence"*.

4. The Trial Chamber then concludes that the accused is not guilty of murder and not guilty of some of the beatings. Where the accused is found guilty of part of the beatings he is guilty of a violation of the laws and customs of war (cruel treatment committed in the context of an armed conflict) and of a crime against humanity (inhumane acts committed during an armed conflict as part of a widespread [or systematic attack on the civilian population]).

III. THE ACCUSED'S DEFENCE OF ALIBI

Dusko Tadic raised a defence of alibi to each of the counts charged, claiming he was somewhere else at the time of the alleged acts. He testified under solemn declaration that he had never been to the Omarska or Keraterm camps nor had he participated in ethnic cleansing in Kozarac. He testified that he had been to Trnopolje on five occasions but was never inside the camp.

According to the Accused, between 23 May and 15 June 1992, he lived with his family in Banja Luka, and visited opstina Prijedor only four times.

Between 15 June and 1 August 1992, he said he worked as a reserve traffic policeman at a traffic checkpoint at Orlovci, close to Prijedor.

From 15 August until 1 November 1992, he said worked in Kozarac as a traffic policeman.

On 15 August 1992, he was elected President of the Local Board of the SDS in Kozarac and appointed as Acting Secretary of the Local Commune of Kozarac. On 9 September 1992, he was elected Secretary of the Local Commune, a decision which became effective on 9 November 1992.

In its findings of fact, the Trial Chamber made the following observations on the Accused's alibi for the crimes alleged in the various paragraphs of the indictment:

Count 1 (paragraph 4 of the Indictment): The events alleged in this paragraph are said to have occurred at various locations in opstina Prijedor between 23 May and 31 December 1992, approximately. According to the Chamber, *"the Defence assertion that the accused was not in Kozarac at this time cannot be accepted. The evidence of the Defence witnesses who happened to be in Kozarac during the attack (. . .) attests only to their not having seen the accused in Kozarac while they were there."*

Counts 5-11 (paragraph 6): For the events alleged, the accused relies exclusively on his defence of alibi. He says that on 18 June 1992, when the three events alleged occurred, he was living in Prijedor and working as a traffic policeman. *"[T]he Trial Chamber does not accept the accused's account of his whereabouts from 15 June to 17 June 1992. (. . .) Accordingly, for the incidents alleged in paragraph 6, the accused's checkpoint duty affords no alibi."*

Counts 12-14 (paragraph 7): For the events alleged in paragraph 7, which occurred on 8, 9 or 10 July 1992, *"the accused has no specific alibi for the late evening and night of 8 or 10 June 1992. (. . .) the Defence evidence as to off-duty days does no more than establish that the accused was generally resident in Prijedor.*

"(. . .) the Trial Chamber rejects the Defence contention that the accused was somehow rendered largely immobile because of the fact that he did not own a car."

Even if the events alleged took place on the night of 9 July 1992, a night when the records of Orlovci checkpoint show him to have been on duty, and *"[e]ven if these records are accepted as accurately reflecting the shifts to which the accused was assigned, they can only establish the hours when the accused was meant to be on duty at the checkpoint; they do not of themselves establish his presence there throughout those hours."*

Counts 15-18 (paragraph 8): The Chamber finds that if the events alleged in this paragraph *"occurred in the afternoon of 27 July 1992, as the evidence of Ermin Strikovic states, the accused has no specific alibi. His checkpoint duty at Orlovci on that date began at 7 p.m. and if the accused had transport available to him he would have had ample time during that day to travel to Omarska from Prijedor, carry out the acts alleged and return in time to take up his checkpoint duties."*

Counts 18-20 (paragraph 9): The events alleged are said to have occurred at the Omarska camp, in late June or early July.

"The Defence contention that the accused was never at the Omarska camp and that, in any event, at the relevant time, his duties with the traffic police precluded him from having committed the acts alleged (. . .) is rejected by the Trial Chamber. Numerous credible witnesses have testified that they saw the accused at the camp and (. . .) the accused's assignment to the Orlovci checkpoint would not preclude him from carrying out what the Prosecution described as his "higher duty" as a traffic policeman to implement ethnic cleansing to achieve a Greater Serbia. Accordingly, the Trial Chamber rejects the accused's alibi and his assertion that he was never at the Omarska camp."

Counts 21-23 (paragraph 10): The events charged in this paragraph appear to have occurred on 7 or 8 July 1992. *"The Trial Chamber finds that the assignment records for the Orlovci checkpoint do not provide the accused with an alibi (. . .) The assignment records reflect that on those nights, the accused was off duty. On 7 July 1992, the accused was off duty after 7 a.m. and offered no testimony regarding his whereabouts. On 8 July 1992 the records reflect that he completed his assignment at 7 p.m. and he likewise offered no testimony regarding his whereabouts at the time these events occurred. Prijedor is about 20 kilometres from the Omarska camp. The travel time is 30-35 minutes by car."*

Counts 24-28 (paragraph 11): This paragraph charges the accused with events occurring around 27 May 1992 in Kozarac. Three witnesses were called by the Prosecution to give evidence about the accused's role, and additional Prosecution witness testimony sought to establish the accused's presence in Kozarac on this day.

While noting inconsistencies between the evidence of these witnesses, the Trial Chamber found that the *"evidence of all or any (. . .) of four Defence witnesses, who had passed through Marsala Tita Street, does not afford an alibi to the accused except to indicate that they did not happen to see the accused in Kozarac on that day while they were there."*

Counts 29-34 (paragraph 12): The events are alleged to have happened around 14 June 1992 in Jaskici and Sivci. The Trial Chamber found that the accused's alibi *"does not deal specifically with 14 June 1992 and (. . .) is generally unspecific as to date in respect of this period".*

IV. THE INAPPLICABILITY OF THE COUNTS CHARGING THE ACCUSED WITH GRAVE BREACHES

The Trial Chamber, by a majority of two to one (Judge McDonald, dissenting), finds that the accused could not be charged with grave breaches under Article 2 because the alleged victims were not protected persons under Article 4 of the Fourth Geneva Convention of 1949.

"For that reason, Article 2 is inapplicable (except in respect of citizens of the Republic of Bosnia and Herzegovina who actually found themselves in the hands of the JNA [Yugoslavia People's Army] before 19 May 1992 or the VJ [Army of the Federal Republic of Yugoslavia] and FRY [Federal Republic of Yugoslavia], after 19 May)". In consequence of this finding, Counts 5, 8, 9, 12, 15, 18, 21, 24, 27, 29 and 32 have been dismissed.

In order for Article 2 to be applicable, the victims must be protected persons, and the conflict must be international in character.

The majority finds that while *"from the beginning of 1992 until 19 May 1992, a state of international armed conflict existed in at least part of the territory of Bosnia and Herzegovina (. . .) between the forces of the Republic of Bosnia and Herzegovina on the one hand and those of the Federal Republic of Yugoslavia (Serbia and Montenegro), being the JNA (later the VJ), working with sundry paramilitary and Bosnian Serb forces, on the other"*, after 19 May 1992, this armed conflict was not of a character to justify the imposition of Article 2 (grave breaches) of the Statute, because the victims were not protected persons, that is, they were not in the hands of a party to the conflict or occupying power of which they were not nationals.

On 19 May 1992, the JNA officially withdrew from the Republic of Bosnia and Herzegovina. *"(. . .) the question for this Trial Chamber is whether, after 19 May 1992, the Federal Republic of Yugoslavia (. . .) by its withdrawal from the territory of the Republic of Bosnia and Herzegovina and notwithstanding its continuing support for the VRS [Army of Republika Srpska], had sufficiently distanced itself from the VRS so that those forces could not be regarded as de facto organs or agents or the VJ and hence of the FRY (. . .)"* If a agency relationship could be proven, then acts committed by the VRS against nationals of the Republic of Bosnia and Herzegovina could be considered to be acts against non-nationals.

In deciding what constitutes agency for the purposes of the applicability of Article 2, the Chamber considered the *Case Concerning Military and Paramilitary Activities in and Against Nicaragua [Nicaragua]*, which was decided by the International Court of Justice.

While noting that that case was concerned with the responsibility of a State and the extant case is concerned with the responsibility of individuals, and that the facts of each case are substantially different, the majority applied the essence of the test which they considered to be laid down in *Nicaragua*. There, the International Court of Justice asked: "whether or not the relationship of the *contras* to the US Government was so much one of dependence on the one side and control on the other that it would be right to equate the contras, for legal purposes, with an organ of the US Government, or as acting on behalf of that Government".

In the context of the extant case, the test would be whether *"the requisite degree of command and control by the VJ, and hence the FRY (. . .) over the VRS is established for the purpose of imputing the acts of those forces operating in opstina Prijedor or the VRS as a whole to the FRY (. . .)."*

According to the Chamber, the Prosecutor must prove that *"the nature of the relationship between the VRS and the government of the FRY, and between the VRS and VJ in particular, was of such a character. In doing so it is neither necessary or sufficient merely to show that the VRS was dependent, even completely dependent, on the VJ and the FRY (. . .) for the necessities of war. It must also be shown that the VJ and the FRY exercised the potential for control inherent in that relationship of dependency or that the VRS has otherwise placed itself under the control of the Government of the FRY."* In other words, the test is one of effective control.

The Trial Chamber found that there were two relationships of especial importance to the determination: (1) that between the General Mladic and the VRS Main Staff and Belgrade; and (2) that between the SDS (and hence RS) and the Government of FRY.

While finding that there was co-ordination between the VRS Main Staff and the VJ Main Staff in Belgrade, the majority held that *"co-ordination is not the same as command and control. The only other evidence submitted by the Prosecution was that, in addition to routing all high-level VRS communications through secure links in Belgrade, a communications link for everyday use was established and maintained between VRS Main Staff Headquarters and the VJ Main Staff in Belgrade. No further evidence was [introduced] by the Prosecution on the nature of this relationship."*

Regarding (2), the majority noted that the political leaders of RS were popularly elected by the Bosnian Serbs of the Republic of Bosnia and Herzegovina, and the independence of RS was declared by a vote of the Bosnian Serb Assembly, and asked whether, in spite of this, it could infer that the necessary degree of effective control was exercised by the FRY over the military operations of the RS armed forces, and find that the VRS was nothing more than a de facto organ or agent of the FRY.

The majority found that there was no evidence that non-Bosnian Serb members of the VRS were specifically charged by Belgrade with the carrying out of certain acts of its behalf.

Secondly, while *"it is clear from the evidence presented that the pay of all 1st Krajina Corps Officers, and presumably of all Senior VRS Commanders as former JNA officers, continued to be received from Belgrade after 19 May 1992, (. . .) such evidence, without more (. . .) establishes nothing more than the potential for control inherent in the relationship of dependency which such financing produced."*

The Trial Chamber noted that *"the military and political objectives of the RS and of the FRY (. . .) were largely complementary"* and dedicated to the creation of a Greater Serbia. Therefore, *"there was little need for the VJ and the Government of the FRY (. . .) to attempt to exercise any real degree of control over, as distinct from co-ordination with, the VRS. (. . .)*

"Thus, while it can be said that the FRY (. . .) through the dependence of the VRS on the supply of matériel by the VJ, had the capability to exercise great influence and perhaps even control over the VRS, there is no evidence on which this Trial Chamber can conclude that the FRY (. . .) and the VJ ever

directed or, for that matter, ever felt the need to attempt to direct, the actual military operations of the VRS, or to influence those operations beyond that which would have flowed naturally from the co-ordination of military objectives and activities by the VRS and VJ at the highest levels. In sum, while (. . .) the evidence available to this Trial Chamber clearly shows that the "various forms of assistance provided" to the armed forces of the RS by the Government of the FRY (. . .) was "crucial to the pursuit of their activities", and (. . .) those forces were almost completely dependent on the supplies of the VJ to carry out offensive operations, evidence that the FRY (. . .) through the VJ "made use of the potential for control inherent in that dependence", or was otherwise given effective control over those forces and which it exercised, is similarly insufficient.

"It is of course possible, on or in spite of the evidence presented, to view the acts of the JNA and the Government of the FRY (. . .) on or about 19 May 1992 as nothing more than a cynical and intentional creation of the objective factors necessary to distance themselves from direct legal responsibility for the acts of the armed forces of the RS, while doing everything to ensure that the material factors necessary to ensure the successful continuation of the armed conflict to achieve the same military and political goals were kept in place. Even if the legal effect of creating such objective factors, which caused no small amount of difficulty to the JNA and the Government of the FRY (. . .) could be vitiated by reason of some fraudulent intention, which this Trial Chamber doubt, that is not the only nor the most reasonable conclusion open on the evidence presented. There is, in short, no evidence on which this Trial Chamber may confidently conclude that the armed forces of the RS and the RS as a whole, were anything more than allies, albeit highly dependent allies, of the Government of the FRY."

Thus, the *"Trial Chamber is, by majority with the Presiding Judge dissenting, of the view that, on the evidence presented to it, after 19 May 1992 the armed forces of the RS could not be considered as de facto organs or agents of the FRY (. . .), either in opstina Prijedor or more generally."*

Separate and Dissenting Opinion of Judge McDonald

The Presiding Judge, Gabrielle Kirk McDonald, found, however, to the contrary. She concluded that at all times relevant to the Indictment, the armed conflict in opstina Prijedor was international in character, that the victims were protected persons and that Article 2 was applicable.

In her separate and dissenting opinion, Judge McDonald notes that the majority purports to apply the essence of the test in the *Nicaragua* case. *"The standard crafted by the majority, however, departs from Nicaragua (. . .). the standard the majority has created is even more demanding."*

According to the Judge: *"(. . .) there are two bases on which the acts of the VRS could be attributed to the FRY (. . .): where the VRS acted as an agent of the FRY (. . .), which could be established by a finding of dependency on the one side and control on the other; or where the VRS was specifically charged by the FRY (. . .) to carry out a particular act on behalf of FRY (. . .) thereby making the act itself attributable to the FRY (. . .) In Nicaragua, the court required a showing of effective control for this latter determination.*

While finding that the *"evidence presented to the Trial Chamber supports a finding of effective control of the VRS by the FRY (. . .) in opstina Prijedor at all times relevant to the charges in the Indictment,"* Judge McDonald states that *"the appropriate test of agency from Nicaragua is one of 'dependency and control' and a showing of effective control is not required"*.

According to Judge McDonald: *"the evidence supports a finding beyond reasonable doubt that the VRS acted as an agent of the FRY (. . .) in regard to the attack and occupation of opstina Prijedor during the times relevant to the charges in the Indictment and the victims are thus protected persons. The dependency of the VRS on and the exercise of control by the FRY (. . .) support this finding of agency under either the majority's standard of effective control or under the more general test of dependency and control.*

(. . .)

"The evidence proves that the creation of the VRS was a legal fiction. The only changes made after the 15 May 1992 Security Council resolution were the transfer of troops, the establishment of a Main Staff of the VRS, and a change in the insignia. There remained the same weapons, the same equipment, the same officers, the same commanders, largely the same troops, the same logistics centres, the same infrastructure, the same source of payments, the same goals and mission, the same tactics, and the same operations. Importantly, the objectives remained the same: to create an ethnically pure Serb State by uniting Serbs in Bosnia and Herzegovina and extending that State from the FRY (. . .) to the Croatian Krajina along the important logistics and supply line that went through opstina Prijedor, thereby necessitating the expulsion of the non-Serb population of the opstina."

"Although there is little evidence that the VRS was formally under the command of Belgrade after 19 May 1992, the VRS clearly continued to operate

as an integrated and instrumental part of the Serbian war effort. This finding is supported by evidence that every VRS unit had been a unit in the JNA, the command and staffs remained virtually the same after the re-designation.

(. . .)

"In addition, the evidence establishes that the VRS, in continuing the JNA operation to take over opstina Prijedor, executed the military operation for the benefit of the FRY (. . .)"

According to Judge McDonald, the evidence supports a finding that *"despite the purported JNA withdrawal from Bosnia and Herzegovina on 19 May 1992, active elements of what had been the JNA and was now rechristened as the VJ operated in tandem with the VRS in Bosnia and Herzegovina. In particular, VJ air crews and aircraft remained in Bosnia and Herzegovina after the purported May withdrawal and worked with the VRS throughout 1992 and 1993. This and other evidence (. . .) provides that there was no material change in the armed forces in opstina Prijedor, and that the conflict remained international after 19 May 1992, with the FRY (. . .) exercising effective control of the operations of the VRS in opstina Prijedor."*

Regarding the relationship between the VRS Commander General Ratko Mladic and the VJ Main Staff in Belgrade, Judge McDonald finds that: *"It is enough that General Mladic, who had been a commander in the JNA, continued to carry out his orders which were issued by the FRY before 19 May 1992, considering the evidence that establishes that there was direct communication between his office and Belgrade."*

Regarding the Majority's finding that the FRY and the VRS were allies, and thus, that "there was no effective control", Judge McDonald finds that *"this supports, rather than vitiates, the status of the VRS as an agent."*

The Judge concludes: *"I question why there should be a requirement that effective control was in fact exercised when the FRY (. . .) was assured that, having transferred officers and enlisted men and provided the matériel, thereby depleting its forces, its plan would be executed. (. . .) The occupation of opstina Prijedor could be accomplished only after the JNA, on behalf of the FRY, set it in motion and gave the VRS the wherewithal to accomplish it. Under such circumstances, there was no need for effective control, however, because the very establishment and continued existence of the VRS is evidence of such control. (. . .) The key issue here is whether the VRS was indeed dependent on and controlled by the FRY (. . .).*

"In summary, the evidence supports a finding beyond reasonable doubt that the VRS acted as an agent of the FRY (...) in regard to the attack and occupation of opstina Prijedor during the times relevant to the charges in the Indictment and the victims are thus protected persons. The dependency of the VRS on and the exercise of control by the FRY (...) support this finding of agency under either the majority's standard of effective control or under the more general test of dependency and control. However, a close reading of Nicaragua leads me to conclude that the effective control standard supports a distinct and separate basis for the attribution of the conduct of non-agents to a State, and that it is not a necessary element for a finding of an agency relationship."

Notes

Introduction

1. Arle Levinson, "Genocide a Thriving Doctrine in 20th Century," *The Star*, September 18, 1995, p. A9.

2. See *Bulletin of the International Tribunal for the Former Yugoslavia*, 8 (1996): 1, quoting Jose Anala Lassa, May 14, 1996.

Chapter 1

1. Telford Taylor, *The Anatomy of the Nuremberg Trials* (1992), p. 27.

2. Telford Taylor, *The Anatomy of the Nuremberg Trials* (1992), p. 29.

3. Telford Taylor, *The Anatomy of the Nuremberg Trials* (1992), pp. 30–31.

4. Joe J. Heydecker and Johannes Leeb, *The Nuremberg Trial,* trans. R.A. Downie (1962), pp. 77–78.

5. Telford Taylor, *The Anatomy of the Nuremberg Trials* (1992), p. 59.

6. Telford Taylor, *The Anatomy of the Nuremberg Trials*, (1992), p. 59.

7. Kevin R. Chaney, "Pitfalls and Imperatives: Applying the Lessons of Nuremberg to the Yugoslavia War Crimes Tribunal," *Dickinson Journal of International Law* 14 (1995): 62.

8. *Agreement for the Prosecution and Punishment of Major War Criminals of the European Axis* (London Agreement), signed at London, August 1945, 82 U.N.T.S. 279, 59 Stat. 1544, E.A.S. No. 472 (entered into force, 8 August 1945); *Charter of the International Military Tribunal* (annexed to the London Agreement) [hereinafter Nuremberg Charter].

9. Telford Taylor, *The Anatomy of the Nuremberg Trials* (1992), p. 61.

10. *Report of Robert H. Jackson, United States Representative to the International Conference on Military Trials* (U.S. Govt. Prt. Office, 1949), pp. v–vi.

11. Telford Taylor, *The Anatomy of the Nuremberg Trials* (1992), p. 64.

12. *Report of Robert H. Jackson, United States Representative to the International Conference on Military Trials* (U.S. Govt. Prt. Office, 1949), pp. v–vi.

13. *Report of Robert H. Jackson, United States Representative to the International Conference on Military Trials* (U.S. Govt. Prt. Office, 1949), pp. x–xi.

14. International Military Tribunal (Nuremberg), "Judgment and Sentences," *American Journal of International Law* 41 (1947): 172, 248.

15. International Military Tribunal (Nuremberg), "Judgment and Sentences," *American Journal of International Law* 41 (1947): 172, 248.

16. Roger Clark, "Crimes Against Humanity at Nuremberg," in *The Nuremberg Trial and International Law,* ed. G. Ginsburgs and V.N. Kudriavtsev (1990), pp. 177, 190–192.

17. M. Cherif Bassiouni, *Crimes Against Humanity in International Criminal Law* (1992), p. 35.

18. Virginia Morris and Michael Scharf, *An Insider's Guide to the International Criminal Tribunal for the Former Yugoslavia* , vol. 1 (1995), pp. 75 n.242, 76 n.243.

19. *The Law of War: A Documentary History* , ed. L. Friedman (1972), p. 779.

20. See *Report to the President from Justice Robert H. Jackson, Chief of Counsel for the United States in the Prosecution of Axis War Criminals,* June 7, 1945, reprinted in *American Journal of International Law* 39 (Supp. 1945): 178, 184.

21. See William V. O'Brien, "The Nuremberg Precedent and the Gulf War," *Virginia Journal of International Law* 31 (1991): 391, 396 n.32.

22. Military Tribunal for the Far East, January 19, 1946, *Bevans* 4: 20.

23. See generally, A. Brackman, *The Other Nuremberg* (1987); R. Conot, *Justice at Nuremberg* (1983); Ann Tusa and John Tusa, *The Nuremberg Trial* (1983); and R. Minear, *Victor's Justice: The Tokyo War Crimes Trial* (1971).

24. See Herbert Kraus, "The Nuremberg Trial of the Major War Criminals: Reflections After Seventeen Years," *DePaul Law Review* 13 (1963): 233, 247; Hans Ehard, "The Nuremberg Trial Against the Major War Criminals and International Law," *American Journal of International Law* 43 (1949): 223, 243; and Carl Haensel, "The Nuremberg Trial Revisited," *DePaul Law Review* 13 (1963): 248, 258.

25. Kevin R. Chaney, "Pitfalls and Imperatives: Applying the Lessons of Nuremberg to the Yugoslavia War Crimes Trials," *Dickinson Journal of International Law* 14 (1996): 57, 73.

26. Telford Taylor, *The Anatomy of the Nuremberg Trials* (1992), pp. 59, 60, 64, 66, 79, 80, 100, 120, and 121.

27. M. Cherif Bassiouni, *Crimes Against Humanity in International Criminal Law* (1992), p. 233.

28. See Max Frankel, *New York Times Magazine,* May 7, 1995, pp. 48–49.

29. Joe J. Heydecker and Johannes Leeb, *The Nuremberg Trial,* trans. R. A. Downie (1962), p. 94 .

30. Telford Taylor, *Anatomy of the Nuremberg Trials* (1992), p. 174.

31. *Maryland v. Craig,* 497 U.S. 836, 846 (1990).

32. Telford Taylor, *Anatomy of the Nuremberg Trials* (1992), pp. 320–321, 627.

33. Ann Tusa and John Tusa, *The Nuremberg Trial* (1984), pp. 477–78.

34. Robert H. Jackson, *Opening Speech for the Prosecution at Nuremberg,* 21 November 1945.

35. Robert H. Jackson, *Report to the President,* October 7, 1946.

36. *Affirmation of the Principles of International Law Recognized by the Charter of the Nuremberg Tribunal,* G.A. Res. 95, 1 U.N. GAOR, U.N. Doc. A/64/Add.1 (1946), p. 188.

37. Geneva Convention for the Amelioration of the Condition of the Wounded and Sick in Armed Forces in the Field, Aug. 12, 1949, 6 U.S.T. 3114, T.I.A.S. No. 3362, 75 U.N.T.S. 31 [hereinafter Geneva Convention I], art. 49; Geneva Convention for the Amelioration of the Condition of the Wounded, Sick, and Shipwrecked Members of Armed Forces at Sea, Aug. 12, 1949, 6 U.S.T. 3217, T.I.A.S. No. 3363, 75 U.N.T.S. 85 [hereinafter Geneva Convention II], art. 50; Geneva Convention Relative to the Treatment of Prisoners of War, Aug. 12, 1949, 6 U.S.T. 3316, T.I.A.S. 3364, 75 U.N.T.S. 135 [hereinafter Geneva Convention III], art. 129; Geneva Convention Relative to the Protection of Civilian Persons in Time of War, Aug. 12, 1949, 6 U.S.T. 3516, T.I.A.S. 3365, 75 U.N.T.S. 287 [hereinafter Geneva Convention IV], art. 146.

38. Convention on the Prevention and Punishment of the Crime of Genocide of 9 December 1948, 78 U.N.T.S. 277 (Article VI) [hereinafter Genocide Convention].

39. *Draft Statute for an International Criminal Court (Annex to the Report of the Committee on International Criminal Jurisdiction),* 7 U.N. GAOR Supp. No. 11, U.N. Doc. A/2136 (1952), p. 21

40. *Revised Draft Statute for an International Criminal Court (Annex to the Report of the Committee on International Criminal Jurisdiction),* 7 U.N. GAOR Supp. No. 11, U.N. Doc. A/2645 (1954) (hereinafter 1953 Draft Statute), p. 21.

41. See *Report of the Int'l. Law Comm'n, 42nd Sess., May 1, 1990–July 28, 1990,* U.N. GAOR Supp. No. 10, U.N. Doc. A/45/10 (1990), p. 40.

42. See Michael Scharf, "The Jury is Still Out on the Need for an International Criminal Court," *Duke Journal of International and Comparative Law* 1 (1991): 135, 139–140 .

43. See *U.N. General Resolution 44/39,* 44 UN GAOR Supp. No. 49, U.N. Doc. A/44/49 (1989), p. 1.

44. "Case Concerning Military and Paramilitary Activities In and Against Nicaragua (Nicaragua v. United States)," *International Court of Justice Reports* 1984: 392 (Jurisdiction of the Court and Admissibility of the Application).

45. Statement by the Legal Adviser, Abraham D. Sofaer, to the Senate Foreign Relations Committee (December 4, 1985), reprinted in Barry E. Carter and Philip R. Trimble, *International Law* (1991), pp. 298–300.

46. Michael P. Scharf, "The Politics of Establishing an International Criminal Court," *Duke Journal of International and Comparative Law* 6 (1995): 167, 171.

47. *United States v. Alvarez-Machain,* 112 S.Ct. 2188 (1982).

48. See United Nations Int'l. Law Comm'n., *Report of The International Law Commission on the Work of its Forty-Second Session: Topical Summary of the Discussion Held in the Sixth Committee,* U.N. Doc. A/CN.4/L.456 (1991), paragraphs 119–156.

49. United States Mission to the United Nations, *Statement by the Honorable Edwin D. Williamson, United States Special Advisor to the United Nations General Assembly in the Sixth Committee*, USUN Press Release #113-(92) (1992).

50. *U.N. General Assembly Resolution 46/54* (1992).

Notes for Chapter 2

1. This history of the Yugoslav conflict is derived from Laura Silber and Allan Little, *Yugoslavia: Death of a Nation* (1996); Arthur L. Clark, *Bosnia: What Every American Should Know* (1996); M. Cherif Bassiouni and Peter Manikas, *The Law of the International Criminal Tribunal for the Former Yugoslavia* (1996); Norman Cigar, *Genocide in Bosnia* (1995); David Rieff, *Slaughterhouse: Bosnia and the Failure of the West* (1995); Misha Glenny, *The Fall of Yugoslavia: The Third Balkan War* (1993); and Robert D. Kaplan, *Balkan Ghosts: A Journey Through History* (1993).

2. Arthur L. Clark, *Bosnia, What Every American Should Know* (1996), p. 77.

3. Carnegie Endowment for International Peace, *The Other Balkan Wars* (1993), p. 151 (originally published in 1914 as *Report of the International Commission to Inquire into the Causes and Conduct of the Balkan Wars*).

4. "Serbia's Ghosts: Why the Serbs See Themselves as the Victims, not the Aggressors," *Newsweek*, April 19, 1993.

5. Gregory Copley, "Hiding Genocide," *Defense and Foreign Affairs Strategic Policy*, December 31, 1992, p. 5.

6. Gregory Copley, "Hiding Genocide," *Defense and Foreign Affairs Strategic Policy*, December 31, 1992, p. 6.

7. Gregory Copley, "Hiding Genocide," *Defense and Foreign Affairs Strategic Policy*, December 31, 1992, p. 6.

8. Misha Glenny, *The Fall of Yugoslavia: The Third Balkan War*, rev. ed. (1994), p. 81.

9. Yiannis Neocleos, "The War in Ex-Yugoslavia and the Connection with the Two World Wars," *American Society of International Law Human Rights Interest Group Newsletter* 6 (1996): 28.

10. Barbara Jelavich, *History of the Balkans* (1983).

11. Patric Brogan, *The Captive Nations: Eastern Europe 1945–1990* (1990), p. 161.

12. Karl Wheeler Soper, "National Security," in *Yugoslavia: A Country Study*, ed. Glen E. Curtis, 3d ed. (1992), pp. 225, 233, 235–37.

13. Warren Zimmermann, *Origins of a Catastrophe: Yugoslavia and its Destroyers—America's Last Ambassador Tells What Happened and Why* (1996), p. 138.

14. Ivo Banac, "The Fearful Asymmetry of War: The Causes and Consequences of Yugoslavia's Demise," *Daedalus* (Spring 1992): 141, 150–51.

15. Anthony Lewis, "War Crimes," (quoting James Ridgeway) in *The Black Book of Bosnia* , ed. Nader Mousavizadeh (1996) , p. 58.

16. Warren Zimmermann, *Origins of a Catastrophe: Yugoslavia and its Destroyers—America's Last Ambassador Tells What Happened and Why* (1996), p. 120.

17. Warren Zimmermann, *Origins of a Catastrophe: Yugoslavia and its Destroyers—America's Last Ambassador Tells What Happened and Why* (1996), p. 120.

18. Laura Silber and Allan Little, *Yugoslavia: Death of a Nation* (1996), p. 150; Anthony Lewis, "War Crimes," in *The Black Book of Bosnia*, ed. Nader Mousavizadeh (1996), p. 61.

19. Warren Zimmermann, *Origins of a Catastrophe: Yugoslavia and its Destroyers—America's Last Ambassador Tells What Happened and Why* (1996), p. 137.

20. Blaine Harden, "Serbs Accused of '91 Croatia Massacre," *Washington Post*, January 25, 1993.

21. See *Security Council Resolution 743* (1992), 21 February 1992.

22. Laura Silber and Allan Little, *Yugoslavia: Death of a Nation* (1996), p. 215.

23. Virginia Morris and Michael P. Scharf, *An Insider's Guide to the International Criminal Tribunal for the Former Yugoslavia*, vol. 1. (1995), p. 19.

24. Warren Zimmermann, *Origins of a Catastrophe: Yugoslavia and its Destroyers—America's Last Ambassador Tells What Happened and Why* (1996), p. 210.

25. Warren Zimmermann, *Origins of a Catastrophe: Yugoslavia and its Destroyers—America's Last Ambassador Tells What Happened and Why* (1996), p. 174.

26. Norman Cigar, *Genocide in Bosnia: The Policy of "Ethnic Cleansing,"* (1995), p. 48.

27. Laura Silber and Allan Little, *Yugoslavia: Death of a Nation* (1995), p. 218.

28. Norman Cigar, *Genocide in Bosnia: The Policy of "Ethnic Cleansing,"* (1995), p. 49.

29. The airlift was temporarily suspended because of such attacks on two hundred occasions between September 1992 and July 1994. See "Sarejevo Airlift in 3rd Year," *The Cleveland Plain Dealer*, July 3, 1994, p. 7-A.

30. *Further Report of the Secretary-General Pursuant to Security Council Resolution 749*, U.N. Doc. S/23900 (1992), para 5.

31. "Prosecute Bosnia's War Criminals," *New York Times*, Wednesday, January 4, 1995, p. A18.

32. Misha Glenny, *The Fall of Yugoslavia: The Third Balkan War* (1992), p. 207.

33. Misha Glenny, *The Fall of Yugoslavia: The Third Balkan War* (1992), p. 208.

34. Quoted in David Owen, *Balkan Odyssey* (1995), p. 19 .

35. Quoted in Laura Silber and Allan Little, *Yugoslavia: Death of a Nation* (1995), p. 250.

36. Laura Silber and Allan Little, *Yugoslavia: Death of a Nation* (1995), p. 250 (quoting Ed Vulliamy of *The Guardian*, who accompanied Penny Marshall to Omarska).

37. See *Security Council Resolution 795*, November 11, 1992.

38. Warren Zimmermann, *Origins of a Catastrophe: Yugoslavia and its Destroyers—America's Last Ambassador Tells What Happened and Why* (1996), p. 197.

39. Norman Cigar, *Genocide in Bosnia* (1995), p. 160.

40. David Owen, *Balkan Odyssey* (1995), p. 12.

41. Anthony Lewis, "War Crimes," in *The Black Book of Bosnia*, ed. Nader Mousavizadeh (1995), p. 63.

42. Warren Zimmermann, *Origins of a Catastrophe: Yugoslavia and its Destroyers—America's Last Ambassador Tells What Happened and Why* (1996), pp. xi–xii.

43. Warren Zimmermann, *Origins of a Catastrophe: Yugoslavia and its Destroyers—America's Last Ambassador Tells What Happened and Why* (1996), p. 216.

44. Iain Guest, *On Trial, The United Nations, War Crimes, and the Former Yugoslavia* (1995), p. 21.

45. Laura Silber and Allan Little, *Yugoslavia: Death of a Nation* (1995), pp. 29–30.

46. Laura Silber and Allan Little, *Yugoslavia: Death of a Nation* (1995), p. 252 (quoting George Kenny).

47. Iain Guest, *On Trial: The United Nations, War Crimes, and the Former Yugoslavia* (1995), p. 33.

48. Iain Guest, *On Trial: The United Nations, War Crimes, and the Former Yugoslavia* (1995), p. 35; see also Jacqueline Frank, "Former State Department Aide Urges U.S. Intervention in Bosnia," *Reuters World Service,* August 28, 1992.

49. *Christian Science Monitor*, May 26, 1993, p. 18; see also, Saul Friedman, "Christopher Assailed; Official: U.S. Downplayed Bosnia Genocide," *Newsday*, February 4, 1994, p. 4.

50. Roger Cohen, "CIA Report Finds Serbs Guilty of Majority of Bosnia War Crimes," *New York Times,* March 9, 1995, pp. A1, A8.

51. Anthony Lewis, "War Crimes," in *The Black Book of Bosnia*, ed. Nader Mousavizadeh (1996), p. 59.

52. Anthony Lewis, "War Crimes," in *The Black Book of Bosnia*, ed. Nader Mousavizadeh (1996), p. 60.

53. Chris Black, "US Options Seen Fewer as Military Avoids Risk," *Boston Globe*, July 23, 1995, p. 12.

54. Iain Guest, *On Trial: The United Nations, War Crimes, and the Former Yugoslavia* (1995), p. 100.

55. Iain Guest, *On Trial: The United Nations, War Crimes, and the Former Yugoslavia* (1995), p. 104 .

56. Serge Schmemann, "From Russia to Serbia, a Current of Sympathy," *New York Times,* January 31, 1993.

57. Iain Guest, *On Trial: The United Nations, War Crimes and the Former Yugoslavia* (1995), p. 111.

58. Norman Cigar, *Genocide in Bosnia* (1995), p. 145.

59. See e.g., David Owen, *Balkan Odyssey* (1995), pp. 10–13.

60. *Security Council Resolution 713*, September 25, 1991.

61. *Security Council Resolution* 727, January 8, 1992. In a U.N. slight of hand, the Resolution merely "decide[d] that the embargo applies in accordance with paragraph 33 of the Secretary-General's Report (S/23363). The referenced paragraph provided: "Indeed, Mr. Vance added that the arms embargo would continue to apply to all areas that have been part of Yugoslavia, any decisions on

the question of the recognition of the independence of certain republics notwithstanding."

62. M. Cherif Bassiouni and Peter Manikas, *The Law of the International Criminal Tribunal for the Former Yugoslavia* (1996), p. 31.

63. Misha Glenny, *The Fall of Yugoslavia: The Third Balkan War* (1993), p. 229.

64. On September 14, 1992, the Security Council adopted Resolution 776, authorizing an expansion of UNPROFOR to protect relief convoys and if necessary respond in self-defense when attacked.

65. John Goshko, "Eagleburger Debuts on the Balkan Crisis," *Washington Post,* August 29, 1992.

66. U.S. General Accounting Office, *Report: Serbia-Montenegro: Implementation of U.N. Economic Sanctions*, (April 1993), p. 4.

67. See generally, Michael P. Scharf and Joshua L. Dorosin, "Interpreting U.N. Sanctions: The Rulings and Role of the Yugoslavia Sanctions Committees," *Brooklyn Journal of International Law* 19 (1993): 781–788.

68. See generally, Michael P. Scharf and Joshua L. Dorosin, "Interpreting U.N. Sanctions: The Rulings and Role of the Yugoslavia Sanctions Committees," *Brooklyn Journal of International Law* 19 (1993): 771–827.

69. Misha Glenny, *The Fall of Yugoslavia: The Third Balkan War* (1992), p. 212.

70. See generally, Michael P. Scharf, "Musical Chairs: The Dissolution of States and Membership in the United Nations," *Cornell International Law Journal* 28 (1995): 30–69.

71. See *Security Council Resolution* 777 (1992).

72. Letter from Carl-August Fleishchhauer, Under-Secretary-General for Legal Affairs, to Kenneth Dadzie, Under-Secretary-General, United Nations Conference on Trade and Development (September 29, 1992), reproduced in Michael P. Scharf, "Musical Chairs: The Dissolution of States and Membership in the United Nations," *Cornell International Law Journal* 28 (1995): 60–61.

73. "Case Concerning Application of the Convention on the Prevention and Punishment of the Crime of Genocide (Bosnia and Hezegovina v. Yugoslavia (Serbia and Montenegro)," 1993 *International Court of Justice Reports* (April 8): 14.

74. United Nations Department of Public Information, "The United Nations and the Situation in the Former Yugoslavia" (1993), p. 13.

75. David Owen, *Balkan Odyssey* (1995), p. 355.

76. David Owen, *Balkan Odyssey* (1995), p. 355.

77. *The Black Book of Bosnia,* ed. Nader Mousavisadeh (1996), p. 175.

Notes for Chapter 3

1. Iain Guest, *On Trial: The United Nations, War Crimes, and the Former Yugoslavia* (1995), p. 52.

2. Iain Guest, *On Trial: The United Nations, War Crimes, and the Former Yugoslavia* (1995), p. 38.

3. See Paul Lewis, "White House Adamant on Balkan War Crimes," *New York Times,* November 3, 1993, p. A-16.

4. See Letter dated 29 June 1993 from the Charge d'Affaires A.I. of the Permanent Mission of Canada to the United Nations addressed to the Secretary-General, S/26016, 30 June 1993.

5. See *United States Submission of Information to the United Nations Security Council in Accordance with Paragraph 5 of Resolution 771 (1992),* September 22, 1992.

6. "Halfway Response to All-Out War," *New York Times* Editorial, October 9, 1992.

7. Iain Guest, *On Trial: The United Nations, War Crimes, and the Former Yugoslavia* (1995), p. 58.

8. *Report of the Secretary-General on the Establishment of the Commission of Experts pursuant to Paragraph 2 of Security Council Resolution 780 (1992),* U.N. Doc. S/24657 (1992).

9. "Going Nowhere: UN War Crimes Commission Bogged Down in Bosnia Death Camp Probe," reprinted in Roy Gutman, *A Witness to Genocide* (1993).

10. Iain Guest, *On Trial: The United Nations, War Crimes, and the Former Yugoslavia* (1995), p. 57.

11. Elaine Sciolino, "U.S. Names Figures to be Prosecuted Over War Crimes," *New York Times International,* December 17, 1992, p. A-1.

12. See e.g., Carla Anne Robbins, "World Again Confronts Moral Issues Involved in War Crimes Trials," *Wall Street Journal,* July 13, 1993, p. A6.

13. Text of Statement of Secretary of State Lawrence Eagleburger at the International Conference on the Former Yugoslavia, December 16, 1992, U.S. Department of State Press Release.

14. Carla Anne Robbins, "World Again Confronts Moral Issues Involved in War Crimes Trials," *Wall Street Journal,* July 13, 1993.

15. M. Cherif Bassiouni, "The Commission of Experts Established Pursuant to Security Council Resolution 780: Investigating Violations of International Humanitarian Law in the Former Yugoslavia," *Occasional Paper No. 2,* International Human Rights Law Institute, DePaul University College of Law (1996), p. 8.

16. Iain Guest, *On Trial: The United Nations, War Crimes, and the Former Yugoslavia* (1995), p. 94.

17. Iain Guest, *On Trial: The United Nations, War Crimes, and the Former Yugoslavia* (1995), p. 94.

18. M. Cherif Bassiouni, "The Commission of Experts Established Pursuant to Security Council Resolution 780: Investigating Violations of International Hu-

manitarian Law in the Former Yugoslavia," *Occasional Paper No. 2*, International Human Rights Law Institute, DePaul University College of Law (1996), p. 8.

19. Iain Guest, *On Trial: The United Nations, War Crimes, and the Former Yugoslavia* (1995), p. 63.

20. Iain Guest, *On Trial: The United Nations, War Crimes, and the Former Yugoslavia* (1995), p. 9.

21. This report was issued as a United Nations document dated February 10, 1993 (U.N. Doc. S/25274), reprinted in Virginia Morris and Michael P. Scharf, *An Insider's Guide the International Criminal Tribunal for the Former Yugoslavia*, vol. 2 (1995), pp. 311–326 .

22. Andrew Kelly, "Head of U.N. War Crimes Panel Resigns," *Reuters World Service*, October 1, 1993.

23. Patrick Bishop, "Britain 'Snubbed War Crimes Team,'" *Daily Telegraph*, December 4, 1993.

24. Patrick Bishop, "Britain 'Snubbed War Crimes Team,'" *Daily Telegraph*, December 4, 1993.

25. "Halfway Response to All-Out War," *New York Times* Editorial, October 9, 1992.

26. Stephanie Nebehay, "U.N. War Crimes Body in Disarray on Anniversary" *Reuters World Service*, October 6, 1993.

27. John Pomfret, "War Crimes' Punishment Seen Distant; Balkan Probe Lacks Funds and Backing," *Washington Post*, November 12, 1993, p. A39; M. Cherif Bassiouni, "The Commission of Experts Established Pursuant to Security Council Resolution 780: Investigating Violations of International Humanitarian Law in the Former Yugoslavia," *Occasional Paper No. 2*, International Human Rights Law Institute, DePaul University College of Law (1996), pp. 10–14.

28. Telephone Interview with M. Cherif Bassiouni, August 8, 1996.

29. Telephone Interview with M. Cherif Bassiouni, August 8, 1996.

30. Telephone Interview with M. Cherif Bassiouni, August 8, 1996.

31. M. Cherif Bassiouni, "The Commission of Experts Established Pursuant to Security Council Resolution 780: Investigating Violations of International Humanitarian Law in the Former Yugoslavia," *Occasional Paper No. 2*, International Human Rights Law Institute, DePaul University College of Law (1996), pp. 13–14.

32. M. Cherif Bassiouni, "The Commission of Experts Established Pursuant to Security Council Resolution 780: Investigating Violations of International Humanitarian Law in the Former Yugoslavia," *Occasional Paper No. 2*, International Human Rights Law Institute, DePaul University College of Law (1996), p. 31.

33. Iain Guest, *On Trial: The United Nations, War Crimes, and the Former Yugoslavia* (1995), pp. 63–64.

34. M. Cherif Bassiouni, "The Commission of Experts Established Pursuant to Security Council Resolution 780: Investigating Violations of International Humanitarian Law in the Former Yugoslavia," *Occasional Paper No. 2*, International Human Rights Law Institute, DePaul University College of Law (1996), pp. 35–37.

35. Iain Guest, *On Trial: The United Nations, War Crimes, and the Former Yugoslavia* (1995), p. 89.

36. Iain Guest, *On Trial: The United Nations, War Crimes, and the Former Yugoslavia* (1995), p. 90.

37. Telephone Interview with M. Cherif Bassiouni, August 8, 1996.

38. Telephone Interview with M. Cherif Bassiouni, August 8, 1996.

39. M. Cherif Bassiouni, "The Commission of Experts Established Pursuant to Security Council Resolution 780: Investigating Violations of International Humanitarian Law in the Former Yugoslavia," *Occasional Paper No. 2*, International Human Rights Law Institute, DePaul University College of Law (1996) p. 67.

40. The 780 Commission's final report is reproduced in U.N. Doc. S/1994/674, May 27, 1994.

41. Reproduced in M. Cherif Bassiouni, "The Commission of Experts Established Pursuant to Security Council Resolution 780: Investigating Violations of International Humanitarian Law in the Former Yugoslavia," *Occasional Paper No. 2*, International Human Rights Law Institute, DePaul University College of Law (1996), pp. 60–61.

42. Telephone Interview with M. Cherif Bassiouni, August 8, 1996.

Notes for Chapter 4

1. The French Report is reproduced in Virginia Morris and Michael Scharf, *An Insider's Guide to the International Criminal Tribunal for the Former Yugoslavia*, vol. 2 (1995), pp. 327–375.

2. See Commission on Human Rights, *Report on the Forty-Ninth Session, 1 February–12 March 1993*, U.N. Doc. E/CN.4/1993/122, p. 49.

3. The CSCE and the Italian reports are reproduced in Virginia Morris and Michael Scharf, *An Insider's Guide to the International Criminal Tribunal for the Former Yugoslavia*, vol. 2 (1995), pp. 211–311, and 375–387, respectively.

4. Resolution 808 is reproduced in Virginia Morris and Michael Scharf, *An Insider's Guide to the International Criminal Tribunal for the Former Yugoslavia*, vol. 2(1995), pp. 157–179.

5. Resolution 808 is reproduced in Virginia Morris and Michael Scharf, *An Insider's Guide to the International Criminal Tribunal for the Former Yugoslavia*, vol. 2(1995), pp. 157–179.

6. The record of debate leading to the adoption of Resolution 808 is reproduced in Virginia Morris and Michael Scharf, *An Insider's Guide to the International Criminal Tribunal for the Former Yugoslavia*, vol. 2 (1995), pp. 159–175.

7. The record of debate leading to the adoption of Resolution 808 is reproduced in Virginia Morris and Michael Scharf, *An Insider's Guide to the International Criminal Tribunal for the Former Yugoslavia*, vol. 2 (1995), pp. 159–175.

8. The proposals of the states and organizations for the Statute of the International Tribunal are reproduced in Virginia Morris and Michael Scharf, *An Insider's Guide to the International Criminal Tribunal for the Former Yugoslavia,* vol. 2 (1995), pp. 209–479.

9. See generally, John R. Crook, "The United Nations Compensation Commission—A New Structure to Enforce State Responsibility," *American Journal of International Law* 86 (1993): 144.

10. Iain Guest, *On Trial: The United Nations, War Crimes, and the Former Yugoslavia* (1995), p. 118.

11. *Report of the Secretary-General Pursuant to Paragraph 2 of Security Council Resolution 808 (1993),* U.N. document S/25704 and Add.1, 3 May 1993, reproduced in Virginia Morris and Michael Scharf, *An Insider's Guide to the International Criminal Tribunal for the Former Yugoslavia,* vol. 2 (1995), pp. 1–39.

12. *Report of the Secretary-General Pursuant to Paragraph 2 of Security Council Resolution 808 (1993),* U.N. document S/25704 and Add.1, 3 May 1993, para 34, reproduced in Virginia Morris and Michael Scharf, *An Insider's Guide to the International Criminal Tribunal for the Former Yugoslavia,* vol. 2 (1995), p. 9.

13. *Report of the Secretary-General Pursuant to Paragraph 2 of Security Council Resolution 808 (1993),* U.N. document S/25704 and Add.1, 3 May 1993, para 47, reproduced in Virginia Morris and Michael Scharf, *An Insider's Guide to the International Criminal Tribunal for the Former Yugoslavia,* vol. 2 (1995), p. 12.

14. For a detailed discussion of the Yamashita case, see M. Cherif Bassiouni, *Crimes Against Humanity in International Law* (1992), p. 380.

15. See Rule for Courts-Martial 916(d), *Manual for Courts-Martial, United States* (1984).

16. See Nikola Srzentic, "Yugoslav Criminal Law," *Yugoslav Survey* 20(3) (1979): 33.

17. See *Provisional Verbatim Record of the Three Thousand Two Hundred and Seventeenth Meeting,* U.N. Doc. S/PV.3217, 25 May 1993 (verbatim transcript of Security Council deliberations on Security Council Resolution 827) reproduced in-Virginia Morris and Michael Scharf, *An Insider's Guide to the International Criminal Tribunal for the Former Yugoslavia,* vol. 2 (1995), pp. 179–208.

18. See *Statement of Ambassador Albright, Provisional Verbatim Record of the Three Thousand Two Hundred and Seventeenth Meeting,* U.N. Doc. S/PV.3217, 25 May 1993, reproduced in Virginia Morris and Michael Scharf, *An Insider's Guide to the International Criminal Tribunal for the Former Yugoslavia,* vol. 2 (1995), pp. 185–189.

19. See James O'Brien, "The International Tribunal for Violations of International Humanitarian Law in the Former Yugoslavia," *American Journal of International Law* 87 (1993): 639, 658.

20. Geoffrey R. Watson, *The Humanitarian Law of the Yugoslavia War Crimes Tribunal: Jurisdiction in* The Prosecutor v. Tadic, unpublished manuscript (1996), p. 32. Watson, who is U.S. Ambassador Madeleine Albright's son-in-law, was present in the Security Council chamber during the voting on Resolution 827.

21. Geoffrey R. Watson, *The Humanitarian Law of the Yugoslavia War Crimes Tribunal: Jurisdiction in* The Prosecutor v. Tadic, unpublished manuscript (1996), p. 32.

22. Iain Guest, *On Trial: The United Nations, War Crimes, and the Former Yugoslavia* (1995), p. 129.

23. Iain Guest, *On Trial: The United Nations, War Crimes, and the Former Yugoslavia* (1995), p. 129.

24. See *Provisional Verbatim Record of the Three Thousand Two Hundred and Seventeenth Meeting,* U.N. Doc. S/PV.3217, 25 May 1993 (verbatim transcript of Security Council deliberations on Security Council Resolution 827) reproduced in Virginia Morris and Michael Scharf, *An Insider's Guide to the International Criminal Tribunal for the Former Yugoslavia,* vol. 2 (1995), p. 201.

25. See *Provisional Verbatim Record of the Three Thousand Two Hundred and Seventeenth Meeting,* U.N. Doc. S/PV.3217, 25 May 1993 (verbatim transcript of Security Council deliberations on Security Council Resolution 827) reproduced in Virginia Morris and Michael Scharf, *An Insider's Guide to the International Criminal Tribunal for the Former Yugoslavia,* vol. 2 (1995), pp. 199–200.

26. David Ottaway, "U.S. Warns Serbs on War Trials," *Washington Post*, January 17, 1994, p. A-19.

27. See generally, John R. Crook, "The United Nations Compensation Commission—A New Structure to Enforce State Responsibility," *American Journal of International Law* 86 (1993): 144.

28. After informal consultations, the list of twenty-three candidates was unanimously adopted by the Security Council in Resolution 857 on 20 August 1993. A report containing the curricula vitae of these candidates was circulated to the members of the General Assembly to facilitate the election process. See U.N. Doc. A/47/1006, 1 September 1993.

29. Judge Abi-Saab resigned in 1995 and was replaced by Fouad Abdel-Moneim Riad, a Professor of Law at Cairo University.

30. Judge de Costil resigned shortly after taking office and was replaced by Claude Jorda, former Prosecutor General for the Court of Appeals in Paris.

31. Iain Guest, *On Trial: The United Nations, War Crimes, and the Former Yugoslavia* (1995), p. 131.

32. See Boris Krivoshei and Serbei Staroselsky, "Russia Will Obey Tribunal on War Crimes in Yugoslavia," *TASS*, September 24, 1993.

33. Iain Guest, *On Trial: The United Nations, War Crimes, and the Former Yugoslavia* (1995), p. 132.

34. Iain Guest, *On Trial: The United Nations, War Crimes, and the Former Yugoslavia* (1995), p. 132.

35. Brenda Sapino, "Gabrielle McDonald's Star Turn," *Texas Lawyer* 11 (October 2, 1995).

36. Brenda Sapino, "Gabrielle McDonald's Star Turn," *Texas Lawyer* 11 (October 2, 1995).

37. "McDonald Described as Open-Minded," *Houston Chronicle*, May 8, 1996, p. 22.

38. William Horne, "The Real Trial of the Century," *The American Lawyer,* September 1995, p. 5.

39. *First Annual Report of the International Tribunal for the Former Yugoslavia,* U.N. Doc. S/1994/1007, August 29, 1994, pp. 15 and 20.

40. The Tribunal's Rules are reproduced in Virginia Morris and Michael Scharf, *An Insider's Guide to the International Criminal Tribunal for the Former Yugoslavia,* vol. 2 (1995), pp. 39–87.

41. William Horne, "The Real Trial of the Century," *The American Lawyer,* September 1995, p. 5.

42. *First Annual Report of the International Tribunal for the Former Yugoslavia,* U.N. Doc. S/1994/1007, August 29, 1994, p. 23.

43. See Rule 22, *United States Proposal for the Rules of Procedure*, reproduced in Virginia Morris and Michael Scharf, *An Insider's Guide to the International Criminal Tribunal for the Former Yugoslavia,* vol. 2 (1995), p. 539.

44. "Comments of the United States on the Tribunal's Rules of Procedure, May 2, 1994," reproduced in *Report on the Proposed Rules of Procedure and Evidence of the International Tribunal to Adjudicate War Crimes in the Former Yugoslavia, Submitted By A Special Task Force of the American Bar Association* (1995), p. 178.

45. See *Statement by the President Made at A Briefing to Members of Diplomatic Missions*, U.N. Doc. IT/29, February 11, 1994 reproduced in Virginia Morris and Michael Scharf, *An Insider's Guide to the International Criminal Tribunal for the Former Yugoslavia,* vol. 2 (1995), p. 652.

46. Rule 101.

47. See *Statement by the President Made at A Briefing to Members of Diplomatic Missions*, U.N. Doc. IT/29, February 11, 1994 reproduced in Virginia Morris and Michael Scharf, *An Insider's Guide to the International Criminal Tribunal for the Former Yugoslavia,* vol. 2 (1995), p. 652.

48. Rule 71.

49. Rule 69.

50. Rule 34.

51. Rule 96.

52. Iain Guest, *On Trial: The United Nations, War Crimes, and the Former Yugoslavia* (1995), p. 133.

53. Rule 96 (as amended on May 1994).

54. *Annual Report of the International Tribunal,* U.N. Doc. S/1994/1007, A/49/342, 29 August 1994, p. 24.

55. Kevin R. Chaney, "Pitfalls and Imperatives: Applying the Lessons of Nuremberg to the Yugoslav War Crimes Trials," *Dickinson Journal of International Law* 14 (1995): 57, 60 .

56. Cedric Thornberry, "Saving the War Crimes Tribunal," *Foreign Policy* 104 (Fall 1996): 78–79 .

57. U.N. Doc. S/25801, May 21, 1993.

58. Article 10 (1) of the Tribunal's Statute, reproduced in Appendix B.

59. Article 25 of the Tribunal's Statute, reproduced in Appendix B.

60. See Rule 27.

Notes for Chapter 5

1. Iain Guest, *On Trial: The United Nations, War Crimes, and the Former Yugoslavia* (1995), p. 145.

2. Iain Guest, *On Trial: The United Nations, War Crimes, and the Former Yugoslavia* (1995), p. 146.

3. James Bone, "U.K. Blocks Choice of War Crimes Prosecutor," *Times* (London), September 4, 1993.

4. Iain Guest, *On Trial: The United Nations, War Crimes, and the Former Yugoslavia* (1995), p. 148.

5. Iain Guest, *On Trial: The United Nations, War Crimes, and the Former Yugoslavia* (1995), p. 146.

6. Stanley Meisler, "Jury Still Out on Bosnian War Crimes Tribunal Created by U.N.," *Los Angeles Times,* December 25, 1993, p. A-5.

7. Stanley Meisler, "Jury Still Out on Bosnian War Crimes Tribunal Created by U.N.," *Los Angeles Times,* December 25, 1993, p. A-5.

8. Telephone Interview with M. Cherif Bassiouni, August 8, 1996.

9. Iain Guest, *On Trial: The United Nations, War Crimes, and the Former Yugoslavia* (1995), p. 146.

10. Iain Guest, *On Trial: The United Nations, War Crimes, and the Former Yugoslavia* (1995), p. 148.

11. Stanley Meisler, "Jury Still Out on Bosnian War Crimes Tribunal Created by U.N.," *Los Angeles Times,* December 25, 1993, p. A-5.

12. Stanley Meisler, "Jury Still Out on Bosnian War Crimes Tribunal Created by U.N.," *Los Angeles Times,* December 25, 1993, p. A-5.

13. Iain Guest, *On Trial: The United Nations, War Crimes, and the Former Yugoslavia* (1995), p. 149.

14. "Venezuelan On War Crimes Panel; Tribunal Will Probe Atrocities in Former Yugoslavia," *Chicago Tribune,* October 22, 1993, p. 10.

15. Roy Gutman, "Tribunal Setback: Prosecutor for War Crimes in Former Yugoslavia Quits," *Newsday,* February 4, 1994, p. 4.

16. David Owen, *Balkan Odyssey* (1995), p. 255.

17. Paul Lewis, "South African Is To Prosecute Balkan War Crimes," *New York Times,* July 9, 1994, p. 2.

18. Stephen Handelman, "Point of War Crimes Tribunal Is To Try Persons, Not Nationalities," *Toronto Star,* July 10, 1994, p. F-9.

19. Iain Guest, *On Trial: The United Nations, War Crimes, and the Former Yugoslavia* (1995), p. 149.

20. Stanley Meisler, "U.N. Names South African Judge as Balkans War Crimes Prosecutor," *Los Angeles Times,* July 9, 1994, p. A-5.

21. Sudarsan Raghavan, "Richard J. Goldstone; A South African Jurist Takes on Balkan and Rwanda Conflicts, Seeking to Punish War Criminals," *Los Angeles Times,* March 14, 1995, p. 5.

22. Evelyn Leopold, "S. African Named as Ex-Yugoslav War Crimes Prosecutor," *Reuters World Service,* July 9, 1994.

23. "U.N. Chief Prosecutor to Quit in 1996," *Deutsche Presse-Agentur,* January 30, 1996.

24. Sudarsan Raghavan, "Richard J. Goldstone; A South African Jurist Takes on Balkan and Rwanda Conflicts, Seeking to Punish War Criminals," *Los Angeles Times,* March 14, 1995, p. 5.

25. *U.N. Security Council Resolution 936 (1994),* 8 July 1994.

26. Stephen Handelman, "Point of War Crimes Tribunal Is To Try Persons, Not Nationalities," *Toronto Star,* July 10, 1994, p. F-9.

27. Stanley Meisler, "U.N. Names South African Judge as Balkans War Crimes Prosecutor," *Los Angeles Times,* July 9, 1994, p. A-5.

28. See Article 32 of the Statute, reproduced in Appendix B.

29. Interview with Thom Warrick, Special Counsel to the Coalition of International Justice, in Brussels, Belgium, July 20, 1996.

30. See Statements of India, Brazil, Zimbabwe, Mexico, Ecuador, and Colombia. *Summary Record of the 70th Meeting of the Fifth Committee,* U.N. Doc. A/C.5/47/SR.70, 25 August 1993; *Summary Record of the 72nd Meeting of the Fifth Committee,* U.N. Doc. A/C.5/47/SR.72, 27 August 1993.

31. *Report of the Secretary-General as Requested by the General Assembly in Resolution 47/235,* U.N. Doc. A/C5/48/44/Add.1, 11 March 1994, p. 6.

32. *General Assembly Resolution 48/241,* April 14, 1994.

33. *Report of the Secretary-General as Requested by the General Assembly in Resolution 47/235,* U.N. Doc. A/C.5/48/44/Add.1, 11 March 1994 (revised cost estimates); *Report of the Secretary-General as Requested by the General Assembly in Resolution 47/235,* U.N. Doc. A/C.5/48/44, 8 December 1993 (original estimate).

34. Prepared Testimony of Thomas Warrick, Special Counsel, Coalition for International Justice Before the House Committee On International Operations and Human Rights, Federal News Service, October 26, 1995.

35. "Prosecute Bosnia's War Criminals," *New York Times,* January 4, 1995, p. A18.

36. Interview with Tom Warrick, Brussels, Belgium, July 20, 1996.

37. Iain Guest, *On Trial: The United Nations, War Crimes and the Former Yugoslavia* (1995), pp. 139–140.

38. William Horne, "The Real Trial of the Century," *The American Lawyer,* September 1995, p. 5.

39. *Washington Weekly Report,* March 18, 1996.

40. Marlise Simons, "Bosnian Rapes Go Untried by the U.N.," *New York Times,* December 7, 1994, p. A12.

41. Prepared Testimony of Thomas Warrick, Special Counsel, Coalition for International Justice Before the House Committee On International Operations and Human Rights, Federal News Service, October 26, 1995.

42. Raymond Bonner, "U.N. Fiscal Woes Are Said to Threaten War Crime Tribunals," *New York Times,* October 4, 1995, p. A8.

43. Raymond Bonner, "U.N. Fiscal Woes Are Said to Threaten War Crime Tribunals," *New York Times,* October 4, 1995, p. A8.

44. *Remarks of Antonio Cassese, 52nd Plenary Meeting of the United Nations General Assembly,* U.N. Doc. A/50/PV.52, November 7, 1995, p. 3.

45. *General Assembly Resolution 49/242,* August 7, 1995.

46. "Effects of Awards of Compensation Made by the United Nations Administrative Tribunal," *International Court of Justice Reports* (1954): 47, 49. ("The function of approving the budget does not mean that the General Assembly has an absolute power to approve or disapprove the expenditure proposed to it; for some part of that expenditure arises out of obligations already incurred by the Organization, and to this extent the General Assembly has no alternative but to honor these engagements").

47. *CSCE Proposal for an International War Crimes Tribunal for the Former Yugoslavia,* U.N. Doc. S/25307, p. 74, reproduced in Virginia Morris and Michael Scharf, *An Insider's Guide to the International Criminal Tribunal for the Former Yugoslavia,* vol. 2 (1995), p. 268.

48. *U.N. Peacekeeping: Lessons Learned in Managing Recent Missions,* United States General Accounting Office Report (December 1993), p. 17.

49. Interview with Justice Richard Goldstone, Brussels, Belgium, July 20, 1996.

50. *Bulletin of the International Criminal Tribunal for the Former Yugoslavia,* No. 4, March 15, 1996.

51. Ed Vulliamy, "In Times of Trial," *The Guardian,* October 31, 1995, p. T6.

52. Minna Schrag, "The Yugoslav Crimes Tribunal: A Prosecutor's View," *Duke Journal of Comparative and International Law* 6 (1995): 192.

53. Press Statement by the Prosecutor, Justice Richard Goldstone, in Conjunction with the Announcement of Indictments on 25 July 1995.

54. Richard J. Goldstone, "The International Tribunal for the Former Yugoslavia: A Case Study in Security Council Action," *Duke Journal of Comparative. and International Law* 6 (1995): 7 .

55. Nader Mousavizadeh, *The Black Book of Bosnia* (1996), p. 189.

56. Bob Woodward, *The Choice* (1996), p. 253.

57. Bob Woodward, *The Choice* (1996), p. 263.

58. Bob Woodward, *The Choice* (1996), p. 263.

59. Bob Woodward, *The Choice* (1996), p. 328.

60. Stephen Engelberg, "Panel Seeks U.S. Pledge on Bosnia War Criminals," *New York Times,* November 3, 1995, p. A1.

61. Stephen Engelberg, "Panel Seeks U.S. Pledge on Bosnia War Criminals," *New York Times,* November 3, 1995, p. A1.

62. See Michael P. Scharf, "Swapping Amnesty for Peace: Was there a Duty to Prosecute International Crimes in Haiti?," *Texas International Law Journal* 31 (1996): 1, 37.

63. Michael P. Scharf, "Swapping Amnesty for Peace: Was there a Duty to

Prosecute International Crimes in Haiti?," *Texas International Law Journal* 31 (1996): 11 n.75.

64. Anthony D'Amato, "Correspondence," *American Journal of International Law* 89 (1995): 94.

65. David Owen, *Balkan Odyssey* (1995), p. 80.

66. Madeleine K. Albright, "War Crimes In Bosnia," *San Francisco Chronicle,* December 4, 1993, p. A22.

67. Roger Cohen, "U.N. in Bosnia: Black Robes Clash with Blue Hats," *New York Times,* April 25, 1995, p. A3.

68. Peter S. Canellos, "Amnesty Plan Worries UN War-Crimes Prosecutor," *Boston Globe,* October 1, 1994, p. 8.

69. Peter S. Canellos, "Amnesty Plan Worries UN War-Crimes Prosecutor," *Boston Globe,* October 1, 1994, p. 8.

70. Elaine Sciolino, "Bosnian Talks Snag on Fate of Two Serbs," *New York Times*, November 17, 1995, p. A3.

71. See *Letter Dated 29 November 1995 from the Permanent Representative of the United States of America to the United Nations addressed to the Secretary-General,* U.N. Doc. A/50/790, S/1995/999, 30 November 1995, p. 4 (General Framework Agreement for Peace in Bosnia and Herzegovina, Article IX).

72. See *Letter Dated 29 November 1995 from the Permanent Representative of the United States of America to the United Nations addressed to the Secretary-General,* U.N. Doc. A/50/790, S/1995/999, 30 November 1995, p. 23 (Agreement on the Military Aspects of the Peace Settlement, Article X).

73. See *Letter Dated 29 November 1995 from the Permanent Representative of the United States of America to the United Nations addressed to the Secretary-General,* U.N. Doc. A/50/790, S/1995/999, 30 November 1995, p. 23 (Agreement on the Military Aspects of the Peace Settlement, Article IX(1)(g)).

74. See *Letter Dated 29 November 1995 from the Permanent Representative of the United States of America to the United Nations addressed to the Secretary-General,* U.N. Doc. A/50/790, S/1995/999, 30 November 1995, p. 63 (Constitution of Bosnia and Herzegovina, Article II (8)).

75. See *Letter Dated 29 November 1995 from the Permanent Representative of the United States of America to the United Nations addressed to the Secretary-General,* U.N. Doc. A/50/790, S/1995/999, 30 November 1995, p. 73 (Constitution of Bosnia and Herzegovina, Article X.

76. Colin Soloway and Stephen J. Hedges, "How Not to Catch a War Criminal," *U.S. News and World Report,* December 9, 1996, p. 63.

77. Dean Murphy, "Bosnia Pact Reported on War Crimes," *Boston Globe,* February 13, 1996, p. 2.

78. Colin Soloway and Stephen J. Hedges, "How Not to Catch a War Criminal," *U.S. News and World Report,* December 9, 1996, p. 63.

79. Interview with Justice Richard Goldstone, Brussels, Belgium, July 20, 1996.

80. Interview with Graham Blewitt, The Hague, Netherlands, July 25, 1996.

Notes for Chapter 6

1. William Horne, "The Real Trial of the Century," *The American Lawyer*, September 1995, p. 5.

2. Robert Block, "First, Catch You a War Criminal," *The Independent,* April 30, 1995, p. 4.

3. William Horne, "The Real Trial of the Century," *The American Lawyer*, September 1995, p. 5.

4. Ed Vulliamy, "In Times of Trial," *The Guardian*, October 31, 1995, p. T6.

5. Stacy Sullivan, "Survivors Deride Defense Claims," *The Times* (London), May 8, 1996.

6. George Rodrigue, "Serbs Systematic in Ridding Region of Muslims, Many Say; Bosnia Corridor Considered Crucial to 'Republic,' " *Dallas Morning News,* December 27, 1992, p. 1A.

7. George Rodrigue, "Serbs Systematic in Ridding Region of Muslims, Many Say; Bosnia Corridor Considered Crucial to 'Republic,'" *Dallas Morning News,* December 27, 1992, p. 1A.

8. George Rodrigue, "Serbs Systematic in Ridding Region of Muslims, Many Say; Bosnia Corridor Considered Crucial to 'Republic,' " *Dallas Morning News,* December 27, 1992, p. 1A.

9. Robert Block, "First, Catch You a War Criminal," *The Independent*, April 30, 1995, p. 4.

10. George Rodrigue, "Serbs Systematic in Ridding Region of Muslims, Many Say; Bosnia Corridor Considered Crucial to 'Republic,' " *Dallas Morning News,* December 27, 1992, p. 1A.

11. Stacy Sullivan, "Serb War Criminal is Innocent Loving Father, Family Say," *The Times* (London), May 13, 1996.

12. William Horne, "The Real Trial of the Century," *The American Lawyer*, September 1995, p. 5.

13. William Horne, "The Real Trial of the Century," *The American Lawyer*, September 1995, p. 5.

14. Robert Block, "First, Catch You a War Criminal," *The Independent*, April 30, 1995, p. 4.

15. Robert Block, "First, Catch You a War Criminal," *The Independent*, April 30, 1995, p. 4.

16. Robert Block, "First, Catch You a War Criminal," *The Independent*, April 30, 1995, p. 4.

17. Dan Fesperman, "Germans Chase Serbian ar Criminals, Amid Familiar Shadows of Own Past," *Baltimore Sun,* February 17, 1994, p. 7A.

18. "Federal Prosecutor's Office Investigating 31 Suspected War Criminals," Associated Press *Worldstream* March 3, 1994.

19. United Press International, February 14, 1994.

20. United Press International, February 14, 1994.

21. United Press International, February 14, 1994.

22. "Alleged Serb War Criminal Arrested in Germany," *Press Association Newsfile*, February 14, 1994.

23. Interview with Graham Blewitt, The Hague, Netherlands, July 25, 1996.

24. Interview with Graham Blewitt, The Hague, Netherlands, July 25, 1996.

25. Interview with Justice Richard Goldstone, Brussels, Belgium, July 20, 1996.

26. Interview with Graham Blewitt, The Hague, Netherlands, July 25, 1996.

27. Interview with Graham Blewitt, The Hague, Netherlands, July 25, 1996.

28. Application for Deferral by the Federal Republic of Germany in the Matter of Dusko Tadic, Submission By the Prosecutor.

29. *Decision of the Trial Chamber on the Application by the Prosecutor for a Formal Request for Deferral to the Competence of the International Criminal Tribunal for the Former Yugoslavia in the Matter of Dusko Tadic*, Case No. IT-94-1-D, November 8, 1994, para. 19.

30. Transcript of Tadic Deferral Hearing, November 8, 1994.

31. Iain Guest, *On Trial: The United Nations, War Crimes, and the Former Yugoslavia* (1995), p. 178.

32. Iain Guest, *On Trial: The United Nations, War Crimes, and the Former Yugoslavia* (1995), p. 178.

33. Transcript of Tadic Deferral Hearing, November 8, 1994.

34. Transcript of Tadic Deferral Hearing, November 8, 1994.

35. Interview with Graham Blewitt, The Hague, Netherlands, July 25, 1996.

36. See Article 4 of the Tribunal's Statute reproduced in Appendix B.

37. Ed Vulliamy, "In Times of Trial," *The Guardian,* October 31, 1995, p. T6.

38. The following background about Michail Wladimiroff is extracted from Malise Simons, "Lawyer Says Defending A Bosnia Serb is No Easy Job," *New York Times,* May 20, 1996, p. A-8.

39. Malise Simons, "Lawyer Says Defending A Bosnia Serb is No Easy Job," *New York Times,* May 20, 1996, p. A-8.

40. Interview with Michail Wladimiroff, The Hague, Netherlands, July 25, 1996.

41. Interview with Michael Wladimiroff, The Hague, Netherlands, July 25, 1996.

42. Interview with Michael Wladimiroff, The Hague, Netherlands, July 25, 1996.

43. Interview with Steven Kay, The Hague, Netherlands, July 25, 1996.

44. Interview with Sylvia de Bertodano, The Hague, Netherlands, July 25, 1996.

45. Ed Vulliamy, "In Times of Trial," *The Guardian,* October 31, 1995, p. T6.

46. Brief of the Prosecutor, quoted in *The Prosecutor v. Tadic,* Case IT-94-I-AR72, 8-10 (Oct. 2, 1995), p. 9.

47. *The Prosecutor v. Tadic,* Case IT-94-I-T, Decision on Jurisdiction, 11 (Aug. 10, 1995).

48. *The Prosecutor v. Tadic,* Case IT-94-I-AR72, 8-10 (Oct. 2, 1995).

49. Geoffrey R. Watson, *The Humanitarian Law of the Yugoslavia War Crimes Tribunal: Jurisdiction in* The Prosecutor v. Tadic, unpublished manuscript (1996), p. 20.

50. Geoffrey R. Watson, *The Humanitarian Law of the Yugoslavia War Crimes Tribunal: Jurisdiction in* The Prosecutor v. Tadic, unpublished manuscript (1996), p. 23.

51. *The Prosecutor v. Tadic,* Case IT-94-1-T, Decision on Jurisdiction (10 August 1995), p. 3.

52. *The Prosecutor v. Tadic,* Case IT-94-I-T, Decision on Jurisdiction (10 August 1995), p. 3.

53. *The Prosecutor v. Tadic,* Case IT-94-I-T, Decision on Jurisdiction (10 August 1995), p. 3.

54. *The Prosecutor v. Tadic,* Case IT-94-I-AR72 (2 October 1995), pp. 16–17.

55. *The Prosecutor v. Tadic,* Case IT-94-I-AR72 (2 October 1995), Separate Opinion of Judge Sidhwa, p. 33.

56. Zand Case (Op. Com., 12 October 1978).

57. *The Prosecutor v. Tadic,* Case IT-94-I-AR72 (2 October 1995), p. 22.

58. *The Prosecutor v. Tadic,* Case IT-94-I-AR72 (2 October 1995), p. 22.

59. *The Prosecutor v. Tadic,* Case IT-94-I-AR72 (2 October 1995), p. 22.

60. *The Prosecutor v. Tadic,* Case IT-94-I-AR72 (2 October 1995), pp. 31–32.

61. *The Prosecutor v. Tadic,* Case IT-94-I-AR72 (2 October 1995), pp. 31–32.

62. *Preliminary Remarks of the International Committee of the Red Cross,* 22 February 1993, reproduced in Virginia Morris and Michael Scharf, *An Insider's Guide to the International Criminal Tribunal for the Former Yugoslavia,* vol. 2 (1995), p. 391.

63. Decision on the Defence Motion for Interlocutory Appeal on Jurisdiction, 2 October 1995, IT Doc. IT-94-1-AR72, p. 68. Judge Li dissented from this conclusion.

64. Geoffrey R. Watson, *The Humanitarian Law of the Yugoslavia War Crimes Tribunal: Jurisdiction in* The Prosecutor v. Tadic, unpublished manuscript (1996), p. 29.

65. Geoffrey R. Watson, *The Humanitarian Law of the Yugoslavia War Crimes Tribunal: Jurisdiction in* The Prosecutor v. Tadic, unpublished manuscript (1996), p. 54.

66. Decision on the Defence Motion for Interlocutory Appeal on Jurisdiction, 2 October 1995, IT Doc. IT-94-1-AR72, para. 88.

67. Decision on the Defense Motion on the Principle of Non-bis-in-idem, *The Prosecutor v. Dusko Tadic,* Case No. IT-94-1-T, November 14, 1995, pp. 4–5.

68. International Tribunal Press Release, CC/PIO/011-E, July 10, 1995.

69. Decision on the Defense Motion on the Form of the Indictment, *The Prosecutor v. Dusko Tadic,* IT-94-1-T, November 14, 1995.

70. Decision on the Defense Motion on the Form of the Indictment, *The Prosecutor v. Dusko Tadic,* IT-94-1-T, November 14, 1995, p. 5.

71. Decision on the Defense Motion on the Form of the Indictment, *The Prosecutor v. Dusko Tadic,* IT-94-1-T, November 14, 1995, p. 5.

72. Decision on the Prosecutor's Motion for Protective Measures for Victims and Witnesses, IT-94-I-T, 10 August 1995.

73. Decision on the Prosecutor's motion Requesting Protective Measures for Witness L, *The Prosecutor v. Dusko Tadic,* IT-94-1-T, November 14, 1995.

74. International Tribunal Press Release, CC/PIO/015-E, August 10, 1995.

75. Brenda Sapino, "Gabrielle McDonald's Star Turn," *Texas Lawyer*, October 2, 1995.

76. Interview with Graham Blewitt, The Hague, Netherlands, July 25, 1996.

77. Monroe Leigh, "Yugoslav Tribunal: Use of Unnamed Witnesses Against Accused," *American Journal of International Law* 90 (1996): 235.

78. Decision on the Prosecutor's Motion for Protective Measures for Victims and Witnesses, IT-94-I-T, 10 August 1995, p. 15.

79. The Nuremberg Tribunal had been severely criticized for allowing the prosecutors to introduce ex parte affidavits against the accused over the objections of their attorneys. See Telford Taylor, *Anatomy of The Nuremberg Trials* (1992), pp. 174 and 241; American Bar Association Section of International Law and Practice, *Report on the International Tribunal to Adjudicate War Crimes Committed in the Former Yugoslavia* (1993), p. 27.

80. Malise Simons, "Lawyer Says Defending A Bosnia Serb is No Easy Job," *New York Times,* May 20, 1996, p. A-8.

Notes for Chapter 7

1. Terry Moran, "A View from the Hague," *The American Lawyer*, June 1996, p. 93.

2. Interview with Michael Keegan, The Hague, Netherlands, July 25, 1996.

3. Trial Chamber II: Order on the Prosecution Motion to Withdraw Counts 2 through 4 of the Indictment Without Prejudice, IT-94-I-T, May 15, 1996.

4. See Chapter 4.

5. Decision on the Defence Motions to Summon and Protect Defence Witnesses, and on the Giving of Evidence by Video-Link, IT-94-I-T, June 25, 1996.

6. Decision on the Defence Motions to Summon and Protect Defence Witnesses, and on the Giving of Evidence by Video-Link, IT-94-I-T, June 25, 1996, p. 7.

7. Decision on the Defence Motions to Summon and Protect Defence Witnesses, and on the Giving of Evidence by Video-Link, IT-94-I-T, June 25, 1996, p. 5.

8. Prosecutor's Pre-Trial Brief, IT-94-I-T, April 10, 1996, p. 1.

9. Response of the Defence to the Prosecutor's Pre-Trial Brief Filed on 10 April 1996, IT-94-I-T, April 23, 1996.

10. Opening Statements by Mr. Grant Niemann and Mr. Michail Wladi-

miroff, IT-94-1-T, 7 May 1996, p. 4 (includes Judge McDonald's announcement of pre-trial rulings).

11. Interview with Justice Richard Goldstone, Brussels, Belgium, July 20, 1996.

12. Interview with Grant Niemann, The Hague, Netherlands, July 25, 1996.

13. John Appleman, *Military Tribunals and International Crimes* (1971), p. ix.

14. Interview with Michail Wladimiroff, The Hague, Netherlands, July 25, 1996.

15. Interview with Michael Wladimiroff, The Hague, Netherlands, July 25, 1996.

16. The descriptions of the highlights of the Tadic trial contained in this chapter are derived both from the author's firsthand observations of parts of the trial at The Hague and from viewing the gavel-to-gavel television coverage of the trial presented by Court TV, as well as daily trial reports prepared by the staff of Court TV. The author thanks Steven Brill, Chairman and Chief Executive Officer of Court TV for granting permission to draw upon the Court TV reports without specific attribution.

17. Walter Goodman, "Sorting out War Crimes and Tangles of History," *New York Times,* May 13, 1996, p. C-14.

18. Interview with Michael Keegan, The Hague, Netherlands, July 25, 1996.

19. Interview with Michail Wladimiroff, The Hague, Netherlands, July 25, 1996.

20. See Defense Motion and Response of the Prosecutor Concerning Hearsay, IT-94-I-T, June 26, 1996, and July 10, 1996.

21. Ed Vulliamy, "Testimony for the Terrorized," *The Guardian*, June 15, 1996, p. 29.

22. Interview with Grant Niemann, The Hague, Netherlands, July 25, 1996.

Notes for Chapter 8

1. The descriptions of the highlights of the Tadic trial contained in this chapter are derived both from the author's firsthand observations of parts of the trial at The Hague and from viewing the gavel-to-gavel television coverage of the trial presented by Court TV, as well as daily trial reports prepared by the staff of Court TV. The author thanks Steven Brill, Chairman and Chief Executive Officer of Court TV for granting permission to draw upon the Court TV reports without specific attribution.

2. Ed Vulliamy, "Secrets and Lies in Bosnia," *The Guardian,* June 13, 1996, p. 15.

3. Interview with Steven Kay, The Hague, Netherlands, July 25, 1996.

4. Interview with Michael Wladimiroff, The Hague, Netherlands, July 25, 1996.

5. As cited in the Prosecution's Response to the Motion On Dismissal of Charges, *The Prosecutor v. Dusko Tadic*, Case No. IT-94-1-T, filed 5 September 1996, at paras. 41 and 42.

6. Gillian Sharpe, Interview with Richard Goldstone, Chief Prosecutor, War Crimes Tribunal, National Public Radio Morning Edition, May 23, 1996, Transcript #1874-9.

7. Bruce Zagaris, "Yugoslav Tribunal Issues New Arrest Warrants Against Karadzic and Mladic and Initiates Investigation Against Serbian President," *International Enforcement Law Reporter* 12(8) (1996): 312–314

8. Decision of Trial Chamber 1, Review of Indictment Pursuant to Rule 61, Radovan Karadzic and Ratko Mladic, Cases No. IT-95-5-R61 and No. IT-95-18-R61, July 11, 1996.

9. Decision of Trial Chamber 1, Review of Indictment Pursuant to Rule 61, Radovan Karadzic and Ratko Mladic, Cases No. IT-95-5-R61 and No. IT-95-18-R61, July 11, 1996, p. 56.

10. Decision of Trial Chamber 1, Review of Indictment Pursuant to Rule 61, Radovan Karadzic and Ratko Mladic, Cases No. IT-95-5-R61 and No. IT-95-18-R61, July 11, 1996, p. 48.

11. Decision of Trial Chamber 1, Review of Indictment Pursuant to Rule 61, Radovan Karadzic and Ratko Mladic, Cases No. IT-95-5-R61 and No. IT-95-18-R61, July 11, 1996, p. 47.

12. Bruce Zagaris, "Yugoslav Tribunal Issues New Arrest Warrants Against Karadzic and Mladic and Initiates Investigation Against Serbian President," *International Enforcement Law Reporter* 12(8) (1996): 312–314

13. Interview with Graham Blewitt, The Hague, Netherlands, July 25, 1996.

14. As reported in "Witness Says He Did Not See Tadic at Castration," *Agence France Presse*, July 30, 1996; Ian Geoghegan, "Key Witness Fails to Place Accused Serb at Omarska," *Reuters World Service*, July 31, 1996.

15. Interview with Michael Keegan, The Hague, Netherlands, July 25, 1996.

16. Interview with Steven Kay, The Hague, Netherlands, July 25, 1996.

17. Interview with Michail Wladimiroff, The Hague, Netherlands, July 25, 1996.

18. "Summary of Decision on Defense Motion on the Non-Admission of Hearsay," *Bulletin of the International Criminal Tribunal for the Former Yugoslavia* 9 (August 14, 1996): 3.

19. "Ex-Camp Guard Testifies About Serb's Atrocities," *The Record*, September 3, 1996, p. 4; "Anonymous Witness Accuses Tadic of Murder and Rape," *Agence France Presse*, September 2, 1996.

Notes for Chapter 9

1. The descriptions of the highlights of the Tadic trial contained in this chapter are derived both from the author's firsthand observations of parts of the trial at The Hague and from viewing the gavel-to-gavel television coverage of the trial presented by Court TV, as well as daily trial reports prepared by the staff of Court TV. The author thanks Steven Brill, Chairman and Chief Executive Officer of Court TV for granting permission to draw upon the Court TV reports without specific attribution.

2. Motion on Dismissal of Charges, *The Prosecutor of the Tribunal v. Dusko Tadic,* Case No. IT-94-I, filed on 20 August 1996; Response to the Motion on Dismissal of Charges, *The Prosecutor of the Tribunal v. Dusko Tadic,* Case No. IT-94-I, filed on 5 September 1996.

3. "Overseers Certify Bosnia Vote Results," *Boston Globe*, September 30, 1996, p. A-7.

4. Judith Ingram, "Muslim Izetbegovic, Declared Winner in Bosnia, Brings New Hope for Unity," *Boston Globe*, September 19, 1996, p. A9.

5. Judith Ingram, "Muslim Izetbegovic, Declared Winner in Bosnia, Brings New Hope for Unity," *Boston Globe,* September 19, 1996, p. A9.

6. "Failure to Implement Dayton Could Bring More Conflict," *Agence France Presse,* September 25, 1996.

7. Security Council Resolution 1074, October 1, 1996.

8. Lynne Terry, "Bosnia, Serbia Sign Diplomatic Pact," *Boston Globe*, October 4, 1996, p. A-2.

9. Interview with Michail Wladimiroff, The Hague, Netherlands, July 25, 1996.

10. "Bosnian Serb Policemen Appear at War Crimes Court by Satellite," *Agence France Presse,* October 15, 1996.

11. "Bosnian Serb Policemen Appear at War Crimes Court by Satellite," *Agence France Presse,* October 15, 1996.

12. "*Lawyer Claims Bosnia War Crimes Witness Lied,*" *Agence France Presse,* October 25, 1996.

13. Mike Corder, "Witness Claims Bosnian Government Forced Him to Lie to Crimes Tribunal," *Associated Press,* October 25, 1996.

14. Mike Corder, "Witness Claims Bosnian Government Forced Him to Lie to Crimes Tribunal," *Associated Press,* October 25, 1996.

15. Mike Corder, "Witness Claims Bosnian Government Forced Him to Lie to Crimes Tribunal," *Associated Press,* October 25, 1996.

16. "War Crimes Tribunal Struggles on Amid Perjury Row," *ANP English Bulletin,* October 29, 1996.

17. Robert Shnayerson, "Judgment at Nuremberg," *Smithsonian*, October 1996, p. 138.

18. William Shakespeare, *Hamlet*, III, ii, 242.

Notes for Chapter 10

1. F.N. Maynard, "Big Dan's Rape Trial," *New Directions for Women*, May/June 1984, p. 7.

2. Opening Statement of Robert Jackson at Nuremberg (1946), p. 6.

3. The full text of the judgment in the Tadic case is available at the Yugoslavia Tribunal's Internet Home Page: http://www.un.org/icty. Both the defense and the prosecution announced that they would appeal the tribunal's judgment.

4. Miker Corder, "U.N. Court Convicts Bosinan Serb," *Associated Press*, May 7, 1997.

5. William Horne, "The Real Trial of the Century," *The American Lawyer*, September, 1995, p. 5.

6. *Annual Report of the International Tribunal for the Prosecution of Persons Responsible for Serious Violations of International Humanitarian Law Committed in the Territory of the Former Yugoslavia Since 1991*, U.N. Doc. S/1994/1007, August 29, 1994, p. 49.

7. Guido de Bruin, "Yugoslavia War Crimes Tribunal Inaugurated in the Hague," *Inter Press Service*, November 17, 1993.

8. See Report to the President from Justice Robert H. Jackson, Chief of Counsel for the United States in the Prosecution of Axis War Criminals, June 7, 1945, reprinted in *American Journal of International Law* 39 (Supp. 1945): 178, 184.

9. Daniel Jonah Goldhagen, *Hitler's Willing Executioners: Ordinary Germans and the Holocaust* (1996), pp. 375–454.

10. Interview with Grant Niemann, The Hague, Netherlands, July 25, 1996.

11. Thomas Hobbes, *Leviathan* (Everyman ed., 1914), Chapter XIII, "Of the Natural Condition of Mankind, as Concerning Their Felicity, and Misery."

12. Interview with Graham Blewitt, The Hague, Netherlands, July 26, 1996.

13. Terry Moran, Court TV Broadcast of the Tadic Trial, September 17, 1996.

14. Daniel Patrick Moynihan, *Pandaemonium: Ethnicity in International Politics* (1993).

15. Warren Zimmermann, *Origins of a Catastrophe: Yugoslavia and its Destroyers—America's Last Ambassador Tells What Happened and Why* (1996), p. xii.

16. William Horne, "The Real Trial of the Century," *The American Lawyer*, September, 1995, p. 5.

17. Interview with Justice Richard Goldstone, Brussels, Belgium, July 20, 1996.

18. William Horne, "The Real Trial of the Century," *The American Lawyer*, September, 1995, p. 5.

19. Interview with Graham Blewitt, The Hague, Netherlands, July 25, 1996.

20. Interview with Grant Niemann, The Hague, Netherlands, July 25, 1996.

21. Interview with Justice Richard Goldstone, Brussels, Belgium, July 20, 1996.

22. "War Crimes Prosecutor Says Tribunal May Have Deterred Violations," *Deutsche Presse-Agentur,* January 26, 1996.

23. "Commentary by Richard Goldstone, Bosnia-Herzegovina: The Responsibility to Act," *Inter Press Service,* June 27, 1996.

24. "Commentary by Richard Goldstone, Bosnia-Herzegovina: The Responsibility to Act," *Inter Press Service,* June 27, 1996.

25. Interview with Graham Blewitt, The Hague, Netherlands, July 26, 1996.

26. Interview with Michail Wladimiroff, The Hague, Netherlands, July 26, 1996.

27. Interview with Grant Niemann, The Hague, Netherlands, July 25, 1996.

28. Interview with Fred Graham, August 20, 1996, New York City.

29. Mark Rice-Oxley, "Tribunal Depends on the Kindness of Foes," *National Law Journal,* June 3, 1996, p. A10.

30. Philip Shenon, "G.I.'s in Bosnia Shun Hunt for War-Crime Suspects," *New York Times International,* March 2, 1996, p. 3.

31. Tribunal Press Release, CC/PIO/027-E, November 24, 1995.

32. Ed Vulliamy, "In Times of Trial," *The Guardian,* October 31, 1995, p. T6.

33. Ed Vulliamy, "In Times of Trial," *The Guardian,* October 31, 1995, p. T6.

34. Jane Perlez, "War Crimes Prosecutor Vents Frustrations," *New York Times,* May 22, 1996, p. A-8.

35. See Donald J. Sears, *To Kill Again: The Motivation and Development of Serial Murder* (1991).

36. John Lichfield, "Sharks Escape as The Hague Tries a Minnow," *The Independent*, May 12, 1996, p. 14.

37. Robert Block, "First Catch You a War Criminal," *The Independent,* April 30, 1995, p. 4.

38. Interview with Justice Richard Goldstone, Brussels, Belgium, July 20, 1996.

39. Interview with Justice Richard Goldstone, Brussels, Belgium, July 20, 1996.

40. Richard Goldstone, "Bosnia-Herzegovina: The Responsibility to Act," *Inter Press Service,* June 27, 1996.

41. Tribunal Press Release, CC/PIO/075-E, May 23, 1995 (Appending Letter from Antonio Cassese to the President of the Security Council dated May 22, 1996).

42. Statement of the President of the Security Council, S/PRST/1996/13, May 8, 1996.

43. Jon Swain, "Serb War Criminals Flaunt Their Freedom," *Sunday Times* (London), June 23, 1996.

44. "Commentary by Richard Goldstone, Bosnia-Herzegovina: The Responsibility to Act," *Inter Press Service,* June 27, 1996.

45. Michael P. Scharf, "Luring Out Humanity's Dark Side," *Boston Globe,* December 1, 1996, p. D2.

46. "Shrugging Off Indictment, Bosnian Serb General Skis," *New York Times International,* Monday, March 11, 1996, p. A3.

47. Jane Perlez, "War Crimes Prosecutor Vents Frustrations," *New York Times,* May 22, 1996, p. A-8.

48. Colin Soloway and Stephen J. Hedges, "How Not to Catch a War Criminal," *U.S. News and World Report,* December 9, 1996, p. 63.

49. Colin Soloway and Stephen J. Hedges, "How Not to Catch a War Criminal," *U.S. News and World Report,* December 9, 1996, p. 63.

50. Interview with Justice Richard Goldstone, Brussels, Belgium, July 20, 1996.

51. Nelson Graves, "Premier-Designate Compares Rwanda to Nazi Genocide," *Reuters World Service,* 26 May 1994.

52. *Security Council Resolution 955,* 8 November 1994.

53. *Security Council Resolution 674* (1990).

54. Statement of Mr. Li Zhaoxing of China at the time of voting on Security Council Resolution 827, which established the Yugoslavia Tribunal. U.N. Doc. S/PV.3217, 25 May 1993, at 33–34. China later abstained on Security Council Resolution 955 (8 November 1994), which established the Rwanda Tribunal.

55. See Report of the International Law Commission on the work of its forty-fifth session, U.N. GAOR, 48th Sess., Supp. No. 10, p. 258, U.N. Doc. A/48/10 (1993); James Crawford, "The ILC's Draft Statute for an International Criminal Tribunal," *American Journal of International Law* 88 (1994): 140; Virginia Morris and Christianne Bourloyannis-Vrailas, "The Work of the Sixth Committee at the Fiftieth Session of the UN General Assembly," *American. Journal of International Law* 90 (1996): 491, 496.

56. See generally, *Comments Received Pursuant to Paragraph 4 of General Assembly Resolution 49/53 on the Establishment of An International Criminal Court, Report of the Secretary-General,* U.N. Doc. A/AC.244/1/Add.2, 31 March 1995, pp. 7–29. (Comments of the Government of the United States of America on Draft Articles for a Statute of an International Criminal Court, March 30, 1995). See also, John F. Harris, "Clinton Pushes for U.N. War Crimes Tribunal," *Washington Post,* Oct. 16, 1995, p. 2.

57. Interview with Justice Richard Goldstone, Brussels, Belgium, July 20, 1996.

58. Interview with Justice Richard Goldstone, Brussels, Belgium, July 20, 1996.

Selected Bibliography

Books

American Bar Association. *Report on the International Tribunal to Adjudicate War Crimes Committed in the Former Yugoslavia*. Chicago, Illinois: American Bar Association, 1993.

———. *Report on the Proposed Rules of Procedure and Evidence of the International Tribunal to Adjudicate War Crimes in the Former Yugoslavia*. Chicago, Illinois: American Bar Association, 1995.

Appleman, John A. *Military Tribunals and International Crimes*. Westport, Connecticut: Greenwood Press, 1971.

Arendt, Hannah. *Eichman in Jerusalem: A Report on the Banality of Evil*. New York: Penguin Books, 1964.

Bassiouni, M. Cherif and Peter Manikas. *The Law of the International Criminal Tribunal For the Former Yugoslavia*. Irvington-on-Hudson, New York: Transnational Publishers, Inc, 1996.

Bassiouni, M. Cherif. *Crimes Against Humanity in International Criminal Law*. Boston: Martinus Nijhoff Publishers, 1992.

———. *A Draft International Criminal Code and Draft Statute for An International Criminal Tribunal*. Boston: Martinus Nijhoff Publishers, 1987.

———, ed. *International Criminal Law*. Irvington-on-Hudson, New York: Transnational Publishers, 1986-1987.

Boyle, Francis A. *The Bosnian People Charge Genocide*. Amherst, Massachusetts: Aletheia Press, 1996.

Brackman, A. *The Other Nuremberg: The Untold Story of the Tokyo War Crimes Trials*. New York: William Morrow & Co., Inc., 1987.

Carnegie Endowment for International Peace. *Unfinished Peace: Report of the International Commission on the Balkans*. Washington, D.C.: The Brookings Institutional Press, 1996.

Cigar, Norman. *Genocide in Bosnia: The Policy of "Ethnic Cleansing."* College Station, Texas: Texas A&M University Press, 1995.

Clark, Arthur L. *Bosnia: What Every American Should Know. New York: Berkley Books*, 1996.

Conot, R. *Justice at Nuremberg*. New York: Harper and Row, 1983.

Ferencz, Benjamin. *An International Criminal Court: A Step Toward World Peace: A Documentary History and Analysis*. Dobbs Ferry, New York: Oceana Publications, 1980.

Friedman, L., ed. *The Law of War: A Documentary History*. New York: Random House, 1972.

Glenny, Misha. *The Fall of Yugoslavia: The Third Balkan War*, revised edition. New York: Penguin Books, 1994.

Goldhagen, Daniel Jonah. *Hitler's Willing Executioners: Ordinary Germans and the Holocaust*. New York: Alfred A. Knopf, Inc., 1996.

Green, Leslie Claude. *The Law Of Armed Conflict and the Enforcement of International Criminal Law*. Irvington-on-Hudson, New York: Transnational Publishers, 1985.

Guest, Iain. *On Trial: The United Nations, War Crimes, and the Former Yugoslavia*. Washington, D.C.: Refugee Policy Group, 1995.

Harris, Whitney R. *Tyranny on Trial: The Evidence at Nuremberg*. Dallas, Texas: Southern Methodist University Press, 1954.

History of the United Nations War Crimes Commission and the Development of the Laws of War. London: Published for the United Nations War Crimes Commission by His Majesty's Stationery Office, 1948.

Kritz, Neil J., ed. *Transitional Justice: How Emerging Democracies Reckon with Former Regimes*, 3 vols. Washington, D.C.: United States Institute of Peace Press, 1995.

Law Reports of Trial of War Criminals, vols. I-XV, selected and prepared by the United Nations War Crimes Commission, published for the United Nations War Crimes Commission by His Majesty's Stationery Office, London, 1949.

Minear, R. *Victor's Justice: Tokyo War Crimes Trial*. Princeton, New Jersey: Princeton University Press, 1971.

Morris, Virginia and Michael P. Scharf. *An Insider's Guide to the International Criminal Tribunal for the Former Yugoslavia,* 2 vols. Irvington-on-Hudson, New York: Transnational Publishers, Inc., 1995.

Moynihan, Daniel Patric. *Pandaemonium: Ethnicity in International Politics.* New York: Oxford University Press, 1993.

Mousavizadeh, Nader, ed. *The Black Book of Bosnia: The Consequences of Appeasement.* New York: Basic Books, 1995.

Nazi Conspiracy and Aggression, Opinion and Judgement. Office of the United States Chief of Counsel for Prosecution of Axis Criminality. Washington, D.C.: United States Government Printing Office, 1947.

Owen, David. *Balkan Odyssey.* Orlando, Florida: Harcourt Brace & Company, 1995.

Paust, Jordan, M. Cherif Bassiouni, Sharon Williams, Michael Scharf, Jimmy Gurulé and Bruce Zagaris. *International Criminal Law: Cases and Materials.* Durham, North Carolina: Carolina Academic Press, 1996.

Roht-Arriaza, Naomi. *Impunity and Human Rights in International Law and Practice.* New York: Oxford University Press, 1995.

Roling, B.V.A. and Antonio Cassese. *The Tokyo Trial and Beyond: Reflections of a Peacemonger.* Cambridge, Massachusetts: Polity Press, 1993.

Rummel, Rudi J. *Death by Government.* New Brunswick, New Jersey: Transactions Publishers, 1994.

Schwartzenberger, G., *The Law of Armed Conflict.* London: Stevens and Sons, Ltd., 1968.

Silber, Laura and Allan Little. *Yugoslavia: Death of a Nation.* New York: TV Books, Inc., distributed by Penguin Books, 1996.

Taylor, Telford. *The Anatomy of the Nuremberg Trials.* New York: Alfred A. Knopf, Inc., 1992.

United Nations. *The Charter and Judgment of the Nuremberg Tribunal: History and Analysis.* Lake Success, New York: United Nations, 1949.

Zimmermann, Warren. *Origins of a Catastrophe: Yugoslavia and Its Destroyers—America's Last Ambassador Tells What Happened and Why.* New York: Times Books, 1996.

Articles

Akahavan, Payam. "Punishing War Crimes in the Former Yugoslavia: A Critical Juncture for the New World Order." *Human Rights Quarterly*, 15 (1993): 264-289.

Aydelott, Danise. "Mass Rape During War: Prosecuting Bosnian Rapists Under International Law." *Emory International Law Review* 7 (1993): 585-631.

Barkey, Drett D. "Bosnia: A Question of Intervention." *Strategic Review* 21(4) (1993): 48-59.

Bassiouni, M. Cherif. "The Time has Come for an International Criminal Court." *Indiana International and Comparative Law Review* 1 (1991): 1-43.

———. "Nuremberg Forty Years After: An Introduction" *Case Western Reserve Journal of International Law* 18(2) (1986): 261-266.

Bassiouni, M. Cherif and Christopher Blakesley. "The Need for an International Criminal Court in the New International World Order." *Vanderbilt Journal of Transnational Law* 25 (1992): 151-182.

Beres, Louis Rene. "Toward Prosecution of Iraqi Crimes Under International Law: Jurisprudential Foundations and Jurisdictional Choices." *California Western International Law Journal* 22 (1991/1992): 127-134.

Blakesley, Christopher L. "Obstacles to the Creation of a Permanent War Crimes Tribunal." *Fletcher Forum of World Affairs* 18 (1994): 77-102 4.

Bourloyannis, Christianne. "The Security Council of the United Nations and the Implementation of International Humanitarian Law." *Denver Journal of International Law & Policy* 20 (1992): 335-355.

Chaney, Kevin R. "Pitfalls and Imperatives: Applying the Lessons of Nuremberg to the Yugoslavia War Crimes Tribunal." *Dickinson Journal of International Law* 14 (1995): 57-94.

Clark, Roger S. "Offenses of International Concern: Multilateral State Treaty Practice in the Forty Years Since Nuremberg." *Nordic Journal of International Law* 51 (1988): 49-118.

Crawford, James. "The ILC's Draft Statute for an International Criminal Tribunal." *American Journal for International Law* 88 (1994): 140-152.

Dadrian, Vahakn N. "Genocide as a Problem of National and International Law: The World War I Armenian Case and Its Contemporary Legal Ramifications." *Yale Journal of International Law* 14(1989): 221.

D'Amato, Anthony, "Peace v. Accountability in Bosnia." *American Journal of International Law* 88 (1994): 500-506.

Daes, Erica-Irene A. "New Types of War Crimes and Crimes Against Humanity: Violations of International Humanitarian and Human Rights Law." *International Geneva Yearbook* 7 (1993): 55-78.

Ferencz, Benjamin B. "Nuremberg Trial Procedure and the Rights of the Accused." *Journal of Criminal Law and Criminology* 39 (1948): 144-151.

———. "An International Criminal Code and Court: Where They Stand and Where They're Going," *Columbia Journal of Transnational Law* 30 (1992): 375-399.

———. "The Nuremberg Precedent and the Prosecution of State-Sponsored Mass Murder." *New York Law School Journal of International and Comparative Law* 3 (1990): 325-332.

Gianais, William N. "The New World Order and the Need for an International Criminal Court." *Fordham International Law Journal* 16 (1992/1993): 88-119.

Graefrath, Bernhard. "Universal Criminal Jurisdiction and An International Criminal Court." *European Journal of International Law* 1 (1990): 67-88.

Greenwood, Christopher. "The International Tribunal for Former Yugoslavia." *International Affairs* 69 (1993): 641-655.

"International Military Tribunal (Nuremberg), Judgment and Sentences," *American Journal of International Law* 41 (1947): 172-344.

Jackson, Robert H. "Report to the President from Justice Robert H. Jackson, Chief of Counsel for the United States in the Prosecution of Axis War Criminals, June 7, 1945," *American Journal of International Law* 39 (Supp. 1945): 178-184.

King, Amy Lou. "Bosnia-Herzegovina, Vance-Owen agenda for a Peaceful Settlement: Did the U.N. Do Too Little, Too Late, To Support This Endeavor?" *Georgia Journal of International and Comparative Law* 32(2) (1993): 347-375.

Kresock, David. "Ethnic Cleansing in the Balkans: The Legal Foundations of Foreign Intervention." *Cornell International Law Journal* 27 (1994): 203-239.

Kunz, Joseph L. "The United Nations Convention on Genocide." *American Journal of International Law* 43 (1949): 738-746.

Lauterpacht, H. "The Law of Nations and the Punishment of War Crimes." *British Year Book of International Law* 21 (1944): 58-95.

Leigh, Monroe. "Yugoslav Tribunal: Use of Unnamed Witnesses Against Accused. *American Journal of International Law* 90 (1996): 235-236.

Meron, Theodor. "Rape as a Crime Under International Humanitarian Law." *American Journal of International Law* 87 (1993): 424-427.

———. "The Case for War Crimes Trial in Yugoslavia." *Foreign Affairs* 72(3) (1993): 122-135.

———. "War Crimes in Yugoslavia and the Development of International Law." *American Journal of International Law* 88 (1994): 78-87.

Moore, John Norton. "War Crimes and the Rule of Law in the Gulf Crisis." *Virginia Journal of International Law* 31 (1991): 403-415.

Nadelmann, Ethan A. "The Role of the United States in the International Enforcement of Criminal Law." *Harvard International Law Journal* 31 (1990): 37-76.

O'Brien, James. "The International Tribunal for Violations of International Humanitarian Law in the Former Yugoslavia," *American Journal of International Law* 87 (1993): 639-659.

O'Brien, William. "The Nuremberg Precedent and the Gulf War." *Virginia Journal of International Law* 31 (1991): 391-401.

Orentlicher, Diane F. "Settling Accounts: The Duty to Prosecute Human Rights Violations of a Prior Regime." 100 *Yale Law Journal* 2537-2614, 1991.

Paust, Jordan. "Applicability of International Criminal Laws to Events in the Former Yugoslavia." *American University Journal of International Law & Policy* 9 (1994): 499-523.

Popovic, Sanya. "The Origins of Yugoslavia's Disintegration and the Prerequisites for Effective International Response." *New Europe Law Review and Political Science Quarterly* (1993): 45-60.

Roht-Arriaza, Naomi. "State Responsibility to Investigate and Prosecute Grave Human Rights Violations in International Law." *California Law Review* 78 (1990): 451-505.

Scharf, Michael P. "Swapping Amnesty for Peace and the Duty to Prosecute Human Rights Crimes in Haiti." *Texas International Law Journal* 31 (1996): 1-42.

———. "Musical Chairs: The Dissolution of States and Membership in the United Nations." *Cornell International Law Journal* 28 (1995): 29-69.

———. "The Politics of Establishing an International Criminal Court." *Duke Journal of Comparative and International Law 6* (1995):167-173.

———. "Getting Serious About an International Criminal Court." *Pace International Law Review* 6 (1994): 103-119.

———. "The Jury Is Still Out on the Need for an International Criminal Court." *Duke Journal of International and Comparative Law* 1 (1991): 135-168.

Scharf, Michael P. and Joshua Dorosin, "Interpreting UN Sanctions: The Rulings and Role of the Yugoslavia Sanctions Committee." *Brooklyn Journal of International Law* 19 (1993): 771-827.

Schwelb, E. "Crimes Against Humanity." *British Year Book of International Law* 23 (1946): 178-206.

Sobchak, Natalie J. "The Aftermath of Nuremberg...The Problems of Suspected War Criminals in America." *New York Law School Journal of Human Rights* 6 (1989): 425-468.

Symposium. "Critical Perspectives on the Nuremberg Trials and State Accountability." *New York Law School Journal of Human Rights* 7 (1996): 453-689.

Symposium. "Nuremberg and the Rule of Law: A Fifty-Year Verdict." *Military Law Review* 149 (1995): 1-302.

Symposium. "The Enforcement of Humanitarian Law." *Duke Journal of Comparative and International Law* 6 (1995): 1-195.

Symposium. "War Crimes." *The Fletcher Forum of World Affairs* 18 (1994): 1-115.

Symposium. "Should There be an International Tribunal for Crimes Against Humanity?" *Pace International Law Review* 6 (1994): 1-197.

Szasz, Paul C. "The Proposed War Crimes Tribunal for Ex-Yugoslavia." *New York University Journal of International Law and Politics* 25 (1993): 405-435.

Tomushcat, Christian. "A System of International Criminal Prosecution is Taking Shape." *International Commission of Jurists: The Review* 50 (1993): 56-70.

"The United Nations Ad Hoc Tribunal for the Former Yugoslavia," *Proceedings*, 87th Annual Meeting of the American Society of International Law (1993): 20-36.

Thornberry, Cedric. "Saving the War Crimes Tribunal." *Foreign Policy* 104 (1996): 72-85.

Webb, John. "Genocide Treaty—Ethnic Cleansing—Substantive and Procedural Hurdles in the Application of the Genocide Convention to Alleged Crimes in the Former Yugoslavia " *Georgia Journal of International Law* 23 (1993): 377-408.

Weller, Mark, "The International Response to the Dissolution of the Socialist Federal Republic of Yugoslavia," *American Journal of International Law* 86 (1992): 569-607.

Index

A Note about the Author

MICHAEL SCHARF holds a JD from Duke University School of Law and served as judicial clerk to Judge Gerald B. Tjoflat of the U.S. Court of Appeals for the Eleventh Circuit before joining the Office of the Legal Adviser of the U.S. Department of State in 1989. While at the State Department, he served as Counsel to the Counter-Terrorism Bureau, Attorney-Adviser for Law Enforcement and Intelligence, Attorney Adviser for United Nations Affairs, and as a member of the United States Delegations to the United Nations General Assembly and to the United Nations Human Rights Commission. In 1993, he received the State Department's Meritorious Honor Award "in recognition of superb performance and exemplary leadership in support of U.S. policy initiatives regarding the former Yugoslavia." He also served as Chairman of the International Law Section of the District of Columbia Bar, as Rapporteur to the Committee of Experts on an International Criminal Court convened under the auspices of the United Nations and International Association of Penal Law, and as an ex-officio member of the American Bar Association's Blue Ribbon Task Force on an International Criminal Court, chaired by former Attorney-General Benjamin Civiletti, and the American Bar Association's Task Force on War Crimes in the Former Yugoslavia, chaired by former State Department Legal Adviser Monroe Leigh. Professor Scharf left the State Department in August 1993 to join the faculty of the New England School of Law, where he serves as Director of the Center for International Law and Policy, and teaches public international law, criminal law, international human rights law and international criminal law. He is also Managing Director of the Public International Law and Policy Group, a non-profit corporation which provides pro bono legal assistance to foreign governments and international organizations including the Office of the Prosecutor of the Yugoslavia Tribunal. During the international trial of Dusko Tadic, Professor Scharf appeared as a frequent guest commentator on Court TV.

Related Works by the Author

International Criminal Law: Cases and Materials (Carolina Academic Press 1996) (with Jordan Paust et al.)

An Insider's Guide to the International Criminal Tribunal for the Former Yugoslavia, 2 vols (Transnational Pub. 1995) (with Virginia Morris)

The International Trial of the Century? A "Cross-Fire" Exchange on the First Case Before the Yugoslavia War Crimes Tribunal, 29 Cornell International Law Journal (1997) (with Valerie Epps)

The Prosecutor v. Dusko Tadic: An Appraisal of the First International War Crimes Trial Since Nuremberg, 60 Albany Law Review (1997)

The Case for a Permanent International Truth Commission, 8 Duke Journal of International and Comparative Law (1997)

Swapping Amnesty For Peace, 31 Texas International Law Journal (1996)

Have We Really Learned the Lessons of Nuremberg, 149 Military Law Review (1996)

UN Mandates: The Letter of the Law, in With No Peace to Keep: United Nations Peacekeeping and the War in the Former Yugoslavia (Grainpress Ltd. 1995) (with Paul Williams)

Musical Chairs: The Dissolution of States and Membership in the United Nations, 28 Cornell International Law Journal (1995)

The Politics of Establishing an International Criminal Court, 6 Duke Journal of Comparative & International Law (1995)

Getting Serious About an International Criminal Court, 6 Pace International Law Review (1994)

Interpreting U.N. Sanctions: The Rulings and Role of the Yugoslavia Sanctions Committee, 19 Brooklyn Journal of International Law (1993)

The Jury is Still Out on the Need for An International Criminal Court, 1 Duke Journal of International & Comparative Law (1991)